D0165927

APPLIED RESEARCH METHODS

IN CRIMINAL JUSTICE AND CRIMINOLOGY

ERIC J. FRITSCH
University of North Texas

CHAD R. TRULSON
University of North Texas

ASHLEY G. BLACKBURN
University of Houston-Downtown

McGraw Hill

Connect
Learn
Succeed™

The McGraw·Hill Companies

APPLIED RESEARCH METHODS IN CRIMINAL JUSTICE AND CRIMINOLOGY

Published by McGraw-Hill, a business unit of The McGraw-Hill Companies, Inc., 1221 Avenue of the Americas, New York, NY 10020. Copyright © 2014 by The McGraw-Hill Companies, Inc. All rights reserved. Printed in the United States of America. No part of this publication may be reproduced or distributed in any form or by any means, or stored in a database or retrieval system, without the prior written consent of The McGraw-Hill Companies, Inc., including, but not limited to, in any network or other electronic storage or transmission, or broadcast for distance learning.

Some ancillaries, including electronic and print components, may not be available to customers outside the United States.

This book is printed on acid-free paper.

1 2 3 4 5 6 7 8 9 0 QVR/QVR 1 0 9 8 7 6 5 4 3

ISBN 978-0-07-802641-6
MHID 0-07-802641-5

Senior Vice President, Products & Markets: *Kurt L. Strand*
Vice President, General Manager, Products & Markets: *Michael Ryan*
Vice President, Content Production & Technology Services: *Kimberly Meriwether David*
Executive Director of Development: *Lisa Pinto*
Managing Director: *Gina Boedeker*
Brand Manager: *Bill Minick*
Managing Developmental Editor: *Sara Jaeger*
Development Editor: *Nicole Bridge*
Marketing Specialist: *Alexandra Schultz*
Editorial Coordinator: *Adina Lonn*
Director, Content Production: *Terri Schiesl*
Senior Project Manager: *Lisa A. Bruflodt*
Senior Project Manager: *Ruma Khurana*
Buyer: *Nichole Birkenholz*
Media Project Manager: *Sridevi Palani*
Cover Designer: *Studio Montage, St. Louis, MO*
Cover Image: *James Woodson/Getty Images; Purestock/Superstock; AndersonRoss/Getty Images; S.Olson/Photo Alto; Design Pics/MonkeyBuisness*
Compositor: *MPS Limited*
Typeface: *10/12 Times*
Printer: *Quad Graphics*

All credits appearing on page or at the end of the book are considered to be an extension of the copyright page.

Library of Congress Cataloging-in-Publication Data

Fritsch, Eric J.
  Applied research methods in criminal justice and criminology / Eric J. Fritsch, Chad R. Trulson, Ashley G. Blackburn.
    pages cm
  ISBN 978-0-07-802641-6 (alk. paper)
  1. Criminology—Research—Methodology. 2. Criminal justice, Administration of—Research—Methodology.
I. Trulson, Chad R. II. Blackburn, Ashley G. III. Title.

HV6024.5.F75 2014
  364.072—dc23

                                                    2012048755

The Internet addresses listed in the text were accurate at the time of publication. The inclusion of a website does not indicate an endorsement by the authors or McGraw-Hill, and McGraw-Hill does not guarantee the accuracy of the information presented at these sites.

www.mhhe.com

DEDICATION

For Cheryl D. and my J-Kids (Jerod, Jacob, Joley, Jadyn, and Jaxon)
    —Eric J. Fritsch

For Gracie Lynn, my beautiful daughter
    —Chad R. Trulson

For Shannon, my husband, and Lorelei, our precious little girl
    —Ashley G. Blackburn

CONTENTS

CHAPTER 3

Sampling Methods 49

CHAPTER 4

Survey Research 67

CHAPTER 8

Putting It All Together: Understanding and Assessing Criminal Justice Research 150

CHAPTER 9

Basic Statistics for Consumers 174

PREFACE

The biggest challenges in teaching research methods are making difficult subjects applicable to students and overcoming student resistance to the course material. Students typically have minimal knowledge of research methods prior to enrolling in the course and typically do not understand why they even have to take the course in the first place. Initially, students fail to see how a solid foundation in research methods will assist them as practitioners in the criminal justice field. This text overcomes these challenges and others by creating a practical, applied, and user-friendly text that focuses on developing students into educated consumers of research.

ORGANIZATION AND FOCUS

In order for students to understand research methods and engage in the course, there must be significant practical application of the material. Research methods must be made real and tangible for the students. This book focuses on applying the concepts learned in the text to real-life examples of research. The reality is that most students will never conduct independent research of their own. However, everyone is exposed to the results of research on a daily basis. One cannot read the daily newspaper or watch the nightly news without hearing about new research results in the medical or other professional fields. Therefore, we developed a textbook that focuses heavily on being educated consumers of research. We believe that students should not only be educated in the concepts of research methods but also need to become educated consumers of research. Students need to develop the skills to critically assess the quality of the research to which they are exposed. The text is not just about the "how to" of research but also focuses on what to look for when evaluating the quality of research.

That we have included only nine chapters in our text is the first indicator of our focus on developing students into educated consumers of research, while the depth of information provided on important topics is the proof. The organization of chapters is practical, comprehensive, and engaging. We have developed a structure that is more nuanced than simply grouping research designs and techniques into chapters. Each chapter builds upon the prior chapters so students can incrementally learn the dynamics of the research process. For instance, Chapter 2 (Getting Started: The Beginnings and Pitfalls of Research) and Chapter 8 (Putting It All Together: Understanding and Assesssing Criminal Justice Research) are powerful examples of the organization of the book, demonstrating that we are constantly providing a clear context and recalling prior material so students can see the big picture of research methods.

Our focus is important to today's students and professors at the typical undergraduate university, in the typical undergraduate criminal justice and criminology program. As mentioned, the great majority of graduates will not be expected to design and carry out a research project. Yet, all students will be expected to know how to read, critique, critically evaluate, and comment on research findings. Whether in their chosen profession or simply in their everyday lives, a focus on producing good consumers of research is the logical and most useful focus for undergraduate students.

Features

Engaging features are consistently presented in each chapter. The features focus on the application of research methods and include those presented below.

- **Chapter Opening Case Studies** provide a practical context for concepts covered in each chapter. Students will review research questions, methodology, results, limitations presented by that particular research design, and the impact on criminal justice. For example, Chapter 9 begins with an overview of a study designed to answer the following research question, "Is gang involvement, along with involvement in gang crime and other risky lifestyles, related to being the victim of a violent crime?" Furthermore, the research question "What are the behavioral and psychological consequences of becoming a prisoner or a prison guard?" is addressed at the beginning of Chapter 2. The standardized format for each chapter opening allows the reader to quickly become familiar with what to expect at the start of each chapter. In addition, the case study is intended to peak the interest of students regarding the topics covered in the chapter.

- **Research in the News** gives students the opportunity to review and assess research studies that are used to report current events. For example, in Chapter 3, a study involving a survey of 10,000 undergraduate students on guns and gun threats on college campuses is presented as the debate over allowing guns on college campuses intensifies. This feature will further illustrate real life examples of criminal justice research and how the studies can influence criminal justice policy. In addition, as this feature appears in later chapters, it is used to revisit and reemphasize topics discussed in earlier ones.

- **Classics in CJ Research** allows students to review classic studies from the earlier days of criminal justice research. The studies presented are the seminal studies on the topic. Classics from the situational obedience studies by Zimbardo and Milgram, to the Minneapolis Domestic Violence Experiment, to the seminal study of the criminal investigation process by Greenwood and Petersilia, and others will be presented in each chapter.

- **What Research Shows: Impacting Criminal Justice Operations** illustrates major research studies that have had an impact on the criminal justice field. Although the practical application of research methods will be demonstrated throughout the text, this feature will illustrate major research studies that have had an impact on the operations of the criminal justice system. For example, the research on the deterrent effect of Scared Straight programs and the impact of prison rape research are discussed in this feature.

Pedagogical Aids

The chapters also contain pedagogical aids to facilitate student learning. Bolded key terms are presented throughout each chapter. These are a critical study tool since research methods is very term-heavy. The bolded key terms can also be used by students as they go back through the text and review for a test. Critical thinking questions are presented at the end of each chapter and provide students an opportunity to review and apply the research concepts covered.

ADDITIONAL INSTRUCTOR RESOURCES

Please visit www.mhhe.com/fritsch for instructor supplements including an Instructor's Manual, Test Bank, and Power Point lecture slides.

ACKNOWLEDGEMENTS

We would like to thank the following reviewers for their valuable comments:

Matt DeLisi, Iowa State University; Craig Hemmens, Missouri State University; Tom Stucky, Indiana University-Purdue University Indianapolis; PJ Verrecchia, York College of Pennsylvania.

We would also like to thank the following staff at McGraw-Hill: Brand Manager Bill Minick, Senior Project Manager Lisa Bruflodt, Senior Project Manager Ruma Khurana, Managing Editor Sara Jaeger, Marketing Specialist Alexandra Schultz, and Development Editor Nicole Bridge.

The Importance of Research Methods and Becoming an Informed Consumer of Research

CASE STUDY

Student Apprehension Regarding Research Methods

Research Study

Understanding and Measuring Student Apprehension in Criminal Justice Research Methods Courses[1]

Research Question

How do we measure disinterest, relevance argumentation, and math anxiety experienced by students enrolled in research methods courses?

Methodology

It is said that "misery loves company," so you are not alone in your apprehension and anxiety regarding your research methods course. The problem of student apprehension and anxiety related to taking a research methods course is not new and has been studied for over 25 years. Previously, such apprehension and anxiety appeared to be caused by math anxiety, especially as it applies to statistics. The authors of this article believe that student apprehension goes beyond math anxiety; that math anxiety is too simplistic of an explanation of student fear of research methods courses. Besides math anxiety, the researchers think that apprehension is caused by student indifference to the subject matter and irrelevance of the course because it does not apply to the "real world." They state that student apprehension in research methods and statistics courses is due to three main factors:

- Disinterest (D.);
- Relevance Argumentation (RA.), and;
- Math Anxiety (MA.).

Taken together, the reconceptualization is known as D.RA.MA., and the combination of these three factors constitutes the D.RA.MA. scale for research methods and statistics courses.

The researchers developed the D.RA.MA. scale by constructing survey questions to measure each factor in the scale (i.e., disinterest, relevance argumentation, and math anxiety). After they developed the survey, they tested it by distributing the survey to three criminal justice classes, totaling 80 students, from a midsized regional comprehensive university in the southern region of the United States. Higher scale scores demonstrate more disinterest, more relevance argumentation, or more math anxiety.

Results

The D.RA.MA. scale consists of 20 survey questions. Ten questions were borrowed from an existing Math Anxiety scale developed by Betz[2]. The researchers then created five items to assess Disinterest and five items intended to measure Relevance Argumentation. The items for the D.RA.MA. scale are illustrated below.

Math Anxiety[3]
- I usually have been at ease in math classes.
- Math does not scare me at all.

1

- I am no good at math.
- I don't think that I could do advanced math.
- Generally, I have been secure about attempting math.
- For some reason, even though I study, math seems unusually hard for me.
- Math has been my worst subject.
- My mind goes blank and I am unable to think clearly when working in mathematics.
- I think I could handle more difficult math.
- I am not the type to do well in mathematics.

Relevance Argumentation[4]
- I will need research methods for my future work.
- I view research methods as a subject that I will rarely use.
- Research methods is not really useful for students who intend to work in Criminal Justice.
- Knowing research methods will help me earn a living.
- Research methods does not reflect the "real world."

Research Disinterest[5]
- I am excited about taking research methods.
- It would not bother me at all to take more research methods courses.
- I expect a research methods class to be boring.
- I don't expect to learn much in research methods.
- I really don't care if I learn anything in research methods, as long as I get the requirement completed.

The Math Anxiety Scale responses for the 80 students ranged from 0 to 30 with a mean of 14, demonstrating a moderate level of math anxiety among the study participants. The responses for Relevance Argumentation ranged from 0 to 12 with a mean of 5.4 while those for Disinterest ranged from 1 to 15 with a mean of 7.0, demonstrating a moderate level of disinterest and relevance argumentation among students regarding research methods. Based on these findings, the study demonstrated that student apprehension regarding research methods courses goes beyond math anxiety and includes two additional factors; disinterest in the subject matter and irrelevance of research methods to the "real world."

Limitations with the Study Procedure

This research study was designed to develop a broader measure of student apprehension in criminal justice research methods courses. Moving beyond just math anxiety, the researchers accomplished their objective by developing the D.RA.MA. scale; adding disinterest and relevance argumentation to the understanding of student apprehension regarding research methods. As is true for all research, this study is not without limitations. The biggest limitation of this study is the limited sample size. Only 80 students completed the survey. Although this is certainly a good start, similar research (i.e., replication) needs to be completed with larger student samples in different locations throughout the country before the actual quality of the D.RA.MA. scale can be determined.

Impact on Criminal Justice

The D.RA.MA. scale developed in this study identifies disinterest and relevance argumentation, in addition to math anxiety, as part of student apprehension and resistance to research methods. A variety of instructional strategies can be inferred from the D.RA.MA. survey. However, it is important for professors to recognize that no single approach will reduce research methods resistance and apprehension for all students. For example, discussing research methods in a popular culture framework may resonate with students and lead to engaged students who are more interested in the subject matter and identify with the relevance of research methods to criminal justice in general and the future careers of students, in particular. This approach may provide an effective means for combating student disinterest and relevance argumentation in criminal justice research methods courses. At a minimum, it is critical for professors to explain the relevance of research methods to the policies and practices of police, courts, and corrections. Students need to realize that research methods are essential tools for assessing agency policies and practices. Professors will always have D.RA.MA.-plagued students, but recognizing the problem and then developing effective strategies to connect with these students is the challenge all professors face. Experimenting with a multitude of teaching strategies to alleviate the math anxiety, relevance argumentation, and disinterest of criminal justice research methods students will result in more effective teaching and learning. ●

What research is and why it is important to be an informed consumer of research

The sources of knowledge development and problems with each

How research methods can dispel myths about crime and the criminal justice system

The steps in the research process

How research has impacted criminal justice operations

INTRODUCTION

As noted in the chapter opening case study, it is expected that you have some anxiety and apprehension about taking this criminal justice research methods course. But, you have taken a significant step toward success in this course by opening up your research methods book, so congratulations are in order. You might have opened this book for a number of reasons. Perhaps it is the first day of class and you are ready to get started on the course material. Perhaps you have a quiz or exam soon. Perhaps the book has been gathering dust on your shelf since the first day of class and you are not doing well in your research methods class and are looking for the book to help with course improvement. Perhaps you are taking a research methods class in the future and are seeing if all the chatter among students is true.

No matter how you got here, two things are probably true. First, you are taking this research methods course because it is a requirement for your major. The bottom line is that most of the students who read this text are required to take a research methods course. While you may think studying research methods is irrelevant to your career goals, unnecessary, overly academic, or perhaps even intimidating, you probably must finish this course in order to graduate. Second, you have heard negative comments about this course. The negative comments mention the difficulty of the course and the relevance of the course (e.g., "I am going to be a police officer, so why do I need to take a research methods course?"). If you are like most students we have experienced in our research methods courses in the past, you are not initially interested in this course and are concerned about whether you will do well in it.

If you are concerned about the course, realize that you are not alone because most students are anxious about taking a research methods course. Also realize that your professor is well aware of student anxiety and apprehension regarding research methods. So, relax and do not think about the entire course and the entire book. Take the course content one chapter, one week

at a time. One of the advantages of taking a research methods course is that you learn about the process of research methods. Each chapter builds upon the previous chapters, illustrating and discussing more about the research process. This is certainly an advantage, but it is also critical that you understand the initial chapters in this book so you are not confused with the content discussed in later chapters. In addition to anxiety and apprehension over the course material, research methods can be boring if you only read and learn about it with no particular purpose in mind. Although examples are prevalent throughout the book, as you read this material, it is recommended that you think about the relevancy and application of the topics covered in this book to your specific criminal justice interests. As you continue to read the book, think about how you might use the information you are reading in your current position or your intended profession.

The goal of this research methods book is to develop you into an informed consumer of research. Most, if not all, of your fellow classmates will never conduct their own research studies. However, every one of you will be exposed to research findings in your professional and personal lives for the remainder of your lives. You are exposed to research findings in the media (e.g., television, newspapers, and online), in personal interaction with others (e.g., friends and family, doctors, and professors), as well as in class. You should challenge yourself for this semester to keep a journal and document exposure to research in your daily life outside of college whether through the nightly news, newspapers, magazine articles, Internet, personal conversations, or other means. At the end of the semester, you will be amazed at the amount of research you are exposed to in a short period of time. This book is focused on research exposure and assisting you to become an educated consumer of research by providing you the skills necessary to differentiate between good and not so good research. Why should you believe research findings if the study is faulty? Without being an educated consumer of research, you will not be able to differentiate between useful and not useful research. This book is designed to remedy this problem.

This book was written to make your first encounter with research methods relevant and successful while providing you the tools necessary to become an educated consumer of research. Therefore, this book is written with the assumption that students have not had a prior class on research methods. In addition, this book assumes that practical and evaluative knowledge of research methods is more useful than theoretical knowledge of the development of research methods and the relationship between theory and research. Since the focus of this book is on consumerism, not researcher training, practical and evaluative knowledge is more useful than theoretical knowledge.

It is also important to understand that the professors who design academic programs in criminal justice at the associate and bachelor level believe that an understanding of research methods is important for students. That is why, more than likely, this research methods course is a required course in your degree program. These professors understand that a solid understanding of research methods will enrich the qualifications of students for employment and performance in their criminal justice careers.

As previously stated, the basic goal of this book is to make students, as future and possibly even current practitioners in the criminal justice system, better informed and more capable consumers of the results of criminal justice research. This goal is based on the belief that an understanding of research methods allows criminal justice practitioners to be better able to make use of the results of research as it applies to their work-related duties. In fact, thousands of research questions are asked and answered each year in research involving criminal justice and criminological topics. In addition, thousands of articles are published, papers presented at conferences, and reports prepared that provide answers to these questions. The ability to understand research gives practitioners knowledge of the most current information in their respective fields and the ability to use this knowledge to improve the effectiveness of criminal justice agencies.

HOW DO WE KNOW WHAT WE KNOW? SOURCES OF KNOWLEDGE

The reality is the understanding of crime and criminal justice system operations by the public is frequently the product of misguided assumptions, distorted interpretations,

outright myths, and hardened ideological positions.[6] This is a bold statement that basically contends that most people's knowledge of crime and criminal justice is inaccurate. But, how do these inaccuracies occur? Most people have learned what they know about crime and criminal justice system operations through some other means besides scientific research results and findings. Some of that knowledge is based on personal experience and common sense. Much of it is based on the information and images supported by politicians, governmental agencies, and especially the media. This section will discuss the mechanisms used to understand crime and criminal justice operations by the public. It is important to note that although this section will focus on the failings of these knowledge sources, they each can be, and certainly are, accurate at times, and thus are valuable sources of knowledge.

Knowledge from Authority

We gain knowledge from parents, teachers, experts, and others who are in positions of authority in our lives. When we accept something as being correct and true just because someone in a position of authority says it is true, we are using what is referred to as **authority knowledge** as a means of knowing. Authorities often expend significant time and effort to learn something, and we can benefit from their experience and work.

However, relying on authority as a means of knowing has limitations. It is easy to overestimate the expertise of other people. A person's expertise is typically limited to a few core areas of significant knowledge; a person is not an expert in all areas. More specifically, criminal justice professors are not experts on all topics related to criminal justice. One professor may be an expert on corrections but know little about policing. If this professor discusses topics in policing in which he is not an expert, we may still assume he is right when he may be wrong. Authority figures may speak on fields they know little about. They can be completely wrong but we may believe them because of their status as an expert. Furthermore, an expert in one area may try to use his authority in an unrelated area. Other times, we have no idea of how the experts arrived at their knowledge. We just know they are experts in the topic area.

As I am writing this, I recall an example of authority knowledge that was wrong during my police academy training in the late 1980s. My academy training was about four years after the U.S. Supreme Court decision in *Tennessee v. Garner*.[7] In this case, the Court limited the use of deadly force by police to defense of life situations and incidents where the suspect committed a violent offense. Prior to the decision, the police in several states could use deadly force on any fleeing suspect accused of a felony offense. One day, the academy class was practicing mock traffic stops. During one of my mock traffic stops, I received information that the vehicle I stopped was stolen. The driver and passenger exited the vehicle and fled on foot. I did not use deadly force (this was a training exercise so was not real) against the suspects and was chastised by my instructor who insisted that I should have shot the suspects as they were fleeing. Training instructors, just like professors, convey authority knowledge but, in this case, the instructor was wrong. I was not legally authorized to use deadly force in the traffic stop scenario despite the insistence of my instructor to the contrary.

Politicians are sometimes taken as a source of authority knowledge about the law, crime, and criminal justice issues. Since they enact laws that directly impact the operations of the criminal justice system, we may assume they are an authority on crime and criminal justice. More specifically, we may assume that politicians know best about how to reduce crime and increase the effectiveness of the criminal justice system. However, history is rife with laws that sounded good on paper but had no impact on crime. For example, there is little evidence that sex offender registration protects the public from sexual predators or acts as a deterrent to repeat sex offenders even though every state has a law requiring convicted sex offenders to register with local authorities. Perhaps politicians are not the criminal justice experts some perceive them to be.

History is also full of criminal justice authorities that we now see as being misinformed. For example, Cesare Lombroso is the father of the positivist school of criminology. He is most readily recognized for his idea that some individuals are born criminal. He stated that criminals have certain unique biological characteristics, including large protruding jaws, high foreheads, flattened noses, and asymmetrical faces, to name a few.[8] These characteristics were similar to those found in primitive humans. Therefore, Lombroso argued that some individuals were genetic "throwbacks" to a more primitive time and were less evolved than other people and thus, were more likely to be criminals. Lombroso's research has been discredited because he failed to compare criminals with noncriminals. By studying only criminals, he found characteristics that were common to criminals. However, if Lombroso had studied a group of noncriminals, he would have discovered that these biological characteristics are just as prevalent among noncriminals. This example involves authority knowledge that is supported by research but the research methods used were flawed. The errors of Lombroso seem obvious now, but what do we know today through authority knowledge that is inaccurate or will be proven wrong in the future?

Knowledge from Tradition

In addition to authority knowledge, people often rely on tradition for knowledge. **Tradition knowledge** relies on the knowledge of the past. Individuals accept something as true because that is the way things have always been so it must be right. A good example of tradition knowledge is preventive/random patrol. Ever since vehicles were brought into the police patrol function, police administrators assumed that having patrol officers drive around randomly in the communities they serve, while they are not answering calls for service, would prevent crime. If you were a patrol officer in the early 1970s and asked your supervisor, "Why do I drive around randomly throughout my assigned area when I am not answering a call for service?" the answer would have been, "That is the way we have always done patrol and random patrol reduces crime through deterrence." The Kansas City Preventive Patrol Experiment challenged the tradition knowledge that preventive/random patrol reduces crime. The results of the study made it clear that the traditional practice of preventive/random patrol had little to no impact on reducing crime. This allowed police departments to develop other patrol deployment strategies such as directed patrol and "hot spots" policing since preventive patrol was seen as ineffective. The development of effective patrol deployment strategies continues today.

Knowledge from Common Sense

We frequently rely on **common sense knowledge** for what we know about crime and the criminal justice system because it "just makes sense." For example, it "just makes sense" that if we send juvenile delinquents on a field trip to prison where they will see first hand the prison environment as well as be yelled at by actual prisoners, they will refrain from future delinquency. That is exactly what the program *Scared Straight*, originally developed in the 1970s, is designed to do. *Scared Straight* programs are still in existence today and are even the premise for the television show *Beyond Scared Straight* on the A&E television network. As originally

RESEARCH STUDY[9]

In the mid-1970s, the number of offenders on probation began to significantly increase. By the mid-1980s, probation was the most frequently used sentence in most states and its use was becoming more common for felons, whereas previously, probation was typically limited to misdemeanor crimes and offenses committed by juveniles. Increasing numbers of felony offenders were being placed on probation because judges had no other alternative forms of punishment. Prisons were already operating above capacity due to rising crime rates. Despite the increase in the use of probation in the 1980s, few empirical studies of probation (particularly its use with felony offenders) had been published. In the early 1980s, the Rand Corporation conducted an extensive study of probation to learn more about the offenders sentenced to probation and the effectiveness of probation as a criminal sanction. At the time the study began, over one-third of California's probation population were convicted felons.[10] This was the first large-scale study of felony probation.

RESEARCH QUESTION

Is it safe to put felons on probation?

METHODOLOGY

Data for the study were obtained from the California Board of Prison Terms (CBPT). The Board had been collecting comprehensive data on all offenders sentenced to prison since 1978 and on a sample of adult males from 17 counties who received probation. From these two data sources, researchers selected a sample of male offenders who had been convicted of the following crimes: robbery, assault, burglary, theft, forgery, and drug offenses. These crimes were selected because an offender could receive either prison or probation if convicted. Approximately 16,500 male felony offenders were included in the study. For each offender, researchers had access to their personal characteristics, information on their crimes, court proceedings, and disposition.

RESULTS

Two main research questions were answered in this study. First, what were the recidivism rates for felony offenders who received probation? When assessing recidivism rates, the study found that the majority of offenders sentenced to probation recidivated during the follow-up period, which averaged 31 months. Overall, 65% of the sample of probationers were re-arrested and 51% were charged with and convicted of another offense. A total of 18% were convicted of a violent crime.

The second research question asked, what were the characteristics of the probationers who recidivated? Property offenders were more likely to recidivate compared to violent or drug offenders. Researchers also discovered that probationers tended to recidivate by committing the same crime that placed them on probation. Rand researchers included time to recidivism in their analysis and found that property and violent offenders recidivated sooner than drug offenders. The median time to the first filed charge was five months for property offenders and eight months for violent offenders.

LIMITATIONS WITH THE STUDY PROCEDURE

The issue of whether or not the findings would generalize to other counties in California and to other states was raised.

created, the program was designed to decrease juvenile delinquency by bringing at-risk and delinquent juveniles into prison where they would be "scared straight" by inmates serving life sentences. Participants in the program were talked to and yelled at by the inmates in an effort to scare them. It was believed that the fear felt by the participants would lead to a discontinuation of their delinquent behavior so that they would not end up in prison themselves. This sounds like a good idea. It makes sense, and the program was initially touted as a success due to anecdotal evidence based on a few delinquents who turned their lives around after participation in the program.

However, evaluations of the program and others like it showed that the program was in fact unsuccessful.

In the initial evaluation of the *Scared Straight* program, Finckenauer used a classic experimental design (discussed in Chapter 5), to evaluate the original "Lifer's Program" at Rahway State Prison in New Jersey where the program was initially developed.[13] Juveniles were randomly assigned to an experimental group that attended the *Scared Straight* program and a control group that did not participate in the program. Results of the evaluation were not positive. Post-test measures revealed that juveniles who were assigned to the experimental group and participated in the program were actually more seriously delinquent afterwards than those who did not participate in the program. Also using an experimental design with random assignment, Yarborough evaluated the "Juvenile Offenders Learn Truth" (JOLT) program

Data for the study came from probation and prison records from two counties in California. These two counties were not randomly selected, but were chosen because of their large probation populations and the willingness of departments to provide information. Further, the probation departments in these counties had experienced significant budget cuts. Supervision may have become compromised as a result and this could have explained why these counties had high rates of recidivism. Studies of probation recidivism in other states have found recidivism rates to be much lower, suggesting the Rand results may not have applied elsewhere.[11] Several studies examining the effectiveness of probation and the factors correlated with probation outcomes were published after 1985. Much of this research failed to produce results consistent with the Rand study.

IMPACT ON CRIMINAL JUSTICE

The Rand study of felony probation received a considerable amount of attention within the field of corrections. According to one scholar, the study was acclaimed as "the most important criminological research to be reported since World War II."[12] The National Institute of Justice disseminated the report to criminal justice agencies across the country and even highlighted the study in their monthly newsletter. Today, the study remains one of the most highly cited pieces of corrections research.

According to Rand researchers, these findings raised serious doubts about the effectiveness of probation for felony offenders. Most of the felons sentenced to probation recidivated and researchers were unable to develop an accurate prediction model to improve the courts' decision-making. The continued use of probation as a sanction for felony offenders appeared to be putting the public at risk. However, without adequate prison space, the courts had no other alternatives besides probation when sentencing offenders.

The researchers made several recommendations to address the limitations of using probation for felony offenders. First, it was recommended that states formally acknowledge that the purpose of probation had changed. Probation was originally used as a means of furthering the goal of rehabilitation in the correctional system. As the United States moved away from that goal in the late 1960s, the expectations of probation changed. Probation was now used as a way to exercise "restrictive supervision" over more serious offenders. Second, probation departments needed to redefine the responsibilities of their probation officers. Probation officers were now expected to be surveillance officers instead of treatment personnel, which required specialized training. In addition, states needed to explore the possibility of broadening the legal authority of its probation officers by allowing them to act as law enforcement officers if necessary. Third, states were advised to adopt a formal client management system that included risk/need assessments of every client. Such a system would help establish uniform, consistent treatment of those on probation and would also help departments allocate their resources efficiently and effectively. Fourth, researchers encouraged states to develop alternative forms of community punishment that offered more public protection than regular probation, which led to the development and use of intensive supervision probation, house arrest, electronic monitoring, day reporting centers, and other intermediate punishments.

at the State Prison of Southern Michigan at Jackson.[14] This program was similar to that of the "Lifer's Program," only with fewer obscenities used by inmates. Post-test measurements were taken at two intervals, three and six months after program completion. Again, results were not positive. Findings revealed no significant differences in delinquency between those juveniles who attended the program and those who did not. Other experiments conducted on *Scared Straight*-type programs further revealed their inability to deter juveniles from further delinquency.[15] Despite the common sense popularity of these programs, the evaluations showed that *Scared Straight* programs do not reduce delinquency and, in some instances, may actually increase delinquency. The programs may actually do more harm than good. I guess that begs the question, "Why do we still do these types of programs?"

Scared Straight programs and other widely held common sense beliefs about crime and the criminal justice system are questionable, based on the available research evidence. Common sense is important in our daily lives and is frequently correct, but, at times, it also contains inaccuracies, misinformation, and even prejudice.

Knowledge from Personal Experience

If you personally see something or if it actually happens to you, then you are likely to accept it as true and gain knowledge from the experience. Gaining knowledge through actual experiences is known as **personal experience knowledge,** and it has a powerful and lasting

Common sense indicates that sending juvenile delinquents on a field trip to prison will keep them from committing future acts of delinquency. Research on Scared Straight *programs indicates they are not effective at deterring delinquency.*

impact on everyone. Personal experiences are essential building blocks of knowledge and of what we believe to be true. The problem with knowledge gained from personal experiences is that personal experiences can be unique and unreliable, which can distort reality and lead us to believe things that are actually false.

How can events that someone personally experienced be wrong? The events are not wrong. Instead, the knowledge gained from the experience is wrong. For example, the research consistently shows that a person's demeanor significantly impacts the decision-making of police officers. During a traffic stop, if a person is rude, disrespectful, and uncooperative to the officer, then the driver is more likely to receive a traffic citation than a warning. That is what the research on police discretion shows. However, if a person was rude and uncooperative to a police officer during a traffic stop and was let go without a citation, the person will gain knowledge from this personal experience. The knowledge gained may include that being disrespectful during future traffic stops will get this person out of future tickets. Not likely. The event is not wrong. Instead, the knowledge gained from the experience is wrong because being disrespectful to the police usually leads to more enforcement action taken by the police, not less.

As a student in criminal justice, you have probably experienced something similar in interaction with friends, relatives, and neighbors. Your knowledge of criminal justice that you have developed in your criminal justice classes is trumped by one experience your friend, relative, or neighbor had with the criminal justice system. They believe they are right because they experienced it. However, there are four errors that occur in the knowledge gained from personal experiences: overgeneralization, selective observation, illogical reasoning, and resistance to change.

Overgeneralization   **Overgeneralization** happens when people conclude that what they have observed in one or a few cases is true for all cases. For example, you may see that a wealthy businesswomen in your community is acquitted of bribery and may conclude that "wealthy people, especially women, are never convicted in our criminal justice system," which is an overgeneralization. It is common to draw conclusions about people and society from our personal interactions, but, in reality, our experiences are limited because we interact with just a small percentage of people in society.

The same is true for practitioners in the criminal justice system. Practitioners have a tendency to believe that because something was done a particular way in their agency, it is done that way in all agencies. That may not be true. Although there are certainly operational similarities across criminal justice agencies, there are also nuances that exist across the over 50,000 criminal justice agencies in the United States. Believing that just because it was that way in your agency, it must be that way in all agencies leads to overgeneralization.

Selective Observation   **Selective observation** is choosing, either consciously or unconsciously, to pay attention to and remember events that support our personal preferences and beliefs. In fact, with selective observation, we will seek out evidence that confirms what we believe to be true and ignore the events that provide contradictory evidence. We are more likely to notice pieces of evidence that reinforce and support our ideology. As applied to the criminal justice system, when we are inclined to be critical of the criminal justice system, it is pretty easy to notice its every failing and ignore its successes. For example, if someone believes the police commonly use excessive force, the person is more likely to pay attention to and remember a police brutality allegation on the nightly news than a police pursuit that led to the apprehension of the suspect without incident on the same nightly news.

The business of background checks on prospective employees is increasing significantly. According to the Society for Human Resource Management, since the events of September 11, 2001, the percentage of companies that conduct criminal history checks during the hiring process has risen past 90%. Employers spend at least $2 billion a year to look into the pasts of their prospective employees. Problems with the business of background checks were identified through research that included a review of thousands of pages of court filings and interviews with dozens of court officials, data providers, lawyers, victims, and regulators.

The business of background checks is a system weakened by the conversion to digital files and compromised by the significant number of private companies that profit by amassing public records and selling them to employers. The private companies create a system in which a computer program scrapes the public files of court systems around the country to retrieve personal data. Basically, these are automated data-mining programs. Today, half the courts in the United States put criminal records on their public websites. So, the data are there for the taking, but the records that are retrieved typically are not checked for errors—errors that would be obvious to human eyes.

The errors can start with a mistake entered into the logs of a law enforcement agency or a court file. The biggest culprits, though, are companies that compile databases using public information. In some instances, their automated formulas misinterpret the information provided them. Other times, records wind up assigned to the wrong people with a common name. Furthermore, when a government agency erases a criminal conviction after a designated period of good behavior, many of the commercial databases don't perform the updates required to purge offenses that have been removed from public record. It is clear that these errors can have substantial ramifications, including damaged reputations and loss of job opportunities.

As another example, if you believe treatment efforts on sex offenders are futile, you will pay attention to and remember each sex offender you hear about that recidivates but will pay little attention to any successes. It is easy to find instances that confirm our beliefs, but with selective observation, the complete picture is not being viewed. Therefore, if we only acknowledge the events that confirm our beliefs and ignore those that challenge them, we are falling victim to selective observation.

Besides selective observation, some of our observations may simply be wrong. Consider eyewitness identification. It is a common practice in the criminal justice system, but research has consistently demonstrated inaccuracies in eyewitness identification. The witness feels certain that the person viewed is the person who committed the offense, but sometimes the witness is wrong. Even when our senses of sight, hearing, taste, touch, and smell are fully operational, our minds have to interpret what we have sensed, which may lead to an inaccurate observation.

Illogical Reasoning **Illogical reasoning** occurs when someone jumps to premature conclusions or presents an argument that is based on invalid assumptions. Premature conclusions occur when we feel we have the answer based on a few pieces of evidence and do not need to seek additional information that may invalidate our conclusion.

Think of a detective who, after examining only a few pieces of evidence, quickly narrows in on a murder suspect. It is common for a detective to assess the initial evidence and make an initial determination of who committed the murder. However, it is hoped that the detective will continue to sort through all the evidence for confirmation or rejection of his original conclusion regarding the murder suspect. Illogical reasoning by jumping to premature conclusions is common in everyday life. We look for evidence to confirm or reject our beliefs and stop when a small amount of evidence is present; we jump to conclusions. If a person states, "I know four people who have dropped out of high school, and each one of them ended up addicted to drugs, so all dropouts abuse drugs," the person is jumping to conclusions.

Illogical reasoning also occurs when an argument, based on invalid assumptions, is presented. Let's revisit the *Scared Straight* example previously discussed. Program developers assumed that brief exposure to the harsh realities of prison would deter juveniles from future delinquency. The *Scared Straight* program is an example of illogical reasoning. Four hours of exposure to prison life is not going to counteract years of delinquency and turn a delinquent into a nondelinquent. The program is based on a false assumption and fails to recognize the substantial risk factors present in the lives of most delinquents that must be mediated before the juvenile can

9

live a crime-free lifestyle. A fear of prison, developed through brief exposure, is not enough to counteract the risk factors present in the lives of most delinquents. Although the *Scared Straight* program sounds good, it is illogical to assume that a brief experience with prison life will have a stronger impact on the decisions made by delinquents than peer support for delinquency, drug abuse, lack of education, poor parental supervision, and other factors that influence delinquency.

Resistance to Change   **Resistance to change** is the reluctance to change our beliefs in light of new, accurate, and valid information to the contrary. Resistance to change is common and it occurs for several reasons. First, even though our personal experience may be counter to our belief system, it is hard to admit we were wrong after we have taken a position on an issue. Even when the research evidence shows otherwise, people who work within programs may still believe they are effective. As previously stated, even though the research evidence shows otherwise, *Scared Straight* programs still exist and there is even a television show devoted to the program. Second, too much devotion to tradition and the argument that this is the way it has always been done inhibits change and hinders our ability to accept new directions and develop new knowledge. Third, uncritical agreement with authority inhibits change. Although authority knowledge is certainly an important means of gaining knowledge, we must critically evaluate the ideas, beliefs, and statements of those in positions of authority and be willing to challenge those statements where necessary. However, people often accept the beliefs of those in positions of authority without question, which hinders change.

Knowledge from Media Portrayals

Television shows, movies, websites, newspapers, and magazine articles are important sources of information. This is especially true for information about crime and the criminal justice system since most people have not had much contact with criminals or the criminal justice system. Instead of gaining knowledge about the criminal justice system through personal experience, most people learn about crime and the operations of the criminal justice system through media outlets. Since the primary goal of many of these media outlets is to entertain, they may not accurately reflect the reality of crime and criminal justice. Despite their inaccuracies, the media has a substantial impact on what people know about crime and the criminal justice system. Most people know what they know about crime and criminal justice through the

media, and this knowledge even has an impact on criminal justice system operations.

An example of the potential impact of the media on the actual operations of the criminal justice system involves the *CSI: Crime Scene Investigation* television shows. The shows have been criticized for their unrealistic portrayal of the role of forensic science in solving criminal cases. Critics claim that *CSI* viewers accept what they see on the show as an accurate representation of how forensic science works. When summoned for jury duty, they bring with them unrealistic expectations of the forensic evidence they will see in trial. When the expected sophisticated forensic evidence is not presented in the real trial, the juror is more likely to vote to acquit the defendant. This phenomenon is known as the **CSI Effect.** Has the research shown that the CSI Effect exists and is impacting the criminal justice system? Most of the research shows that the CSI Effect does not exist and thus does not impact juror decision-making, but other research has shown that viewers of *CSI* have higher expectations related to evidence presented at trial.[17]

There are several instances in which media attention on a particular topic created the idea that a major problem existed when it did not. An example is **Halloween sadism.** Halloween sadism is the practice of giving contaminated treats to children during trick or treating.[18] In 1985, Joel Best wrote an article entitled, "The Myth of the Halloween Sadist."[19] His article reviewed press coverage of Halloween sadism in the leading papers in the three largest metropolitan areas (*New York Times, Los Angeles Times*, and *Chicago Tribune*) from 1958–1984. Although the belief in Halloween sadism is widespread, Best found few reported incidents and few reports of children being injured by Halloween sadism. Follow-ups on these reported incidents led to the conclusion that most of these reports were hoaxes. Best concluded, "I have been unable to find a substantiated report of a child being killed or seriously injured by a contaminated treat picked up in the course of trick or treating."[20] Since 1985, Best has kept his research up to date and has come to the same conclusion. Halloween sadism is an urban legend; it is a story that is told as true, even though there is little or no evidence that the events in the story ever occurred.

DISPELLING MYTHS: THE POWER OF RESEARCH METHODS

In the prior section, sources of knowledge were discussed along with the limitations of each. A researcher (e.g., criminologist), ideally, takes no knowledge claim

The press release from Oregon State University is titled "Beer Compound Shows Potent Promise in Prostate Cancer Battle." The press release leads to several newspaper articles throughout the country written on the preventative nature of drinking beer on prostate cancer development with titles such as "Beer Protects Your Prostate" and "Beer May Help Men Ward Off Prostate Cancer." By the titles alone, this sounds great; one of the main ingredients in beer appears to thwart prostate cancer.

The study that generated these headlines was conducted by a group of researchers at Oregon State University using cultured cells with purified compounds in a laboratory setting. The research showed that xanthohumol, a compound found in hops, slowed the growth of prostate cancer cells and also the growth of cells that cause enlarged prostates. But you would have to drink more than 17 pints of beer to consume a medically effective dose of xanthohumol, which is almost a case of beer. In addition, although the research is promising, further study is necessary to determine xanthohumol's true impact on prostate cancer.

These are the types of headlines that people pay attention to and want to believe as true, even if disproven by later research. People want to believe that there are health benefits to alcohol consumption. You have probably heard about the health benefits of drinking red wine, but here is something you should consider. Recently, the University of Connecticut released a statement describing an extensive research misconduct investigation involving a member of its faculty. The investigation was sparked by an anonymous allegation of research irregularities. The comprehensive report of the investigation, which totals approximately 60,000 pages, concludes that the professor is guilty of 145 counts of fabrication and falsification of data. The professor had gained international notoriety for his research into the beneficial properties of resveratrol, which is found in red wine, especially its impact on aging. Obviously, this throws his research conclusions, that red wine has a beneficial impact on the aging process, into question.

---

for granted, but instead relies on research methods to discover the truth. In the attempt to generate new knowledge, a researcher is skeptical of knowledge that is generated by the sources discussed in the prior section, and this skepticism leads to the questioning of conventional thinking. Through this process, existing knowledge claims are discredited, modified, or substantiated. Research methods provide the researcher with the tools necessary to test current knowledge and discover new knowledge.

Although knowledge developed through research methods is by no means perfect and infallible, it is definitely a more systematic, structured, precise, and evidence-based process than the knowledge sources previously discussed. However, researchers should not dismiss all knowledge from the prior sources discussed, because, as mentioned, these sources of knowledge are sometimes accurate and certainly have their place in the development of knowledge. Researchers should guard against an elitist mind-set in which all knowledge, unless it is research-based knowledge, is dismissed.

To further discuss the importance of research methods in the development of knowledge, this section will discuss myths about crime and criminal justice. **Myths** are beliefs that are based on emotion rather than rigorous analysis. Take the myth of the Halloween sadist previously discussed. Many believe that there are real examples of children being harmed by razor blades, poison, or other nefarious objects placed in Halloween candy. This belief has changed the practices of many parents on Halloween; not allowing their children to trick-or-treat in their neighborhood and forbidding them from going to the doors of strangers. After careful analysis by Best, there is not a single, known example of children being seriously injured or killed by contaminated candy given by strangers. The Halloween sadist is a myth but it is still perpetuated today, and as the definition states, it is a belief based upon emotion rather than rigorous analysis. People accept myths as accurate knowledge of reality when, in fact, the knowledge is false.

The power of research is the ability to dispel myths. If someone were to assess the research literature on a myth or do their own research, she would find that the knowledge based on the myth is wrong. Perceived reality is contradicted by the facts developed through research. But that does not mean that the myth still doesn't exist. It is important to keep in mind that the perpetuation and acceptance of myths by the public, politicians, and criminal justice personnel has contributed to the failure of criminal justice practices and policies designed to reduce crime and improve the operations of the criminal justice system. In this section, a detailed example of a

MYTHS ABOUT CRIME

Some additional myths about crime that research does not support include:

- Crime statistics accurately show what crimes are being committed and what crimes are most harmful.[22]
- Most criminals—especially the dangerous ones—are mentally ill.[23]
- White-collar crime is only about financial loss and does not hurt anyone.[24]
- Serial murderers are middle-aged, white males.[25]
- Criminals are significantly different from noncriminals.[26]
- People are more likely to be a victim of violent crime committed by a stranger than by someone they know.[27]
- Older adults are more likely to be victimized than people in any other age group.[28]
- Sex offender registration protects the public from sexual predators.[29]
- Juvenile crime rates are significantly increasing.[30]
- Only the most violent juveniles are tried as adults.[31]

myth about crime, police, courts, and corrections will be presented to demonstrate how the myth has been dispelled through research. In addition, several additional myths about crime, police, courts, and corrections will be briefly presented.

Myths about Crime—Drug Users Are Violent

The myth of drug users as violent offenders continues to be perpetuated by media accounts of violent drug users. The public sees drug users as violent offenders who commit violent crimes to get money for drugs or who commit violent crimes while under the intoxicating properties of drugs. The public also recognizes the violent nature of the drug business with gangs and cartels using violence to protect their turf. In May 2012, extensive media attention was given to the case of the Miami man who ate the face of a homeless man for an agonizing 18 minutes until police shot and killed the suspect. The police believed that the suspect was high on the street drug known as "bath salts." This horrific case definitely leaves the image in the public's mind about the relationship between violence and drug use.

In recent years, media reports have focused on the relationship between methamphetamine use and violence; before then it was crack cocaine use and violence.[32] However, media portrayals regarding the violent tendencies of drug users date back to the 1930s and the release of *Reefer Madness*. In 1985, Goldstein suggested that drugs and violence could be related in three different ways:

1. violence could be the direct result of drug ingestion;
2. violence could be a product of the instability of drug market activity; and

3. violence could be the consequence of people having a compulsive need for drugs or money for drugs.[33]

So, what does the research show? Studies have found that homicides related to crack cocaine were usually the product of the instability of drug market activity (i.e., buying and selling drugs can be a violent activity) and rarely the result of drug ingestion.[34] After an extensive review of research studies on alcohol, drugs, and violence, Parker and Auerhahn concluded, "Despite a number of published statements to the contrary, we find no significant evidence suggesting that drug use is associated with violence. There is substantial evidence to suggest that alcohol use is significantly associated with violence of all kinds."[35] The reality is not everyone who uses drugs becomes violent and users who do become violent do not do so every time they use drugs; therefore, the relationship between violence and drug use is a myth.

Myths about Police—Female Police Officers Do Not Perform as Well as Males

Female police officers still face the myth that they cannot perform as well as male police officers. Throughout history, females have faced significant difficulties even becoming police officers. In the past, it was common for police agencies to require all police applicants to meet a minimum height requirement to be considered for employment. The minimum height requirement was 5'8" for most agencies, which limited the ability of females to successfully meet the minimum standards to become a police officer. Even if women could meet the minimum height requirements, they were typically faced with a physical-abilities test that emphasized upper body

Some additional myths about the police that research does not support include:

- Police target minorities for traffic stops and arrests.[36]
- Most crimes are solved through forensic science.[37]
- COMPSTAT reduces crime.[38]
- Intensive law enforcement efforts at the street level will lead to the control of illicit drug use and abuse.[39]
- Police work primarily entails responding to crimes in progress or crimes that have just occurred.[40]
- Police presence reduces crime.[41]
- Detectives are most responsible for solving crimes and arresting offenders.[42]

strength (e.g., push-ups and bench presses). Women failed these tests more often than men, and thus were not eligible to be police officers. Minimum height requirements are no longer used in law enforcement, but the perception that female police officers are not as good as males still exists. Today, the myth that women cannot be effective police officers is based largely on the belief that the need to demonstrate superior physical strength is a daily, common occurrence in law enforcement along with the belief that police work is routinely dangerous, violent, and crime-related.

So, what does the research show? On occasion, it is useful for police officers to be able to overpower suspects by demonstrating superior physical strength, but those types of activities are rare in law enforcement. In addition, it is fairly rare for a police officer to have to deal with a dangerous and violent encounter or even an incident involving a crime. The Police Services Study conducted in the 1970s analyzed 26,418 calls for service in three metropolitan areas and found that only 19% of calls for service involve crime and only 2% of the total calls for service involve violent crime.[43] This research study was among the first to assess the types of calls for service received by police agencies.

Despite the belief that women do not make good police officers, consistent research findings show that women are extremely capable as police officers, and in some respects, outperform their male counterparts.[44] Research has demonstrated several advantages to the hiring, retention, and promotion of women in law enforcement. First, female officers are as competent as their male counterparts. Research does not show any consistent differences in how male and female patrol officers perform their duties. Second, female officers are less likely to use excessive force. Research has shown that female patrol officers are less likely to be involved in high-speed pursuits, incidents of deadly force, and the use of excessive

force. Female officers are more capable at calming potentially violent situations through communication and also demonstrate heightened levels of caution. Third, female officers can help implement community-oriented policing. Studies have shown that female officers are more supportive of the community-policing philosophy than are their male counterparts. Fourth, female officers can improve law enforcement's response to violence

Despite the belief that women do not make good police officers, research findings show that women are extremely capable as police officers, and in some respects, outperform their male counterparts.

MYTHS ABOUT COURTS

Some additional myths about courts that research does not support include:

- Many criminals escape justice because of the exclusionary rule.[45]

- Subjecting juvenile offenders to harsh punishments can reduce crime committed by juveniles.[46]

- Public opinion is overwhelmingly in favor of imprisonment and harsh punishment for offenders.[47]

- The death penalty brings closure and a sense of justice to the family and friends of murder victims.[48]

- Insanity is a common verdict in criminal courts in the United States.[49]

- Eyewitness identification is reliable evidence.[50]

- Most people who commit crimes based on hatred, bias, or discrimination face hate crime charges and longer sentencing.[51]

---

against women. Studies have shown that female officers are more patient and understanding in handling domestic violence calls, and female victims of domestic violence are more likely to provide positive evaluations of female officers than their male counterparts.[52]

Myths about Courts—The Death Penalty Is Administered Fairly

According to a recent Gallup poll, 52% of Americans say the death penalty is applied fairly in the United States, the lowest mark in almost 40 years.[53] The issue of fairness and the death penalty typically concerns whether the punishment is equally imposed on offenders who are equally deserving based on legal factors (i.e., similar offense, similar prior criminal history, similar aggravating circumstances, and similar mitigating circumstances).[54] Unfairness can be shown if similarly situated offenders are more or less likely to receive death sentences based on age, gender, and race.

So, what does the research show? First, has research shown that a defendant's age influences his or her chances of being sentenced to death? A study of about 5,000 homicides, controlling for legally relevant variables, found that defendants over the age of 25 were more than twice as likely to receive the death penalty in comparison to those 25 years of age or younger.[55]

Second, has research shown that a defendant's gender influences his or her chance of being sentenced to death? Capital punishment is almost exclusively reserved for male defendants. On December 31, 2010, there were 3,158 prisoners under a sentence of death in the United States: 58 were women, or 1.8%.[56] However, women account for 10–12% of all murders in the United States.[57] One research study found that male defendants were 2.6 times more likely than females to receive a death sentence after controlling for legally relevant factors.[58]

Third, has research shown that a defendant's race influences his or her chance of being sentenced to death? Most of the research on the biased nature of the death penalty has focused on racial inequities in the sentence. Although some research has shown that a defendant's race has an impact on the likelihood of receiving a death sentence, a significant amount of research has shown that the race of the victim has the most substantial impact on death sentences. The research evidence clearly shows that offenders who murder white victims are more likely to receive a death sentence than offenders who murder black victims.[59] When assessing the race of both the victim and offender, the composition most likely to receive the death penalty is when a black offender murders a white victim.[60]

Myths about Corrections—Imprisonment Is the Most Severe Form of Punishment

It seems clear that besides the death penalty, the most severe punishment available in our criminal justice system is to lock up offenders in prison. On a continuum, it is perceived that sentence severity increases as one moves from fines, to probation, to intermediate sanctions such as boot camps, and finally, to incarceration in prison. The public and politicians support this perception as well.

So, what does the research show? What do criminals think is the most severe form of punishment? A growing body of research has assessed how convicted offenders perceive and experience the severity of sentences in our criminal justice system.[61] Research suggests that alternatives to incarceration in prison (i.e., probation and intermediate sanctions) are perceived by many offenders as more severe due to a greater risk of program failure (e.g., probation revocation). In comparison, serving prison time is easier.[62]

Some additional myths about corrections that research does not support include:

- Punishing criminals reduces crime.[63]
- Prisons are too lenient in their day-to-day operations (prisons as country clubs).[64]
- Prisons can be self-supporting if only prisoners were forced to work.[65]
- Private prisons are more cost effective than state-run prisons.[66]
- Focus of community corrections is rehabilitation rather than punishment.[67]

- Correctional rehabilitation does not work.[68]
- Drug offenders are treated leniently by the criminal justice system.[69]
- Most death row inmates will be executed eventually.[70]
- If correctional sanctions are severe enough, people will think twice about committing crimes.[71]
- Sexual violence against and exploitation of inmates of the same gender are primarily the result of lack of heterosexual opportunities.[72]

For example, one study found that about one-third of nonviolent offenders given the option of participating in an Intensive Supervision Probation (ISP) program, chose prison instead because the prospects of working every day and submitting to random drug tests was more punitive than serving time in prison.[73] Prisoners also stated that they would likely be caught violating probation conditions (i.e., high risk of program failure) and be sent to prison anyway.[74] In another research study involving survey responses from 415 inmates serving a brief prison sentence for a nonviolent crime, prison was considered the eighth most severe sanction, with only community service and probation seen as less punitive. Electronic monitoring (seventh), intensive supervision probation (sixth), halfway house (fifth), intermittent incarceration (fourth), day reporting (third), county jail (second), and boot camp (first) were all rated by inmates as more severe sanctions than prison.[75]

WHAT IS RESEARCH AND WHY IS IT IMPORTANT TO BE AN INFORMED CONSUMER OF RESEARCH?

We probably should have started the chapter with the question "What is research?" but we wanted to initially lay a foundation for the question with a discussion of the problems with how knowledge is developed and the power of research in discovering the truth. **Research methods** are tools that allow criminology and criminal justice researchers to systematically study crime and the criminal justice system. The study of research methods is the study of the basic rules, appropriate techniques,

and relevant procedures for conducting research. Research methods provide the tools necessary to approach issues in criminal justice from a rigorous standpoint and challenge opinions based solely on nonscientific observations and experiences. Similarly, **research** is the scientific investigation of an issue, problem, or subject utilizing research methods. Research is a means of knowledge development that is designed to assist in discovering answers to research questions and leads to the creation of new questions.

How Is Knowledge Development through Research Different?

Previously, sources of knowledge development were discussed, including authority, tradition, common sense, personal experience, and media portrayals. The problems generated by each knowledge source were also discussed. Research is another source of knowledge development, but it is different than those previously discussed in several ways. First, research relies on logical and systematic methods and observations to answer questions. Researchers use systematic, well-established research practices to seek answers to their questions. The methods and observations are completed in such a way that others can inspect and assess the methods and observations and offer feedback and criticism. Researchers develop, refine, and report their understanding of crime and the criminal justice system more systematically than the public does through casual observation. Those who conduct scientific research employ much more rigorous methods to gather the information/knowledge they are seeking.

Second, in order to prove that a research finding is correct, a researcher must be able to replicate the finding using the same methods. Only through replication can we have confidence in our original finding. For researchers, it may be important to replicate findings many times over so that we are assured our original finding was not a coincidence or chance occurrence. The Minneapolis Domestic Violence Experiment is an example of this and will be discussed in detail in Chapter 5. In the experiment, the researchers found that arrests for domestic violence lead to fewer repeat incidences in comparison to separation of the people involved and mediation. Five replication studies were conducted and none were able to replicate the findings in the Minneapolis study. In fact, three of the replications found that those arrested for domestic violence had higher levels of continued domestic violence, so arrest did not have the deterrent effect found in the Minneapolis study.

Third, research is objective. Objectivity indicates a neutral and nonbiased perspective when conducting research. Although there are examples to the contrary, the researcher should not have a vested interest in what findings are discovered from the research. The researcher is expected to remain objective and report the findings of the study regardless of whether the findings support their personal opinion or agenda. In addition, research ensures objectivity by allowing others to examine and be critical of the methodology, findings, and results of research studies.

It should be clear that using research methods to answer questions about crime and the criminal justice system will greatly reduce the errors in the development of knowledge previously discussed. For example, research methods reduces the likelihood of overgeneralization by using systematic procedures for selecting individuals or groups to study that are representative of the individuals or groups that we wish to generalize. This is the topic of Chapter 3, which covers sampling procedures. In addition, research methods reduces the risk of selective observation by requiring that we measure and observe our research subjects systematically.

Being an Informed Consumer of Research

Criminal justice and criminological research is important for several reasons. First, it can provide better and more objective information. Second, it can promote better decision-making. Today, more than ever, we live in a world driven by data and in which there is an increasing dependence on the assessment of data when making decisions. As well as possible, research ensures that our decisions are based on data and not on an arbitrary or personal basis. Third, it allows for the objective assessment of programs. Fourth, it has often been the source of innovation within criminal justice agencies. Fifth, it can be directly relevant to criminal justice practice and have a significant impact on criminal justice operations.

Before we apply research results to practices in the criminal justice system, and before we even accept those research results as reasonable, we need to be able to know whether or not they are worthwhile. In other words, should we believe the results of the study? Research has its own limitations, so we need to evaluate research results and the methods used to produce them, and we do so through critical evaluation. Critical evaluation involves identifying both positive and negative aspects of the research study—both the good and the bad. Critical evaluation involves comparing the methodology used in the research with the standards established in research methods.

Through critical evaluation, consumers of research break studies down into their essential elements. What are the research questions and hypotheses? What were the independent and dependent variables? What research design was used? Was probability sampling used? What data-gathering procedures were employed? What type of data analysis was conducted and what conclusions were made? These are some of the questions that are asked by informed consumers of research. The evaluation of research ranges from the manner in which one obtains an idea to the ways in which one writes about the research results, and understanding each step in the research process is useful in our attempts to consume research conducted by others. Located between these two activities are issues concerning ethics, sampling, research design, data analyses, and interpretations.

The research design and procedures are typically the most critically evaluated aspects of research and will likewise receive the greatest amount of attention in this text. Informed consumers of research don't just take the results of a research study at face value because the study is in an academic journal or written by someone with a Ph.D. Instead, informed consumers critically evaluate research. Taking what is learned throughout this text, critical evaluation of research is covered in Chapter 8, and upon completing this text, it is hoped that you will be an informed consumer of research and will put your research knowledge to use throughout your career.

Although many students will never undertake their own research, all will be governed by policies based upon research and exposed to research findings in their chosen professional positions. Most government agencies, including the criminal justice system, as well as private industry, routinely rely on data analysis. Criminal justice students employed with these agencies will be challenged if not prepared for quantitative tasks. Unfortunately, it is not unusual to find students as well as professionals in criminal justice who are unable to fully understand research reports and journal articles in their own field.

Beyond our criminal justice careers, we are all exposed to and use research to help us understand issues and to make personal decisions. For example, we know that cigarette smoking causes lung cancer and has other significant health impacts, so we don't smoke. Your doctor tells you that your cholesterol is too high and you need to limit your red meat intake because research shows that consumption of red meat raises cholesterol; so, you quit eating red meat. That is why not all the examples in this text are criminal justice research examples. Some come from the medical field while others come from psychology and other disciplines. This is to remind you that you are probably exposed to much more research than you thought on day one of this class.

Overall, knowledge of research methods will allow you to more appropriately consider and consume information that is important to your career in criminal justice. It will help you better understand the process of asking and answering a question systematically and be a better consumer of the kind of information that you really need to be the best criminal justice professional you can. Once familiar with research methods, your anxiety about reviewing technical reports and research findings can be minimized. As discussed in the next section, research methods involve a process and once you understand the process, you can apply your knowledge to any research study, even those in other disciplines.

THE RESEARCH PROCESS

One of the nice things about studying research methods is it is about learning a process. Research methods can be seen as a sequential process with the first step being followed by the second step, and so on. There are certainly times when the order of the steps may be modified, but researchers typically follow the same process for each research study they complete regardless of the research topic (as depicted in Figure 2.1 in Chapter 2). Very simply, a research problem or question is identified, and a methodology is selected, developed, and implemented to answer the research question. This sequential process is one of the advantages of understanding research methods, because once you understand the process, you can apply that process to any research question that interests you. In addition, research methods are the same across disciplines. So, sampling is the same in business as it is in health education and as it is in criminal justice. Certainly the use of a particular method will be more common in one discipline in comparison to another, but the protocol for implementing the method to complete the research study is the same. For example, field research (discussed in Chapter 6) is used much more frequently in anthropology than in criminal justice. However, the research protocol to implement field research is the same whether you are studying an indigenous Indian tribe in South America in anthropology or a group of heroin users in St. Louis in criminal justice.

Some authors have presented the research process as a wheel or circle, with no specific beginning or end. Typically, the research process begins with the selection of a research problem and the development of research questions or hypotheses (discussed further in Chapter 2). It is common for the results of previous research to generate new research questions and hypotheses for the researcher. This suggests that research is cyclical, a vibrant and continuous process. When a research study answers one question, the result is often the generation of additional questions, which plunges the researcher right back into the research process to complete additional research to answer these new questions.

In this section, a brief overview of the research process will be presented. The chapters that follow address various aspects of the research process, but it is critical that you keep in mind the overall research process as you read this book, which is why is it presented here. Although you will probably not be expected to conduct a research study on your own, it is important for an educated consumer of research to understand the steps in the research process. The steps are presented in chronological order and appear neatly ordered. In practice, the researcher can go back and forth between the steps in the research process.

Step 1: Select a Topic and Conduct a Literature Review

The first step in the research process is typically the identification of a problem or topic that the researcher is interested in studying. Research topics can arise from a wide variety of sources, including the findings of a current study, a question that a criminal justice agency needs to have answered, or the result of intellectual curiosity. Once the researcher has identified a particular problem or topic, the researcher assesses the current state of the literature related to the problem or topic. The researcher will often spend a considerable amount of time in determining what the existing literature has to say about the topic. Has the topic already been studied to the point that the questions in which the researcher is interested have been sufficiently answered? If so, can the researcher approach the subject from a previously unexamined perspective? Many times, research topics have been previously explored but not brought to completion. If this is the case, it is certainly reasonable to examine the topic again. It is even appropriate to replicate a previous study to determine whether the findings reported in the prior research continue to be true in different settings with different participants. This step in the research process is also discussed in Chapter 2.

Step 2: Develop a Research Question

After a topic has been identified and a comprehensive literature review has been completed on the topic, the next step is the development of a research question or questions. The research question marks the beginning of your research study and is critical to the remaining steps in the research process. The research question determines the research plan and methodology that will be employed in the study, the data that will be collected, and the data analysis that will be performed. Basically, the remaining steps in the process are completed in order to answer the research question or questions established in this step. The development of research questions is discussed in more detail in Chapter 2.

Step 3: Develop a Hypothesis

After the research questions have been established, the next step is the formulation of **hypotheses,** which are statements about the expected relationship between two **variables.** For example, a hypothesis may state that there is no relationship between heavy metal music preference and violent delinquency. The two variables stated in the hypothesis are music preference and violent delinquency. Hypothesis development is discussed in more detail in Chapter 2.

Step 4: Operationalize Concepts

Operationalization involves the process of giving the concepts in your study a working definition and determining how each concept in your study will be

measured. For example, in Step 3, the variables were music preference and violent delinquency. The process of operationalization involves determining how music preference and violent delinquency will be measured. Operationalization is further discussed in Chapter 2.

Step 5: Develop the Research Plan and Methodology

The next step is to develop the methodology that will be employed to answer the research questions and test the hypotheses. The research methodology is the blueprint for the study, which outlines how the research is to be conducted. The research questions will determine the appropriate methodology for the study. The research design selected should be driven by the research questions asked. In other words, the research questions dictate the methods used to answer them. The methodology is basically a research plan on how the research questions will be answered and will detail:

1. What group, subjects, or population will be studied and selected? Sampling will be discussed in Chapter 3.

3. What research design will be used to collect data to answer the research questions? Various research designs will be covered in Chapters 4–7.

You need to have familiarity with all research designs so that you can become an educated consumer of research. A survey cannot answer all research questions, so knowing a lot about surveys but not other research designs will not serve you well as you assess research studies. There are several common designs used in criminal justice and criminology research. Brief descriptions of several common research designs are presented below, but each is discussed in detail in later chapters.

Survey Research   **Survey research** is one of the most common research designs employed in criminal justice research. It obtains data directly from research participants by asking them questions and is often conducted through self-administered questionnaires and personal interviews. For example, a professor might have her students complete a survey during class to understand the relationship between drug use and self-esteem. Survey research is discussed in Chapter 4.

Experimental Design   **Experimental designs** are used when researchers are interested in determining whether a program, policy, practice, or intervention is effective. For example, a researcher may use an experimental design to determine if boot camps are effective at reducing juvenile delinquency. Experimental design is discussed in Chapter 5.

Field Research   **Field research** involves researchers studying individuals or groups of individuals in their natural environment. The researcher is observing closely or acting as part of the group under study and is able to describe in depth not only the subject's behaviors, but also consider the motivations that drive those behaviors. For example, if a researcher wanted to learn more about gangs and their activities, he may "hang out" with a gang in order to observe their behavior. Field research is discussed in Chapter 6.

Case Studies   A **case study** is an in-depth analysis of one or a few illustrative cases. This design allows the story behind an individual, a particular offender, to be told and then information from cases studies can be extrapolated to a larger group. Often these studies require the review and analysis of documents such as police reports and court records and interviews with the offender and others. For example, a researcher may explore the life history of a serial killer to try and understand why the offender killed. Case studies are discussed in Chapter 6.

Secondary Data Analysis   **Secondary data analysis** occurs when researchers obtain and reanalyze data that was originally collected for a different purpose. This can include reanalyzing data collected from a prior research study, using criminal justice agency records to answer a research question, or historical research. For example, a researcher using secondary data analysis may analyze inmate files from a nearby prison to understand the relationship between custody level assignment and disciplinary violations inside prison. Secondary data analysis is discussed in Chapter 7.

Content Analysis   **Content analysis** requires the assessment of content contained in mass communication outlets such as newspapers, television, magazines, and the like. In this research design, documents, publications, or presentations are reviewed and analyzed. For example, a researcher utilizing content analysis might review true crime books involving murder to see how the characteristics of the offender and victim in the true crime books match reality as depicted in the FBI's Supplemental Homicide Reports. Content analysis is discussed in Chapter 7.

Despite the options these designs offer, other research designs are available and will be discussed later in the text. Ultimately, the design used will depend on the nature of the study and the research questions asked.

Step 6: Execute the Research Plan and Collect Data

The next step in the research process is the collection of the data based on the research design developed. For example, if a survey is developed to study the relationship between gang membership and violent delinquency, the distribution and collection of surveys from a group of high school students would occur in this step. Data collection is discussed in several chapters throughout this text.

Step 7: Analyze Data

After the data have been collected, the next phase in the research process involves analyzing the data through various and appropriate statistical techniques. The most common means for data analysis today is through the use of a computer and statistically oriented software. Data analysis and statistics are discussed in Chapter 9.

Step 8: Report Findings, Results, and Limitations

Reporting and interpreting the results of the study make up the final step in the research process. The findings and results of the study can be communicated through reports, journals, books, or computer presentations. At this step, the results are reported and the research questions are answered. In addition, an assessment is made regarding the support or lack of support for the hypotheses tested. It is also at this stage that the researcher can pose additional research questions that may now need to be answered as a result of the research study. In addition, the limitations of the study, as well as the impact those limitations may have on the results of the study, will be described by the researcher. All research has limitations, so it is incumbent on the researcher to identify those limitations for the reader. The process of assessing the quality of research will be discussed in Chapter 8.

RESEARCH IN ACTION: IMPACTING CRIMINAL JUSTICE OPERATIONS

Research in the criminal justice system has had significant impacts on its operations. The following sections provide an example of research that has significantly impacted each of the three main components of the criminal justice system: police, courts, and corrections. The purpose of this section is to demonstrate that research has aided the positive development and progression of the criminal justice system.

Police Research Example[76]

The efforts of criminal justice researchers in policing have been important and have created the initial and critical foundation necessary for the further development of effective and productive law enforcement. One seminal study asked: How important is it for the police to respond quickly when a citizen calls? The importance of rapid response was conveyed in a 1973 National Commission on Productivity Report despite the fact that there was very little empirical evidence upon which to base this assumption. In fact, the Commission stated "there is no definitive relationship between response time and deterrence, but professional judgment and logic do suggest that the two are related in a strong enough manner to make more rapid response important."[77] Basically the Commission members were stating that we don't have any research evidence that response times are important, but we "know" that they are. Police departments allocated substantial resources to the patrol function and deployed officers in an effort to improve response time through the use of the 9-1-1 telephone number, computer-assisted dispatch, and beat assignment systems. Officers were typically assigned to a patrol beat. When the officers were not answering calls for service, they remained in their assigned beats so they could immediately respond to an emergency.

The data for the project were collected as part of a larger experiment on preventive patrol carried out in Kansas City, Missouri, between October 1972 and September 1973.[78] To determine the impact of response time, researchers speculated that the following variables would be influenced by response time: 1) the outcome of the response, 2) citizen satisfaction with response time, and 3) citizen satisfaction with the responding officer. Several data sources were used in the study. First, surveys were completed after all citizen-initiated calls (excluding automobile accidents) that involved contact with a police officer. The survey instrument consisted of questions to assess the length of time to respond to a call and the outcome of the call (i.e., arrest). Over 1,100 surveys were completed. Second, a follow-up survey was mailed to citizens whom the police had contacted during their response. These surveys asked questions to assess citizen satisfaction with response time and outcome. Over 425 of these surveys were returned.

The data collected during the study showed that response time did not determine whether or not the police made an arrest or recovered stolen property. This was the most surprising finding from the study because it challenged one of the basic underlying principles of police patrol. Researchers attributed the lack of significance to the fact that most citizens waited before calling the police. Rapid response simply did not matter in situations where citizens delayed in reporting the crime.

Rapid response time was not only believed to be important in determining the outcome of a response (i.e., more likely to lead to an arrest), it was also considered an important predictor of citizen satisfaction. Data from the study showed that when the police arrived sooner than expected, citizens were more satisfied with response time. However, subsequent research has shown that citizens are also satisfied with a delayed response as long as the dispatcher sets a reasonable expectation for when the patrol officer will arrive. Response time was also the best predictor of how satisfied a citizen was with the responding officer. It was further revealed that citizens became dissatisfied with the police when they were not informed of the outcome (i.e., someone was arrested). Again, these findings indicate the need for dispatchers and patrol officers to communicate with complainants regarding when they should expect an officer to arrive and the outcome of the call.

Based on the results of the response time study, the researchers concluded that rapid response was not as important as police administrators had thought. Response time was not related to an officer's ability to make an arrest or recover stolen property. Results from the response time study challenged traditional beliefs about the allocation of patrol in our communities. Based on tradition knowledge, as previously discussed, rapidly responding to calls for service is what the police had always done since they started using patrol vehicles. In addition, common sense, as previously discussed, played a role in the practice of rapid response to calls for service; it just made sense that if a patrol officer arrives sooner, she will be more likely to make an arrest.

Prior to the research, police departments operated under the assumption that rapid response was a crucial factor in the ability of an officer to solve a crime and an important predictor of citizen satisfaction. In response to the research on rapid response, many police departments changed the way they responded to calls for service. Many departments adopted a **differential police response** approach. Differential police response protocols allow police departments to prioritize calls and rapidly dispatch an officer only when an immediate response is needed (i.e., crimes in progress). For crimes in progress, rapid response is critical and may reduce the injuries sustained by the victim as well, but these emergency calls usually account for less than 2% of all 9-1-1 calls for police service. For nonemergency calls, an officer is either dispatched at a later time when the officer is available or a report is taken over the phone or through some other means. Differential police response has been shown to save departments money and give patrol officers more time to engage in community-oriented and proactive policing activities. The benefits for a department are not at the expense of the public. In fact, a study by Robert Worden found a high degree of citizen satisfaction with differential police response.[79]

Courts Research Example[80]

Research on the courts component of the criminal justice system, while far from complete, has produced direct effects on the operations of the criminal justice system. The study reviewed in this section asked the following research question: Are jurors able to understand different legal rules for establishing a defendant's criminal responsibility? The study described below explored the issue of criminal responsibility as it applies to the insanity defense in the United States. For several years, the *M'Naghten* rule was the legal rule applied in all courts of the United States. Under *M'Naghten*, criminal responsibility was absent when the offender did not understand the nature of his actions due to failure to distinguish "right" from "wrong." This is known as the "right/wrong test" for criminal responsibility. The case of *Durham v. United States* was heard in the U.S. Court of Appeals for the District of Columbia and offered an alternative test for criminal responsibility and insanity. The legal rule emerging from *Durham* was that criminal responsibility was absent if the offense was a product of mental disease or defect. This ruling provided psychiatrists with a more important role at trial because of the requirement that the behavior be linked to a mental disorder that only a psychiatrist could officially determine.

At the time of Simon's 1967 study, most courts across the country still followed the *M'Naghten* rule. Questions arose, however, regarding whether juries differed in their understanding of *M'Naghten* versus *Durham* and, in turn, whether this resulted in differences in their ability to make informed decisions regarding criminal responsibility in cases involving the insanity defense. The study was designed to determine the effect of different legal rules on jurors' decision-making in cases where the defense was insanity. There was a question of whether there was a difference between the rules to the extent that jurors understood each rule and could capably apply it.

Simon conducted an experimental study on jury deliberations in cases where the only defense was insanity.[81] Utilizing a mock jury approach, Simon took the transcripts of two actual trials with one reflecting the use of the *M'Naghten* rule and the other the *Durham* rule. Both cases were renamed and the transcripts were edited to constitute a trial of 60–90 minutes in length. These edited transcripts were then recorded, with University of Chicago Law School faculty as the attorneys, judges, and witnesses involved in each case. Groups of 12 jurors listened to each trial with instruction provided at the end regarding the particular rule of law (*M'Naghten* or *Durham*) for determining criminal responsibility. Each juror submitted a written statement with his or her initial decision on the case before jury deliberations, and the juries' final decisions after deliberation were also reported.

Simon found significant differences in the verdicts across the two groups (*M'Naghten* rule applied and *Durham* rule applied) even when the case was the same. For the *M'Naghten* version of the case, the psychiatrists stated that the defendant was mentally ill yet knew right from wrong during the crime. These statements/instructions should have led to a guilty verdict on the part of the mock jury. As expected, the *M'Naghten* juries delivered guilty verdicts in 19 of the 20 trials, with one hung jury. For the *Durham* version of the case, the psychiatrists stated that the crime resulted from the defendant's mental illness, which should have lead to acquittal. However, the defendant was acquitted in only five of the 26 *Durham* trials. Twenty-six groups of 12 jurors were exposed to the *Durham* version of the trial and the case was the same each time. Simon interpreted these results as suggesting that jurors were unambiguous in their interpretations and applications of *M'Naghten* (due to the consistency in guilty verdicts), but they were less clear on the elements of *Durham* and how to apply it (reflected by the mix of guilty, not guilty, and hung verdicts).[82]

Steffensmeier, Ulmer, and Kramer[83] hypothesized that African Americans overall were not likely to be treated more harshly than white defendants by the courts because it was only particular subgroups of minority defendants that fit with court actors' stereotypes of "more dangerous" offenders. In particular, they argued that younger African American males not only fulfilled this stereotype more than any other age, race, and gender combination, they were also more likely to be perceived by judges as being able to handle incarceration better than other subgroups.

In order to test their hypotheses, the researchers examined sentencing data from Pennsylvania spanning four years (1989–1992). Almost 139,000 cases were examined. The sentences they examined included whether a convicted defendant was incarcerated in prison or jail, and the length of incarceration in prison or jail. The researchers found that offense severity and prior record were the most important predictors of whether a convicted defendant was incarcerated and the length of incarceration. The authors found that the highest likelihood of incarceration and the longest sentences for males were distributed to African Americans aged 18–29 years. Their analysis of females revealed that white females were much less likely than African American females to be incarcerated, regardless of the age group examined. Taken altogether, the analysis revealed that African American males aged 18–29 years maintained the highest odds of incarceration and the longest sentences relative to any other race, sex, and age group.

Overall, this research showed that judges focused primarily on legal factors (offense severity and prior record) when determining the sentences of convicted offenders. These are the factors we expect judges to consider when making sentencing decisions. However, the research also found that judges base their decisions in part on extralegal factors, particularly the interaction of a defendant's age, race, and gender. This research expanded our knowledge beyond the impact of singular factors on sentencing to expose the interaction effects of several variables (race, gender, and age). Court personnel are aware of these interaction effects based on this study, and others that followed, as well as their personal experiences in the criminal justice system. Identification and recognition of inequities in our justice system (in this case that young, African American males are punished more severely in our justice system) is the first step in mitigating this inequity.

After Simon's study, most states rejected the *Durham* test. Recall her finding that the *Durham* rule produced inconsistent verdicts. She interpreted this finding as *Durham* being no better than providing no guidance to jurors on how to decide the issue of insanity. The observation helped to fuel arguments against the use of *Durham*, which, in turn, contributed to its demise as a legal rule. Today, only New Hampshire uses a version of the *Durham* rule in insanity cases.

Corrections Research Example[84]

Although the research in corrections is far from complete, it has contributed greatly to the development of innovative programs and the professional development of correctional personnel. The contributions of academic and policy-oriented research can be seen across the whole range of correctional functions from pretrial services through probation, institutional corrections, and parole.

Rehabilitation remained the goal of our correctional system until the early 1970s, when the efficacy of rehabilitation was questioned. Violent crime was on the rise, and many politicians placed the blame on the criminal justice system. Some believed the system was too lenient on offenders. Interest in researching the effectiveness of correctional treatment remained low until 1974 when an article written by Robert Martinson and published in *Public Interest* titled "What Works? Questions and Answers about Prison Reform" generated enormous political and public attention to the effectiveness of correctional treatment.[85]

Over a six-month period, Martinson and his colleagues reviewed all of the existing literature on correctional treatment published in English from 1945 to 1967. Each of the articles was evaluated according to traditional standards of social science research. Only studies that utilized an experimental design, included a sufficient sample size, and could be replicated were selected for review. A total of 231 studies examining a variety of different types of treatment were chosen, including educational and vocational training, individual and group counseling, therapeutic milieus, medical treatment, differences in length and type of incarceration, and community corrections. All of the treatment studies included at least one measure of offender recidivism, such as whether or not offenders were rearrested or violated their parole. The recidivism measures were used to examine the success or failure of a program in terms of reducing crime.

After reviewing all 231 studies, Martinson reported that there was no consistent evidence that correctional treatment reduced recidivism. Specifically, he wrote, "with few and isolated exceptions, the rehabilitative efforts that

What does research show regarding the punishment risks of young black males?

have been reported so far have had no appreciable effect on recidivism."[86] Martinson further indicated that the lack of empirical support for correctional treatment could be a consequence of poorly implemented programs. If the quality of the programs were improved, the results may have proved more favorable, but this conclusion was for the most part ignored by the media and policy-makers.

Martinson's report became commonly referred to as "nothing works" and was subsequently used as the definitive study detailing the failures of rehabilitation. The article had implications beyond questioning whether or not specific types of correctional treatment reduced recidivism. The entire philosophy of rehabilitation was now in doubt because of Martinson's conclusion that "our present strategies . . . cannot overcome, or even appreciably reduce, the powerful tendencies of offenders to continue in criminal behavior."[87]

Martinson's article provided policy makers the evidence to justify spending cuts on rehabilitative programs. Furthermore, it allowed politicians to respond to growing concerns about crime with punitive, get-tough strategies. States began implementing strict mandatory sentences that resulted in more criminals being sent to prison and for longer periods of time. Over the next several years, Martinson's article was used over and over to support abandoning efforts to treat offenders until rehabilitation became virtually nonexistent in our correctional system.

CHAPTER SUMMARY

This chapter began with a discussion of sources of knowledge development and the problems with each. To depict the importance of research methods in knowledge development, myths about crime and the criminal justice system were reviewed along with research studies that have dispelled myths. As the introductory chapter in this text, this chapter also provided an overview of the steps in the research process from selecting a topic and conducting a literature review at the beginning of a research study to reporting findings, results, and limitations at the end of the study. Examples of actual research studies in the areas of police, courts, and corrections were also provided in this chapter to demonstrate the research process in action and to illustrate how research has significantly impacted practices within the criminal justice system. In addition, this chapter demonstrated the critical importance of becoming an informed consumer of research in both your personal and professional lives.

CRITICAL THINKING QUESTIONS

1. What are the primary sources of knowledge development, and what are the problems with each?

2. How is knowledge developed through research methods different from other sources of knowledge?

3. What myths about crime and criminal justice have been dispelled through research? Give an example of a research study that dispelled a myth.

4. Why is it important to be an informed consumer of research?

5. What are the steps in the research process, and what activities occur at each step?

KEY TERMS

authority knowledge: Knowledge developed when we accept something as being correct and true just because someone in a position of authority says it is true

case study: An in-depth analysis of one or a few illustrative cases

common sense knowledge: Knowledge developed when the information "just makes sense"

content analysis: A method requiring the analyzing of content contained in mass communication outlets such as newspapers, television, magazines, and the like

CSI Effect: Due to the unrealistic portrayal of the role of forensic science in solving criminal cases in television shows, jurors are more likely to vote to acquit a defendant when the expected sophisticated forensic evidence is not presented

differential police response: Methods that allow police departments to prioritize calls and rapidly dispatch an officer only when an immediate response is needed (i.e., crimes in progress)

experimental designs: Used when researchers are interested in determining whether a program, policy, practice, or intervention is effective

field research: Research that involves researchers studying individuals or groups of individuals in their natural environment

Halloween sadism: The practice of giving contaminated treats to children during trick or treating

hypotheses: Statements about the expected relationship between two concepts

illogical reasoning: Occurs when someone jumps to premature conclusions or presents an argument that is based on invalid assumptions

myths: Beliefs that are based on emotion rather than rigorous analysis

operationalization: The process of giving a concept a working definition; determining how each concept in your study will be measured

overgeneralization: Occurs when people conclude that what they have observed in one or a few cases is true for all cases

personal experience knowledge: Knowledge developed through actual experiences

research: The scientific investigation of an issue, problem, or subject utilizing research methods

research methods: The tools that allow criminology and criminal justice researchers to systematically study crime and the criminal justice system and include the basic rules, appropriate techniques, and relevant procedures for conducting research

resistance to change: The reluctance to change our beliefs in light of new, accurate, and valid information to the contrary

secondary data analysis: Occurs when researchers obtain and reanalyze data that were originally collected for a different purpose

selective observation: Choosing, either consciously or unconsciously, to pay attention to and remember events that support our personal preferences and beliefs

survey research: Obtaining data directly from research participants by asking them questions, often conducted through self-administered questionnaires and personal interviews

tradition knowledge: Knowledge developed when we accept something as true because that is the way things have always been, so it must be right

variables: Concepts that have been given a working definition and can take on different values

ENDNOTES

1   Briggs, Lisa T., Stephen E. Brown, Robert B. Gardner, and Robert L. Davidson. (2009). "D.RA.MA: An extended conceptualization of student anxiety in criminal justice research methods courses." *Journal of Criminal Justice Education* 20 (3), 217–226.

2   Betz, N. E. (1978). "Prevalence, distribution, and correlates of math anxiety in college students. *Journal of Counseling Psychology* 25 (5), 441–448.

3   Briggs, et al., 2009, p. 221.

4   Ibid, p. 221.

5   Ibid, p. 221.

6   Kappeler, Victor E., and Gary W. Potter. (2005). *The mythology of crime and criminal justice*. Prospect Heights, IL: Waveland.

7   *Tennessee v. Garner*, 471 U.S. 1 (1985).

8   Lombroso-Ferrero, Gina. (1911). Criminal man, according to the classification of Cesare Lombroso. New York: Putnam.

9   This study was included in Amy B. Thistlethwaite and John D. Wooldredge. (2010). *Forty studies that changed criminal justice: Explorations into the history of criminal justice research.* Upper Saddle River, NJ: Prentice Hall.

10 Petersilia, J., S. Turner, J. Kahan, and J. Peterson. (1985). *Granting felons probation: Public risks and alternatives.* Santa Monica, CA: Rand.

11 Vito, G. (1986). "Felony probation and recidivism: Replication and response." *Federal Probation* 50, 17–25.

12 Conrad, J. (1985). "Research and development in corrections." *Federal Probation* 49, 69–71.

13 Finckenauer, James O. (1982). *Scared straight! and the panacea phenomenon.* Englewood Cliffs, NJ: Prentice Hall.

14 Yarborough, J.C. (1979). Evaluation of JOLT (Juvenile Offenders Learn Truth) as a deterrence program. Lansing, MI: Michigan Department of Corrections.

15 Petrosino, Anthony, Carolyn Turpin-Petrosino, and James O. Finckenauer. (2000). "Well-meaning programs can have harmful effects! Lessons from experiments of programs such as Scared Straight," *Crime & Delinquency* 46, 354–379.

16 Robertson, Jordan. "I'm being punished for living right": Background check system is haunted by errors. December 20, 2011. http://finance.yahoo.com/news /ap-impact-criminal-past-isnt-182335059.html. Retrieved on December 29, 2011.

17 Shelton, D. E. (2008). "The 'CSI Effect': Does it really exist?" *NIJ Journal* 259 [NCJ 221501].

18 Best, Joel. (2011). "Halloween sadism: The evidence." http://dspace.udel.edu:8080/dspace/bitstream/handle/ 19716/726/Halloween%20sadism.revised%20thru%20 2011.pdf?sequence=6. Retrieved on May 7, 2012.

19 Best, Joel. (1985, November). "The myth of the Halloween sadist. *Psychology Today* 19 (11), p. 14.

20 Ibid.

21 "Beer compound shows potent promise in prostate cancer battle." Press release from Oregon State University May 30, 2006. http://oregonstate.edu/ua/ncs/archives/2006/ may/beer-compound-shows-potent-promise-prostate -cancer-battle. Retrieved on January 6, 2012; Colgate, Emily C., Cristobal L. Miranda, Jan F. Stevens, Tammy M. Bray, and Emily Ho. (2007). "Xanthohumol, a prenylflavonoid derived from hops induces apoptosis and inhibits NF-kappaB activation in prostate epithelial cells," *Cancer Letters* 246, 201–209; "Health benefits of red wine exaggerated" http://health.yahoo.net/articles /nutrition/health-benefits-red-wine-exaggerated. Retrieved on January 14, 2012; "Scientific journals notified following research misconduct investigation." January 11, 2012.

http://today.uconn.edu/blog/2012/01/scientific-journals -notified-following-research-misconduct-investigation/. Retrieved on January 14, 2012.

22 Pepinsky, Hal. "The myth that crime and criminality can be measured." 3–11 in Bohm, Robert M., and Jeffrey T. Walker. (2006). *Demystifying crime and criminal justice.* Los Angeles: Roxbury.

23 Bullock, Jennifer L., and Bruce A. Arrigo. "The myth that mental illness causes crime." 12–19 in Bohm, Robert M., and Jeffrey T. Walker. (2006). *Demystifying crime and criminal justice.* Los Angeles: Roxbury.

24 Friedrichs, David O. "The myth that white-collar crime is only about financial loss." 20–28 in Bohm, Robert M., and Jeffrey T. Walker. (2006). *Demystifying crime and criminal justice.* Los Angeles: Roxbury.

25 Kuhns III, Joseph B., and Charisse T. M. Coston. "The myth that serial murderers are disproportionately white males." 37–44 in Bohm, Robert M., and Jeffrey T. Walker. (2006). *Demystifying crime and criminal justice.* Los Angeles: Roxbury.

26 Longmire, Dennis R., Jacqueline Buffington-Vollum, and Scott Vollum. "The myth of positive differentiation in the classification of dangerous offenders." 123–131 in Bohm, Robert M., and Jeffrey T. Walker. (2006). *Demystifying crime and criminal justice.* Los Angeles: Roxbury.

27 Masters, Ruth E., Lori Beth Way, Phyllis B. Gerstenfeld, Bernadette T. Muscat, Michael Hooper, John P. J. Dussich, Lester Pincu, and Candice A. Skrapec. (2013). *CJ realities and challenges,* 2nd ed. New York: McGraw-Hill.

28 Ibid.

29 Ibid.

30 Ibid.

31 Ibid.

32 Brownstein, Henry H. "The myth of drug users as violent offenders." 45–53 in Bohm, Robert M., and Jeffrey T. Walker. (2006). *Demystifying crime and criminal justice.* Los Angeles: Roxbury.

33 Goldstein, P. (1985). "The drugs/violence nexus: A tripartite conceptual framework." *Journal of Drug Issues* 15, 493–506.

34 Goldstein, P., H. Brownstein, and P. Ryan. (1992). "Drug-related homicide in New York City: 1984 and 1988." *Crime & Delinquency* 38, 459–476.

35 Parker, R., and K. Auerhahn. (1998). "Alcohol, drugs, and violence." *Annual Review of Sociology* 24, 291–311, p. 291.

36 Buerger, Michael. "The myth of racial profiling." 97–103 in Bohm, Robert M., and Jeffrey T. Walker. (2006). *Demystifying crime and criminal justice.* Los Angeles: Roxbury.

37 Cordner, Gary, and Kathryn E. Scarborough. "The myth that science solves crimes." 104–110 in Bohm, Robert M., and Jeffrey T. Walker. (2006). *Demystifying crime and criminal justice*. Los Angeles: Roxbury.

38 Willis, James J., Stephen D. Mastrofski, and David Weisburd. "The myth that COMPSTAT reduces crime and transforms police organizations." 111–119 in Bohm, Robert M., and Jeffrey T. Walker. (2006). *Demystifying crime and criminal justice*. Los Angeles: Roxbury.

39 Masters, et al., 2013.

40 Ibid.

41 Ibid.

42 Ibid.

43 Scott, Eric J. (1981). Calls for service: Citizen demand and initial police response. Washington, DC: Government Printing Office.

44 Lersch, Kim. "The myth of policewomen on patrol." 89–96 in Bohm, Robert M., and Jeffrey T. Walker. (2006). *Demystifying crime and criminal justice*. Los Angeles: Roxbury.

45 Janikowski, Richard. "The myth that the exclusionary rule allows many criminals to escape justice." 132–139 in Bohm, Robert M., and Jeffrey T. Walker. (2006). *Demystifying crime and criminal justice*. Los Angeles: Roxbury.

46 Bishop, Donna M. "The myth that harsh punishments reduce juvenile crime." 140–148 in Bohm, Robert M., and Jeffrey T. Walker. (2006). *Demystifying crime and criminal justice*. Los Angeles: Roxbury .

47 Immarigeon, Russ. "The myth that public attitudes are punitive." 149–157 in Bohm, Robert M., and Jeffrey T. Walker. (2006). *Demystifying crime and criminal justice*. Los Angeles: Roxbury.

48 Acker, James R. "The myth of closure and capital punishment." 167–175 in Bohm, Robert M., and Jeffrey T. Walker. (2006). *Demystifying crime and criminal justice*. Los Angeles: Roxbury.

49 Masters, et al., 2013.

50 Ibid.

51 Ibid.

52 Lersch, 2006.

53 Newport, Frank. "In U.S., support for death penalty falls to 39-year low." October 13, 2011. http://www.gallup.com/poll/150089/support-death-penalty-falls-year-low.aspx. Retrieved on April 16, 2012.

54 Applegate, Brandon. "The myth that the death penalty is administered fairly." 158–166 in Bohm, Robert M., and Jeffrey T. Walker. (2006). *Demystifying crime and criminal justice*. Los Angeles: Roxbury.

55 Williams, M. R., and J. E. Holcomb. (2001). "Racial disparity and death sentences in Ohio." *Journal of Criminal Justice* 29, 207–218.

56 Snell, Tracy L. (2011, December). Capital punishment, 2010—statistical tables. Washington, DC: Bureau of Justice Statistics.

57 Applegate, 2006.

58 Williams and Holcomb, 2001.

59 Applegate, 2006.

60 Ibid.

61 Wood, Peter B. "The myth that imprisonment is the most severe form of punishment." 192–200 in Bohm, Robert M., and Jeffrey T. Walker. (2006). *Demystifying crime and criminal justice*. Los Angeles: Roxbury.

62 Ibid.

63 Michalowski, Raymond. "The myth that punishment reduces crime." 179–191 in Bohm, Robert M., and Jeffrey T. Walker. (2006). *Demystifying crime and criminal justice*. Los Angeles: Roxbury.

64 McShane, Marilyn, Frank P. Williams III, and Beth Pelz. "The myth of prisons as country clubs." 201–208 in Bohm, Robert M., and Jeffrey T. Walker. (2006). *Demystifying crime and criminal justice*. Los Angeles: Roxbury.

65 Parker, Mary. "The myth that prisons can be self-supporting." 209–213 in Bohm, Robert M., and Jeffrey T. Walker. (2006). *Demystifying crime and criminal justice*. Los Angeles: Roxbury.

66 Blakely, Curtis, and John Ortiz Smykla. "Correctional privatization and the myth of inherent efficiency." 214–220 in Bohm, Robert M., and Jeffrey T. Walker. (2006). *Demystifying crime and criminal justice*. Los Angeles: Roxbury.

67 Jones, G. Mark. "The myth that the focus of community corrections is rehabilitation." 221–226 in Bohm, Robert M., and Jeffrey T. Walker. (2006). *Demystifying crime and criminal justice*. Los Angeles: Roxbury.

68 Cullen, Francis T., and Paula Smith. "The myth that correctional rehabilitation does not work." 227–238 in Bohm, Robert M., and Jeffrey T. Walker. (2006). *Demystifying crime and criminal justice*. Los Angeles: Roxbury.

69 Masters, et al., 2013.

70 Ibid.

71 Ibid.

72 Ibid.

73 Petersilia, Joan. (1990). "When probation becomes more dreaded than prison. *Federal Probation* 54, 23–27.

74 Ibid.

75 Wood, P. B., and H. G. Grasmick. (1999). "Toward the development of punishment equivalencies: Male and female inmates rate the severity of alternative sanctions compared to prison." *Justice Quarterly* 16, 19–50.

76 Example is excerpted from Amy B. Thistlethwaite and John D. Wooldredge. (2010). Forty studies that changed

criminal justice: Explorations into the history of criminal justice research. Upper Saddle River, NJ: Prentice Hall. This is an excellent book that demonstrates the impact research has had on criminal justice operations.

77 National Commission on Productivity. (1973). Opportunities for improving productivity in police services. Washington, DC: United States Government Printing Office, p. 19.

78 Pate, T., A. Ferrara, R. Bowers, and J. Lorence. (1976). Police response time: Its determinants and effects. Washington, DC: Police Foundation.

79 Worden, R. (1993). "Toward equity and efficiency in law enforcement: Differential police response. *American Journal of Police* 12, 1–32.

80 Example is excerpted from Amy B. Thistlethwaite and John D. Wooldredge. (2010). Forty studies that changed criminal justice: Explorations into the history of criminal justice research. Upper Saddle River, NJ: Prentice Hall.

81 Simon, R. (1967). *The jury and the defense of insanity.* Boston: Little, Brown.

82 Ibid.

83 Steffensmeier, D., J. Ulmer, & J. Kramer. (1998). "The interaction of race, gender, and age in criminal sentencing: The punishment cost of being young, black, and male. *Criminology* 36, 763–797.

84 Example is excerpted from Amy B. Thistlethwaite and John D. Wooldredge. (2010). Forty studies that changed criminal justice: Explorations into the history of criminal justice research. Upper Saddle River, NJ: Prentice Hall.

85 Martinson, R. (1974). "What works? Questions and answers about prison reform." *The Public Interest* 10, 22–54.

86 Ibid, p. 25.

87 Ibid, p. 49.

Chapter 2

Getting Started: The Beginnings and Pitfalls of Research

Stanford Prison Experiment

Research Question

What are the behavioral and psychological consequences of becoming a prisoner or a prison guard?

The Experiment and Basic Design

The Stanford Prison Experiment began on August 14, 1971.[1] The experiment was scheduled to last for two weeks but, due to ethical concerns, was shut down after only six days. The experiment was conducted in the basement of the psychology department building on the Stanford University campus where Dr. Philip Zimbardo and his research team had re-created or "simulated" the prison environment. The purpose was to simulate not only the physical features and discomforts of a prison environment, but also the mental rigors of incarceration to determine its effects on participants. University offices were converted into the "Stanford County Jail" with three prison cells, a guard room, the warden's office, and the superintendent's office. The hallway served as the recreation yard, and there was a small closet that served as solitary confinement, or "the hole." There was a hidden camera set up to record the study as it progressed.

Experimental Procedure

An advertisement was placed in the city newspaper to recruit participants. The researchers received more than 70 applications from which 24 individuals were selected. Prior to beginning the experiment, the participants were examined for mental health issues, medical disabilities, and histories of crime and/or drug use. Once the researchers

determined there were no psychological differences among the participants, there was random assignment of participants into the prisoner group and the guard group. The warden was played by an undergraduate student and two other psychology students played prison staff roles. Dr. Zimbardo acted as the superintendent and, prior to the prisoners' arrival, he called a meeting with prison guards to explain their role. While not allowed to physically abuse the prisoners, guards were instructed to instill feelings of boredom, frustration, fear, and suffering. The goal was to make prisoners feel powerless and totally controlled by their environment. To enhance realism, guards wore military style uniforms and carried a whistle and billy club, or baton, signifying their power and authority.

To begin, participants randomly selected to play prisoners were told to be at their homes at a certain time. Local police, working with Dr. Zimbardo, picked up these participants and arrested them in front of their families and neighbors. Once detained, they were booked, fingerprinted, and blindfolded before being transported to the basement prison. Once inside the simulated prison, their clothes were taken, they were deloused with a spray, and they were given a uniform with an identifying number. They were also made to wear a chain around their leg to remind them of their status.

Once prisoners and guards were interacting with one another, signs that the environment was impacting their behavior became quickly evident. The first day passed without incident but the second day began with inmate rebellion. Guards responded by stripping the inmates and taking their beds. One inmate who protested loudly was put in the "hole." Because they were outnumbered, the guards began to use psychological responses such as providing privileges for good behavior. At first the inmate group showed solidarity in their rebellion, however, as the days passed, this solidarity diminished. Prisoner 8612 was the first to complain of health issues and to request release. "Superintendent" Zimbardo responded by asking him to return to the prison and be a snitch in order to receive additional privileges. When Prisoner 8612 returned, he told the other prisoners that they could not quit. This initiated a sense of hopelessness among the prisoners, that they would not be released no matter how much they rebelled. Not long after returning, Prisoner 8612 began showing signs of severe psychological stress and uncontrollable rage. No longer able to ignore him, and only 36 hours into the experiment, Prisoner 8612 had to be released.

Over the next few days, there was a visitation period during which prisoners' families came to the basement prison, a preemptive strike by the staff and guards against a possible escape attempt, a visit from a priest, and a visit from a lawyer. Even with all this, the guards' harassment and humiliation of inmates increased. When Prisoner 819 protested, he was verbally harassed and placed in the hole. When he met with the priest, he began to cry uncontrollably. "Superintendent" Zimbardo brought him to a "rest and relaxation" room. While in the room, the guards had the other prisoners verbally berate Prisoner 819. When "Superintendent" Zimbardo returned to the room, Prisoner 819 was crying again. Although release was an option, the prisoner instead wanted to return to the prison to show the other prisoners that he could be a model inmate. Eventually, after Dr. Zimbardo reminded Prisoner 819 who he was, and that the prison was not real, he decided to leave. In replacement, a new prisoner, Prisoner 416, joined the experiment. He rebelled from the outset, going on a hunger strike immediately. By this point, however, the other prisoners had become acclimated to their environment and refused to join Prisoner 416 in his protest. Upon continuing his food strike, Prisoner 416 was placed in the "hole." He was continually harassed and was eventually left in solitary confinement overnight due to his refusal to eat. The next morning, a graduate student not participating in the experiment came to Dr. Zimbardo and expressed outrage at the way the participants, particularly the prisoners, were being treated. Prior to this point, Dr. Zimbardo and the other participants were so caught up in their roles that they could not separate reality from the experiment. It was only when an outsider responded that Dr. Zimbardo realized the study must be discontinued.

Results

While the study did not last as long as intended, only six days instead of two weeks, the results did reveal psychological consequences of the simulated prison environment. After his visit, the priest mentioned that the prisoners were acting like "first timers" based on the fear and emotion he witnessed. In general there were three types of prisoner responses observed during the study. The prisoners would (a) rebel, (b) passively react, and/or (c) take on the role of model prisoner. Not only were prisoners affected, the prison guards were also changed during the experiment, acting in ways they would not have outside of their prison guard role. There were three types of guard personas observed during the study, (a) the good guard who tried to help the prisoners, (b) the tough but fair guard, and (c) the sadistic guard who reveled in his role, taking joy in the humiliation and harassment he was asked to impart on the prisoners. The effects were so prominent that Dr. Zimbardo himself recalls being caught up in his role as prison superintendent, again showing the impact an environment, even a simulated environment, can have on a person's psyche.

Problems with the Experimental Procedure

Although the Stanford Prison Experiment took place 40 years ago, it remains a prominent example of how social science experiments, though well intended, can turn unethical and be damaging to participants. Based on the extensive interviews and surveys conducted after the experiment, it was found that the participants had suffered during their time in the experiment. For one participant, Prisoner 8612, the experience impacted his life significantly as he went on to become a prison psychologist. The lack of control and understanding he felt drove him to study psychology and eventually to apply his knowledge to the real prison environment. Because Dr. Zimbardo was caught up in his dual roles of lead researcher and prison superintendent, he admits he lost sight of the effects the study was having on the participants. Although it was recognized that suffering resulted from the experiment, in hindsight, Dr. Zimbardo has discussed the good to come from the study. First, he insists that the participants were able to overcome and rebound from their experience because they were otherwise healthy, as shown by the battery of tests given prior to the study beginning. Also, the study stands as a testament to the "power of the situation" and just how impactful situational elements can be to those involved. Finally, due to the results, Dr. Zimbardo was able to make many suggestions for prison reform. He contends that although there were costs to conducting the study, there were also benefits that should not be overlooked. ●

To demonstrate an understanding of the ethical nature of research

To discuss the guidelines put in place to reduce harm to research participants

To describe what it means to be a social scientist

To formulate a research question

To explain the process of sharing research through written work

INTRODUCTION

Most of the chapters in this text will speak specifically to different forms of sampling, data collection, and data analysis. To begin, however, it is important to understand how research is guided by ethics and how approval to conduct research can be impacted by design. Perhaps the bottom line is that if ethics are not considered at the outset of a research study, there is the possibility that the research will never begin.

The Stanford Prison Experiment is one of the most well-known and widely discussed social science experiments, particularly because of how it impacted those who participated. Due to this and research resulting in more severe consequences, there developed a realization of how research subjects can be negatively affected by their participation. As a result, many safeguards have been put in place to protect human subjects in the research process.

ETHICAL ISSUES IN CRIMINAL JUSTICE RESEARCH

"It's all relative." Have you heard this saying before? If so, you know this reference infers that time and place impact how events are viewed by individuals and societies as a whole. **Ethical relativism** refers to the belief that how we think about ethics varies from one time to another, one place to another, and from one person to another. What was considered ethical in the 1800s may be very different from what is considered ethical in the 21st century. **Ethics** can be defined as those recognized rules of conduct that govern a particular group. This group may be aligned on cultural grounds, professional grounds, or otherwise brought together by common interests.

Most professional disciplines have an established code of ethics. In fact, without a code of ethics in place, organizations and individuals may be seen as unprofessional. The American Medical Association,[2] the American Bar Association,[3] and others have published codes to which members of the discipline must adhere. Criminal justice professionals have established codes, and this

also includes criminal justice researchers. In general, there are two broad types of ethical guidelines for those conducting research in criminal justice. First, there are internal guidelines. These are guidelines or codes of ethics developed within the discipline or perhaps by an individual university. External guidelines, on the other hand, may include legal codes, constitutions, or even precedent case law. Each of these limits and guides the behaviors of those conducting research in criminal justice. Compliance with these limits and guidelines falls to one or more monitoring agencies. For example, Institutional Review Boards employed by universities are responsible for monitoring research conducted by university faculty. The criminal justice system generally, and federal and state agencies specifically, are also responsible for protecting human subjects. For example, the U.S. Department of Health and Human Services[4] has a major role concerning ethical guidelines for researchers.

There are many reasons why studying ethics is important to researchers, particularly those in criminal justice. First, researchers may be privy to confidential and personal information about their participants. This information may include mental health records, abuse histories, and criminal histories among other sensitive information. Second, findings of criminal justice research may be used to guide public policy. This means that research has consequences for public agencies, including law enforcement agencies, the courts, and corrections departments. Therefore, researchers must ensure that their research is not misleading. Criminal justice research may also have negative implications for those involved as participants. These implications may be physical, psychological, social, financial, or professional. Indeed, in the Stanford Prison Experiment, the participants, particularly the mock prisoners, were faced with psychological distress during and after the experiment.

Unethical Research

While research with severe consequences will be presented to you, more common examples of unethical behavior in research include activities that are not life

Judgment at Nuremberg: Eight of 24 Defendants during the Nuremberg Trials at Nuremberg's Palace of Justice, circa 1945 and 1946.

threatening. For example, students are often warned against plagiarism when completing writing assignments for their classes. Researchers are also expected to submit original work and to not take credit for someone else's work or ideas. Second, research fraud occurs when researchers report findings that are fabricated or when they do not report limitations to their work that could impact the interpretation of the findings being reported. Additionally, if researchers misuse or misappropriate funds they have been given to support research endeavors, it would constitute unethical behavior. Again, while not necessarily causing bodily harm or immense psychological distress, these and other behaviors are indeed unethical and can have grave professional consequences for those found to be engaging in such deception. While codes of ethics exist today based on the knowledge that research may be harmful to individuals, it has taken years for such guidelines to develop. During this time, history has seen many unethical research studies undertaken, including those in social science.

Research for Purposes of Science and Medicine   Some of the most visible examples of unethical research come from the Nazi occupation of Germany. During World War II, the Nazis performed countless harmful medical studies, including the testing of new drugs that exposed test subjects to diseases and to poisons, and subjecting participants to extreme temperatures and altitudes.[5] Additionally, prisoners in concentration camps underwent mutilating surgeries and post-mortem dissection, among other atrocities.

Following the war, these horrific acts came to light and led to international regulation of medical experimentation. Such studies were not only present in Nazi Germany, however. The United States has also faced its fair share of unethical research. The Tuskegee Syphilis Study,[6] which began in the 1930s, is a well-known example of unethical biomedical research that also led to the development of ethical rules of conduct and protections for human subjects. The goal of this study was to see how syphilis affected the infected person. Although a cure, penicillin, was discovered during the time of the study, the U.S. Public Health Service withheld the medication from 425 uneducated black men who had tested positive for syphilis. These men were not told of their diagnosis and were also not told that they were participating in research. While they were offered free medical care, they were not actually being treated, causing the men to suffer and eventually lose their life to the infection. In the 1940s through the 1970s, U.S. government officials were also sponsoring thousands of harmful experiments, including those involving radiation. While the government officials claimed their activities were in the interest of national defense, participants were not made aware of the experiments and therefore were not willing participants.

Another example involves chronically ill patients at New York City's Jewish Chronic Disease Hospital.[7] In the 1960s, researchers were interested in studying transplant rejection and began to inject chronically ill patients with live cancer cells. While researchers claimed to have received oral consent from the patients, there was no documentation. Further, the patients were not told they were being injected with live cancer cells. Despite the fact that the researchers in this study were convicted of fraud, deceit, and unprofessional conduct for their actions, the principal researcher was later elected vice president of the American Cancer Society. Also in the 1960s, researchers at New York's Willowbrook State Hospital[8] began deliberately injecting patients, mentally defective children, with the hepatitis virus. The virus was also being passed through fecal matter and spread quickly from resident to resident. Researchers claimed that since the virus would have spread anyway, it was best to give it to the patients under controlled conditions.

A final example involves the use of prison inmates as test subjects. In his book, *Acres of Skin: Human Experiments at Holmesburg Prison*, Allen Hornblum (1999)[9] gives a detailed and harrowing account of the human experimentation occurring in the 1960s and 1970s among inmates incarcerated at Holmesburg Prison located outside of Philadelphia. These experiments included the testing of all sorts of products from perfumes and deodorants to new medications and chemical agents. As harmless as some of these experiments may have seemed at first, they left many inmates with long-lasting physical and psychological scars. When asked why they participated in the experiments, the majority of inmates responded that the monetary reward was worth the risk. Unfortunately for some, the consequences of their participation as test subjects ended up being more harmful than they had anticipated. At times this was because the researchers were not truthful with the test subjects about the possible outcomes of the tests. Eventually, the testing of experimental products and chemicals on prisoners—many of whom may have been coerced through payment and experimented on without informed consent—fell out of favor. Lawsuits began to appear and outsiders looking in brought the debate to the public's attention generally and to the attention of legislators specifically. However, it was not until the mid-1970s that these experiments were finally halted. It would be a decade before such experiments on inmates were made illegal.

These research abuses represent some of the most serious and egregious but unfortunately, they are not the only examples that exist. The use of shock therapy, the testing of drugs such as LSD for their truth serum potential, and the many experiments that involve withholding potential helpful medications from control group participants have all come under great scrutiny by the public. Due to the actions of these researchers and others, there now exist limitations on human subject research, some of which were developed prior to the unethical studies discussed above yet not followed. Before discussing those restrictions, however, there are a few examples of unethical research endeavors in the social sciences that must be discussed.

Research for Purposes of Social Science   Medical researchers are not the only ones who have engaged in illegal or extremely unethical research. Social science researchers have conducted their own share of ethically questionable research studies. The Stanford Prison Experiment represents one such case. Around the same time, Laud Humphreys and Stanley Milgram conducted two of the most well-known examples of ethically questionable social science research.

As a doctoral student in the 1960s, Laud Humphreys[10] was interested in studying the sexual encounters of homosexual males in public restrooms for purposes of completing his dissertation. For his study, Humphreys decided to act as a "watchqueen," or voyeur, when these activities were taking place. He then followed unknowing participants to their cars and copied their license plate numbers. Humphreys used this information to find the participants' home addresses and, once he had this information, went to their homes disguised as a researcher interested in interviewing the men concerning their mental health. His findings were published in a popular and controversial work entitled, *Tearoom Trade: Impersonal Sex in Public Places* (1975). The ethical question resulting from Humphreys's activities was whether it was right to put those individuals who engaged in these sexual encounters at risk of being discovered by their loved ones without their permission. After all, Humphreys never asked for the participants' informed consent to participate in his study. The other questions raised concerned the appropriate nature of field research and when it is acceptable to use deception for the purpose of conducting such research.

Also in the 1960s, Stanley Milgram was a psychologist employed at Yale University. His study on obedience is another experiment that engendered a great deal of controversy once made public.[11] The study was driven by Milgram's interest in the horrific activities that took place during World War II in Germany, particularly those driving the Holocaust. Knowing how soldiers and others carried out the orders given to them, he wanted to examine how far individual study participants would go in harming another when told to do so by an authority figure. To do so, Milgram set up an experiment for which volunteers were paid to act as a "teacher." They were given four dollars for one hour of their time. These "teachers" were monitored and given instructions by an authority figure, the experimenter, who instructed them to give shocks to the "learner," a member of the research team. The shocks increased in strength from 15 to 450 volts with the number of questions the "learner" answered incorrectly. Shocks at the highest level on the electroshock machine were marked XXX, signifying danger.

The "learner" was in a different room from the "teacher," or test subject, and, while the "learner" was not actually being shocked, he feigned harm by yelling and protesting the shocks. The experimenter used pre-scripted encouragements to prod the "teachers" to continue with the test despite the "learner's" protests.

Two classic studies of situational obedience have been discussed in this chapter, as relates to methodology and ethical controversy surrounding the impact on research participants. The opening case study provided an overview of Zimbardo's Stanford Prison Experiment, which was conducted in the early 1970s. As you may remember, for this study, college students were recruited to participate and were given the role of inmate or prison guard in a simulated prison environment. Also discussed in this chapter was a study conducted by Stanley Milgram in the early 1960s in which participants were directed by a "researcher" to shock a person (the "learner"), with whom they did not have visual contact, with increasing severity when the "learner" answered questions incorrectly. Unknown to the participant, the "researcher" and the "learner," the person pretending to be shocked, were both a part of the study. The purpose of the study was to see whether and how much the participant would increase the severity of the shock based on the direction of the "researcher," or authority figure, even when confronted with shouts of pain and refusals to go further from the "learner." Both of these studies were conducted to examine situational obedience to authority and the lengths that individuals would go in certain situations if only because they were told to do so by someone they perceived to have authority.

Recently the Milgram study was re-created by *ABC News: Primetime* in collaboration with Santa Clara University.[12] After consulting with the American Psychological Association about what precautions needed to be taken, researchers were able to stem the psychological impact on the participant by reducing the severity of the "shocks" given to the "learner." The re-creation, which included 70 participants, was also unique in that it included female participants and tested participants when partnered with someone else to see if the influence of the partner would outweigh the influence of the authority figure (i.e., the "researcher"). While over 45 years had passed since the original study by Milgram, the results were strikingly similar. Over half of the men and women, 65% and 73% respectively, followed the "researcher's" advice to increase the severity. In Milgram's original study, 65% of the male participants followed the instructions of the authority figure, giving increasingly dangerous shocks to the "learner."

A practical application of these findings, particularly the Stanford Prison Experiment, was made recently when the brutality at the hands of U.S. military personnel was revealed at Abu Ghraib in Iraq.[13] While there exist those who object to this argument,[14] Zimbardo and others have discussed the "power of the situation" and how, while under normal conditions these soldiers would not have committed acts of torture, it was the unique situation they were in that influenced their behavior. Similarly, Milgram's study was in part based on an interest in Nazi Germany and how Nazi soldiers could act so inhumanely to fellow German citizenry under authority of the Third Reich. Especially today, as the world continues to see war as a common occurrence, it would not be surprising if additional applications of social science research regarding authority or situation-bound behavioral explanations take shape.

Although initially unsure, many of the "teachers" continued with the shocks after being told to do so by the experimenter. After the experiment, the "teachers," or test subjects, suffered emotional distress about what they had done. While a debriefing process was thought to have stemmed these feelings among the participants, the study continues to be used as an example of how social science experiments can cause harm to human subjects. Even with these consequences, however, the importance of this study continues to be felt today. As an example, the torturous activities that took place at Abu Ghraib in Iraq between 2004 and 2006 left the public wondering how far U.S. soldiers would go if given orders that were unethical and whether receiving the order from a commanding officer lessened their responsibility.

RESTRICTIONS ON THE STUDY OF HUMAN SUBJECTS

In 1946 the doctors responsible for the Nazi experiments were brought to trial in Nuremberg, Germany. At these trials, the doctors were found guilty as war criminals of torture, murder, and other offenses. Resulting from these trials was the Nuremburg Code.[15] This Code was a 10-item directive putting forth instructions for human experimentation. The Code directed that researchers must gain voluntary consent from human test subjects prior to using them in medical research. Among other items, researchers must also have a humanitarian purpose for conducting their research and must experiment on animals first if at all possible. The Nuremburg Code was the first international code for conduct of research and protections for human research participants. Following the creation of the Nuremburg Code, in 1948 the United Nations adopted the Universal Declaration on Human Rights,[16] which entitled each human to certain rights and freedoms. Following the adoption of this Declaration, there was a push for human rights in all aspects, including research involving human subjects. In 1964, the World Medical Association passed the Declaration of Helsinki,[17] which further outlined ethical principles for medical research involving human subjects. While slow to develop, these international codes and declarations made it clear that medical researchers conducting research with human subjects were no longer free to do whatever they pleased.

HEW Guidelines

In 1971, the U.S. Department of Health, Education, and Welfare (HEW)[18] put forth guidelines for research with human subjects. These original guidelines were similar to a "*Miranda* warning"[19] for researchers and directed them to gain not only voluntary consent, but also informed consent by

- giving a fair explanation of the procedures to be followed,

- providing a description of the potential risks and benefits of participating in the study,

- disclosing alternative procedures for conducting the research,

- offering to answer any questions concerning the study, and

- instructing the participants that they are free to withdraw their consent at any time without penalty.

When implemented, these guidelines applied only to federally funded research, although individual states also adopted similar provisions in order to keep federal funding. Like states, universities receive federal funding and therefore must also abide by the research guidelines. As much research is conducted by those working at universities, these guidelines impact the majority of research being carried out today. While most public entities are bound by these guidelines, private organizations and agencies are not. While they cannot violate the law (e.g., kill someone) in the name of research, they are free to conduct research without following ethical guidelines as long as they are not receiving federal funds.

National Commission for the Protections of Human Subjects

Although the HEW guidelines were in effect, it was not until 1974 with the National Research Act that the HEW was required to codify the previous policy into federal regulations. Following this directive, the HEW formed the National Commission for the Protections of Human Subjects of Biomedical and Behavioral Research. Members of this Commission drafted the 1979 *Belmont Report: Ethical Principles and Guidelines for the Protection of Human Subjects,* or the *Belmont Report*[20] for short. A key area for the drafters was to resolve the issue of informed consent for field researchers. The argument was that social science research has lower risks than medical research and therefore should have fewer restrictions. As was mentioned above, while social science research is not in the same category as biomedical research regarding potential harm, the possibility of harm to social science test subjects does exist. Therefore, the *Belmont Report* included three important principles for researchers. The first principle, the principle of respect for persons, directed researchers to treat human subjects as autonomous; subjects must be given information about the study so that they can make informed decisions as to whether or not they want to participate. This principle recognized that those persons with diminished autonomy (e.g., children, mentally disabled) may need additional protection beyond informed consent. The second principle, the principle of beneficence, stated that researchers must maximize the benefits of research and minimize any and all possible harm to research subjects. The final principle, the principle of justice, concerned the selection of human subjects and stated that risks and benefits must be dispersed equally. For example, researchers could not include men only for beneficial research with little risk and women for high-risk studies. When feasible, selection should be as equal as possible with regard to gender, race and ethnicity, age, socioeconomic status, and the like. Following the *Belmont Report,* decisions regarding research on human subjects have been decentralized. Specific to researchers at universities, these decisions are made by an Institutional Review Board.

Institutional Review Boards

Institutional Review Boards (IRBs) were originally created in 1974 for federally funded research under the first HEW guidelines.[21] They exist today to check for compliance of both federally funded and nonfunded research. For nonfunded research, board members are responsible for ensuring that research complies with federal and state laws governing the protection of human research subjects. In order to do this, IRBs review research proposals and may approve a protocol, ask for appropriate modifications, disapprove, or terminate all research activities falling under their jurisdiction. The IRB's authority is limited, however, to the evaluation of safety and risk. It is not the role of the IRB to decide whether a proposed research project is worthwhile or not, but instead to determine whether the research design is harmful to participants, and generally, whether the benefits outweigh the risks of the research.

Based on their review, the IRB can require modifications to the research design or require that researchers provide additional information to participants. In order to be approved by the IRB, researchers must show that their research minimizes risk through design, that the benefits outweigh the risks involved, and that there will be an equitable selection of subjects. Researchers must also show that they will seek and obtain informed consent and that the consent is documented appropriately, most likely on a consent form. Additionally, researchers must have a plan for monitoring the data collection process to ensure it is conducted according to plan and also that adequate provisions exist to protect privacy of the participating subjects and maintain confidentiality of the data. While these are generally the items IRBs require in order to approve research, there may be additional protections for vulnerable populations, which will be discussed later. Once a proposal is approved by the IRB, annual reviews of continuing research are conducted to confirm that the research has not deviated from its original design. Members of the IRB are also responsible for investigating suspected or alleged violations of research protocol, complaints by research participants, and violations of institutional policy. These investigations may be conducted through an audit and, if researchers are found to be not following their proposed design, they may face penalties.

Because of their duties, members of IRBs must be neutral and objective. Decision-makers should have no interest in the research study under review. Generally an IRB will have at least five members from various disciplines with one member being an expert on vulnerable populations. IRBs should also be demographically diverse and have at least one member who is not affiliated with the institution. This may be a community member. Can you think of a reason why it is important to have a

nonaffiliated member? Most importantly, it lends to objectivity of the IRB's review process.

There are two general types of IRB review of proposed research. A full board review is only necessary for certain proposals in which the risk to the participants is more than minimal. This means that there is more risk than the human subject would encounter in her normal daily activities. Proposals involving **vulnerable populations** (e.g., prison inmates, terminally ill patients) always require a full board review. Again, the purpose of such a review is to assess whether the anticipated benefits of the research justify anyone taking the risks involved. In a full board review situation, the majority of the board must give approval. Other than approval, the board may disapprove, approve with appropriate revisions, or decline review due to the proposal not meeting the standards of research needing review. The second type of review is an expedited review. This is the most common and is used for certain types of research where the risk is no more than minimal. For an expedited review, the research can be approved by the IRB chairperson; a meeting of the full board is not required. As long as they do not involve vulnerable populations, there are also research projects that may be exempt from IRB approval. These generally include observations of nonsensitive public behavior and the use of secondary data if publicly available or de-identified (i.e., research subjects cannot be identified from information collected by the researchers and are thus anonymous) by the original researchers.

Informed Consent

Informed consent is a cornerstone of research with human subjects.[22] It is a process in which participants are told accurate and relevant information about the study in a way that is easy to understand. This includes the disclosure of known risks, benefits, alternative procedures, and the offer to answer any questions the participant may have. Study participants must also be informed that they can withdraw their consent at any time without penalty. Having all of this information at the outset allows the participants to make an informed decision about their participation. Once informed, the participant must provide consent. In order to consent, a person must be competent. Persons must be competent in order to comprehend what they are being told. Persons may not be competent for reasons including age and mental capacity. If competent, and once informed, the participant must agree to participate in the research study. This agreement must be voluntary in that participants must not be coerced or in any way feel pressured to participate. Informed consent is always an issue with vulnerable populations[23] due to unique risks to these persons and also the question of whether they are able to fully consent voluntarily. Because of this, special precautions are necessary. While you have seen the term "vulnerable population" above, it is now time to describe these populations. First, due to their capacity for understanding, children cannot give informed consent. In order to have children participate as human subjects, researchers must have consent and assent. Researchers would first request consent from the parent or guardian following the informed consent procedures outlined above. Following, children over age seven must assent, or agree, to participating. If they do not assent, they cannot be forced to participate even though the parent or guardian has given his consent. Vulnerable populations also include those with questionable capacity to consent such as the mentally ill, the mentally deficient, and those under the influence of controlled substances. The terminally ill are also seen as vulnerable particularly because they may be willing to participate in risky research, including drug trials that may be harmful to them. Additionally, comatose patients and the fetuses of pregnant women are vulnerable, as they are unable to give consent. Finally, due to the relationships involved, prisoners, students, and employees are also considered vulnerable. Prisoners may feel like they have to participate because of their situation, that there may be a penalty or negative consequence if they do not or that they may receive leniency if they do participate. The same goes for students and employees, especially if the research is being conducted or suggested by their teachers or employers. In these situations, there is a coercive influence that precludes consent from being voluntary and therefore extra precaution is normally required. While this is the case, researchers quite frequently conduct research using students as participants. You may have even participated in research being conducted by your professor or another professor or graduate student on campus. When this happens, it is especially important that the participants are made aware that there will not be negative consequences for nonparticipation. Some researchers may offer extra credit or other incentives to increase student participation. Incentives are often left to the discretion of the researcher; however, negative consequences should never be a consideration. IRBs will ultimately govern how student subjects are recruited and what they are promised as well as how they are informed that there will not be negative repercussions for nonparticipation.

SENSITIVE ISSUES IN CRIMINAL JUSTICE

Besides the vulnerability of their subjects, there are other issues criminal justice researchers must take into consideration regarding risk. Stigmatization is one of these issues. Studies of illegal behavior, lifestyle, or victimization may stigmatize a person. For example, if researchers enter a prison to conduct research on prison rape, those inmates who participate may be looked at suspiciously by other inmates, particularly if the participant has been victimized in the past. Following the study, that inmate may face repercussions from a victimizer who thinks they have "snitched." Likewise, researchers must also be careful not to single out participants in the free community. For example, if children in a class are singled out for experimental sessions with a school counselor over a period of time, those children may be teased by the others.

Monetary Reward

Another issue that may arise is the payment of participants by researchers for their participation. Think for example about a homeless man offered ten dollars to participate in a research study. If he was not offered ten dollars, would he have been just as likely to participate? Payment can come in many forms. It may be monetary, it could be a gift, it could even be extra credit in class. Officially there are no clear rules on payment, whether it should be used, and, if used, how much should be paid. Research proposals involving payment are examined on a case-by-case basis by IRBs.

Methodological Considerations

As communities within the United States are particularly diverse, one methodological consideration is a possible language barrier between researchers and research participants. Researchers must be careful to properly prepare for their subjects. This may mean having surveys in multiple languages or having a multilingual staff. Other considerations that must be made concern the type of research being conducted. Research may disrupt the routine of an agency. What if a researcher wants to survey 500 inmates? If approved, the state correctional agency must rework their entire daily schedule to have a place for the surveys to be administered and to pull the sample of inmates needed to participate. Undoubtedly, this is not an easy task. What about research that may involve the withholding of beneficial treatment? As you will learn in Chapter 5, an experimental design generally involves the use of a control group that does not receive the treatment being given. If this is beneficial treatment, such as medication that may serve as a cure to a currently terminal illness, is it fair to withhold it from those participants? Another challenging issue involves the observation of or participation with those under study. Because the researcher is there, the participants may feel like they need to impress or show off and this may lead to their acting out in a delinquent or criminal manner. Therefore, the research may be the reason why criminal acts occur. Additionally, research may uncover criminal behavior. Interviewing or surveying individuals about their offending backgrounds may lead to issues of confidentiality, which will be discussed next.

Confidentiality and Anonymity

Especially important in criminal justice research are issues of confidentiality and anonymity related to participation as a research subject and the information shared as a result. Confidentiality infers that, although the researcher may be able to link the information given on a survey or during an interview to the particular research participant who gave it, this link will not be revealed in the publication of the findings. Results may be given in aggregate, or group, form but information will not be linked back to the individual participants. Even if participants do not give identifying information during the study, they may have been asked to sign an informed consent form from which the researcher has access to their name. Confidentiality maintains that the researcher will not release these names, that their participation will be kept secret. Anonymity infers that the participant's

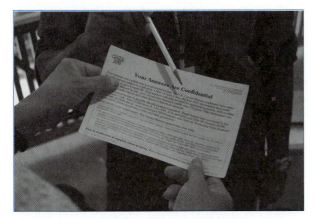

A 2010 Census interviewer explains a confidentiality notice to a household resident prior to her participation in the Census interview.

identity will not be known, even to the researcher. For example, research subjects may be asked to participate in an online survey. Consent is assumed by completion of the survey and there are no questions included in the survey that ask for respondent's personal or identifying information (e.g., name, address). Therefore, even the researcher does not know who participated in the survey, leaving participation completely anonymous.

Procedures for ensuring confidentiality include keeping data in places where only the principal researcher has access. This may be on a password-protected computer or in a locked file cabinet. Researchers may also substitute code numbers for names so that, if breached, participant responses cannot be traced back to the individuals from which they came. Additionally, any hard copies of data files or analytic results should be disposed of properly by shredding or otherwise destroying. It is not enough to put these in the recycling or trash bin. It is important for researchers that all research staff be educated on issues of confidentiality and anonymity so that, when made, these promises are not broken.

Certificates of Confidentiality

Now, you may be wondering about confidentiality and whether there may be consequences for keeping research data confidential. While **shield laws**, which extend government immunity from prosecution for not divulging confidential and anonymous research information in court, do exist (see the 1973 Omnibus Crime Control and Safe Streets Act, Section 524[a]), with some exceptions, these generally apply to federally funded research only. However, there is generally no recognized privilege between researchers and their participants, and therefore, researchers may be subpoenaed to testify about what a research subject has told them. Here, a researcher may have to make a decision between testifying and protecting confidentiality. If they choose to protect confidentiality, they may face penalties, including possible jail time, although this happens infrequently. The U.S. Department of Health and Human Services has taken a step to protect researchers in this regard. **Certificates of Confidentiality**[24] can now be applied for by researchers using human subjects for sensitive research. These certificates "protect against compulsory legal demands, such as court orders and subpoenas, for identifying information or identifying characteristics of a research participant" and the authority of the certificate has generally been upheld when challenged in a court setting.[25] There may also be negative consequences for the researcher if they decide not to keep the confidentiality they promised. Future subjects may no

WHAT RESEARCH SHOWS: IMPACTING CRIMINAL JUSTICE OPERATIONS
Crime Prediction Software

Nationwide, there is a new trend taking place, the use of computer-aided prediction in the prevention of criminal acts. From the East Coast to the West Coast, these programs are being utilized by criminal justice officials to respond to criminal behavior before it happens. As controversial as it may be to make life-altering decisions based on something that may happen instead of something that has happened, the use of computer-based prediction systems seems to be a welcome addition to the criminal justice tool box.

Dr. Richard Berk, Professor of Criminology and Statistics at the University of Pennsylvania, has developed one such program that is currently being used in cities like Philadelphia, Baltimore, and Washington D.C.[26] Dr. Berk's prediction software has been utilized to predict which individuals serving a sentence under community supervision (i.e., probation or parole) are more likely to commit future offenses such as murder. Being able to predict which offenders are at higher risk, either for future offending or victimization, can inform community supervision officers as to the level of supervision they should provide. Dr. Berk contends his software can also be useful in sentencing decision, including how much bail should be set for a certain offender.

Other software programs have been implemented by criminal justice agencies across the country. The Florida State Department of Juvenile Justice uses such software to determine which juvenile offenders are at highest risk for recidivism.[27] Identified offenders are given a specialized treatment plan based on their high-risk status. Additionally, in Santa Cruz, California, law enforcement has begun to use prediction software to determine where in the city they should focus their efforts to prevent crimes from occurring.[28] These location-specific projection programs work by analyzing crime-related data and identifying patterns as to which locations in the city are at highest risk for law breaking to occur on any given day.

While prediction systems have existed for decades, these were generally based on offender history, scales, and other survey responses in need of individual interpretation. Computer software provides an advantage: the ability to sort and analyze this information in a much shorter time frame. As many of these software products are still being tested in cities in which they have been implemented, research will show whether others (individuals or locations) were missed by the programs. Determining the ability of these programs to effectively predict high-risk elements should be the next step in their continued use.

---

longer trust that the researcher will keep promises of confidentiality and therefore may be less than truthful when participating in research studies under their supervision. Beyond criminal liability, there are other ways in which researchers may be held liable for their research findings. Researchers may also be sued in civil court for libel or slander. Additionally, researchers may face financial, professional, social, and personal consequences for the research they conduct and the findings that result.

So far, this chapter has provided discussion concerning the ethicality of research and the use of human subjects. Now it is time to introduce the reader more generally to research with particular attention to some basic principles of research. Indeed, one of the first steps in understanding research methods from a consumer standpoint is to become familiar with the language of research.

A LANGUAGE ALL ITS OWN

As discussed in Chapter 1, we are all consumers and producers of research whether we know it or not. While this is the case, when you pick up a research article for the first time and begin to read about the methods used by the authors, you may feel a bit "lost in translation." Anything can be confusing until you are exposed to it—this is particularly true concerning research methods. Until you have been taught this language and how to apply it, approaching research can be daunting and intimidating. However, once you become familiar with the terms and processes that are utilized by researchers, you will be much more comfortable deciphering what a researcher or an author of a research article is trying to tell you.

Criminology as a Social Science

Criminology is a social science. This means that in order to study a social phenomenon, crime, we apply the scientific method. Sometimes we rely on our faith or philosophy to make sense of the world. However, philosophy or theology and science are quite different. Theology is sometimes quite subjective and propositions therefore cannot be scientifically measured or proven. For example, if one were to say that a crime occurs because the criminal is possessed by the devil, how do we prove this? Scientific principles indicate the ability to measure, replicate, and verify. In order to measure something, we must be able to observe it. As with the devil example, how can we measure the devil's work if we cannot observe the devil? Next, in order to prove that a research finding or measurement is not a mistake, a researcher must be able to replicate the finding using the same methods. Only through replication can we have confidence in our original findings. For social science research, it may be important to replicate findings many times over so that we are assured our original finding was not a coincidence or chance occurrence. Finally, not only is it important to reveal a connection between two phenomena, it is also important to verify that this connection is real. Ultimately, you cannot verify your findings unless you are able to measure and replicate. Only through repeated measures can we verify that the results found are true. For example, if a researcher wanted to study the relationship between low socioeconomic status and crime, they could measure this in a number of ways. Researchers could survey prison inmates or arrestees to ask them about their income and previous employment. Researchers could also use official statistics and plot arrests or calls for assistance on maps in order to see if there are more arrests in areas that are known to be low income. In order to replicate, these surveys or maps could be conducted or developed across a number of cities and/or states. Following these replications, researchers would review the data to determine if the findings from the original study were verified.

Social Science as a Discipline

While these three steps (measurement, replication, and verification) describe the scientific method, it is important to recognize that social sciences are different from hard, or physical, sciences. In research for physical sciences (e.g., physics, biology, or chemistry), there may be less replication needed to prove something is true. One only needs to stick their hand in boiling water once to know that it is going to burn. Although you can replicate this, you may be certain that the result will be the same no matter whose hand it is or where you are boiling the water. The other major difference is related to this expectation. Physical sciences are governed by laws and principles such as Newton's Universal Law of Gravitation. When certain conditions are present, certain things always happen. When an apple breaks away from the tree, it always falls to the ground. The social sciences, including criminology, are different in this regard. These disciplines operate on more **probabilistic** notions. This means that something is more or less likely to occur when certain conditions are present or not present. Social scientists can never be 100% certain that any event will occur; only that something is

more or less likely to occur given the conditions. For example, it is not realistic to expect that everyone who grows up in a single parent household will become delinquent. While that condition may put a child more at risk for delinquency due to the fact that there may be less supervision, among other things, not everyone who grows up in a single parent household will turn to delinquency. In fact, many individuals from single parent households go on to be very successful. You may have been raised by a single parent and instead of committing crime, you are enrolled in a class about studying crime. In criminology we are often looking for risk factors, the conditions that make something more or less likely to occur. When we seek to understand criminality and why it occurs, it is particularly important to realize that we will never be able to predict with certainty the cause of criminality in all cases. Instead, we attempt to find those conditions that make crime more likely than not and focus on those when creating programs and policies to deter or respond to crime.

Objectivity

Objectivity indicates a neutral and nonbiased perspective when conducting research. It is truly a foundation on which scientific research is based. Objectivity is the opposite of subjectivity, which refers to one's beliefs, opinions, and perspective. If researchers are subjective instead of objective, their prejudgments and biases may creep into their research design and consequently impact the findings. Therefore, while it is not unethical to have opinions and judgments, it is important that these do not impact researchers when carrying out their research. For example, if a researcher has a great disdain for sex offenders and he is placed in charge of evaluating a sex offender treatment program, can you see how his feelings may impact his findings? It could even be that the researcher consciously or subconsciously sets up the research to show that the treatment program is not working or to minimize the positive results of the program so that it is no longer used with the intention that sex offenders will serve longer sentences instead of being rehabilitated and released. As another example, it is often suggested that researchers do not study groups of which they are a member. This could be that the researcher is too close to the group under study and will not recognize when things happen that are unnatural. It may be very difficult to maintain their objectivity when observing their friends, family members, or colleagues. So, while it is only natural to have opinions and feelings based on past experiences, it is important to recognize these and to ensure that they do impact our research endeavors.

Categorizing Research

Over time, different types of research have begun to be categorized based on

- methodology utilized by the researchers to collect and analyze the data;
- how research results will be utilized; and/or
- intentions of the researchers.

First, there are two major types of research based on the methodology used to collect the data. **Methodology** indicates the methods used to gather information. You will learn about many different types of methodology while reading the chapters that follow, including types of sampling procedures, experimental designs, the use of surveys and interviews, and the use of observation and participation, among others. **Qualitative research** incorporates methods that are sensitizing. This type of research involves developing a deeper understanding about a particular group or activity. For qualitative research, researchers may live with the group under study. They may participate in their activities as if they were a member of the group or they may observe the activities as an outsider looking in. The point is to immerse oneself into the lifestyle of those under study so that you can truly understand their perspective. Earlier in this chapter, Humphrey's study of sex in public restrooms was discussed. This is an example of a researcher actually participating, as a "watchqueen," in the activities under observation. Chapter 6 will discuss this study and others involving qualitative methodologies in more detail. **Quantitative research,** on the other hand, implies that researchers will be counting and measuring some phenomenon. Researchers will take a **concept** such as crime and will attempt to put a numerical value on it. Can you think of ways that crime can be measured numerically? Quantitative research on crime could be conducted using arrest rates, calls to the police, victimization rates, and many other types of numerical measurement. Based on these methodologies, the main difference between quantitative and qualitative research is that qualitative research attempts to explore "why" things occur the way they do and quantitative research examines "what" has occurred. So, quantitative research examines what the evidence shows while qualitative research explores why the evidence shows what it does. It should be noted, however, that research projects do not necessarily have to be one or the other. In some cases, researchers combine both qualitative and quantitative methodologies in their research.

Research can also be categorized by how the results of the study will be utilized. **Pure research** refers to research conducted to develop or further develop a discipline. Its goal is to achieve new knowledge for the sake of achieving new knowledge. The development of a new theory to explain criminality would be an example of pure research. The other category is called **applied research.** Applied research has more practical concerns. Usually this type of research is conducted to answer questions currently impacting a certain field, perhaps to address immediate policy concerns or to determine whether a program will be continued or terminated. Much of the research you will encounter as a criminal justice professional will be applied in some way. It could be that the chief of police is interested in understanding how mandatory arrest policies impact domestic violence victims or that the director of a community supervision department is interested in knowing which programs aid probationers in successfully completing their sentence. In answering these questions through research, one would be using a more applied approach.

Similar to pure and applied research, another way research can be categorized is by its intention, or the reason for which it's being conducted. There are four general categories. First, for descriptive research, researchers seek to describe a particular phenomenon. This type of research is not intended to understand the cause or to explain why something is occurring; it only provides a description of what is happening. For example, a researcher may want to determine what age group is most crime prone and whether this is the same for females and males. This type of research will most likely be quantitative in nature. For the second category, exploratory research, researchers seek to grasp what is going on regarding a particular phenomenon. For example, a researcher may want to better understand the process of prison gang formation, reasons why the gang forms, how members are recruited, and the like. This type of research may involve qualitative methodologies and is useful when there is little information available on a particular subject. For the third category, explanatory research, researchers seek to identify causes and effects related to a certain topic. For example, a researcher may be interested in the relationship between poverty and crime. Explanatory research determines whether something is more or less likely, so the question that may be posed is whether crime is more or less likely in high poverty areas. Finally, evaluation research is conducted to determine the impact of a program or policy. It may determine whether a program is cost effective, whether it was properly implemented, or whether it worked as intended. For example, evaluation research may examine whether a zero tolerance policy has decreased misconduct among students in a certain school district or whether a juvenile offender program, such as a boot camp, has been successful in reducing recidivism.

The Role of Theory in Research

Some of you may have already taken a course in criminological theory and therefore have been introduced to the terms paradigm and theory. For those of you who have not, a **paradigm** is a school of thought. A paradigm is an umbrella term under which information can be organized. There are three main paradigms under which criminological theories are structured in criminology. There is the classical paradigm, the positivist paradigm, and the critical paradigm. Under each of these paradigms there are many theories developed along similar ideas. For example, under the positivist paradigm, the overriding theoretical perspective woven into each theory is that crime is predetermined, or caused by something outside of an individual's control. This cause may be biological, psychological, or sociological in nature. A **theory** has been defined as "a set of interconnected statements or propositions that explain how two or more events or factors are related to one another."[29] One quality of a useful theory is that it has been empirically verified, that is, it has been tested many times to verify that its propositions are true. Therefore, a great deal of research in criminology is theory driven.

Whether you are developing and testing theory or deriving a new research project not related to theory, you must have a critical eye. Critical thinking is imperative to good research. There are two general foundations to critical thinking that lend to research design. The first is deduction. **Deduction** is the process of first utilizing a theory and its tenets to then develop a specific hypothesis. The aim of deductive thinking is to test a particular hypothesis in order to confirm whether the propositions of the broader theory are true. For example, labeling theorists contend that once an individual is labeled in a negative fashion, such as a criminal or addict, they internalize this label and act accordingly. Researchers may test this theory by determining if individuals who are formally processed through the criminal justice system (i.e., arrested and convicted) are more likely than those who are diverted and handled informally (i.e. no conviction on record if diversion program completed successfully) to reoffend. If those who are formally processed are more likely to reoffend, controlling for other factors, this lends support to labeling theory. **Induction** works

the opposite way. Inductive thinking involves applying what is known about one or a few cases to an entire group. Findings from exploratory research may then result in a theory regarding the group or topic under study. For example, in a qualitative study of one Mafioso, his characteristics and activities may be applied to all individuals involved in organized criminal enterprises. Interestingly, at the beginning of a research project, we are often using deductive and inductive reasoning without even knowing it.

Creating a Question and Hypothesizing

When a researcher begins a research project, one of the first steps is choosing a research question. Oftentimes this first step can be overwhelming as our interests may be quite broad. For example, you may be interested in researching human trafficking; however, this is a very broad topic and would need to be narrowed in order to sustain a workable research study. Research questions related to this topic may relate to offenders, victims,

FIGURE 2.1 | Steps in the Research Process

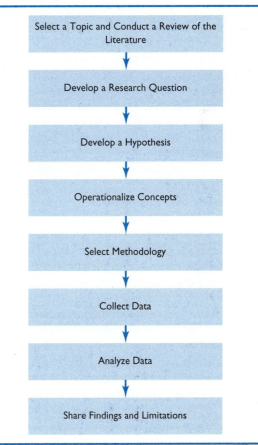

services available for victims, consequences of victimization, or government responses. Furthermore, you may want to focus on one specific country. This may be a source country or a destination county. As you can see, this topic, like many others, has many layers that can be explored. If you have a choice of topic, it is good to select something you are interested in. That way, you are more likely to be interested in answering the question you pose instead of feeling like the project is only a means to an end. In other situations, such as evaluating a program for your employer, it may be very easy to decide what the research question is in that the questions have really been provided for you based on the need of the organization or agency for which you are employed.

For purposes of our discussion, let's ask the question "Is there a relationship between type of victimization (i.e., human trafficking or not) and likelihood of reporting to law enforcement?" Once you have figured out what your research question will be, the next step is to determine the concepts important to your question. The process of developing concepts involves putting a tag or name on some event. Concepts may include trafficking, victimization, poverty, and reporting among others. After developing your question and understanding which concepts are employed in answering the question, you will develop a hypothesis. **Hypotheses** are statements about the expected relationship between two concepts. These are often based on previous research findings and may be derived from a particular theory. There are two types of hypotheses, the research hypothesis and the null hypothesis. The research hypothesis states the expected relationship in positive terms. In the case of reporting human trafficking victimization, the research hypothesis could be that being a human trafficking victim makes one less likely to report the victimization to the police. The null hypothesis, on the other hand, assumes that there will be no relationship between the concepts in question, that is, type of victimization is unrelated to official reporting. The best way to remain neutral and objective in research is to assume the null hypothesis is correct.

Once you have developed your research questions and hypotheses, the next step is **operationalization**. Through this process, you are giving the concept in question a working definition, or determining how each concept in your study will be measured. For the example question regarding human trafficking and official reporting, you may operationalize human trafficking as a person being brought from one country to another for means of forced labor, using force or coercion. Poverty may be measured by income or employment prior to being trafficked. Official

reporting could be measured by whether the victim reported her victimization to law enforcement either in the source or destination country. What if you were interested in the relationship between intelligence and crime? How would you quantitatively, or numerically, measure intelligence? What if you were interested in the relationship between being a problem student and delinquency? How would you determine who is a problem student? The process of operationalization is key to your research project. If you do not know how a concept is to be measured, you cannot begin to collect your information. Further, operationalizing your concepts will often lead you to the type of information you need. For example, if you are interested in problem students and you want to measure this by how many disciplinary infractions each student has received, you may ask the students through questionnaire or interview about their history of disciplinary infractions or you may go to the dean of students or other administrators in order to get official records regarding which students have been disciplined formally.

Once you have determined how the concepts should be operationalized, they become variables. **Variables** signify concepts that have been given a measurement. As with types of research, variables can be quantitative or qualitative, depending on the type of measurement. For example, if you are measuring trafficking by how many victims are trafficked to a particular country annually, it is a quantitative measurement; however, if you are measuring why victims are trafficked to that particular country, this would be more qualitative. There are two types of variables important to your research. The **independent variable** is the cause. It determines, or precedes the other variable in time. The **dependent variable** is the outcome. In the case of type of victimization and official reporting, if you hypothesize that type of victimization (i.e., human trafficking) makes one less likely to officially report the victimization, then your independent variable will be human trafficking and your dependent variable will be official reporting. As another example, if you think that intelligence makes one more likely to succeed, the independent variable would be intelligence and the dependent variable would be success. It is important to note that the role of the variable may change depending on the research project in question. For example, in a study that asks whether poverty causes crime, poverty is the independent variable and crime is the dependent variable. However, in a study that asks whether crime causes poverty, it would be the opposite. Crime would serve as the independent variable and poverty as the dependent variable. Can you think of a scenario in which crime causes poverty?

Besides independent and dependent variables, there are also extraneous factors or correlates that should be taken into consideration when conducting research. These are factors that relate to, but do not cause the outcome. For example, weather is often cited as a correlate to crime. In the summer months, crime is often higher. Can you think why this may be? Usually individuals are outside more, and thus more vulnerable to victimization. So, does warmer weather cause crime? No; however, it is a factor that is related to vulnerability. In the human trafficking example, it could be that in the victim's home country law enforcement officials are corrupt and therefore they are unlikely to report. In that case, official reporting would be related to perceptions of law enforcement rather than to the type of victimization the victim has experienced. There are many other extraneous factors in social science research, and it is important to understand how these may impact your study and your study findings.

Reliability and Validity

Reliability and validity are two very important concepts that you should be aware of when designing your study and analyzing your data. These two terms will be revisited throughout this text, but for now a general explanation will be provided so that the concepts are no longer foreign to you. Oftentimes researchers must rely on others for information. For example, if you are using official data, you must trust that law enforcement officials and others were truthful in their reporting. You also must take into consideration that not all crimes come to the attention of law enforcement and therefore are not counted in official data. These unreported offenses are often called the *dark figure of crime*. Researchers attempt to measure the dark figure of crime by using self-report data. Researchers may ask respondents how many times they have committed criminal acts or how many times they have been victimized. However, there are issues with self-report data as well. For example, it is difficult to know whether a respondent is being totally truthful when completing your survey or responding to your interview question. Each of these issues relates to reliability and validity of your findings. Reliability and validity address the quality of a study's methodology and therefore also pertain to the quality and believability of the findings resulting from the study.

Reliability pertains to ensuring that the responses you receive when utilizing questionnaires or interviews are reliable, that if you ask the same person the same question at a different time, you will get a similar answer. To determine whether responses are reliable, there are steps that can be taken. For surveys or interviews, you may ask the same questions in different ways. For example, you may ask about a respondent's grade point average and later ask him if he is a good student. Reliability may also be an issue when you have more than one person coding or analyzing information. In Chapter 7, you will learn more about this relating to content analysis and issues of interrater reliability.

As for validity, there are many different types of validity in research; some impact the research design while others impact the measuring instrument. Validity refers to the accurateness of your measurement. Validity may relate to factors that threaten an experimental design and therefore impact your findings. In Chapter 5, you will be introduced to many internal validity threats, including selection bias, history, and maturation. The presence of these factors may explain away the relationship you find between your independent and dependent variable, thereby making it spurious, or false. There also exist external validity threats that affect the ways in which your findings can be used. In Chapter 3, you will learn about sampling and how researchers often use a representative subset of a population instead of studying the entire population. When using a sample, it is always best if researchers can generalize their findings back to the larger population; however, this is not always possible. For example, if you do not have a representative sample, you cannot generalize your findings back to the larger population. Additionally, validity plays a role in survey research. A researcher must determine if their research instrument, or survey, and the questions included are valid, whether they are measuring what they intended to measure. For example, a classic question utilized in research to measure fear of crime is, "Are you afraid to walk alone at night near your home?" This may be problematic, however, because this fear, if it exists, may not be directly related to crime. Can you think of what else this question may be measuring other than fear of being victimized? Your instrument has to include the right questions in order to illicit the responses needed. If a question does not measure what you intended to measure, then it is not valid. There are four types of validity related to research instruments that will be discussed further in Chapter 4. These are face validity, content validity, construct validity, and pragmatic validity. As you will learn in Chapter 4, there is much work that goes into creating a research instrument prior to administering it. Ultimately, if the researcher does not have a valid, reliable response or is not measuring what she intended to measure, her efforts will be wasted.

Examining the "CSI Effect"

While in years past most people in the United States did not give a second thought to criminal investigative techniques, today many are fascinated by the process based on what they have learned from film and television. One television show in particular, *CSI: Crime Scene Investigation (CSI)*, has been discussed and researched as to its relevance and impact on our culture. Specifically, researchers have expressed interest in examining how shows like *CSI* and others have influenced decision-making when taking part in the criminal justice process.

One study conducted in 2006 did just that, surveying 1,027 randomly summoned jurors as to their television viewing habits and how these may have impacted what they expect from the trial process.[30] Focusing on forensic scientific evidence in particular, 46% of jurors in the study expected that such evidence would be a part of every criminal case that came before the court. Over 20% of the sample expected to see DNA in every case, 36% expected to see fingerprint evidence in every case, and 32% expected that firearms laboratory evidence would be a part of every criminal trial. Viewers of *CSI* were also more likely to have higher expectations related to evidence presented at trial. According to the researchers, the good news stemming from the study was that respondents did not rely solely on such evidence for conviction or acquittal. Other factors, such as victim or witness testimony, also influenced decision-making, even among frequent viewers of *CSI*.

The potential for television shows, whether documentary-based like *48 Hours Mystery* or fictional like *CSI* or the *Law & Order* franchises, to impact our daily lives has been recognized, especially as these shows increase their viewership. Researchers are interested in examining this phenomenon from many angles, not only exploring how perceptions based on what is presented as reality on television impact the criminal justice process but also how it may impact criminal justice education. For example, how many of your fellow classmates were influenced by what they have viewed on television when selecting a criminal justice class or even criminal justice as a college major and how well did their expectations match the reality? These and other questions can be addressed through research and, as viewership continues to grow and more television shows are created, it is likely that we will see increased study on what now has been so popularly coined the "CSI Effect."

INFORMATION LITERACY AND THE STRUCTURE OF RESEARCH PAPERS

Now that you have been introduced to the language of research, it is time to examine the process of how research is shared with others. When one is developing a research report, paper, or article, there are generally five sections that should be incorporated. First will be the introduction section. This section is very important because it is the first chance the writer has to catch the readers' attention and to let them know why the information or research being presented is worth their attention. Usually, this section is not very long compared to the length of the report; however, included will be the major details that will be examined in the report, including the research question(s) being explored. Following the introduction section is typically a literature review. The literature review is where the writer provides the reader insight on any previous research that has been conducted on the topic. This is also where the writer will make the case for his hypotheses, as hypotheses are usually developed based on the findings of past research, assuming past research exists on the topic. The third section is generally called the methodology section. In the methodology section, the writer provides the details of the study

Often researchers begin the research process by finding information related to their topic in books, articles, and/or from reputable online sources.

for the reader, including the procedures used to answer the research question(s). The research question(s) and hypotheses driving the study should be reiterated and the process of data collection, including the population of interest, the sampling procedure, the method of data collection, and the plan of analysis, should be described. The next section relays the findings or results of the research being conducted. In a qualitative study, the writer may describe his observations or the activities he was able to participate in. If a quantitative piece, the writer may include tables presenting the statistical results of the analysis of data utilized. Research articles or papers on research studies should generally conclude with the fifth section, where the writer discusses his findings in terms of their importance. In this section, limitations that may have impacted the study should be noted. Program or policy implications related to the findings may also be given. The writer may also suggest areas for future research related to the topic. All in all, this is where the writer emphasizes the point of the research project for the reader. While this is a basic structure for research reports and papers, it is always best to check with your professor, employer, or editor prior to beginning any writing so that you are aware of the structure they expect.

As mentioned above, the first step in developing a research project is choosing a research topic and, from that topic, selecting one or more research questions. There exists, an unlimited number of topics for researchers to examine. It is also important to remember the significance of replication so, even if a topic has been researched, an attempt to replicate previous findings is a valid research project. For those of you who may be unsure of a topic, you may begin your search by reading local, national, or international news reports to see if you become inspired by a topic covered or you may also want to dive into the academic literature for ideas.

Regardless of whether you have a topic or you are looking for a topic, you will need to make yourself familiar with academic and particularly the empirical research that has been published. As a student, you may have already conducted literature searches for research papers you were asked to write for other courses. Irrespective of whether you are writing a research paper, an empirical research or evaluation report, a thesis or dissertation, or an academic research article, you will begin by familiarizing yourself with the related literature. There are many places to find literature; however, you must be careful in distinguishing scholarly publications from nonscholarly works. Primary sources are always best. Primary sources include published books,

journal articles, and some government reports. Secondary sources include textbooks, encyclopedias, and news reports. Secondary sources usually involve summaries of primary source work and, while they may offer suitable information related to the research design, they often do not provide the detail you need to write a quality literature review. Another term you may hear when beginning a literature search is **peer review.** Peer review is a form of quality control most commonly related to academic journals. If a journal follows a peer review process, when a manuscript is submitted it is sent out to be reviewed by experts in the field to determine whether the manuscript is suitable for publication. Publication outlets that are not peer reviewed do not garner as much respect from the academic community as there is less control for quality of the material published.

Books and academic journals can often be found in print in your library, although as we move further into the electronic age, many of these sources can also be found online through your library. For example, your library may subscribe to electronic journals or to research databases such as EBSCOhost and ERIC through which you can search for individual books and articles by subject, keyword, author, or other search terms. If you are looking for a book or journal that your library does not own or subscribe to, you may look into whether your library has an interlibrary loan system. This would allow you to borrow the book or obtain the journal article from another library through your library membership. Online searching has become more prevalent, and in many cases, can provide you with information that you otherwise could not obtain. It is important, however, to be able to ascertain whether the information you find online is reputable. As an example, many students rely on general websites for information; however, did you realize that on many websites, anyone can submit information? There are entries on numerous websites that are complete works of fiction. The bottom line is that not everything you find online is reliable and you may end up with misinformation if you are not careful. Reputable websites may include government websites, university websites, and some organization websites such as the National Criminal Justice Reference Service website, the Bureau of Justice Statistics website, and the National Institute of Justice website. For example, if you are searching for information on services available to victims of domestic violence, it may be best to go to the service organization's website to obtain information about the services they provide. You may also visit the website for the U.S. Department of Justice, Office for

The Controversy Regarding Embryonic Stem Cell Research

One recent example of the controversial nature of research, in this case medical research, pertains to the use of human embryonic stem cells in medical studies. Stem cells, as they are commonly known, are cells within the body that have unique capabilities, namely the ability to regenerate growth.[31] Medical researchers have long touted stem cell use for treating injuries and diseases such as heart disease and diabetes, which have become more common the United States in recent years.

The majority of the embryonic stem cells used for medical research are obtained from embryos that were donated after not being used in *in vitro* fertilization procedures. These embryos are destroyed in the process of acquiring the stem cells needed for study. The ethical or moral issue regarding the use of stem cells relates to whether a human embryo constitutes "life." This is quite similar to the controversy surrounding abortion.

Under President George W. Bush, there existed a ban against federal funding for stem cell research. As such research is often costly to conduct, this ban severely limited the ability of medical researchers to conduct stem cell studies. In 2009, President Obama reversed this ban, allowing for federal funds to be used for promising stem cell research.[32] The executive order signed by President Obama also required the National Institutes of Health (NIH) to develop ethical guidelines for stem cell research.[33]

The most recent turn of events for stem cell research was a lawsuit brought on by two researchers, James Sherley and Theresa Deisher, against the use of embryonic stem cells.[34] This case hinged on a piece of legislation known as the Dickey-Wicker amendment, passed by Congress in 1996, which prohibited the use of federal funds for research in which embryos would be discarded or destroyed. While Chief Judge Royce Lamberth for the U.S. District Court in Washington at first sided with the researchers, placing a temporary ban on funding for such research, in July 2011 the chief judge reversed his decision and dismissed the lawsuit brought before the court.

There is no doubt that this case is not the last that will come before the court regarding embryonic stem cell research. As with abortion, the ethical divide regarding the destruction of embryos does not seem to be lessening. It is important to note that this discussion has centered on the use of federal funding only and that stem cell research conducted with private funds remains relatively unaffected by such rulings. The change in federal policy brought on by President Obama, however, has certainly allowed for more studies using embryonic stem cells by increasing the funding sources for such research. As long as the NIH and all other appropriate guidelines are followed, such research is now considered an acceptable means to better understand the use of embryonic stem cells in medical treatments.

Violence Against Women for information about services for domestic violence victims. So, as these examples show, while quality information can be found online, you must be smart about where you are searching and you must view everything with a critical eye to ensure the provider of the information is trustworthy. Once you have collected a solid foundation of information related to your topic, you then must read through this information to grasp what has been found previously and what issues exist that remain to be examined. Unless you have a true understanding of your topic and the information available, your review of the literature will be lacking and you may have a difficult time developing a quality research question.

C H A P T E R   S U M M A R Y

This chapter has provided the reader the basic information needed to begin the process of being an informed consumer of research. First, the ethical and sometimes unethical nature of research in criminal justice was discussed. Much has been learned from unethical research of the past and, while occurrences of unethical research still arise, these are few and far between due to the regulations and monitoring now in place. As oftentimes our research involves human subjects, it is important that researchers not forget the guidelines put in place to keep research participants safe from harm. Along with a discussion regarding research ethics, this chapter also has presented the basic language of research and the knowledge one needs to embark on a research project. The chapters that follow will provide the information you need to further develop your understanding of research methods. So, while you have come far, there is still a long way to go to understanding the various elements of research. It is important to remember, however, that you are probably already familiar with much of this information; you just have never thought of it from a researcher's perspective.

CRITICAL THINKING QUESTIONS

1. Name and describe three examples of research studies that were deemed unethical after being conducted. What were the reasons these studies were deemed unethical?

2. What is the role of IRBs and why is it important to have them?

3. What does it mean to have informed consent from a research participant?

4. Why is it important for a researcher to be objective?

5. Describe the research process from the creation of a research question to variable development.

KEY TERMS

applied research: Practical research that may involve evaluating existing or proposed policies or programs

Certificates of Confidentiality: Certificates awarded by the U.S. Department of Health and Human Services to protect researchers from court orders to identify information or characteristics of a research participant

concept: A clear idea regarding a particular subject (e.g., crime) based on that subject's characteristics

deduction: The process of using a theory and its tenets to develop one or more specific hypotheses

dependent variable: The outcome variable; the variable dependent on what occurs with the independent variable

ethical relativism: The belief that how we think about ethics varies from one time to another, one place to another, and from one person to another

ethics: Recognized rules of conduct that govern a particular group

hypotheses: Statements about the expected relationship between two concepts

independent variable: The variable that determines and precedes the other variable in time

induction: The process of applying what is known about one or a few cases to an entire group

informed consent: Voluntary consent required from competent research participants after participants have been given accurate and relevant information about the study regarding procedures and possible risks and benefits to participation

institutional review board (IRB): A group of individuals selected to review research proposals to check compliance with federal and state law; determines whether research should be conducted based on a risk-benefit ratio

methodology: The techniques utilized to gather information or data for research purposes

operationalization: The process of giving a concept a working definition; determining how each concept in your study will be measured

paradigm: School of thought; way to organize information within a discipline

peer review: A form of quality control most commonly related to academic journals; process by which submitted manuscripts are sent out to be reviewed by experts in the field to determine whether the manuscript is suitable for publication

probabilistic: An event or outcome is more or less likely when certain conditions are present or not present

pure research: Research conducted to achieve new knowledge in the development of a discipline

qualitative research: Research that is sensitizing or helps to develop a better understanding about a particular group or activity for which there exists little information; qualitative research is more descriptive and less numerical

quantitative research: Research that involves a numerical measurement of some phenomenon

shield laws: Laws extending government immunity from prosecution for not divulging confidential and anonymous research information in court

theory: A statement explaining how two or more factors are related to one another

variable: An operationalized concept allowing for specific measurement

vulnerable populations: Regarding informed consent, those populations for which there are unique risks and a question of whether their consent is fully voluntary or not coerced; examples include prison inmates and terminally ill patients

ENDNOTES

1 Zimbardo, P., Producer/Director. [Videotape]. (1991). Quiet Rage: The Stanford Prison Experiment. California: Philip Zimbardo.

2 See American Medical Association's Code of Medical Ethics. http://www.ama-assn.org/ama/pub/physician -resources/medical-ethics/code-medical-ethics.page.

3   See American Bar Association's Model Rules of Professional Conduct. http://www.americanbar.org/groups /professional_responsibility/publications/model_rules_of _professional_conduct/model_rules_of_professional _conduct_table_of_contents.html

4   See http://www.hhs.gov/ohrp/ for more information on U.S. Department of Health and Human Services Office of Human Research Protections.

5   Heydecker, J. J., & Leeb, J. (1975). *The Nuremberg Trial: A history of Nazi Germany as revealed through the testimony at Nuremberg.* Santa Barbara, CA: Greenwood.

6   Centers for Disease Control and Prevention. (2011). U.S. Public Health Service Syphilis Study at Tuskegee. http:// www.cdc.gov/tuskegee/

7   Mulford, R.D. (1967). Experimentation on human beings. *Stanford Law Review,* 20(1), 99–117.

8   Krugman, S. (1986). The Willowbrook Hepatitis Studies revisited: Ethical aspects. *Reviews of Infectious Diseases,* 8(1), 157–162.

9   Hornblum, A.M. (1999). *Acres of skin: Human experiments at Holmesburg Prison.* New York: Routledge.

10 Humphreys, L. (1975). *Tearoom trade: Impersonal sex in public places.* Piscataway, NJ: Aldine Transactions.

11 Milgram, S. (1963). Behavioral study of obedience. *Journal of Abnormal and Social Psychology,* 67(4), 371–378.

12 Borge, C. (2007, Jan. 3). Basic instincts: The science of evil. ABC News/Primetime. http://abcnews.go.com /Primetime/story?id=2765416&page=1. Watch WebCast of Episode on ABC News website: http://abcnews.go.com /Primetime/video?id=2769000.

13 Schwartz, J. (2004, May 6). Simulated prison in '71 showed a fine line between 'normal' and 'monster'. *The New York Times.* http://www.nytimes.com/2004/05/06 /international/middleeast/06PSYC.html?ex=13992624 00&en=91f8144cdf7dd44a&ei=5007&partner=USER LAND. Also see links on The Stanford Prison Experiment Related Links webpage: http://www.prisonexp .org/links.htm.

14 See Saletan, W. (2004 May 12). Situationist ethics: The Stanford Prison Experiment doesn't explain Abu Ghraib. Slate. http://www.slate.com/id/2100419/.

15 For full text, go to http://www.research.buffalo.edu/rsp /irb/forms/nuremberg_code.pdf.

16 For full text, see the United Nations website http://www .un.org/en/documents/udhr/.

17 For full text, see the World Medical Association website http://www.wma.net/en/30publications/10policies/b3/.

18 U.S. Department of Health and Human Services. (2004). Guidelines for the conduct of research involving human subjects at the National Institutes of Health. http://www .nccamwatch.org/research/human_guidelines.pdf.

19 Hagan, F. (2006). *Research methods in criminal justice and criminology* (p. 47). Boston: Allyn and Bacon.

20 For full text see the National Institutes of Health webpage http:// hhs.gov/ohrp/humansubjects/guidance/belmont .html.

21 Office for Human Research Protections. (1993). IRB Guidebook. http://www.hhs.gov/ohrp/archive/irb/irb _guidebook.htm.

22 See U.S. Department of Health and Human Services Informed Consent webpage http://www.hhs.gov/ohrp /policy/consent/index.html.

23 See U.S. Department of Health and Human Services Vulnerable Populations webpage http://www.hhs.gov/ohrp /policy/populations/index.html.

24 U.S. Department of Health and Human Services. (2003). Guidance on Certificates of Confidentiality. http://www .hhs.gov/ohrp/policy/certconf.pdf.

25 National Institutes of Health. (2009). Frequently Asked Questions: Certificates of Confidentiality. http://grants .nih.gov/grants/policy/coc/faqs.htm#278.

26 Bland, Eric. (2010 Aug. 22). Software predicts criminal behavior: Program helps law enforcement determine who is most likely to commit crime. ABC News. http://abcnews.go.com/Technology/software-predicts -criminal-behavior/story?id=11448231.

27 Higginbotham, S. (2010 April 14). Hmmm…software that predicts if you will do crime and time. GIGAOM. http:// gigaom.com/2010/04/14/predictive-analysis-ibm/.

28 Goode, E. (2011 Aug. 15). Sending the police before there's a crime. *The New York Times.* http://www.nytimes .com/2011/08/16/us/16police.html.

29 Curran, D. J., & Renzetti, C. M. (2001) *Theories of crime* (p. 2). Boston: Allyn & Bacon.

30 Shelton, D.E. (2008). The 'CSI Effect': Does it really exist? *NIJ Journal,* 259 [NCJ 221501], https://www.ncjrs .gov/pdffiles1/nij/221501.pdf.

31 National Institutes of Health. (2009). Stem cell basics. NIH. http://stemcells.nih.gov/info/basics/defaultpage.asp.

32 Childs, D. (2009 March 9). Obama reverses course, lifts stem cell ban. ABC News. http://abcnews.go.com/Health /Politics/story?id=7023990&page=1.

33 National Institutes of Health. (2009). National Institutes of Health Guidelines for Human Stem Cell Research. http://stemcells.nih.gov/policy/2009guidelines.htm.

34 Rovner. J. (2011 July 27). Judge dismisses lawsuit challenging stem-cell research funding. NPR. http://www.npr .org/blogs/health/2011/07/27/138760069/judge-dismisses -lawsuit-challenging-stem-cell-research-funding.

Sampling Methods

CASE STUDY

Rehabilitation versus Incarceration of Juvenile Offenders

Research Study

Public Preferences for Rehabilitation versus Incarceration of Juvenile Offenders[1]

Research Question

Is the public willing to pay more in taxes for rehabilitation or incarceration as a response to serious juvenile crime?

Methodology

Through a process known as random digit dialing, the researchers of this study randomly sampled 29,532 telephone numbers from four states (Illinois, Louisiana, Pennsylvania, and Washington). Random digit dialing is a variation of probability sampling (discussed later in this chapter) where researchers utilize a computer program that randomly dials the last four digits of a phone number in a known area code. With this variation of sampling, all phone numbers within a given area code have an equal chance at selection for the sample.

Following the random number selection process, researchers excluded randomly chosen phone numbers that corresponded to fax machines, businesses, government organizations, nonworking numbers, and so on. After excluding these phone numbers, a total of 7,132 eligible phone numbers remained. Of the remaining eligible phone numbers, 2,282 telephone interviews were eventually completed across the four states for an overall response rate of 32%.

The survey instrument administered to respondents inquired about rehabilitation versus incarceration for serious juvenile offenders, as related to an increase in household taxes. Of those respondents who agreed to participate in the telephone survey, one-half were randomly assigned the rehabilitation scenario and one-half were randomly assigned to receive the incarceration scenario. The hypothetical rehabilitation versus incarceration scenarios are as follows:

(Rehabilitation Scenario) "Currently in [state] juvenile offenders who commit serious crimes such as robbery are put in jail for about one year. Suppose [state] citizens were asked to approve the addition of a rehabilitation program to the sentence for these sorts of crimes. Similar programs have reduced youth crime by 30%. Youths in these programs are also more likely to graduate from high school and get jobs. If the change is approved, this new law would cost your household an additional $100 per year in taxes."

(Incarceration Scenario) "Currently in [state] juvenile offenders who commit serious crimes such as robbery are put in jail for about one year. Suppose [state] citizens were asked to vote on a change in the law that would increase the sentence for these sorts of crimes by one additional year, making the average length of jail time two years. The additional year will not only impose more punishment but also reduce youth crime by about 30% by keeping juvenile offenders off the street for another year. If the change is approved, this new law would cost your household an additional $100 per year in taxes."

After receiving one of the initial scenarios, respondents were asked: "Would you be willing to pay the additional $100 in taxes for this change in the law?" Those who answered "yes" were then asked if they would be willing to pay $200 for the same change. Those respondents who originally answered "no" to the $100 increase were asked if they would be willing to pay $50 for the same change in the law. Based on the survey, four potential outcomes were measured among respondents: 1) those who said no to $100 and no to $50, 2) those who said yes to $50 but no to $100, 3) those who said yes to $100 but no to $200, and 4) those who said yes to $100 and yes to $200.

Results

Across four states and 2,282 completed telephone interviews, the results of the survey revealed respondents were willing to pay (WTP) more for rehabilitation than incarceration for serious juvenile offenders. Among respondents who were randomly chosen to receive the rehabilitation scenario, 28.5% were not willing to pay any additional taxes. Conversely, roughly 70% were willing to pay at least $50, with nearly 65% willing to pay $100–$200. Among respondents randomly chosen to receive the incarceration scenario, 39% were not willing to pay any additional taxes. Roughly 60% of respondents who received the incarceration scenario were willing to pay at least $50. In short, more respondents were willing to pay (and pay more) for rehabilitation than incarceration for serious juvenile offenders.

Limitations with the Study Procedure

Specific to sampling, perhaps the greatest limitation with this study lies in the relatively high nonresponse rate. In this study, the overall response rate was 32%. This means that nearly 70% of all eligible phone numbers, and hence the perspectives of roughly 70% of randomly sampled persons associated with those phone numbers, were not able to be assessed in the current study. High rates of nonresponse effectively reduce sample size, increase sampling error (the difference in results expected between surveying a sample versus the whole population), and call into question the generalizability of findings since the random sample becomes less representative of the larger population. One relevant question to be considered with high nonresponse is whether those individuals who were eligible to participate in the survey but did not, differ from those who were eligible and did participate. It is possible, for example, that those who were randomly chosen to participate in the telephone interview but did not may hold significantly different attitudes towards rehabilitation versus incarceration compared to those who ultimately participated in the survey. And, if those who refused participation in the survey hold widely different opinions of rehabilitation versus incarceration relative to increasing taxes, the sample (and their results) cannot be said to be representative of the larger population. In sum, such a high rate of nonresponse affects both the representativeness of the sample and hence the ability to generalize the results to the larger population of interest. As discussed in detail in the chapter, a primary advantage of a representative sample is the ability to generalize or apply the results from the sample to the larger population. If in fact large numbers of the sample refuse to participate, this may inhibit the ability of researchers to generalize sample findings to the larger population and may call into question results of a study based on a low response rate.

Beyond response rates and sample sizes, it is important to note other general limitations with survey research such as that highlighted in the current study. As acknowledged by the study authors, it is possible that the hypothetical scenario failed to elicit "real" responses and feelings on rehabilitation versus incarceration from respondents because the scenario was hypothetical, and not a real or genuine proposed change in the law in the states examined. Moreover, surveys in general are replete with potential limitations. While these issues are covered in detail in Chapter 4, it is important to note that surveys may fail to elicit "considered" answers to questions. This potential is particularly relevant in telephone interviews, which are rarely planned ahead of time and therefore respondents might be contacted during a time where they are rushed or otherwise unable or unwilling to provide completely considered answers. More broadly, respondents may not have completely understood the questions being asked. If there was any confusion on the part of the respondents, this could have affected their responses to the questions and ultimately the outcome of the study. Again, these are general limitations of surveys and not necessarily specific to this study. However, such potentials should be considered when interpreting survey results.

Although no research study is perfect, to become an informed consumer of research it is important to be aware of potential limitations not only in sampling, but in response rates and general research methodology. Although this chapter focuses on sampling, knowledge of additional areas often associated with sampling, such as survey limitations, nonresponse or nonparticipation by respondents, and concerns about representativeness and generalizability, allows a clearer picture of the entire research process of which sampling is only one part. In large part, being an informed consumer of research requires more than an understanding of research results; it also requires knowledge of how the results were produced in the first place.

Impact on Criminal Justice

There are many ways in which the highlighted study is important to criminal justice. In one way, this study is important because it was a partial replication of a previous study.[2] Although certain aspects of the current study were modified, the researchers utilized an identical survey instrument. Fully or partially replicating previous research by using the same survey instrument can allow researchers to verify the results of previous studies and have more confidence that the findings are indeed "true" or valid, and not some aberration due to problems in sampling or otherwise.

This study is also important from a policy standpoint. Public opinion often finds its way into policy discussions regarding the will of the public toward any number of pressing criminal justice issues, such as the juvenile death penalty, life without parole for juveniles, and in the current research, whether the public is willing to pay more in taxes for rehabilitation versus incarceration. The current research has the potential to inform the public policy process regarding the desired treatment of serious juvenile offenders and whether or not the public supports funding such treatment with additional taxes.

From a methodological point of view, random digit dialing is an interesting sampling variation as used in conjunction with survey research. Random digit dialing has

the potential to reach individuals that may be unknown in more traditional population lists or sampling frames, such as phone books, voter registration records, and others. Inasmuch as a phone number selected via random digit dialing serves as a proxy for a person, random digit dialing remedies the problem of unlisted phone numbers and has the ability to capture those individuals who do not have "land" lines but only cell phones, and therefore are not listed in a phone book. As a result, random digit dialing is a viable sampling variation to identify the largest possible number of individuals in the population to be sampled when telephone surveys are utilized. ●

IN THIS CHAPTER YOU WILL LEARN

About the process of sampling and why it is important to the research process

The difference between a sample and a population

That there are two general types of samples—probability and non-probability samples

About the difference between probability and non-probability samples

About important concepts related to sampling, such as representativeness and generalizability

About basic procedures in drawing a sample

That random selection is a key component in probability samples

That the type of sampling required in a research study is highly related to the research question of interest

INTRODUCTION

The case study highlighted above provides one example of how **sampling** can be utilized in a research study. While not all studies require sampling, in those that do, sampling is a critical consideration in evaluating the results of the study. And when the sampling process breaks down in some way, it can seriously impact the results. It is therefore critical that research consumers have specific knowledge about sampling, including but not limited to the different types of sampling and problems that may directly or indirectly be associated with sampling. The goal of this chapter is to provide that critical insight.

Chapter 3 begins by examining several areas relevant to sampling. This section includes a focus on what sampling is and why researchers typically utilize a sample instead of an entire population. It then discusses the importance of randomness to the sampling process. Although random sampling is not always desired or needed in every research study that must utilize a form of sampling, it is a critical part of many research studies. This section then examines two additional areas relevant to sampling. These areas include the key concepts of **representativeness** and **generalizability,** and a brief discussion about sample size and sampling error.

The second section of this chapter examines different types of sampling methods known as **probability sampling methods.** Although probability sampling methods each have their own distinct features, the consistent link between all of them is that each member of a particular **population** has an equal chance at being selected for the **sample.** When researchers are interested in generalizing or applying the research results obtained from the sample to the larger population from which it was drawn (such as in the highlighted study beginning this chapter), probability samples are superior.

Chapter 3 then explores **non-probability sampling methods.** As opposed to probability sampling methods, non-probability sampling methods do not ensure that every member of a particular population has an equal chance at being selected for the sample. There are various situations in which a non-probability sample may be utilized and be appropriate for a particular research study. Although the various non-probability samples are unique and useful in their own way, the consistent theme among non-probability samples is that the results produced from studies utilizing this form of sampling do not generalize to a larger population. This is because not everyone in the larger population had an equal chance at being selected for the research study.

CLASSICS IN CJ RESEARCH
A Snowball's Chance in Hell: Doing Fieldwork with Active Residential Burglars[3]

RESEARCH STUDY

METHODOLOGY

The general methodology for this study was to interview active residential burglars about their criminal careers (e.g., number of burglaries, age at first burglary). A main goal of this study was also to shed light on the process of researching active criminals—locating active offenders, obtaining their cooperation, and maintaining an ongoing relationship throughout the study period.

Perhaps the most interesting part of the study was the process of locating active offenders to interview. Unlike prison inmates or police officers or other known populations, there is no list of active offenders, replete with phone numbers and addresses. For this study, the researchers located their sample members by utilizing a form of non-probability sampling normally employed to contact research participants who are not readily known or otherwise absent from a convenient sampling frame. This type of non-probability sampling is called snowball sampling. Procedurally, to facilitate the sample of active residential burglars, the researchers first hired an ex-offender with ties to the criminal world. The ex-offender first approached known criminal associates. The ex-offender then contacted several law-abiding but street-smart friends, explaining that the research was confidential and no police involvement would occur. The ex-offender also explained to the contacts that individuals who took part in the study would be paid a small sum of money.

Over time, the criminal (e.g., low level fence; small time criminal, crack addict) and noncriminal contacts (e.g., youth worker) recruited by the ex-offender were able to identify and make contact with several active residential burglars. Upon their participation, these burglars also referred other residential burglars. In essence, the sample of active residential burglars snowballed through this sort of referral process that started with one ex-offender. All in all, 105 active residential burglars participated in the study.

RESULTS

One goal of the research was to shed light on the offending careers of the residential burglars. Based on their interview questions, the researchers found that the active residential burglars averaged 10 or fewer burglaries a year over the course of their offending careers. They also found extremes among this average. For example, the researchers uncovered a group of extreme offenders, roughly 7% of the sample, who committed in excess of 50 burglaries per year.

Another key finding from this study linked to the arrest patterns of the active burglars. Although most members of the burglar sample had previously been arrested, the researchers did uncover a subgroup of burglars who had not been previously arrested but who had committed a large amount of residential burglaries. Among other things, the results revealed a number of criminals who were not only quite successful in their residential burglary careers, but also successful at avoiding official detection.

Beyond the specific findings relative to the offending patterns of active residential burglars, it is important to note that the qualitative nature of this study also produced important insight. For example, through the process of snowball sampling, the researchers explored ways in which to successfully locate,

WHAT IS SAMPLING?

Generally, sampling refers to a process of selecting a smaller group from a larger group "in the hope that studying this smaller group (the sample) will reveal important things about the larger group (the population)."[4] In some forms of sampling, such as probability sampling, the goal is that the smaller sample is representative of the larger population. For example, officials at your university might select a random sample of criminal justice students and ask their opinion on whether students should have the right to carry weapons on campus. In selecting a sample randomly, university officials' goal is that the results obtained from the sample of students would be similar to the results obtained if all criminal justice students (the population) were asked their opinion on this topic. If the **randomly drawn sample** is representative of the population, the opinion results

obtained from the sample of criminal justice students can then inform about the opinions of the entire population.

It is noteworthy to consider that sampling is certainly not limited to the social sciences. Indeed, smaller subsets of larger populations are taken in any number of scientific contexts so that researchers might learn things about some larger population. Consider environmental researchers who take core samples from glaciers in Antarctica. Environmental researchers drill deep into the glaciers with hollowed tubes to take core samples of snow and ice that have been compressed over many years. The resulting core samples are then analyzed to gather data in such areas as temperature change and atmospheric conditions over the age of the frozen core samples. Or consider beer brew masters. Brew masters also engage in a process where once a beer batch has fermented and is processed, they take a sample from the massive swirling vats of beer to determine whether the contact, and recruit hard-to-access active criminal populations. The researchers also explored the difficulty of working with active criminals, developing trusting relationships, and in general, gathering data in ways that are relatively "extreme" compared to other approaches.

LIMITATIONS WITH THE STUDY PROCEDURE

Because this was a qualitative research study, an argument could be made that the results may not generalize to all active residential burglars. Indeed, because the sample of burglars was obtained via snowball sampling, a non-probability technique, there is no way to guarantee that the 105 burglars were "representative" of all residential burglars. This is because the sample was not randomly drawn from a larger population. As mentioned, however, it must be considered that no easy or complete list or sampling frame of active residential burglars is in existence. The very nature of this hard-to-access population virtually excludes all other sampling methods in efforts to understand the offending careers of active residential burglars.

The researchers also note some potential limitations. One limitation centered on defining eligible members for the sample. The researchers limited their sample to individuals who were residential burglars and who were currently active, meaning they had committed a residential burglary in the past two weeks. While these sample inclusion criteria appear simple, the researchers note that "in the field" sometimes the burglars were evasive about their activities. To verify their eligibility for the study, the researchers had to rely on confirmation by other burglars. On a broad level then, the limitation associated with this study is one that can be levied at any study where questions are asked of individuals—the ability to trust the responses of others.

IMPACT ON CRIMINAL JUSTICE

This study impacted criminal justice in that it represented one of very few qualitative research studies in criminal justice. As noted by the authors, many criminologists at the time shied away (and perhaps still do) from this type of research based on the belief that it was impractical. Importantly, the authors showed through a unique sampling scheme that this research can be conducted on a practical basis. This research may have also spurred others to conduct qualitative research in criminal justice settings and with other less-researched criminal justice populations.

This research was also only one of a handful of studies that contacted, recruited, and fostered the cooperation of active criminals, as opposed to known criminals such as confined prisoners. Gaining the trust of active criminal populations is extremely difficult because these groups are often highly suspicious of outsiders. The researchers in this case were able to garner the trust of 105 active offenders and interview them about the frequency of their criminality. Their research uncovered a number of important insights about the active criminal. For example, the researchers uncovered a subset of extremely active and successful burglars adept at avoiding apprehension by criminal justice authorities. In other words, there are some criminals for which that old credence "crime pays" rings true. The finding also sheds some light on the notion that official estimates of crime, for example, may significantly underestimate the true level of crime.

Researchers taking ice samples at the South Pole. Ice core samples can be utilized to study changes in the atmosphere. Researchers do not need to gather the entire "population" of ice to determine this, but only need to sample.

smaller sample (small glass of beer) passes muster. In essence, the small glass of beer serves as a sample of knowledge about how the larger vat of beer (or the population) might taste. The examples above also demonstrate that samples and populations need not be animate objects—samples can be produced from any number of different populations.

In both instances above, researchers as drillers or brew masters are interested in getting a smaller but representative sample of a larger population. Because these researchers are concerned with representativeness, their techniques are in ways variants of probability sampling. For example, the brew master wants to be able to generalize or apply the results of the sample beer to the larger vat of beer. Provided the sample was drawn in a way that makes it representative of the larger vat of beer, such a process negates the need for the brew master to drink hundreds and hundreds of gallons of beer to determine the quality of the batch! In many forms of sampling, especially forms of probability sampling, the nature of the sampling process allows the researcher to take a smaller but representative sample of a larger population of individuals and retrieve results that would be similar as if he or she had utilized the larger population.

Uses of Sampling

Sampling methods can be used in any number of the different research designs that are discussed in Chapters 4–6 of this text. For example, sampling can first be used to retrieve a small representative subset of individuals from a larger population. These individuals might then be randomly assigned to experimental and control groups in an experimental design as discussed in Chapter 5. Sampling can also be used as a tool to select a smaller but representative portion of individuals from a larger population for the administration of surveys, whether they are telephone, Internet, face-to-face, or mail surveys. Sampling can also be used in qualitative research as covered in Chapter 6. However, the nature of qualitative research lends itself best to non-probability sampling methods.

The bottom line is that sampling is utilized in a number of different research designs. Although the type of sampling used will vary depending on the goal of the study, sampling does have a place in many research studies in and beyond the social sciences. It is also important to understand that the nature of the research will determine whether the type of sampling required is probability- or non-probability–based sampling. This should become clearer in the sections that examine different types of probability and non-probability samples later in this chapter.

Why Sample?

We've hinted at the fact that utilizing a sample can lead to research results that would be similar to results if researchers instead examined the entire population. This is certainly a justification for sampling since it is generally easier and less tedious than utilizing an entire population. For example, consider the study highlighted at the beginning of the chapter where researchers were interested in citizen preferences for rehabilitation versus incarceration for serious juvenile offenders in four different states (Pennsylvania, Washington, Illinois, and Louisiana). The combined population of these four states is just over 35 million individuals. Instead of drawing a sample, suppose the researchers wished to conduct telephone interviews with the entire population of eligible phone numbers in each of these four states. The number of telephone surveys to be conducted among the eligible and participating

population would be prohibitive in a number of areas—time, expense, staff needs, and length of time required to complete, analyze, and report results. In short, it would simply not be feasible for a small research team to conduct such a study with an entire population.

The good news is that sampling, under certain conditions, allows researchers to retrieve results from a sample that are similar to the results that would have been obtained by utilizing the entire population. Although there will be some degree of difference between the results produced from a sample compared to an entire population (called sampling error), this error can be estimated and considered. In short, taking a smaller representative sample of a larger population is often as sufficient as surveying or otherwise utilizing the entire population in a research study.

Representativeness and Generalizability

Two foundations of sampling are representativeness and generalizability. This is particularly true when researchers utilize probability sampling methods, because a major goal of probability sampling is that the sample is representative of the larger population. Representativeness is achieved when the sample provides an accurate picture of the larger population. And if the sample represents the larger population, the results from the sample can then be used to make generalizations about the larger population.

Consider a hypothetical population of criminal justice students at a large university. Let's say the criminal justice student population comprises 2,500 students, half males and half females. Suppose researchers randomly sampled approximately 500 criminal justice students, and 85% of the sample turned out to be males and only 15% females. Based only on gender, it is clear that this sample does not accurately represent the larger population of criminal justice students. Therefore, any results produced from the 500-person criminal justice sample cannot accurately be generalized back to the larger population. In fact, the results produced were almost entirely responses from males. The results may well represent the population of male criminal justice students at the university, but the results would not generalize to all criminal justice students in the population. In sum, samples can only be generalized back to what they represent—in this case, male criminal justice students and not all criminal justice students at the university.

The previous discussion brings up the issue of generalizing to a specific population and that of generalizing results beyond a particular population. If a sample is representative of a specific population, researchers can be

Each year, dozens of national, state, and local agencies enter into agreements with various contractors to conduct telephone surveys that address a number of issues. Apparently, however, the method employed by the calling contractors of being "polite but persistent" is enough to make some respondents boil over with anger. Recently, the Centers for Disease Control (CDC), and their contractor, the National Opinion Research Center (NORC), have drawn the ire of several citizens. According to one news article, those contacted by NORC on behalf of CDC via random digit dialing have slammed down phones, blown boat horns into the receiver, and cursed profusely in response to what they feel are aggressive, untimely, and repeated calls to participate in surveys.

The CDC says that citizen complaints are rare among the 1 million or more telephone calls and 100,000 interviews that NORC conducts each year on their behalf. There is even a website that tracks complaints about NORC, www.800notes.com, complaints that clearly show the annoyance of many citizens. Some respondents have gone to great lengths to show their displeasure with the continued calls. One respondent, for example, explained in a post that she was going to provide false information and tie up employees by talking about her day.

Although respondents may register their number with DO NOT CALL registries, government researchers and surveyors are exempt from having to acknowledge the list. And despite the fact that individuals do not have to answer survey questions, it appears that such a denial is not enough to stop some surveyors.

1. Visit the website www.800notes.com and view some of the comments posted. What are your feelings toward repeated calls from a research or survey organization that identified your phone number via random digit dialing?

2. Based on what you know about human subjects' consent and research participant rights, what are your feelings on repeated "cold calls" based on random digit dialing?

Adapted from JoNel Aleccia, Dial it down: Pesky CDC callers incite fury. Retrieved on May 12, 2011, at http://www.msnbc.com.

---

confident that the results of a study generalize or apply back to the specific population from which they selected their sample. For example, if the sample of 500 criminal justice students above accurately represented the criminal justice student population by gender, we might say that any results produced from surveying the 500 criminal justice students reflects the results that would have been found by gender if the whole population of 2,500 criminal justice students was surveyed.

Generalizing results from a representative sample to a specific population does not mean that the results automatically generalize to all similar populations. For example, the opinions on carrying personal weapons on campus from a representative sample of criminal justice students at one Texas university may represent well the opinions of all criminal justice students on that campus. But their opinions may be much different from those of students at a university in Iowa, or criminal justice students in Norway. Perhaps the bottom line is that consumers must be attuned to notions of representativeness and generalizability and must be very cautious of research findings that purport to generalize well beyond the specific population and sample utilized in a research study. Only through replication with different samples from varying populations can more confidence be attached to such broad claims of generalizability between different populations.

Sampling Error and Sample Size

Inasmuch as the results from a probability sample are meant to be a close approximation of what would actually be found if an entire population were utilized, there is certain to be some degree of difference in the results produced from a sample compared to a population. For example, survey results from a sample of citizens on attitudes toward rehabilitation versus incarceration will not likely be exactly identical to the overall survey results if an entire state population of citizens was surveyed.

The difference in results or outcomes between a sample and a population is called **sampling error.** Researchers expect there to be a difference between the sample results and the results from an entire population, even when the sample is representative of the population. The good news is that this margin of error can be estimated and considered in research. For an example, go watch any major news program and be attuned to survey results from national surveys. During election time, for example, major news networks broadcast any number of survey or poll results from random samples of U.S. citizens, often called scientific surveys to denote the samples were randomly chosen, and hence, probability samples of some sort. Results from such polls are usually graphically displayed with bar or pie charts and show the percent of Americans in favor or opposed to a particular candidate or issue. Results are usually accompanied by an indicator, such as "margin of error $+/- 3\%$" or some other variation. Such an indicator means that results can vary up or down three percentage points. For example, suppose a survey of randomly selected citizens revealed a presidential approval rating of 47% with a margin of error $+/- 3\%$. Considering the error or difference produced by utilizing a sample instead of an entire population ($+/- 3\%$), the approval could be as high as 50% or as low as 44%. These statistics noted above are an indicator of sampling error, or the expected difference in results produced by sampling versus surveying the entire U.S. population. In short, we know that there will be some degree of error by using a sample; the major question is how much error. Sampling error gives us that indication.

One of the most important factors related to the degree of sampling error is sample size. A general rule is the larger the sample, the lower the sampling error. This is because as the sample gets larger, it more closely approximates the population, and therefore error or difference between the sample and population decreases. When the sample is equal to the population, the error is zero, because the sample is the population! Conversely, very small samples are less representative of the population, results are less generalizable to the population as a whole, and sampling error is greater. Of course, one must consider that even if an entire population was selected to participate in a survey, some eligible participants would not respond, other persons in the population would be unable to be reached or would be unknown (e.g., homeless individuals), and these issues are relevant to consider in discussions of sample versus population, and sampling error. But as a very general rule, the larger the sample, the less sampling error.

Students often wonder about the appropriate sample size for a particular research study. Based on the previous discussion, it would seem that the larger the sample, the better. This is generally true when considering the notion of sampling error. However, constraints of the research process—high costs, staffing, tight deadlines—might mean that a larger sample is not feasible. Study constraints notwithstanding, there is no clear-cut rule concerning what constitutes the appropriate sample size. Sample size depends on a number of considerations: size of the population, how much variability exists in the population, and demands of certain statistical techniques, among others.

Consider the issue of population variability. Instead of a social science survey, consider how large a sample of the world population we might need to take to determine what a human heart looks like. There are variations in human hearts to be sure based on age and lifestyle and many other considerations, but there is no need to cut into hundreds of people to come to a conclusion of what a human heart looks like. This is because when it comes to human hearts, there is not a lot of variability in the population. Very small samples in this example would suffice and would be representative of the population and therefore generalizable to the population as a whole. The sample size situation is different when we want to ask people their opinions on any number of issues—people who are spread across different cultures and geographies and who each have unique influences and life experiences. As opposed to a human heart, a larger sample is needed because there is much more diversity in the population.

The bottom line is that sample size is less important than obtaining a representative sample. An extremely large unrepresentative sample is much less useful than a more modest sample size that is representative of a particular population. In this way, samples are akin to gifts—bigger is not always better!

PROBABILITY SAMPLING METHODS

The key feature that makes probability sampling methods different from non-probability sampling methods lies in how the sample is selected. In probability sampling methods, selection of the sample is accomplished through a random process such that every member of the population has an equal chance at selection for the sample. To ensure that every member of the population has an equal chance at selection, probability sampling techniques require a random and unbiased process for selection. Researchers must have access to a complete listing of the population, also called a sampling frame. In many cases, researchers might not have access to a list of the population. Researchers might also not have the resources, need, or motivation to utilize a complete list of the population, even if it were available. In these cases, non-probability samples are utilized. Such samples are not comprised of individuals with an equal chance at being selected for the sample.

Before delving into the various probability and non-probability sampling techniques, it is important to briefly revisit the notion of representativeness and generalizability. Researchers who are interested in generalizing sample results to a larger population must ensure that the sample is not biased and is an adequate representation of the population. Accomplishing representativeness, and hence generalizability, is the province of probability sampling techniques. The four probability sampling techniques are examined below.

Simple Random Sampling

Simple random samples are simply samples drawn randomly from a larger population. The key to selecting a simple random sample is that every member of the population has an equal chance at being selected for the sample—no one individual or group of individuals has a greater or lesser chance of getting selected than another individual or group of individuals.

The procedure for drawing a simple random sample is relatively straightforward, as with other forms of probability sampling (see Figure 3.1). First, the researcher must identify the target population from where the sample will be drawn. Selecting a **target population** is obviously driven by the aim of a particular research study. For example, if a researcher wishes to elicit the opinions of undergraduate criminal justice students at a large southern university, the population would be all undergraduate criminal justice students enrolled at the university. In another example, if the goal is to elicit the opinions of residents in Dade County, Florida, the population would be residents of Dade County, Florida.

Once the target population is identified, the researcher must obtain a listing of the population. Obtaining a listing of the population is one of the more difficult, yet crucial, parts of probability sampling. This list of the population is often called a **sampling frame.** Because a sampling frame is a list of the population, sampling frames come in many

James Brown, the host of "The NFL Today" and "Inside the NFL," promotes the importance of the 2010 Census. Instead of sampling members of the U.S. Population, the U.S. Census is one effort to reach the entire population.

forms. For example, general sampling frames might include phone books, voter registration records, census contacts, or records from the department of motor vehicles. Each of these sampling frames includes members of a certain population, for example, residents of a city or county or other regional indicator. If a researcher wished to survey undergraduate criminal justice students for their opinions on carrying weapons on campus, the sampling frame would be a listing of all criminal justice students—by name or student number or some other indicator.

One crucial consideration involved in the use of a sampling frame is that it be a complete listing of the population. Sampling frames that do not include all members of a target population are problematic. In cases where the sampling frame is incomplete in some way, any samples drawn from the sampling frame may not be truly representative of the population. For example, if a researcher used a phone book as a sampling frame of county residents, there is likely to be a substantial number of members from the population missing because not all residents have phones. In these cases, the true representativeness of the sample could be called into question, and hence, the generalizability of results produced from the sample. Conversely, a target population and sampling frame of all enrolled undergraduate criminal justice students at a particular university is likely to be complete. Nonetheless, an important step in selecting a simple random sample, and all probability samples, is the presence of a complete sampling frame.

FIGURE 3.1 | Simple Random Sampling

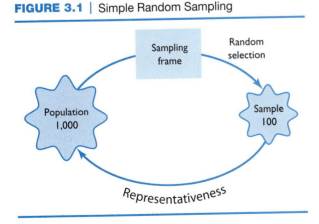

Once a sampling frame is identified, the process of selecting a simple random sample requires that members of the population be selected in a way that each member has an equal chance of selection. In essence, members of the population must be selected randomly. There are a number of different ways to draw a random sample—flipping a coin, rolling a die, or using a lottery type machine. Perhaps the most common way of randomly selecting a sample from a population is through the use of a computer program. A variety of statistical software packages exist (e.g., Statistical Package for the Social Sciences [SPSS]) that will randomly draw a sample from an identified list of the population. Note, for example, that the case study that began this chapter was a form of random selection via computer—**random digit dialing.** As opposed to using a phone book, however, the researchers utilized a computer program that randomly dialed the last four digits of phone numbers in the area codes among the specified states. Such a process means that every member of the population had an equal chance of having their phone number dialed. Unfortunately, those without a phone number could not be considered for the sample.

Whether members of a sample are selected by computer or some other random selection procedure, what can be ensured is that each member of the sample had an equal chance at selection. One problem with simple random samples, however, is that despite being randomly drawn, it cannot be ensured that the sample is representative of the population. In short, just because everyone in the population had an equal chance at being selected does not mean the sample automatically will represent the population. It is possible, for example, that by a chance occurrence the sample could be highly unrepresentative of the population. Consider, for example, the flipping of a coin. It is possible that flipping a regular coin over 100 times could result in the coin landing on heads 100 times, or 85 times, or 75 times— well beyond the 50 times we would expect by probability. Such an imbalance could occur simply by chance. The same problem could occur with simple random sampling. A population of 500 that included 50% males and 50% females could, by chance, result in a simple random sample with highly imbalanced proportions of one gender or the other. For example, a 200-person sample from this population that included 75% males would not be representative of the population—but this could occur, by chance.

In sum, simple random samples ensure that each member has an equal chance at being selected, but such samples do not guarantee representativeness of the population on known categories of information among the population (e.g., race, gender, age). Provided researchers have

information on the population, it is possible to examine whether the sample indeed is an accurate reflection of the population. This is only possible on information to which the researchers are privy, however. For example, if researchers did not know the gender breakdown of the entire population, they would not be able to examine whether the sample is truly representative of the population. Because of the potential chance occurrence of nonrepresentativeness posed by simple random samples, researchers might choose to utilize a stratified random sampling technique.

Stratified Random Sampling

Stratified random sampling is quite similar to simple random sampling (see Figure 3.2 below). The major difference in a stratified sample versus a simple random sample is that the sampling frame is divided up into different strata, based on characteristics of the population. From there, smaller random samples are taken from each strata and then combined into a singular sample. This technique ensures that the final sample is representative of the population based on certain characteristics such as age, race, gender, or whatever is of interest in the research study.

Suppose we wished to conduct a survey on the alcohol drinking behaviors of undergraduates at your college. Let's say we are most interested in determining whether alcohol consumption differs based upon credit-hour classification: freshman, sophomore, junior, and senior. The population of the college is 4,000 individuals, and we want to take a sample of 100 persons. Based on our knowledge of the population, we know the proportion breakdowns of each classification: freshman (20%), sophomore (25%), junior (25%), and senior (30%). To ensure

FIGURE 3.2 | Stratified Random Sampling (Proportionate)

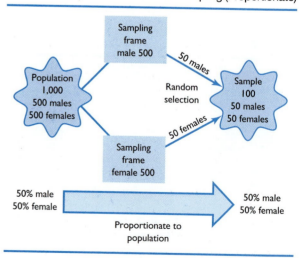

WHAT RESEARCH SHOWS: IMPACTING CRIMINAL JUSTICE OPERATIONS
The Impact of Prison Rape Research

In 2003, the Prison Rape Elimination Act (PREA) was signed into law and became the first federal law dealing with sexual victimization in prisons and other confinement facilities. Spurred by PREA, dozens of research studies have been conducted over the last several years, addressing a variety of topics related to sexual victimization in prisons. For the most part, these studies have employed self-report surveys and examinations of official data collected by correctional agencies. Among other goals, the intent of such research is to understand the nature and extent of sexual victimization in prison with the goal of decreasing this form of violence behind bars. And because of the insight provided by these research studies, correctional agencies have developed or are developing a number of methods to help decrease the sexual victimization of prisoners and are having a substantial impact on correctional system operation.

One of the best sources of information on the strategies used by correctional agencies to address prison sexual victimization following PREA comes from the Urban Institute. The study was meant to provide a national-level picture of what is being done to address prison sexual victimization following PREA, and also to identify specific practices that appear promising in addressing this problem. To assess what correctional agencies are doing in the aftermath of PREA, Urban Institute researchers surveyed state correctional administrators, conducted phone interviews with 58 department of corrections representatives, and conducted case studies in 11 different states.

Overall, results from the Urban Institute study revealed that correctional agencies are responding to PREA's call to identify and help reduce sexual victimization in prisons. Their study identified several new or developing policies, including enhanced data collection efforts to understand the extent of sexual victimization in prison, prevention efforts that include the hiring of special staff to deal with inmate reports of sexual victimization, and educational efforts for inmates on how to prevent sexual victimization, among others.

One example highlighted was the Texas prison system's "Safe Prisons Program." Developed following PREA, the Safe Prisons Program was created to address sexual victimization and other forms of violence and disorder in Texas prisons and includes components of data analysis, incident monitoring, staff training, and policy development. The program also includes a database to track perpetrators and victims of violence. Moreover, a special prosecution unit was developed to ease the burden on the local district attorney from prosecuting crimes that occurred in prison.

The research by the Urban Institute, and others, has not only shed light on a significant problem in correctional environments but has also spurred the development of significant correctional policy to help tackle this problem.

Zweig, J., Naser, R., Blackmore, J., & Schaffer, M. (2006). Addressing sexual violence in prisons: A national snapshot of approaches and highlights of innovative strategies. Washington, D.C.: Urban Institute.

that our sample of 100 is representative of the population, we first must divide the sampling frame (a list of the student population) into four different strata consistent with the classifications for which we are interested. In essence, we are taking a list of the population of students (the sampling frame), and breaking up this larger sampling frame into four different sampling frames (freshman, sophomore, junior, and senior) to represent each classification. Once we have four sampling frames corresponding to all freshman, sophomores, juniors, and seniors, we then take a random sample from each of the four sampling frames. The size of the random sample from each sampling frame is proportionate to each classification's proportion of the population. For example, in our desired sample of 100 students, 20 freshman will be randomly selected from the freshman sampling frame, 25 sophomores will be randomly selected from the sophomore sampling frame,

25 juniors, and 30 seniors. This will result in a sample of 100 students, with each classification represented in the sample exactly to their proportion in the population.

The process above is an example of **proportionate stratified sampling.** In proportionate stratified sampling, each predetermined category of the sample (in this case freshman to senior) is represented in the sample exactly proportionate to their percentage of the population. For example, freshman make up 20% of the population, and likewise make up 20% of the final sample. The example above suggests that samples can be stratified based on any number of factors for which researchers have information about the population. For example, the sample could have been stratified by gender and credit-hour classification. To do this, the sampling frame of the entire population would be broken down into multiple sampling frames consistent with gender and classification:

freshman women, freshman men, sophomore women, sophomore men, and so on. From there, the sample would simply be randomly selected from each strata, and the number of members in the sample from each strata would be proportionate to their existence in the population. For example, if freshman women make up 10% of the population, and we wish to take a final sample of 100 across gender and classification, 10 freshman women, or 10%, would be included in the final sample. At its essence, stratified sampling is a method researchers use to break down the population into particular sampling frames, and then take a random sample from each sampling frame to create a sample that is perfectly representative of the population (at least on the strata).

As a final note, sometimes researchers are interested in taking a sample from a larger population where one group or strata is overrepresented compared to the group's proportion of the population. Of course, this smacks against all that has been learned thus far about representativeness. Indeed, in these situations, researchers are actually taking an unrepresentative sample of the population, and they do so on purpose. In some cases researchers do this when a group or strata of interest is so small that drawing a sample proportionate to the group's membership in the population would result in a sample that is relatively meaningless if comparisons were to be made among other groups. For example, in the hypothetical study on alcohol consumption by credit-hour classification, suppose that freshmen made up only 1% of the population of 4,000 students, sophomores equaled 33%, juniors equaled 33%, and seniors equaled 33%. Among 4,000 students, this would equal only 40 students as the population of freshman. If the population was stratified by classification, and samples proportionate to the population were drawn from those strata, in a 100-person sample, only 1 freshman would be selected. While this 1-person sample would technically represent the proportion of freshmen in the population, this one person would not likely be representative of all 40 freshmen in the population relative to alcohol consumption. What if this one freshman, for example, drank a case of beer a day! This would probably not be an accurate representation of the freshman class. To correct for such extreme imbalances, researchers may oversample the small group, also considered disproportionate stratified sampling. Although it sounds counterintuitive, in some situations researchers must sample in a way that is unrepresentative to ensure adequate representation of a particular group in a sample.

Systematic Random Sampling

Systematic random sampling is another form of probability sampling. Like simple random and stratified random samples, systematic sampling utilizes a random process in the selection of the sample (see Figure 3.3 below). Systematic sampling involves a few basic, but important, steps to ensure that each member of the sample has an equal chance at being selected.

Systematic sampling begins with some sort of list or grouping, and members or items on the list or in the grouping are selected in intervals. The interval is often referred to as taking "every n^{th} individual." This means that one portion of selecting the sample entails taking every 5th, or 6th, or some other "n^{th}".

Consider taking a 50-person sample from a 100-person criminal justice class. In this scenario, the professor likely has a list of student names or student ID numbers. Or, the professor could simply line up all the students in front of the class (we are assuming all, of course, are in attendance for a complete population of the class).

Utilizing the student lineup, the professor has to first calculate the sampling interval, or n^{th} value. To determine this interval, the professor simply divides the population (100) by the number of individuals desired in

FIGURE 3.3 | Systematic Sampling

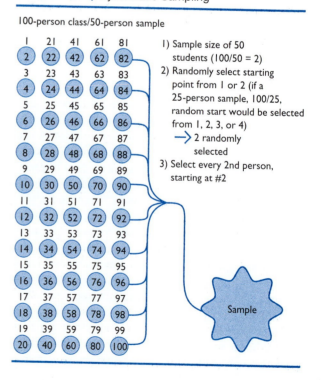

100-person class/50-person sample

1) Sample size of 50 students (100/50 = 2)
2) Randomly select starting point from 1 or 2 (if a 25-person sample, 100/25, random start would be selected from 1, 2, 3, or 4)
   → 2 randomly selected
3) Select every 2nd person, starting at #2

Sample

the sample (50). In this example, the sampling interval is 2 (100/50 = 2). This means every 2nd person will be selected.

The next step to a systematic sample is critical and is what makes it a probability sample. Instead of automatically starting at the top of the list (or front of the lineup), and picking every 2nd person, the professor must begin with a random starting point. A traditional way to pick a random starting point is to take all of the numbers involved in the interval (1 or 2 in this example), and randomly pick one of the numbers. If the professor picks 1, he or she will start at #1 in the lineup and then take every 2nd person—1, 3, 5, 7, 9, and so on. If the professor picks 2, he or she will start at #2 and take every second person in the student lineup—2, 4, 6, 8, 10, and so on. An alternative method would be to take 100 numbers, select a number, and then proceed by taking every second person. For example, if the number 6 were chosen, the sample would consist of 6, 8, 10, 12, and so on. In each example, the outcome is essentially the same. In this latter example, once the professor reaches the end of the student lineup, he or she could simply continue selecting every 2nd person by starting at the beginning of the student lineup until the 50-person sample has been achieved.

By using a random start, the professor ensures that each member of the class population has an equal chance at being selected for the sample. But to further ensure that systematic sampling results in an equal probability of selection, the professor must be sure that the student lineup is not sorted in any particular way that might lead to bias. For example, if the professor sorted the students in such a way that all even-numbered students had the highest class grades and odd-numbered students had the lowest class grades, a resulting sample might be highly biased and not representative of the class as a whole. Such is the case in any form of systematic sampling procedure—it must be ensured that the elements to be sampled are randomly arranged, and do not follow a particular pattern.

Cluster/Multistage Random Sampling

It is sometimes the case that researchers wish to take a sample of individuals dispersed across wide geographical areas. For example, suppose a researcher wanted to conduct a paper-and-pencil survey with a representative sample of 5,000 prison inmates across the sprawling state of Texas. Texas incarcerates more than 150,000 inmates spread across more than 100 incarceration facilities. Because Texas is so large and prison inmates are dispersed all over the state, the thought of drawing a representative sample is a daunting task.

Cluster sampling is a way to narrow down the process of sampling to help ensure that samples are representative of the large population of focus. In this way, cluster sampling first begins by narrowing down large geographic areas—whether they are states, census tracts, or any other large area—into more manageable parts. From there, a series of random samples are drawn of different units, for example, randomly selected prison facilities, randomly selected housing areas within those prison facilities, and finally, randomly selected inmates from the housing areas. The series of random samples implicates the multistage part of cluster/multistage sampling—multiple random samples (see Figure 3.4 below).

Operationally, the first step in the hypothetical prison inmates study would be to narrow down the state of Texas by breaking it down into manageable clusters. Although methods vary, perhaps the state of Texas could be broken down into areas based upon the regions in which prison facilities are located located (**or N, S, E, and W as in Figure 3.4**). For example, the Texas Department of Criminal Justice is divided into six regions. This could be an initial clustering of the state of Texas. Next, the researcher might obtain a listing of all prison facilities located within each of the six regions. This list serves as a sort of sampling frame. From there, the researcher may choose to draw a simple random sample of five prison facilities in each region, for a total of 30 prison facilities across the state. Note that instead of a simple random sample, the researcher could have stratified the list of prison facilities by any number of measures, such as size, type of inmate population, and so on.

Once the 30 prison facilities are randomly selected, the researcher continues to select random samples. For

FIGURE 3.4 | Cluster/Multistage Sampling

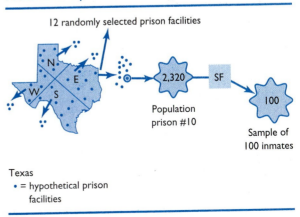

12 randomly selected prison facilities

Population prison #10

Sample of 100 inmates

Texas
• = hypothetical prison facilities

example, the researcher might obtain a list of all inmates at each of the 30 prison facilities. Once the sampling frame of each facility is obtained, the researcher then selects a random sample of inmates from each facility. In this hypothetical study, this would equal approximately 167 inmates sampled from each of the 30 randomly selected prison facilities for a total of approximately 5,000 inmates.

As before, any number of steps could be added to the process above. For example, separate housing areas could be randomly sampled within each of the 30 prison facilities. Then, inmates could be randomly chosen from the sampled housing areas. Still further, in each stage, proportionate or disproportionate stratification could occur to help make the sample as representative of the population as possible. As can be seen, cluster/multistage sampling can become tedious. In reality, however, cluster/multistage sampling can be boiled down to the successive drawing of random samples from populations that are large and widely dispersed.

NON-PROBABILITY SAMPLING METHODS

As opposed to probability sampling techniques, non-probability samples are not drawn through a random and unbiased procedure. There are many potential reasons that might preclude utilizing a random sample. A main reason is that a ready-made list of the population simply may not be available. For example, suppose a researcher was interested in studying the subculture of hoboes. Although the town of Britt, Iowa, holds the National Hobo Convention each year, there is little in the way of a complete list of hoboes. Moreover, even if Britt kept a list of all hoboes who attend the National Convention, this list would certainly not be complete and capture all hoboes in America. In this situation, the researcher may only have access to a defined number of hoboes. As previously mentioned, a research team may not have the resources, need, or motivation to utilize a complete list of the population, even if it was available. In some cases, those who utilize non-probability sampling techniques are actually interested in a sample that does not necessarily represent some larger population. In these cases, non-probability samples are utilized. Such samples are comprised of individuals from known or unknown populations who did not have an equal chance at being selected for the sample.

At this juncture it is important to note the potential issues faced when members of a particular sample are selected through non-probability sampling methods. Regardless of the reasons for selecting a non-probability sample, the important point to consider is that the resulting sample is likely not representative of a larger population. Absent representativeness, the results generated from a non-probability sample cannot be generalized to a larger population. An examination of different non-probability samples may make it clearer why a researcher might want to utilize these sampling techniques, as opposed to a probability sampling technique.

Convenience Sampling

Perhaps the most basic of all sampling techniques is **convenience sampling** (also called accidental or haphazard or person-on-the-street sampling). With convenience sampling, individuals in the sample are chosen based on convenience. In this way, it is a form of first-come, first-serve sampling.

Convenience sampling is perhaps the most common form of sampling consumed by the average citizen. Local news casts, for example, that stop people on the street and ask their opinion on any number of topics are typically convenience samples. The advent of the Internet has made surveys based on convenience sampling ever-present. Go visit any 10 websites from sporting websites to governmental research organizations to magazine websites and you are sure to have abundant opportunities to take a survey on any pressing issue. These surveys may come in the form of more aggressive pop-ups, or more passive enticements to complete a survey. Regardless, all of these forms of gathering data are based on convenience sampling—anyone can respond, and usually, multiple times.

The obvious problem with convenience sampling is that it is likely the sample is not representative of the larger population. This does not mean that convenience sampling is not useful. However, if the sample does not represent the population, the results from the sample cannot be generalized to the larger population. This is the critical piece of knowledge that should be understood by research consumers. In many cases, results generated from convenience samples are portrayed to represent the attitudes, opinions, and perspectives of the larger population. This is erroneous. Survey results from a convenience sample, in reality, only represent and hence are generalizable to the sample. For example, suppose a local news crew was on your campus today and stopped 100 students on their way to class to ask their

In a study of guns and gun threats on college campuses, researchers Miller, Hemenway, and Wechsler surveyed a random sample of more than 10,000 undergraduate students from 119 four-year colleges in the U.S. Utilizing a mailed questionnaire, survey questions specifically asked whether respondents possessed a working firearm at college and also whether they had been threatened with a gun at college. Results of the survey revealed that just over 4% of students had a working firearm at college and just under 2% had been threatened with a gun while at school. Interestingly, the researchers revealed that students most likely to have a gun and/or have been threatened with a gun were male, lived off campus, binge drank, and engaged in risky or aggressive behavior after drinking.

This study is interesting in and of itself, but it seems particularly relevant as state legislatures are increasingly debating the merits of allowing guns on college campuses. In Texas, for example, the state senate voted in May 2011 to allow guns on campus for individuals who have completed a state-mandated concealed handgun course. Because the bill allowing guns on college campuses is heavily favored in the Texas House, and by Governor Rick Perry, it appears that Texas college students may have the opportunity to come to class strapped, locked and loaded.

1. Based on the research findings by Miller and colleagues, do you feel comfortable with a law allowing college students to carry concealed guns on campus?

2. Take time to look up research and commentary concerning guns on college campuses. Based on your research, has this changed your opinion on allowing college students to carry concealed guns on campus?

Miller, M., Hemenway, D., & Wechsler, H. (2002). Guns and gun threats at college. *Journal of American College Health, 51*, 57–65

opinions regarding whether students should be able to carry concealed handguns on campus. Suppose the local news crew revealed that 90% of students they surveyed believed that concealed handguns should be allowed on campus. What if 90 out of 100 students who believed guns should be allowed on campus just exited an organizational meeting of a group whose members' sole purpose is to promote the carrying of weapons on campus. The result from this survey would surely represent the feelings of the convenience sample, but the results might be completely different from students on the campus as a whole if they were instead selected randomly.

Convenience sampling has its uses in the research process. However, results generated from a convenience sample are not likely generalizable to the larger population from which the sample was obtained. As a result, data produced from a convenience sample is quite limited to the specific attributes of the sample and often must be interpreted with some caution.

Purposive Sampling

Purposive sampling (also called judgmental sampling) is aptly named because the researcher is specifically interested in the attributes of the particular sample that was purposely chosen for its characteristics. It is also called judgmental sampling because the researcher is using his or her judgment in selecting a sample that is specific to the goal of the research. A case in point might be the selection of mock jury samples by individuals who work as jury consultants. Jury consultants may, for example, choose members of a sample based on factors such as age, income, education, or anything else that might be useful. Once a particular sample of mock jury members is chosen on these criteria, the jury consultant may present particular pieces of evidence and survey sample members on their feelings toward guilt or innocence at particular phases of evidence presentation. Such consultants might further modify certain variables, such as the method of presentation, the type of presentation, who presents the material, and any other factor so that the jury consultant can examine the impact of these changes on mock juror opinions of guilt and innocence.

In this example, the jury consultant is specifically interested in selecting mock jury members who have particular attributes. Information obtained from a mock jury sample can be used in any number of ways, particularly in voir dire proceedings in which the defense, for example, may attempt to select or strike jurors based on certain characteristics that have been found to influence juror opinions. For example, if through the mock jury trials, high-income individuals were more likely to vote for conviction of a residential burglar than individuals of low income, the jury consultant may recommend to defense lawyers to avoid selecting jurors of a high-income bracket.

No matter how purposive sampling is utilized, the goal of the individual selecting the sample is to be very purposive in selecting the particular sample needed. There is little interest in selecting a representative sample from a larger population; rather, the interest lies in selecting a specific sample that fulfills the goal of the research.

Quota Sampling

Quota sampling is quite similar to convenience sampling. The one major difference is that quota samples are based on some known characteristic of the population. For example, suppose researchers were interested in the opinions of students at a mid-size college on whether students should be allowed to conceal and carry guns on campus. Instead of simply surveying students on a first-come, first-serve basis as in convenience sampling, suppose the researchers were interested in making sure the sample at least reflected the gender composition of the population on campus. For example, at the campus of interest, the student population of 5,000 is evenly split, 50% female and 50% male. The researchers want to take a sample of 100 students. In a quota sample, the researchers will simply ensure that 50 opinion surveys are given to women, and 50 surveys are given to males—largely on a convenience basis. In short, the researchers are interested in obtaining a quota based on the gender composition of the college population.

Although quota sampling is slightly more rigorous than convenience sampling, it is not by much. Despite the fact that researchers are ensuring that the sample is reflective of the proportion of students in the population by gender or some other known characteristic, the sample is still essentially convenience based. As a result, every member of the campus population does not have an equal chance at being selected, and thus, is not representative of the larger college population. Because it is not representative, the results generated from the quota sample do not represent the college population.

Snowball Sampling

Snowball sampling is a non-probability sampling technique utilized when one is attempting to study hard-to-access populations, or more typically, populations whose members are not easily identifiable. For example, there is likely no sampling frame or list (at least not a public one) that contains members of a particular subculture from which to draw a sample. Such groups could range from gang members to those involved in an underground fight club. In a general way, snowball sampling might be considered referral sampling. Because members of a particular population may not be easily identifiable, the researcher attempts to initiate contact with one known

Snowball sampling is often utilized to make contact with hard-to-access populations, such as gang members.

member, and through referral, is introduced to subsequent members of the group. Through this referral process, the sample begins to snowball, or grow.

As with all non-probability samples, something to consider with snowball samples is that the end sample may not be representative of the entire population. This is because each member of the population did not have an equal chance at being selected for the sample. In many cases of snowball sampling, the researcher may ultimately only be privy to a small number of members from a larger population. Because representativeness cannot be ensured, neither can generalizability.

Noting the above, recall the many purposes of research: describe, explore, explain, apply, and evaluate. In many cases of non-probability sampling, and specifically with snowball sampling, researchers are interested in exploring a lesser known topic in hopes that future research can delve further. In this way, sometimes non-probability sampling is utilized to provide an overall explanation of a particular area—a sort of starting point on which to build future research efforts.

CHAPTER SUMMARY

This chapter covered forms of probability and non-probability sampling. Probability sampling is used when the goal of a research study is to obtain an accurate representation of the population for the purposes of generalizability. Whether the population consists of students, city residents, or others, probability sampling techniques ensure that each member of the known population has an equal chance at selection. Simply ensuring that each member of a particular population has an equal chance at selection does not ensure representativeness. And, a representative sample does not ensure results from the sample will generalize to different places and times. However, probability sampling makes achieving the goals of representativeness and generalizability more likely than non-probability samples. Although probability samples are superior to

non-probability samples when the goal is representativeness and generalizability, this should not be taken to mean that non-probability samples are not useful in research methods. Non-probability samples—samples in which each member of a particular population does not have an equal chance of selection—are often very useful in particular research studies.

In an overall view, both probability and non-probability sampling techniques should be viewed as a set of tools. Sometimes the right tool is a probability sampling technique, and sometimes the right tool is a non-probability sampling technique. In many cases, the tool used is highly dependent upon the research question that is being asked. Knowing which tool is appropriate to a particular research question is a good step on the path to becoming an informed consumer of research.

CRITICAL THINKING QUESTIONS

1. What is the difference between probability and non-probability samples?

2. What are some reasons a researcher would utilize a sample instead of a population?

3. What is sampling error?

4. What is the difference between representativeness and generalizability?

5. What is more important: sample size or representativeness? Explain your thoughts.

KEY TERMS

cluster/multistage sampling: A type of probability sampling in which large geographical areas are clustered, or divided, into smaller parts. From there, random samples of individuals or groups or locations are taken in successive or multiple steps. For example, breaking a state down into regions would be a form of clustering. From there, taking a simple or stratified or systematic random sample of schools from each cluster would be one stage of sampling. A next stage of sampling might be randomly selecting students from each randomly selected school

convenience sampling: A form of non-probability sampling in which the sample is composed of persons of first contact. Also known as accidental or haphazard sampling, or person-on-the-street sampling

generalizability: In reference to sampling, refers to the ability of the sample findings to generalize or be applied to the larger population. For example, let's say the findings of a sample survey on attitudes toward the death

penalty reveal the majority of the sample is in support of the death penalty. If the sample is a good representation of the population, the results from this survey can be generalized or applied to the population

non-probability sampling methods: As opposed to probability sampling methods, non-probability sampling methods include those sampling techniques in which every member of the population *does not* have an equal chance at being selected for the sample

population: A population is a complete group. A population could be all students at a university, all members of a city, or all members of a church. A defining feature of a population is that it be complete

probability sampling methods: As opposed to non-probability sampling methods, probability sampling methods include those sampling techniques where every member of the population has an equal chance at being selected for the sample. Such procedures increase the probability that the sample is representative of the population, and hence, that the results produced from the sample are generalizable to the population

proportionate stratified sampling: A sampling method in which each predetermined category of the sample is represented in the sample exactly proportionate to their percentage or fraction of the total population

purposive sampling: As a non-probability sample, purposive sampling involves the researcher selecting a specific or purposeful sample based on the needs of the research. If a researcher was interested in the techniques of residential burglars, their sample would be focused only on such burglars

quota sampling: Similar to convenience sampling, quota sampling does involve taking into account a known characteristic of the population. For example, if 50% of the population is female, and the researcher wants a 100-person sample to survey, the researcher must survey exactly 50 females in a quota sample. Once the quota of 50 females is met, no other females will be surveyed

random digit dialing: A sampling process involving phone numbers where a computer randomly dials the last 4 digits of a telephone number in a given area code using a known prefix. Random digit dialing, in this way, can help remedy the problem of unlisted phone numbers or numbers for which there is no so-called phone book (e.g., cell phones)

randomly drawn sample: A sample for which each member of the population has an equal chance at being selected. Samples not drawn through a random process are those in which each member of the population does not have an equal chance at being selected for the sample

representativeness: In probability sampling processes, representativeness occurs when the smaller sample is an accurate representation of the larger population

sample: A sample is a smaller part of a population

sampling: The process of selecting a smaller group from a larger group. In probability sampling, for example, a smaller group or sample of individuals is taken from the larger group or population. The goal is that the smaller

sample accurately represents the population, despite being smaller in number

sampling error: The percentage of error or difference in using a sample instead of an entire population

sampling frame: A complete list of the population that the researcher will use to take a sample. If the sampling frame does not include each member of the population, and hence is not complete, a researcher must question how those who are listed on the sampling frame differ from those who are not accounted for on the sampling frame

simple random samples: As a form of probability sampling, simple random samples are samples randomly drawn from a larger population. Although each member of the population has an equal chance at being selected for the sample, this form of sample cannot guarantee representativeness

snowball sampling: A non-probability sampling technique utilized when a researcher is attempting to study hard to access populations. It is also referred to as referral sampling. In snowball sampling a researcher makes a contact, and that contact refers another, and so on. After time, the sample snowballs or gets larger. Because there is no ready to use sampling frame for some populations (e.g., gang members), researchers must use contacts and referrals to get a sample

stratified random sampling: Stratified sampling is a form of probability sampling where several simple random samples are taken from a population that has been divided up into strata, such as age, race, gender, or any number of strata based on information about the population

systematic random sampling: Systematic random sampling involves selecting every nth person (e.g., 5th, 10th, etc.) from a list. To be considered a probability sample, the starting point on the list must be chosen at random

target population: The population of interest for a particular research study (e.g., all prison inmates, all domestic violence arrestees)

ENDNOTES

1. Piquero, A., and L. Steinberg. (2010). "Public preferences for rehabilitation versus incarceration of juvenile offenders." *Journal of Criminal Justice,* 38, 1–6.
2. Nagin, D., A. S. Piquero, E. S. Scott, and L. Steinburg. (2006). "Public preferences for rehabilitation versus incarceration of juvenile offenders: Evidence from a contingent valuation survey." *Criminology and Public Policy,* 5, 301–326.
3. Wright, R., S. H. Decker, A. K. Redfern, and D. L. Smith. (1992). "A snowball's chance in hell: Doing fieldwork with active residential burglars." *Journal of Research in Crime and Delinquency, 29,* 148–161.
4. Vogt, W.P. (1993). Dictionary of statistics and methodology: A nontechnical guide for the social sciences. Newbury Park, CA: Sage, p. 200.

Chapter 4

Survey Research

CASE STUDY

National Crime Victimization Survey

Research Study

Criminal Victimization in the United States[1]

Research Question

How many violent and property crime victimizations occurred in the United States in 2010?

Methodology

The results of the National Crime Victimization Survey (NCVS) are provided on an annual basis by the U.S. Census Bureau and serve as an alternative to the Uniform Crime Reports. The NCVS collects information on the violent crimes of rape or sexual assault, robbery, aggravated assault, and simple assault, and the property crimes of household burglary, motor vehicle theft, and theft. The results are derived from a nationally representative sample of U.S. households selected through a stratified, multistage cluster sampling process (see Chapter 3). The survey results are based on data gathered from residents living throughout the United States, including persons living in group quarters, such as dormitories, rooming houses, and religious group dwellings. Armed Forces personnel living in military barracks and institutionalized persons, such as prison inmates, are not included in the survey.

Each housing unit selected for the NCVS remains in the sample for 3 years, with each of the seven interviews taking place at 6-month intervals. An NCVS interviewer's first contact with a household selected for the survey is in person and the survey is completed through a face-to-face interview. The interviewer may conduct subsequent interviews by telephone. To elicit more accurate reporting of incidents, the NCVS uses a self-report method that includes a direct interview with each person 12 years or older in the household. In 2010, 40,974 households and 73,283 individuals age 12 and older were interviewed for the NCVS. Each household was interviewed twice during the year. The response rate was 92.3% of households and 87.5% of eligible individuals.

The NCVS has been collecting data on personal and household victimization since 1973. The data include type of crime, month, time and location of the crime, relationship between victim and offender, characteristics of the offender, self-protective actions taken by the victim during the incident and results of those actions, consequences of the victimization, type of property lost, whether the crime was reported to the police and reasons for reporting or not reporting, and offender use of weapons, drugs, and alcohol. Basic demographic information such as age, race, gender, and income is also collected to enable analysis of victimization by various subpopulations.

Results

During 2010, U.S. residents age 12 or older experienced an estimated 18.7 million violent and property crime victimizations, down from 20.1 million in 2009 and 24.2 million in 2001. The criminal victimizations in 2010 included an estimated 3.8 million violent victimizations and 14.8 million property victimizations. Violent and serious violent victimizations (includes rape or sexual assault, robbery, and aggravated assault) declined by nearly 34% between 2001 and 2010.

From 2001 to 2010, weapon violence (26% to 22%) and stranger-perpetrated violence (44% to 39%) declined. Between 2001 and 2010, about 6% to 9% of all violent victimizations were committed with firearms. This percentage has remained stable since 2004. The percentage of victims of violent crimes who suffered an injury during the victimization increased from 24% in 2008 to 29% in 2010. About 50% of all violent victimizations and nearly 40% of property crimes were reported to the police in 2010. These percentages have remained stable over the past 10 years. Males (15.7 per 1,000 population) and females (14.2 per 1,000 population) had similar rates of violent victimization during 2010.

Limitations with the Study Procedure

While rape or sexual assault significantly increased from 2009 to 2010, you should be cautious in interpreting this change because the estimates of rape/sexual assault are based on a small number of cases reported to the interviewers. Small changes in the number of victimizations can result in large year-to-year percentage changes. For instance, the 2010 estimate of rape or sexual assault is based on 57 reported cases compared to 36 reported cases in 2009. This represents an increase of 21 actual cases but also represents a 49.6% increase in the national estimate of rape or sexual assault from 2009 to 2010. The measurement of rape or sexual assault represents one of the most serious challenges in the field of victimization research. Rape and sexual assault remain sensitive subjects that are difficult to ask about in the survey context.

Any time national estimates are derived from a sample rather than the entire population, as is the case with the NCVS, because of sampling error it is important to be cautious when drawing conclusions about the size of one population estimate in comparison to another (e.g., does aggravated assault occur more frequently than robbery?) or about whether population estimates are changing over time (e.g., did robbery increase or decrease in the past year?). Although one figure may be larger than another, the NCVS estimates are based on responses from a sample of the population. Therefore, each estimate has some degree of sampling error. The sampling error of a population estimate depends on several factors, including the amount of variation in the responses, the size and representativeness of the sample, and the size of the subgroup for which the estimate is computed, as illustrated in the rape or sexual assault example previously discussed.

In addition to sampling error, the NCVS results are subject to non-sampling error. While substantial care is taken in the NCVS to reduce the sources of non-sampling error throughout all the survey operations, an unknown amount of non-sampling error still remains. A major source of non-sampling error includes the inability of the respondents to recall in detail the crimes that occurred during the six months prior to the interview. The NCVS uses a 6-month reference period. Respondents are asked to report victimization experiences occurring in the last 6 months. Generally, respondents are able to recall more accurately an event that occurred within 3 months of the interview rather than one that occurred within 6 months. Research indicates that assault is recalled with the least accuracy of any crime measured by the NCVS. This may be related to the tendency of victims to not report crimes committed by offenders who are not strangers, especially if they are relatives. Recall problems may result in an understatement of the actual rate of assault.

However, a shorter reference period would require more field interviews per year, increasing the data collection costs significantly. These increased costs would have to be balanced by cost reductions elsewhere (sample size is often considered). Reducing sample size however, reduces the precision of estimates of relatively rare crimes such as rape or sexual assault. In light of these trade-offs of cost and precision, a reference period of 6 months is used for the NCVS.

Other sources of non-sampling error can result from other types of response mistakes, including errors in reporting incidents as crimes, misclassification of crimes, systematic data errors introduced by the interviewer, and errors made in coding and processing the data.

Impact on Criminal Justice

The NCVS is one of the two national sources of crime data in the United States. The NCVS is generally viewed as a more reliable and valid measure of crime than the Uniform Crime Reports. The data from the NCVS survey are particularly useful for calculating crime rates, both aggregated and disaggregated, and for determining changes in crime rates from year to year. In addition, the NCVS is the primary source of information on the characteristics of criminal victimization and on the number and types of crimes not reported to law enforcement authorities. It provides the largest national forum for victims to describe the impact of crime and the characteristics of violent offenders. ●

IN THIS CHAPTER YOU WILL LEARN

Why nonresponse is a major source of survey error and how nonresponse impacts survey results

The four main mechanisms for assessing validity as well as how to increase the validity of survey questions and responses

How to assess the reliability of survey questions and responses as well as ways to increase reliability

The methods in which surveys are distributed and the strengths and weaknesses of each

INTRODUCTION

Survey research involves the collection of information from individuals through their responses to questions, and represents one of the most widely used research tools in crime and criminal justice studies. Surveys are one of the most common ways to obtain information about attitudes and behaviors and involve collecting information from people via self-administered surveys, telephone interviews, face-to-face interviews, and more recently Internet and e-mail–based surveys.

In survey research, the main way of collecting information is by asking people questions. Their answers constitute the data to be analyzed. For example, the U.S. Census is a self-administered survey where individuals receive surveys in the mail and are asked to fill them out and send them back to the U.S. Census Bureau. In addition to the counting of people, the U.S. Census collects data about the race, age, household composition, education, type of housing, and many other characteristics of the people counted. As presented in the introductory case study, the NCVS is another example of a large-scale survey where data is collected via face-to-face and telephone interviews.

Most people are familiar with surveys, especially those that involve the measurement of public opinion for newspaper and magazine articles, the measurement of political perceptions and opinions involving politicians, and marketing research designed to understand consumer preferences and interests. In fact, we are inundated with surveys in our daily lives. From the restaurant that offers you a free appetizer on a future visit for completing a telephone survey about your experience, to the call center that wants your feedback on the performance of the customer service representative at the conclusion of your phone call, to solicitations to complete online surveys regarding your website experience, to the evaluation of your professor at the end of the semester, we don't have to look far for an example of a survey in our daily lives.

The same is true for research in criminology and criminal justice. Surveys are frequently the data collection method of choice to answer research questions. For example, if we want to know whether the police officers in our local police department prefer to work 8-, 10-, or 12-hour shifts, we can survey them to address this issue. If we want to determine the level of fear of crime on a college campus, we can survey students, faculty, staff, and visitors to gauge their level of fear of crime. If we want to know if the public agrees with recent U.S. Supreme Court decisions, we can survey residents and ask them their opinion. If we want to understand how correctional officers view their roles and interactions with inmates, we can survey the officers regarding the topic. If we want to identify the extent, causes, and consequences of bullying, we can survey students to better understand bullying. Overall, surveys can be used to answer a wide range of research questions involving crime and the operation of the criminal justice system.

Three characteristics of surveys make them a preferable source of data collection in comparison to other sources.[2] First, probability sampling is typically used in surveys, which enables the research consumer to have confidence that the sample is not a biased one and is a reflection of the larger population. Data from research studies using a probability sample are definitely preferred over data from a non-probability sample, such as those who attend a college class or happen to be convenient to survey. Second, standardized measurement (i.e., each respondent is asked the same questions in the same manner) ensures that comparable information is obtained about everyone who responds to the survey. Standardized measurement produces meaningful statistics and comparisons of respondents (e.g., how are juveniles who are chronically truant different from juveniles who are not?). Third, the development of a survey ensures that all the data needed for a given analysis are available. For example, you may find in your literature that parental supervision is an important factor that distinguishes truants from nontruants. Since you are creating the survey, you can be sure to ask questions about the respondent's level of parental supervision so the relationship between truancy and parental supervision can be addressed in your study.

Survey Components

Surveys bring together sampling, question design, and methods of survey distribution. It is important to note that each of these activities has many applications outside of surveys, but their presence is essential to quality surveys. For consumers of research, it is important to understand how the details of each component of a survey can affect its precision, consistency, and accuracy (i.e., its reliability and validity). How the sample is selected, which questions are asked, and the procedures used to collect the answers all impact the quality of the survey and its results.[3]

Sampling   With the U.S. Census as an exception, survey information is typically collected from a sample of the population, rather than from every member of the population. The ability to select a sample that is representative of the whole population was a significant development that made surveys a useful research tool. The keys to good sampling are finding a way to give all (or nearly all) members of the population the same (or a known) chance of being selected and using probability sampling methods for choosing the sample.[4]

Every survey involves a number of decisions that have the potential to enhance or detract from the accuracy of the survey results. With respect to sampling, critical issues include the following: the choice of whether or not to use a probability sample, the size of the sample, the sampling technique utilized, and the rate of response (the percentage of those sampled who respond to the survey). Since sampling was covered in detail in Chapter 3, it will not be revisited in this chapter. At this point, realize that probability sampling techniques are typically used in surveys. Therefore, the material covered in Chapter 3 is applicable to survey development and distribution. This chapter will discuss the response rate for surveys since it directly applies to surveys and was not covered in Chapter 3.

Survey Question Design

In surveys, the questions measure the concepts and variables under study. Survey question design is a critical element of survey research. Sticking with the theme of this book regarding the development of educated consumers of research, the focus on question design in this chapter will not be on how to write survey questions but on strategies for evaluating the quality of the questions. Survey researchers evaluate questions to find out if they are well understood by the respondents and if the answers are meaningful. In other words, the reliability and validity of the survey questions must be assessed in determining the quality of the survey. The researcher must decide the extent to which previous literature regarding the reliability and validity of questions will be drawn upon in the development of the survey as well as the process for question evaluation.

Methods of Survey Distribution

Surveys can be distributed through several means, including face-to-face or telephone interviews or through self-administered means via the mail or Internet. Some surveys have respondents answer self-administered questions while others use an interviewer to ask questions and record answers. When interviewers are used, it is important to avoid having them influence the answers given by the respondents. The decision about which mode of data collection to use has important cost implications and affects the quality of the data that will be collected.[5]

The National Crime Victimization Survey and other surveys are administered through face-to-face interviews.

The three components of survey development (i.e., sampling, question design, and methods of distribution) are interrelated because the quality of the survey data will not be better than the most error-prone feature of the survey design. A large sample size will not make up for a low rate of response. Similarly, a high response rate will not compensate for unreliable and invalid survey questions. Survey researchers must focus on each component of the survey, including sampling, question design, and method of distribution, because weaknesses in one area cannot be rectified by the strengths of another area.

Since sampling has already been covered in Chapter 3, this chapter discusses question design and methods of survey distribution. A concentrated effort is made to discuss the realities and the practical problems with the decisions made by survey researchers. The goal is to provide a comprehensive overview of the sources of error in surveys and the range of methodological issues that arise when using surveys. Although survey research is a common way to solicit information from a wide variety of individuals, it is not without its limitations, which will be discussed throughout this chapter. We begin our discussion with an overview of the sources of error in survey research.

ISSUES IN SURVEY DEVELOPMENT: NONRESPONSE AND SURVEY DESIGN

Sampling error, as discussed in Chapter 3, occurs because the sample drawn from a population will not exactly match the population. For example, survey results from a sample of citizens on attitudes toward the use of the death penalty will not be identical to the overall survey results if an entire state population of citizens was surveyed. As discussed in Chapter 3, the difference in survey results between a sample and a population is called sampling error. Researchers expect there to be a difference between the sample results and the results from an entire population, even when the sample is representative of the population. They just try to minimize the error as much as possible.

When a sample is drawn, it is inevitable that the sample will differ from the population from which it was drawn. The way the sample is drawn (e.g., probability vs. non-probability sampling) can affect how closely the sample is likely to mirror the characteristics of the population. Regardless of the sophistication of the sampling strategy, by chance, the sample will differ slightly from what it would look like if it was an exact mirror image of the population. One of the goals of survey research is to minimize the random, by chance differences between the sample and the population.

Nonresponse

Nonresponse is a major source of survey error. There are three categories of nonrespondents (i.e., those selected to be in a sample who do not actually respond to the survey)[6]:

1. Those who did not receive the survey, thereby not giving them a chance to respond to the survey. For example, this includes mailed surveys that are undeliverable due to bad addresses and telephone surveys that fail to call when the potential respondent is available to answer the phone.

2. Those who receive the survey but refuse to complete it. For example, this includes potential respondents who refuse to participate in the NCVS even though their household has been selected for participation. In 2010, 7.7% of the sampled households refused to participate in the survey.[7]

3. Those asked to participate in the survey but are unable to perform the task required of them. This includes people who are too ill to be interviewed, who have language barriers, or whose reading and writing skills preclude them from completing a self-administered survey.

Failure to collect survey data from a high percentage of those selected to be in a sample is a major source of survey error.[8] When it comes to surveys, the quality of the results not only depends on how well the sample is a close approximation of the population but also how well those who respond to the survey reflect the total population. The method of distribution that a researcher decides to use can have a major influence on the response rate and the extent to which nonrespondents introduce bias into the results. As discussed later in this chapter, some methods of distribution (e.g., face-to-face interviews) have higher response rates than other distribution methods (e.g., mailed surveys). Overall, a low response rate will bias the sample, which means that the nonresponse makes the respondents systematically different from the population from which they were drawn, thereby producing biased results. For example, let's say we surveyed 100 physicians on the effects of energy drinks on general health, and 50 returned the survey, for a response rate of 50%. The question we should consider is, "How do the 50% who did not respond differ from the 50% who did?" In this circumstance, if we had the other 50% of the responses, they might totally change the results of the study.

Calculating Response Rates   In assessing the quality of a research project that used a survey to collect data, the **response rate** is a basic parameter for evaluating a project. Simply, the response rate is the number of people who respond to the survey divided by the number of people sampled. The denominator includes all people in the sample who were selected as a potential survey respondent but did not respond for whatever reason. This includes the three categories of nonrespondents previously listed, including those who do not receive the survey, those who receive the survey but refuse to participate, and those who are asked to participate in the survey but are unable to perform the task required of them.

Since the response rate is a simple way to assess the quality of a study involving a survey, researchers want to demonstrate a high response rate. To this end, some researchers do not include some of the categories of nonrespondents in the calculation of the response rate, which artificially inflates the response rate for the study. Most commonly, the category of nonrespondents that are excluded from the response rate calculation are those who did not receive the survey.

For example, let's say that a sample of 1,000 college students has been selected for a survey, designed to be completed via telephone interviews, on criminal victimization on campus. In this fictitious study, 500 students completed the survey, 100 students refused to complete the survey and hung up on the interviewer, while another 400 never answered their phone despite numerous calls. What is the response rate? Based on the discussion above, the response rate is 50%. The response rate is the number of people who complete the survey (i.e., 500) divided by the number of people sampled (i.e., 1,000). However, some researchers will exclude the 400 potential respondents who were in the sample but never answered their phone despite repeated attempts. With this exclusion, the response rate is now 83.3%, which is much higher, and therefore better, because the researcher has only included those who completed the survey and those who refused to do so in the response rate (i.e., 500/600).

As an educated consumer of research, you need to be cautious when interpreting response rates. It is important to specifically know how the reported response rate was calculated. As illustrated in the example, differences in the way response rates are calculated can make comparisons across studies difficult. Instead of reporting a response rate, some researchers will report a "completion rate," which excludes those who did not receive the survey from the calculation. In our above example, the completion rate is 83.3% because the 400 students who never answered the phone are excluded in the calculation. The completion rate will always be higher than the response rate as outlined above, which includes selected but uncontacted individuals in the denominator. Although a response rate seems simple to calculate, be sure to remember that it is important to understand how the response rate was calculated before you decide if the response rate is high.

The Impact of Nonresponse

You may now be wondering what is an acceptable response rate. Babbie[9] has suggested that a 50% response rate is adequate, 60% is good, and 70% is very good. Besides focusing on the numeric value of the response rate and how it fits with Babbie's categorization, it is more important to determine if those who did respond are a representative cross section of the sampled group than it is to have a high response rate. In other words, it is critical for the survey researcher to assess if there are significant differences between the respondents and the sample.

In addition, ideally, a researcher will have meaningful information on those who did not respond. Demographic variables such as education, race, ethnicity, gender, age, and income may be helpful in assessing differences between respondents and nonrespondents. An assessment could show that those who did respond to the survey were quite similar in terms of education, race, ethnicity, gender, age, and income to those who did not respond. If the respondents and nonrespondents are quite

similar, a researcher could legitimately analyze the results of a survey even if the response rate was extremely low (e.g., 10%). Basically, the effect of nonresponse on survey results depends on the percentage not responding and the extent to which those not responding are biased (i.e., systematically different from the population). Again, the issue isn't specifically about the response rate, but more critically about whether the respondents and nonrespondents are similar or different on key characteristics that are related to the research questions.

Another issue that needs to be considered in determining the adequacy of the response rate is the population studied. You would expect a higher response rate from a survey of students in the Introduction to Criminal Justice course at your university than from a citizen survey in the same community, even though the topic may be the same. The students probably have a preexisting relationship with the researcher, which, coupled with the use of a group-administered survey (discussed later in this chapter), will lead to a higher response rate in comparison to a survey that is mailed to community residents. In addition, individuals that have an interest in the survey topic are more likely to respond to a survey than those who are less interested. Therefore, you can expect a higher response rate from a survey of police chiefs in California regarding the role of municipal police departments in fighting terrorism than from a survey of California residents on the same topic. Therefore, the adequacy of a response rate is more complex than merely looking at the number and determining how it measures up to Babbie's stated standards.

An example of significant bias from low response and poor sampling where the respondents were significantly different from the population is the classic *Literary Digest* presidential poll in 1936. The survey, which was administered via mail, predicted a victory for Alf Landon in an election that Franklin Roosevelt won by a huge margin. The sample of addresses for the mailed survey was selected from telephone books. At the time, not everyone had a telephone so most voters were not listed in the telephone book. In addition, Republicans (those in Landon's party) were much more likely to have telephones in 1936. Furthermore, only a minority of those asked to return questionnaires did so, which also led to the inaccurate survey results.

Overall, nonresponse is a problematic source of survey error. As the response rate decreases, it becomes more likely that the nonrespondents will differ from the survey respondents. When there are significant differences between respondents and nonrespondents, each group represents biased subgroups of the total population.

WHAT RESEARCH SHOWS: IMPACTING CRIMINAL JUSTICE OPERATIONS

What Causes Inmates to Riot?[10]

Early research into the causes of prison riots focused primarily upon the deprivations that are part of the prison environment. Gresham Sykes[11] provided one of the first analyses of prison riots when he explored the causes of two riots that took place at the New Jersey State Prison in the spring of 1952. Sykes attributed the riots to changes in the inmate social system that had stripped the inmates of their control. Based on his observations, Sykes believed that the transfer of power from the inmate social system to prison staff exaggerated the deprivations experienced by inmates and contributed to the riots. His insights, however, failed to provide a complete understanding of why inmates rioted. Overcrowding, poor living conditions, lack of programming, guard brutality, poor administration, and a concentration of violence-prone inmates have all been cited as contributing factors to riots despite the fact that these conditions also exist in prisons where no riots have ever taken place. Further, Sykes' explanations of prison riots were based on a case study (see Chapter 6) from a single prison facility where a riots had occurred.

In an effort to formulate a more comprehensive explanation for why inmates riot, Richard Wilsnack examined data from 48 state prisons. Included in his sample were prisons that had experienced a riot, some other type of collective inmate violence (e.g., work stoppage and hunger strikes), as well as prisons with no reported collective violence. He was the first to conduct a large-scale quantitative study of collective inmate violence. He created a 160-question survey that was mailed to 51 correctional institutions, including the largest state prison institution for each state and the District of Columbia. All of the prisons housed adult males convicted of felony crimes and were medium or maximum security facilities. Institutions were selected to be representative of the types of prisons where riots were most likely to occur. Only three states—Alabama, Kansas, and Mississippi—failed to respond to the survey, for a response rate of 94%. To improve the reliability of responses, questions were constructed in such a way that respondents had to provide only simple replies.

Twelve of the prisons surveyed reported a riot during the study period. The study identified several contributing factors to the riots. First, an analysis of prison conditions revealed that inmate deprivation, disorganization, and conflict existed in prisons where riots had taken place. Three-fourths of the prisons reporting a riot had experienced an increase in inmate assault and/or had at least one occurrence of an inmate assault on a guard. Second, administrative instability and conflict were related to prison riots. Three-fourths of the prisons reporting a riot had experienced major administrative changes (i.e., turnover or extended absences) and conflict among staff members. While a shortage of correctional staff was not related to the occurrence of a riot, low salaries and high staff turnover were found to be associated. Third, external pressures existed in prisons where riots had taken place. Wilsnack found that pressure and publicity from outside of the prison were also related to the occurrence of a riot. All of the riots had taken place in institutions where legislators and concerned citizens had tried to influence prison operations. In addition, 80% of these institutions had received some type of media coverage prior to the riot. Overall, riots were more likely to occur in maximum security prisons with overcrowding and unoccupied inmates. Furthermore, riots were more likely to occur in facilities where inmates of different ages, convictions, and prior records were all housed together. Wilsnack's findings did not support Sykes' contention that riots occurred as a result of a disruption of the inmate social structure.

Wilsnack's quantitative study of inmate collective violence enhanced our understanding of prison riots and other forms of collective prison disturbances. Despite the difficulties in researching prison riots, our understanding of the causes has grown significantly over the past several decades. Researchers have uncovered many of the conditions associated with prison riots and several theories have been developed to explain their occurrence. Prison administrators today are better equipped to respond to prison riots with emergency response teams. These teams consist of officers trained in hostage negotiation and disturbance control.

This body of research has also helped prison administrators develop preventative measures to reduce the likelihood of riots. Regular security audits, consistent enforcement of rules and procedures, maintaining effective communication between inmates, staff, and administrators, providing inmates with structured activities and appropriate programs, and using inmate classification systems are all important strategies for preventing the occurrence of riots.[12] The number of prison riots has significantly declined since the 1970s, despite the large increases in the number of inmates. According to Useem and Piehl,[13] this trend can be attributed to more effective prison management.

Bias means that in some systematic way the individuals responding to a survey are different from the overall population. Therefore, the results based on the survey respondents are not reflective of the overall population.

Although we can calculate a response rate, we usually do not know for sure the impact of nonresponse on the survey results. Perhaps the strongest argument for efforts to increase response rates is credibility.[14] When response

Research on prison riots has led to an understanding of the factors that lead to collective violence in prisons and strategies to reduce the incidence of prison riots.

rates are high, there is only a small potential for error due to nonresponse to have a significant impact on the survey results. When response rates are low, there is great potential for error due to nonresponse to have a significant impact on the survey results. Finally, a low response rate also provides critics of the survey results an easy, intuitive basis on which to say the data are not credible.

Survey Question Design

Designing a good survey instrument involves selecting survey questions that are needed to answer your research questions. As discussed in Chapter 1, one of the initial steps in any research project is to develop a research question or questions. The same is true for survey research. Since responses to the survey questions are the data collected in surveys, the survey responses are used to answer your research questions. Therefore, it is critical that questions included in the survey are able to answer your research question. For example, if your research question is, "Is there a relationship between parental supervision and chronic truancy?" you need to ask survey questions that can measure the variables identified in

the research question: parental supervision and chronic truancy. Designing a question for a survey instrument is designing a measure.

Besides the recognition that the survey questions must be able to be used to answer the research questions, how do researchers know what to ask on a survey? When building a questionnaire, a survey researcher has two sources for survey questions. First, the researcher can include survey questions that have been used in other surveys. When another researcher has already designed a quality set of questions to measure a variable in your research question, it is recommended that you use the items from the preexisting survey, with a few caveats. First, the existing survey questions must be reliable and valid, which will be discussed in the next section. For now, this basically means that the survey questions must be a quality measurement of the variable. For example, if you are creating a survey to address criminal victimization on your campus, a great starting point for developing the survey questions is to use the NCVS, covered in the chapter opening case study, as a template for your survey questions. You can certainly modify the questions to meet your specific needs, but the NCVS is a high-quality measurement of criminal victimization and so it is a reasonable place to start when creating the survey questions. Second, you need to provide appropriate citation to the original developer of the survey questions in the research manuscript. For example, Rosenberg[15] developed a measure of self-esteem that is the most often used measure of self-esteem in survey research. In order to use the 10-question measure of self-esteem or a modified version, the researcher must provide appropriate citation to its original source.

A good source for prior surveys on a wide range of topics is the Inter-University Consortium for Political and Social Research (ICPSR) at the University of Michigan.[16] Your university probably belongs to the ICPSR. ICPSR is a website depository where major social and political survey files are archived. If your university belongs to ICPSR, you can get codebooks for any study on file at ICPSR. The codebooks include the actual survey questions asked and the response formats used. The studies archived at the ICPSR cover a wide range of criminal justice and criminology topics, so it is a good starting place if you are ever tasked with developing a survey.

Second, when building a questionnaire, a researcher can include items that she has personally constructed. This is the favored option when a satisfactory measure of the variable does not already exist or the variables in the research question are unique. Despite the discussion

RESEARCH IN THE NEWS
Want a Job? Check the Spelling on Your Facebook Profile.[17]

When it comes to looking for jobs, you better put your best Facebook forward. Recruiters are looking, and frankly, they are not impressed with your poor grammar or posts about your latest unforgettable exploits, according to a new survey. The survey was conducted by social recruiting platform Jobvite. The company surveyed more than 1,000 human resources and recruitment professionals on their social recruiting activities and intentions with over 800 responding to the survey. Respondents answered questions using an online survey tool.

In addition to checking your résumé, nearly 3 out of 4 hiring managers and recruiters check candidates' social profiles, even if they are not provided on your résumé, with some of the content garnering negative reactions. Content that recruiters especially frown on includes references to using illegal drugs (78% negative) and posts of a sexual nature (67% negative). Profanity in posts and tweets garnered a 61% negative reaction, and almost half (47%) reacted negatively to posts about alcohol consumption. Worse than drinking, grammar or spelling mistakes on social profiles saw a 54% negative reaction from respondents. However, recruiters and hiring managers tend to be neutral in their reactions to political opinions (62% neutral) and religious posts (53% neutral).

above, do not think that every good question about a topic has already been asked. And do not think that the questions perfectly suiting your purposes have already been formulated. Finally, it is certainly reasonable to use both options (i.e., prior surveys and personally constructed items) when constructing a survey. As you are reading and evaluating survey research, the researcher should inform you about the source of the questions: whether based upon prior surveys or if questions were developed by the researcher.

Survey Questions and Answers: The Presence of Error

In order to conceptualize the error associated with answers to survey questions, it important to address what a survey is designed to measure. At its most basic, surveys try to measure two items: objective facts and subjective states. Objective facts include the number of times a person has been arrested, whether or not a person has used marijuana in the past week, and whether or not a person has been the victim of theft in the past 6 months. Subjective states include a person's level of attachment to his parents and a person's viewpoint on the primary purpose of prisons.

As will be discussed in the next section, the way we assess the answers to a survey question is to measure how well they correspond to the truth. If you are asking survey respondents about objective facts (e.g., how many times have you been arrested?), you can obtain independent information (e.g., criminal history information from a statewide database) against which to evaluate the answers to the survey question. Unfortunately, there is no objective way to verify or evaluate a person's report about a subjective state (e.g., viewpoint on the primary purpose of prisons). There is no way to independently assess whether the person is telling the truth, which can cause error in the survey results.

A defining characteristic of survey research is that answers to the survey questions are used as the measurements of the concepts and variables in the study. The extent to which those answers are good measures of the concepts and variables is obviously a critical dimension of the quality of survey results. The extent to which the answers are not good measures creates survey error. Survey error comes from several areas, including misunderstanding the question, not having the information needed to answer, and distorting answers in order to look good, to name a few.[18] For example, respondents typically underreport how much alcohol they drink and overstate their income. Survey results of alcohol consumption and income are likely to be biased (i.e., systematically different from the true scores). The issue is that to the extent that answers are impacted by factors other than the facts on which the answer should be based, there is error in the answer.[19] The next section discusses the quality of the survey measurement and related error by discussing reliability and validity.

SURVEY MEASUREMENT QUALITY: VALIDITY AND RELIABILITY

Assessing the quality (i.e., accuracy and consistency) of a survey measurement is a critical part of the research process. A survey researcher can spend days developing what he views as an excellent survey, but if the survey questions and responses are not accurate and consistent, the results of the study are questionable. Accurate and consistent survey questions and responses are essential to getting accurate results and making conclusions that reflect the true reality of the topic being studied. Specifically, the two key components of survey quality are reliability and validity. In order to be a high-quality measurement, survey questions and responses must be both reliable and valid. Reliability is necessary for quality measurement, but not sufficient. A quality measure must also be valid. Similarly, just because a measure is valid doesn't necessarily mean it is reliable, and validity means little if the measure used is not reliable.

Validity addresses the accuracy of the measurement and refers to the extent to which researchers measure what they planned to measure. Validity refers to the accuracy and trustworthiness of survey instruments, data, and findings. The question asked when assessing validity is: "Are the survey questions measuring what they are intended to measure?"

Reliability addresses the consistency of a measurement and refers to whether or not you get the same answer if you use an instrument to measure something more than once. For example, if a police radar gun is used to measure the speed of two vehicles going the same speed and the same results are obtained, then the radar gun is reliable. Similarly, if a breathalyzer is administered to two individuals with the same blood alcohol level and the breathalyzer gets the same results each time, then the breathalyzer is reliable. In these cases, the radar gun is a reliable measure of the speed of automobiles, and the breathalyzer is a reliable measure of blood alcohol content (i.e., level of intoxication).

As previously discussed, surveys generally assess two different types of information: objective facts and subjective states. Generally, it is easier to accurately and consistently measure objective facts than subjective states. For example, it is easier to accurately and consistently measure a survey respondent's gender, race, ethnicity, and education level (i.e., objective facts) than it is to measure a survey respondent's opinion (i.e., subjective state) regarding the level and quality of police service provided to the community. The extent to which a survey is unreliable and invalid creates measurement error, which is a persistent problem in criminal justice and criminology research. One of the major sources of error in research studies is poor quality of the measurements.

Both validity and reliability must be present for high-quality research results. This section will address ways to measure and increase the validity and reliability of a measurement. It is important to note that validity and reliability do not just apply to survey research but to measurement completed in all research designs, including experimental designs (Chapter 5), field research (Chapter 6), case studies (Chapter 6), secondary data analysis (Chapter 7), and content analysis (Chapter 7). Since this is the first chapter to discuss measurement, a comprehensive review of validity and reliability is presented here. As you proceed through the remainder of this book, keep in mind that validity and reliability apply to all types of measurement that are completed in research studies.

Assessing Validity

Validity addresses the accuracy of the measurement and refers to the extent to which the survey questions and responses measure what they were supposed to measure. In other words, are the survey questions and responses good indicators of what the researchers are trying to study? Stated another way, are the survey questions and responses measuring what they are intended to measure? There are numerous ways to assess the validity of measures. The ways range from simply asking if the measures seem like logical and common sense ways to measure the concepts and variables (i.e., face validity) to the complexity of determining whether the measures fit the theoretical constructs of the concept being measured (i.e., construct validity). Even though researchers may use sophisticated ways to assess the validity of their measures, concerns about the validity of the measure may still persist because of the complexity of the concepts studied by criminal justice and criminology researchers. In addition, validity is never proven; instead, invalidity is reduced, and when this occurs researchers express greater confidence in their data and the results of their study. There are several ways of assessing if the measures used in a study are valid: face, content, criterion-related, and construct validity. The different means of assessing validity vary by complexity and subjectivity.

Face Validity
Face validity, the simplest and most subjective means to measure validity, assesses whether the survey questions are a logical and common sense way to measure the concept. Basically, face validity involves an assessment of the survey questions to see if on "face value" the questions seem to be measuring the concepts and variables they are supposed to be measuring. Face validity answers the simple question, "Do the survey questions look like they measure what they are supposed to be measuring?" For example, if a researcher is measuring fear of crime, does the survey instrument ask questions about specific types of crime and the level of fear for each? If so, the survey has face validity.

Face validity is sometimes developed based on establishing a consensus among researchers that the measure is a valid way to measure the concept. For example, if researchers generally agree that asking someone "How many times have you been arrested?" is a valid measure of prior arrests, then, until proven otherwise, the question is a valid measure of prior arrests. However, because face validity is entirely a matter of judgment, there can be great disagreement among researchers and consumers of research about whether a survey question has face validity.

Content Validity Content validity is subjective, just like face validity, but is somewhat more complex than face validity. It occurs when the survey questions measure the full breadth and depth of the concept being studied. For example, let's say that when you have completed Chapters 1–4 of this book, you are scheduled to take an exam over Chapters 1–4. What if when you take the exam, your professor only asks questions about sampling, which is covered in Chapter 3? You would probably argue that the test was not fair and was not a good measure of your knowledge of Chapters 1–4 because it only covered Chapter 3. What you are stating is that the test, as a measurement of knowledge of the material covered in Chapters 1–4, lacks content validity. In order to have content validity, the test should have included questions over Chapters 1, 2, 3, and 4.

As another example, there exists a traditional measure of fear of crime that lacks content validity. Traditionally, fear of crime was measured in surveys based on the response to the question, "How safe do you feel walking alone in your neighborhood at night?" This question lacks content validity because it does not measure the full breadth and depth of someone's fear of crime. It is basically limited to fear of street crimes like robbery and assault, but does not include crimes that people fear but occur in their residences, such as sexual assault, family violence, burglary, and theft. Also, the question is limited to your neighborhood, whereas you may have a high level of fear of crime but it is due to getting off late at night from your job and having to walk through a deserted parking garage to get to your car. Furthermore, the question is time dependent, only asking about fear of crime at night.

When it comes to criminal justice and criminology research, content validity is difficult to obtain because researchers are trying to measure complex concepts. When studying criminal offending, it is difficult to ask about all types of crimes; there are just too many. Similarly, when studying drug use, it is difficult to ask about all types of drugs. However, just as discussed with face validity, consensus among researchers is used to determine content validity.

Criterion-Related Validity Criterion-related validity is more complex and less subjective than face and content validity. Criterion-related validity is assessed by determining the strength of the relationship between the responses to the survey and another measurement, the criterion, to which it should be related if the measurement is valid. For example, let's say that you want to create a measure of self-esteem. As previously mentioned in this chapter, the 10-question measure of self-esteem created by Rosenberg in the 1960s is a valid measure of self-esteem. You create a 16-question measure of self-esteem but will want to determine if the measure is valid. You can give a sample of people a survey that includes both the Rosenberg questions and your new questions about self-esteem. You can then determine the relationship between the responses to your measure of self-esteem in comparison to Rosenberg's questions, the criteria. If individuals that have high self-esteem according to Rosenberg's measure consistently have high self-esteem according to your new measure of self-esteem, then your measure has criterion-related validity. If individuals have high self-esteem according to Rosenberg's measure but consistently have low self-esteem according to your new measure, then your measurement of self-esteem lacks criterion-related validity.

As another example, you may be interested in pursuing law school after completing your bachelor's degree. Admission committees at law schools use the Law School Admission Test (LSAT) to predict success in law school. They prefer to admit students with high LSAT scores because they believe those are the students most likely to do well in law school. If there is a strong relationship between the LSAT score and success in law school as measured by law school grades, then the LSAT has high criterion-related validity. The LSAT is related to something that it should be related to, in this case, law school grades.

There are two types of criterion-related validity: concurrent and predictive validity. A measurement has high criterion-related validity, more specifically high concurrent validity, when there is a strong relationship between a new measure and a measure that is known to be valid. The example above regarding Rosenberg and a new measure of self-esteem is an example of concurrent validity. Concurrent validity occurs when an experimental measure (e.g., your new self-esteem measurement) and a valid measure (e.g., Rosenberg's self-esteem scale) measure the same thing at the same time (i.e., concurrently).

Concurrent validity is also assessed when a response to a survey item is compared to the same information from a different data source. For example, let's say your professor asks your current grade point average on a self-administered survey. Then, your professor uses your university's information system to obtain your official GPA. The more these two numbers correspond (i.e., your stated GPA and your official GPA), the higher the concurrent validity of the survey measurement of GPA. In criminal justice and criminology research, this process can occur to validate survey information that is also stored by criminal justice agencies such as prior arrests, convictions, and incarcerations, to name a few.

Another way to assess concurrent validity is to use what is sometimes referred to as the known group comparison technique. Let's say that you want to develop a measure of religiosity because you want to study the impact of religious beliefs on delinquent activities. Although valid measures of religiosity exist, you want to develop your own measure. After you have developed the survey questions, you administer the survey to members of the clergy and members of Atheist Alliance International (AAI). If your survey measure of religiosity shows that the members of the clergy have high levels of religiosity and members of AAI have low levels of religiosity, then you have established the concurrent validity of your measure. The items in your survey measurement are measuring what they were intended to measure (i.e., level of religious beliefs). If the measurement doesn't differentiate the level of religious beliefs between members of the clergy and AAI, then there is something wrong with your survey questions.

Another type of criterion-related validity assesses how accurately a measurement predicts some future, rather than current, outcome similar to the example previously discussed regarding the LSAT as a prediction of law school success. This type of validity is referred to as predictive validity. Let's say that you develop a set of survey items that is designed to determine if someone will be a successful police officer. A local police department decides to assist you with your study and allows you to issue your survey to the current police recruit academy class of 175 cadets. You track these police recruits for the next three years after completion of the police academy and field training program. If the individuals who scored highest on your survey while in the academy are also the most likely to have received promotions, excellent performance evaluation reviews, and fewer disciplinary infractions, then your measure has predictive validity. Police departments can now use this measurement tool to screen potential police officers with confidence in its ability to predict future success.

We frequently use measures in the criminal justice system to make decisions, including whether a crime can be solved, whether someone should be let out of jail on bail, whether a person should be released from prison on parole, and whether a person should be placed on a general probation caseload or a specialized caseload. These measures are only as good as their level of predictive validity; ability to predict some future outcome. If they have predictive validity, then we can have confidence in the predictive accuracy of the measurement.

Construct Validity   Another way of assessing the accuracy of a measure is to determine its **construct validity.** Similar to criterion-related validity, construct validity is more complex and less subjective than face and content validity. Construct validity assesses the extent to which a particular measure relates to other measures consistent with theoretically derived hypotheses concerning the concepts/variables that are being measured. Since construct validity is based on theory, it is favored by researchers.

For example, prior research has established a relationship between self-esteem and delinquency. Juveniles with high self-esteem are less likely to commit delinquent acts than juveniles with low self-esteem. You want to conduct a research study to test the following hypothesis: There is a relationship between self-esteem and delinquency. As presented in prior examples, let's say that you want to create your own measure of self-esteem instead of using Rosenberg's validated measure. You create your new 16-item measure of self-esteem and use a prior validated measure of delinquency. You administer the survey to the 8th graders in the middle school closest to your residence. The results show that those with high levels of self-esteem are less likely to commit acts of delinquency and those with low levels of self-esteem are more likely to commit acts of delinquency. This is exactly what was expected based on your theoretically derived hypothesis regarding the relationship between self-esteem and delinquency. Therefore, your new measure of self-esteem has construct validity. If the survey results would have shown that those most likely to be delinquent also have the highest levels of self-esteem, then your measurement of self-esteem would lack construct

FIGURE 4.1 | Mechanisms for Assessing Validity

Mechanism	Question	Simple/Complex	Subjective/Objective
Face Validity	Do the survey questions look like they measure what they are supposed to be measuring?	Simple	Subjective
Content Validity	Do the questions appear to measure the full depth and breadth of the concept?	Simple	Subjective
Criterion-Related Validity	What is the strength of the relationship between the responses to the survey and the measurement, the criterion, to which it should be related if the measurement is valid? Includes concurrent and predictive validity.	Complex	Objective
Construct Validity	What is the extent to which a particular measure relates to other measures consistent with theoretically derived hypotheses concerning the concepts that are being measured?	Complex	Objective

validity and the results of the study would be suspect. As depicted in the example, construct validity is based on actual research results and is not obtained until after the data has been collected and analyzed. Other researchers can begin to use your measure of self-esteem because you have shown that it has construct validity.

Increasing Validity

Now that we have presented the main approaches to assessing validity, we turn our attention to discussing ways to increase the validity of a survey instrument. As previously discussed, it is certainly reasonable for a researcher to use measures that have already been established as valid. If you are studying victimization on your college campus, it is certainly reasonable to develop your survey based on the National Crime Victimization Survey since the validity of this measurement has already been established. Even though a researcher may be using a previously established measure, there are validity issues that must be addressed in every research study. This section will discuss the major validity issues and the suggested means to overcome them, thereby increasing the validity of a research study. As an educated consumer of research, you should be aware of these issues as you review research reports. One significant validity issue with survey research is whether respondents are telling the truth.

Are the Respondents Telling the Truth? Aiding Respondent Recall   Recall that validity is addressing the accuracy of the measurement. Survey responses are usually accurate and truthful when the survey questions ask about a behavior or incident that is easily remembered.

Most offenders can easily remember how many times they have been arrested in the past month, but it is more difficult for a drug abuser to remember how many times they have used illicit drugs in the past month. It is likely that the number of arrests in the past month will be a more accurate response than the number of times an abuser has used drugs in the past month.

It is clear that a respondent's ability to accurately recall events declines over time and accurately recalling events typically takes more time than the few seconds that a respondent has to answer a survey question. As discussed in the chapter opening case study, a major source of error of the National Crime Victimization Survey (NCVS) includes the inability of the respondents to recall in detail the crimes that occurred during the 6 months prior to the interview. The NCVS uses a 6-month reference period. Respondents are asked to report victimization experiences occurring in the last 6 months. Generally, respondents are able to recall more accurately an event that occurred within 3 months of the interview rather than one that occurred within 6 months. Research indicates that assault is recalled with the least accuracy of any crime measured by the NCVS. Recall problems may result in an underestimate of the actual rate of assault.

Survey researchers recognize that memory is less trustworthy than once assumed. In response, strategies have been developed to maximize respondent recall. Survey researchers should be as specific and recent as possible when asking about past events. You can improve accuracy by making the recall period for the survey questions recent. The problem of forgetting becomes increasingly serious as the respondent is asked to recall events stretching over a longer period of time.

In addition, the researcher should clearly specify the behavior asked about. The complexity of respondent recall does not mean that survey researchers cannot ask about past events. Instead, survey researchers need to customize questions to shorten the recall period and interpret results cautiously as the recall period grows larger.

In addition, many respondents will telescope their responses. **Telescoping** occurs when a respondent brings behaviors and actions that occurred outside the recall period into the recall period. For example, let's say that a person was assaulted 8 months ago and has not been assaulted since that time. The person is answering a survey question that asks "How many times have you been assaulted in the past 6 months?" and the survey respondent answers "one time." The respondent has telescoped the victimization into the 6-month time frame even though it occurred 8 months ago and was outside the time frame provided by the researcher. Telescoping responses leads to overreporting of recent events and underreporting of distant events.

Are the Respondents Telling the Truth? Asking Embarrassing and Stigmatizing Questions

People have a tendency to underreport embarrassing or stigmatizing events (e.g., hitting their children, being a sexual assault victim, and lying on their tax return). Criminal justice research asks about many potentially embarrassing and stigmatizing topics such as criminal offending, victimization, drug use, alcohol consumption, mental illness, and prison rape, to name a few, thus making truthful reporting a challenge in criminal justice research. Respondents may be embarrassed or afraid to give truthful answers and thus, underreport behaviors or attitudes they wish to hide from others. As an educated consumer of research, you need to be aware of and assess the strategies a researcher uses to increase the honesty of survey responses.

Dishonest answers can be difficult to detect, so what strategies exist to increase the honesty and therefore, accuracy of survey responses? First, researchers should inform respondents that their responses are, at a minimum, confidential, and if possible, anonymous. Anonymity infers that the survey respondent's identity will not be known by the researcher. For example, if a professor hands out a survey in her class to the 150 people in attendance, asks them to respond to the survey and hand them to the end of the seating row where they are picked up by the professor, the surveys are anonymous. The professor does not know who filled out a particular survey. Anonymously collecting survey information, especially if it is of a sensitive or criminal nature, is one of the simplest ways to increase the honesty of responses. Respondents

It is difficult to get drug users and others who engage in stigmatizing behaviors to answer survey questions truthfully, which impacts the validity of the results. What strategies exist to increase the truthfulness of responses?

will be more honest regarding sensitive or embarrassing topics when they know their responses cannot be used to harm or embarrass them.

Confidentiality infers that although the researcher may be able to link the information given on a survey or during an interview to the particular research participant who gave it, this link will not be released to anyone else besides members of the research team. For example, a researcher who does face-to-face interviews will certainly know the identity of the respondent but promises to keep the responses in confidence.

Second, survey researchers should try to ensure that sensitive questions are asked in a nonjudgmental way. The researcher should minimize any sense of judgment and maximize the importance of accuracy. Careful attention should be paid to the wording of the introduction and the question to ensure that nothing negative about the behavior is implied to the respondent. The researcher needs to be very careful about any cues respondents are receiving about how their answers will be interpreted. These questions must be asked with great care and great empathy.

Third, the survey researcher should use a self-administered data collection procedure (discussed later in this chapter). It is generally agreed that having respondents answer questions in a self-administered form, on paper or directly into a computer, rather than having an interviewer ask the questions, will produce more honest answers. For surveys dealing with sensitive topics, a mail survey, Internet survey, or group administration survey should be considered. A face-to-face interview can also include some self-administered questions where a respondent is given a set of sensitive questions to answer in a booklet or directly into a computer. A similar strategy can be used with telephone surveys where answers to sensitive questions are entered directly into a computer using the touch-tone feature on the telephone.

Fourth, respondents feel more comfortable answering potentially sensitive questions when the responses are provided as categorical ranges rather than as a specific number. For example, a researcher may get a more honest answer if instead of asking, "What is your annual income?" the researcher provides the respondent with ranges of income from which to choose a response (e.g., less than $20,000, $20,000–$35,000). A respondent's age can be collected with categorical ranges, instead of a specific age, as well. Especially with demographic characteristics, the more sensitive the question, the better it is to use response categories instead of specific numeric values.

Fifth, the survey researcher can use a randomized response technique (RRT), which allows the researcher to ask about illegal and sensitive behaviors and obtain accurate estimates of the frequency of the behavior. Here's how it works. Let's say you are interested in the frequency of excessive force used by correctional officers. You are conducting face-to-face interviews with a sample of correctional officers at a prison unit. Your interviewers define excessive force for each respondent. But instead of your interviewers asking correctional officers the question directly, they give each respondent a randomization device, such as a coin. They ask the respondent to flip the coin. They tell the respondent not to tell them the results of the coin toss. Then they instruct the respondent as follows: "Say Yes if either of the following is true: Your coin came up heads, or you have used excessive force against an inmate in the last month."

If the respondent says yes, the interviewer does not know which question is being answered. Did the correctional officer say yes because the coin landed on heads or because the officer has used excessive force against an inmate in the last month? If this procedure was repeated with 100 respondents, based on probability theory, you would expect 50 out of 100 to say "Yes," simply because their coin toss came up heads. Therefore, if you find that 68% of the respondents say "Yes" to this question, you estimate that the 18% above the expected 50% represents correctional officers who used excessive force against inmates in the past month. Thus your finding is that 18% of correctional officers use excessive force against inmates in any given month.

Sixth, although this will be discussed in a later section of this chapter, realize that researchers can use one of the reliability tests, such as split-half reliability, to detect untruthful responses. Researchers ask the same or similar questions in different sections of a survey to determine if respondents were truthful in their responses. Surveys in which the truthfulness of the respondent is questioned should be discarded from the study prior to analysis.

Are the Respondents Telling the Truth? Social Desirability   People have a tendency to overreport something if it makes them look good (e.g., willingness to intervene in a crime to protect someone). Survey researchers call this overreporting **social desirability bias.** Social desirability bias occurs when respondents provide answers to survey questions that do not necessarily reflect the respondent's beliefs but that reflect social norms. If social desirability bias is widespread, it can have a significant impact on the results of the study.

One of the best examples of social desirability bias is LaPiere's[20] study of attitudes and behaviors towards hotel and restaurant service of Chinese people. Beginning in 1930 and continuing for two years thereafter, LaPiere traveled across the United States in an automobile with a young Chinese student and his wife. The early 1930s was a time when the general attitude of Americans toward Chinese residents was negative and was well documented in several social distance studies completed at the time. There was a national negative stereotype of Chinese citizens at the time, and the social norms of the time were to react negatively to individuals of Chinese descent. Discrimination against Chinese residents was common as well.

LaPiere discovered substantial differences between the stated attitude of survey respondents and actual behavior. During their extensive travels, the Chinese couple was received at 66 hotels, auto camps, and "tourist homes," and was only refused service at one. Similarly, they were provided service in 184 restaurants and cafes throughout the United States and were never refused service. To assess differences between stated attitude and behavior, LaPiere completed a mailed survey six months after departure from 22 of the hotels and 43 of

CLASSICS IN CJ RESEARCH
The Relationship Between Correctional Officers' Race and their Attitudes

RESEARCH STUDY[21]

Historically, correctional officers were white, uneducated, conservative males who lived in the rural areas where most prisons were located. Beginning in the 1950s, prison populations started to change as more urban blacks were sent to prison. Racial tensions between inmates and guards escalated. Black inmates had not only become more prevalent in number, they stood as a unified group against the guards who perceived them as a greater threat compared to the white inmates. Many reformers advocated increasing the number of black prison guards as a way to reduce conflict and antagonism between guards and inmates. The assumption was that black guards would be able to relate better to the black inmates because they shared similar backgrounds. Whether or not the attitudes held by black prison guards toward inmates were any different from those held by white guards remained an untested assumption until the late 1970s when James Jacobs and Lawrence Kraft conducted an empirical test of correctional officers' attitudes.

The authors tested the following five hypotheses:

1. Black guards have more sympathetic attitudes toward inmates compared to white guards.

2. Black guards are more supportive of rehabilitation compared to white guards.

3. Black guards convey less support for their superiors compared to white guards.

4. Black guards are less committed to institutional goals compared to white guards.

5. Black guards are less committed to their occupations compared to white guards.

RESEARCH QUESTION

Is there a relationship between correctional officers' race and their attitudes toward inmates, correctional goals, administrators, and correctional officer roles?

METHODOLOGY

The authors administered a survey to a sample of 252 guards from Stateville and Joliet prisons who were attending in-service training. Both prisons were maximum-security facilities within seven miles of each other. Three-fourths of the inmate populations in both prisons were black, and most of the prisoners came from the Chicago area (the prisons were 35 miles southwest of the city). At the time the survey was administered, 12% of the correctional officers employed by the Illinois Department of Corrections were black and most of them were working at Stateville and Joliet.

The survey was administered to guards while they attended in-service training at the Correctional Academy between the summer of 1974 and fall of 1975; 165 white guards and 66 black guards completed the survey; 21 guards were excluded from the sample because they did not indicate their race and/or rank on the questionnaire. Prison guards were group-administered an anonymous survey and asked to respond to a series of questions that consisted of both closed-ended and open-ended questions.

Specifically, inmate orientation consisted of a 10-item measure, one question open-ended and the other nine closed-ended, which asked questions such as, "Inmates try to take advantage of officers whenever they can." Job orientation consisted of a 7-item measure, which asked all closed-ended questions such as, "Although understanding may be important in helping inmates, what is really needed is strictness." Staff orientation was a 3-item measure, all closed-ended questions such as, "When I began, the veterans were friendly and helped me learn." System orientation was a 5-item measure, one question open-ended and the other four closed-ended, such as, "Why are there so many members of minority groups in prison?" Job commitment was a 9-item measure with all closed-ended questions such as, "Thinking ahead five years from now, do you think you will still be a correctional officer?"

RESULTS

The results of the study for each hypothesis are presented below.

1. Hypothesis: Black guards have more sympathetic attitudes toward inmates compared to white guards.

   Study finding: Black prison guards did not express attitudes that were more sympathetic toward inmates compared to white guards. The responses of black guards to several questions actually revealed less sympathy. The hypothesis was rejected.

2. Hypothesis: Black guards are more supportive of rehabilitation compared to white guards.

   Study finding: Black and white prison guards both indicated that rehabilitation was the primary purpose of prison, but when asked what the "primary purpose of prison should be," more black guards than white guards chose punishment. The hypothesis was rejected.

3. Hypothesis: Black guards convey less support for their superiors compared to white guards.

   Study finding: Black prison guards responded more favorably to their superiors than white guards even though most of the prison administrators and supervisors at the two prisons were white. The hypothesis was rejected.

4. Hypothesis: Black guards are less committed to institutional goals compared to white guards.

   Study finding: Black officers do not support a more relaxed correctional process. The majority of both races disagreed with the statement that "correctional officers should be rough with inmates occasionally to let them know who is boss," but blacks more often gave approval to the statement. The hypothesis was rejected.

5. Hypothesis: Black guards are less committed to their occupations compared to white guards.

   Study finding: The responses of both black and white guards indicated a strong sense of institutional commitment. Two-thirds of the guards sampled responded that they planned to be working at the prison for at least the next five years. Many of the guards expressed a preference for their current occupation over other alternative options such as private security and police work. The hypothesis was rejected.

Overall, the conclusion was there were no consistent differences by race in guards' attitudes toward prisoners, staff, correctional goals, or their occupation. According to the study authors, "There is nothing in these responses to suggest that black guards treat inmates with greater respect or sensitivity. They do not hold more rehabilitative views. Nor have they aligned themselves with the inmates against the administration."[22]

LIMITATIONS WITH THE STUDY PROCEDURE

Jacobs and Kraft recognized one of the potential validity issues with their questions was social desirability. Guards' responses may have been self-serving. Respondents may have provided "socially desirable" answers. The guards may have responded to the questions in terms of how they felt they should respond, not based on their own personal feelings. The extent that social desirability influenced the guards' responses was not known. As discussed in this chapter, social desirability is a source of measurement error that threatens the validity of a researcher's measures. Survey questions are valid only if they correctly assess the phenomenon under study; in this case, the guards' attitudes toward prisoners, staff, correctional goals, and their occupation.

Another limitation of this study is that the sample of prison guards was not randomly selected. A non-probability sampling method was used to draw the sample. As discussed in Chapter 3, since a non-probability sampling method was used, in this case purposive sampling, the sample of prison guards selected for this study are likely not representative of a larger population. Jacobs and Kraft purposely chose prison guards from Joliet and Stateville prisons who were completing in-service training at the state's Correctional Academy because most of the black

prison guards in Illinois worked at these two prison facilities. However, since non-probability sampling was used, the sample may not even be representative of all prison guards in these two prison facilities and is even less likely to be representative of prison guards in Illinois or the United States. Therefore, the results may not be generalizable to these other populations.

Reliability issues may have arose with the wording of some of the survey questions as well. For example, in the inmate orientation scale, Jacobs and Kraft asked "in your opinion, when just considered as people, how similar are guards and prisoners?" The question was supposed to mean how similar is the prison guard answering the question to the inmates. Respondents may have understood the question differently with some respondents having answered in terms of *other* guards or *most* guards, not themselves personally. Therefore, it may be misleading to consider this item an indicator of perceived distance between self-as-guard and prisoners.

IMPACT ON CRIMINAL JUSTICE

Jacobs and Kraft recommended that recruitment of minority guards was itself an important societal goal, because it expanded job opportunities in an area where minorities had been traditionally excluded. For this reason alone increasing the proportion of black guards is socially justifiable as well as legally compelled. The study discovered, though, that we should not unquestioningly accept the belief that this change in demographic composition of the work force will automatically have a major impact on the atmosphere of the prison.

Neither black nor white guards displayed attitudes that indicated they were more "inmate oriented." The similarities suggested that the attitudes might have been formed as a result of their socialization into the prison environment. Just as police officers develop "working personalities" that influence their interactions with the public, guards display certain attitudes and behaviors toward inmates. Numerous studies published after Jacobs and Kraft have identified various organizational influences on guards' attitudes.

The number of black correctional officers employed in prisons across the United States has increased in the years since Jacobs and Kraft published their study. Jacobs and Kraft were the first to explore the influence of race on correctional officer attitudes and, since then, numerous studies of correctional officers' attitudes have been published. The debate over whether or not hiring more black correctional officers will ease racial tensions between officers and inmates continues due to contradictory research findings, but according to Jurik,[23] it would be unrealistic to expect significant improvements to the prison environment by simply hiring officers with particular demographic characteristics.

the restaurants they visited and asked "Will you accept members of the Chinese race as guests in your establishment?" To his bewilderment, 91% of the hotels and 93% of the restaurants answered "No," even though he had a personal experience with each of the establishments where all but one provided service to the Chinese couple. Simply stated, he discovered what people say is not always what they do.

LaPiere's study certainly illustrates the difference that occurs sometimes between stated attitudes on surveys and actual behaviors. Just because someone says they would or would not do something on a survey, does not necessarily mean that will relate to the respondents' actions. In this case, LaPiere observed substantial discrepancies between attitudes and behaviors.

This study is also a reflection of social desirability bias. At the time, the social norms dictated a negative reaction to individuals of Chinese descent. When presented with a question about whether they would provide service to someone of Chinese descent, almost all of the respondents reflected the social norms at the time and responded "no." As stated above, social desirability bias occurs when respondents provide answers to survey questions that do not necessarily reflect the respondent's beliefs but instead reflect social norms, and that is certainly the case in LaPiere's study.

In order to detect social desirability, some survey researchers include the same or similar questions in different sections of a survey to determine if respondents were truthful in their responses, as previously mentioned. Researchers can also build in questions that are likely to identify respondents who are giving socially desirable answers. For example, the researcher may ask survey questions that include words such as "always" and "never." People rarely "always" or "never" do or feel something, so respondents who routinely select these responses are probably depicting social desirability bias. Another way to detect social desirability bias is to include unlikely choices in the closed-ended survey questions. Surveys in which the truthfulness of the respondent is questioned should be discarded from the study prior to analysis.

Increasing Validity: Using Scales and Indexes

Recall that validity addresses the accuracy of the measurement and refers to the extent to which the survey questions and responses measure what they are supposed to measure. One way of increasing the validity of your survey questions and responses is to ask multiple

questions to measure the same concept, especially if the concept is complex. You do not need to ask five different questions to measure a respondent's age. But, what about measuring parental attachment? You could have one question in your survey that asks, "What is your level of parental attachment?" but there are validity issues with asking just one question to measure a complex concept. As an alternative, you could ask the following 11 questions to measure parental attachment:

How often would you say that…

1. You get along well with your mother?
2. You feel that you can really trust your mother?
3. Your mother does not understand you?
4. Your mother is too demanding?
5. You really enjoy your mother?
6. You have a lot of respect for your mother?
7. Your mother interferes with your activities?
8. You think your mother is terrific?
9. You feel very angry toward your mother?
10. You feel violent toward your mother?
11. You feel proud of your mother?

The response categories for each question can be almost never, sometimes, most of the time, almost always.

Which is a better, more valid measure? Certainly, the measurement of parental attachment that asks 11 different questions is a higher quality measurement than just asking one question. In fact, the questions above were used by Bjerregaard and Smith[24] in their assessment of gender differences in gang participation. Their measurement of parental attachment is an adaptation of Hudson's[25] *Child's Attitude Toward Mother (Father) Index*, a well-standardized and validated index in the family assessment literature. By asking multiple questions to measure a complex concept, the researcher is able to even out response idiosyncrasies and improve the validity of the measurement.

Therefore, to measure a complex concept, researchers construct scales and indexes. These words are often used interchangeably in research methods, but they are actually different, so we will make some distinctions between the two. An **index** is a set of items that measure some underlying concept. Creating an index involves developing a set of items that, taken together, are indicators of the underlying concept you are attempting to measure. For example, every weekday the Dow Jones Industrial Index (DJJI) is reported on the nightly news. The DJJI is a set of numerous stocks that are combined to create a single number. Rosenberg's self-esteem measure, which was previously discussed, is an index. It uses 10 questions to measure the underlying concept of self-esteem. Similarly, the 11 parental attachment questions listed above form an index. The 11 items, taken together, are indicators of the underlying concept of parental attachment. So, when multiple questions are used to measure a complex concept, an index has been created.

What does a researcher do with the responses to the individual questions that make up the index? The researcher calculates an overall index score by summing the responses to all of the questions. The score serves as the indicator of your level of the concept being measured. Let's use the parental attachment index as an example. Each of the 11 questions had four possible response categories: almost never, sometimes, most of the time, almost always. Almost never is coded as 1, sometimes is coded as 2, most of the time is coded as 3, and almost always is coded as 4. Each respondent's answers to all questions are summed to get a single number that represents the respondent's level of parental attachment. The scores range from 11 (i.e., answered each question as "almost never") to 44 (i.e., answered each question as "almost always") with a higher score representing a higher level of parental attachment. One respondent may have a score of 22 on the parental attachment index while another respondent may have a score of 37, the latter having a higher level of parental attachment than the former.

If you tried to do the scoring of the parental attachment index on your own, you may have run into a problem. Some of the questions are positive (e.g., you get along with your mother) and some are negative (e.g. your mother is too demanding). A response of "almost always" on the first question in the previous sentence demonstrates a high level of parental attachment, but a response of "almost always" on the second question in the previous sentence demonstrates a low level of parental attachment. How does a researcher deal with this issue? The answer is the researcher reverse codes the negative statements. Instead of using the 1-4 coding scheme discussed in the last paragraph, the researcher reverses the code for the negative items. In this case, almost never is coded as 4, sometimes is coded as 3, most of the time is coded as 2, and almost always is coded as 1. Therefore, when a respondent answers "almost never" to the "your mother is too demanding" question, the answer is coded as a 4, which demonstrates a high level of parental attachment.

A **scale** is a set of questions that are ordered in some sequence. The researcher is seeking a pattern from the respondent's answers to the set of questions, rather than a simple summation of the individual question responses, as happens with indexes. For example, Guttman scales are used by survey researchers and are ordered in such a way that agreement with a particular item indicates agreement with all the items that come earlier in the ordered set of statements. Consider the following Guttman Scale regarding immigration.

Place a check next to each statement you agree with

_____ I would be comfortable with the United States expanding immigration.

_____ I would be comfortable with new immigrants moving into my city.

_____ I would be comfortable with new immigrants moving onto my block.

_____ I would be comfortable with new immigrants moving next door to me.

_____ I would be comfortable with a new immigrant dating my child.

_____ I would be comfortable with a new immigrant marrying my child.

The items are ordered so that agreement with the fourth item would also indicate a strong likelihood of agreement with the first three statements. If the respondent is not comfortable with new immigrants moving into his city, then he is definitely not going to be comfortable with new immigrants moving next door.

You have probably also heard someone say "On a scale of 1 to 10 ...." For example, it is common for health care providers to ask patients to rate their pain on a scale of 1 to 10. You have probably also heard someone mention the term Likert scale. Scales are used to measure the intensity of your response. Just like the pain scale measuring the intensity of your pain, a Likert scale measures the intensity of your response. A Likert scale measures the intensity of your preference or opinion and is typically measured on a five-point scale, such as "strongly agree," "agree," "neither agree nor disagree," "disagree," and "strongly disagree." Responses to several questions using a Likert scale are often combined to form an index. Now, you probably understand why the words "index" and "scale" are used interchangeably by many people. The word "scale" is used more frequently than "index." Although there are differences between the two terms, the key is to understand how scales and indexes are used in criminal justice and criminology research rather than worrying about whether the research study you are reviewing used a scale or an index. Also, remember that complex concepts should be measured by numerous questions.

Assessing Reliability

In our everyday lives, we use the terms reliable and unreliable to describe our cars, friends, and technology, among others. If your car starts every time you are ready to leave, then it is reliable. If your friend never helps you when you request assistance, then he or she is considered unreliable. If your cell phone routinely drops calls, then it is unreliable. Basically, reliable, as it has been used in these examples, involves consistency. For example, does your car consistently start? As another example, if you measure your weight on your bathroom scale five times in a row and receive the same result, then the scale is a reliable measure of weight. The scale has consistently measured your weight. Stepping on your bathroom scale three times in a row and getting readings of 108, 212, and 157 pounds is inconsistent, unreliable, and as a result, not very useful.

We also use the term to describe items in criminal justice as previously mentioned. For example, if a police radar gun is used to measure the speed of two vehicles going the same speed and the same results are obtained, then the radar gun is reliable. Similarly, if a breathalyzer is administered to two individuals with the same blood alcohol level and the breathalyzer gets the same results each time, then the breathalyzer is reliable. In these cases, the radar gun is a reliable measure of the speed of automobiles, and the breathalyzer is a reliable measure of blood alcohol content (i.e., level of intoxication).

Researchers use the term in roughly the same way to describe the measures they use in their research. Reliability, from a research standpoint, addresses the consistency of a measurement. It refers to whether or not you get the same result if you use an instrument to measure something more than once. It is the researcher's expectation that there will not be different results each time the measure is used, assuming that nothing has changed in what is being measured. When a researcher obtains different results on different measurements, then there is random error in the measurement process and the results must be evaluated with caution.

Just as with validity, there are some common ways for researchers to assess the reliability of their measures, but the assessment used depends on which aspect of reliability they are interested in. There are three different aspects of reliability that are of interest to criminal justice researchers: 1) reliability over time; 2) reliability over raters or observers; and, 3) reliability over items. The survey researcher could administer the same survey to the same respondents twice to assess consistency. This is known as test-retest reliability and is used when the researcher is interested in reliability over time. The survey researcher could have two different persons gather observations and assess the consistency between the two. This is known as interrater reliability and is used when the researcher is interested in reliability over raters or observers. Frequently, researchers assess reliability of their measures by dividing the survey into two halves and comparing the results of each half. This is known as split-half reliability and is used when the researcher is interested in reliability over items. Each of the three common ways to assess the reliability of a survey instrument is discussed in the next sections.

Test-Retest Reliability—Reliability over Time   If a researcher is interested in the reliability of a survey instrument over time, she can use **test-retest reliability**. Utilizing test-retest reliability, a measurement is reliable over time if the same measurement is repeated using the same subjects and yields the same results. Let's use the Scholastic Aptitude Test (SAT) as an example. If we administer the SAT to 100 high school seniors tomorrow and then administered the SAT to the same 100 seniors two days later, we would expect each student to get similar results on each test (assuming learning did not take place from the first administration to the second). If the results are quite similar, then the SAT is highly reliable; if not, then the SAT is unreliable. To assess the level of reliability of a measurement using test-retest reliability, the researcher must use the same measurement on the same subjects. If the researcher gets the same results each time, then the measurement is highly reliable and a quality measure. If the researcher gets different results each time, then the measurement has low reliability.

Since it is common for surveys to be used in cross-sectional designs (see Chapter 5), and thus, the sample only surveyed once, test-retest reliability is used infrequently to assess the reliability of a survey. However, the process is fairly easy to complete because all the researcher needs to do is give the same survey to the same subjects within a short period of time. For example, if a researcher wanted to determine the reliability of her fear of crime survey on your campus, she could administer the survey to a classroom of students on Tuesday and the same students on Thursday. If the results for each respondent are the same, then the fear of crime survey has high reliability. If the results are substantially different, then the fear of crime survey has low reliability unless something substantial has occurred on campus (e.g., a robbery and sexual assault) or in the news that can explain the substantial differences over a two-day period.

Interrater Reliability—Reliability over Raters

A measurement is reliable if someone else using the same measurement in the same situation produces almost identical results. Furthermore, a measurement is reliable if the same results are obtained time after time, even when the measurement is used by different people. Consider a blood pressure cuff. If five nurses take your blood pressure within the span of a few minutes using the same blood pressure cuff and each nurse gets the same results, then the blood pressure cuff is reliable (i.e., consistent results across different raters). The raters in this example are the nurses. The five nurses arrived at the same result, so the measurement tool (i.e., blood pressure cuff) is reliable.

Interrater reliability is particularly challenging in field research (see Chapter 6) and content analysis (see Chapter 7) where there has to be substantial agreement among those who are reading and coding the documents in content analysis or observing the behavior in field research. As it applies to surveys, interrater reliability is assessed in telephone and face-to-face interviews where the interaction between the respondent and the interviewer (i.e., rater) can influence responses. In addition, when open-ended questions are used, regardless of how the survey is administered, it becomes important that the data collected are interpreted in consistent ways. If the individuals coding the data consistently agree, then interrater reliability is high.

Split-Half Reliability—Reliability over Items

A popular way of determining the reliability of a survey measurement is to assess the internal consistency of the measure. This assessment is done on indexes (i.e., when a set of survey items are developed to measure some underlying concept) by comparing answers by a respondent. A measurement is reliable over items when the items contained in the index consistently measure the underlying concept. Consider the 11-question parental attachment index, previously discussed, used by Bjerregaard and Smith.[26] Each of the 11 questions was designed to measure parental attachment. Low scores indicated low parental

attachment and high scores indicated high parental attachment. How does a researcher determine the reliability, or what is sometimes referred to as the internal consistency, of the survey items?

Utilizing the **split-half reliability** technique, the researcher would split the items in half. This is accomplished by either selecting the responses to the first five questions and placing them in one group and placing the next five in another, or the odd-numbered questions and responses in one group and the even-numbered ones in another, or randomly selecting two sets of five. The researcher then compares the scores of the two halves on parental attachment for each respondent. If five of the items for a respondent indicate low parental attachment, then the other five should be consistent and also show low parental attachment. If the two halves correspond with one another over and over, then the index developed to measure parental attachment is a reliable one.

A statistic called **Cronbach's alpha** is often used to assess the internal consistency/reliability of an index. The closer Cronbach's alpha is to 1.0, the more reliable it is. The internal consistency coefficient should be at least +.60 and preferably above +.70. In an article by Bjerregaard and Smith, the authors stated, "The reliability coefficient for this scale is 0.86"[27] so the measure of parental attachment was reliable. As a consumer of research you should look for an internal consistency coefficient if the researcher uses an index. Most likely what you will see is Cronbach's alpha, which above +.70 demonstrates a reliable measure.

Increasing Reliability

One goal of a good measure is to increase question reliability. In this section, specific ways that researchers can improve the reliability of survey questions and responses will be discussed. The focus of this section is to make you an informed consumer of research regarding reliability, not describe all the nuances of question design so you can build your own survey.

Increasing Reliability: Ensuring Consistent Meaning for All Respondents

One step toward increasing reliability is to make sure each respondent in a sample is asked the same set of questions. But increasing reliability is not as simple as making sure each survey respondent is asked the same questions. Each question should mean the same thing to all respondents so each respondent interprets what is being asked in the same way. Ensuring consistent meaning for all respondents leads to consistent responses to the survey questions, thus increasing reliability. If two respondents understand the question to mean different things, their answers may be different for that reason alone, which can negatively impact the results of the study. To the extent that there is inconsistency across respondents, error is introduced, and the measurement is less reliable.

One potential problem you need to assess is whether the survey includes words that are universally understood. When surveys are done on the general population, a researcher needs to remember that those sampled will have a wide range of educational and cultural backgrounds. The researcher needs to be careful in wording the questions so they are easily understood by all participants. Also, when conducting research on a criminal justice topic, the researcher needs to be careful to not use jargon and acronyms that are used in the criminal justice system. In addition, the survey researcher needs to be sure to adequately define and describe any terms that may be uncommonly used in the general population and those terms that are sometimes used incorrectly in the general population. For example, although some have a general understanding of what activities comprise certain types of crime, it is a good idea to define each crime included in a survey. It is common for people to use burglary and robbery interchangeably, but from a survey standpoint, the researcher needs to make sure that it is clear to the respondent what activity constitutes burglary and what activity constitutes robbery by defining each crime.

Besides being sure to define any unfamiliar words used in a survey, the researcher needs to be cautious when using terms or concepts that can have multiple meanings. For example, the term "recidivism" holds multiple meanings in criminal justice research. For example, recidivism is the continuation of criminal activity, but it is measured various ways in criminal justice research. In a self-report survey, recidivism can mean any subsequent criminal activity regardless of whether the offense was reported to the police or the perpetrator was arrested. Also, if a sex offender commits a theft, is he a recidivist? The answer to this question depends on how you define recidivism. Some researchers require the subsequent offense to be as serious or more serious than the original offense to be included as recidivism. Some researchers only consider reincarceration as recidivism, while others expand it to include reconvictions, and some expand it even further by including all subsequent arrests as recidivism. Since there is so much variation in how recidivism is defined and measured, a survey researcher needs to make sure the definition of recidivism is clear in the survey so all respondents will interpret the term in the same way.

What is the reliability issue with the following survey question: Do you favor or oppose gun control legislation? The problem is that respondents will interpret the term "gun control legislation" differently, so the question will not mean the same thing to all respondents. The term "gun control legislation" encompasses many legislative strategies to control guns and there is no way of knowing which strategy the respondents are thinking about while answering the question. Gun control legislation can mean banning the legal sale of certain kinds of guns such as automatic weapons, requiring people to register their guns, limiting the number of guns that people may own, limiting which people may possess guns, or implementing a waiting period before the purchase of a gun, among others. The problem is when a respondent says "yes" they favor gun control legislation, the researcher has no way of knowing which strategy is supported by the respondent. The responses cannot be interpreted without assuming what respondents think the question means. Respondents will undoubtedly interpret this question differently. As written, the question is unreliable because it does not mean the same thing to all respondents. The solution to this problem is fairly simple. The researcher should ask a separate survey question for each gun control strategy she is interested in studying. These separate specific questions will be reliable because they will be consistently understood by all respondents and interpreted by researchers. For example, one of the survey questions can be "Do you favor legislation that limits the number of guns a person may own?" This is a reliable question that will be consistently understood by all respondents.

Increasing Reliability: Additional Question Characteristics   In addition to ensuring that the question means the same thing to every respondent, there are three additional characteristics of a reliable question that you should be familiar with as you assess research articles. First, in order to be a reliable question, the researcher's side of the question and answer process is entirely scripted so that the questions, as written, fully prepare a respondent to answer questions. In face-to-face and telephone interviews, it is important to give interviewers a script so that they can read the questions exactly as worded. Second, the kinds of answers that constitute an appropriate response to the question are communicated consistently to all respondents. The respondents should have the same perception of what constitutes an adequate answer to the question The simplest way to give respondents the same perceptions of what constitutes an adequate answer is to provide them with a list of acceptable answers by using closed-ended questions. With closed-ended questions, the respondent has to choose one of a set of appropriate responses provided by the researcher. Third, a survey question should ask only one question, not two or more. For example, a researcher should not ask the question, "Do you want to graduate from college and become a police officer?" A respondent could want to do one but not the other. When asked two questions at once, respondents will have to decide which to answer, and the survey researcher will have to assume what the respondent's answer means.

SURVEY DISTRIBUTION METHODS

A survey researcher must decide how to distribute the survey to the sample. Until the 1970s, most academic and government surveys were completed through face-to-face interviews.[28] When telephone ownership became nearly universal in the United States, telephone interviewing became a common mechanism to distribute surveys.[29] The newest means of survey distribution is through the Internet. There are five main mechanisms to distribute a survey: mail, group-administered, Internet, face-to-face, and telephone. Each survey distribution method will be discussed in this section. The strengths and weaknesses of each distribution method will also be discussed. Survey researchers need to consider the strengths and weaknesses of each method of distribution as they decide which distribution methods works best for their research questions and survey.

Self-Administered Surveys

Self-administered surveys involve the distribution of surveys for respondents to complete on their own. Self-administered surveys include those distributed by mail, group-administered surveys, and surveys distributed via the Internet. Self-administered surveys involve minimal (i.e., group-administered) or no personal contact (i.e., mail and Internet surveys) between the researcher and the respondent. With self-administered surveys, surveys can be mailed to the sample, distributed to a large group of people in one location, or can be sent through e-mail or placed on the Internet. One of the main advantages of self-administered surveys is that the collection of sensitive, stigmatizing, and embarrassing information is more

likely to be valid, as previously discussed, since respondents do not have to share their responses directly with an interviewer. However, one of the main disadvantages is that there may be a discrepancy between what people report they do and what they actually do, as previously discussed when the topic of social desirability was addressed. A survey researcher must weigh the strengths and weaknesses of each type of self-administered survey when determining the best method of distribution for their survey.

Mailed Surveys
Since only a valid mailing address is required, a common method to distribute surveys is to mail the survey to the sample.

The major strengths of mail surveys are listed below.

1. Mail surveys are fairly inexpensive to complete. Since there are no interviewers to pay, the costs of a mail survey are typically much lower than a face-to-face or a telephone interview. The main cost is the printing and mailing of the surveys and the return postage for the survey responses. In addition, mail surveys can be accomplished with minimal staff and office space.

2. Mail surveys can be easily distributed to a geographically dispersed sample.

3. Mail surveys provide respondents ample time to give thoughtful answers and even to refer to other documents that may be needed to answer the survey questions.

The major weaknesses of mail surveys are listed below.

1. Mail surveys typically have lower response rates than other methods of survey distribution.

2. Mail surveys require complete and easy-to-understand instructions since there is no personal interaction between the survey researcher and the respondent. If the instructions are unclear or the survey questions are confusing to the sample, the researcher will face significant reliability issues, which will impact the results of the study as previously discussed.

3. With mail surveys, the researcher has no control over who actually completes the survey. The survey researcher may restrict the survey to only adults between the ages of 18 and 35, but that does not necessarily reflect who actually answered the survey.

RESEARCH IN THE NEWS
Survey Shows More Teens Using Synthetic Drugs[30]

Nearly one in nine high school seniors have gotten high in the past year on synthetic drugs, such as K2 or Spice, second only to the number of teens who have used marijuana, according to the Monitoring the Future survey. The survey, conducted annually by the University of Michigan, questions 47,000 students in the 8th, 10th, and 12th grades in 400 public and private schools throughout the United States. The survey is group-administered to students in their normal classrooms. It is sponsored by the National Institute of Drug Abuse and the National Institutes of Health.

Monitoring the Future, the nation's most comprehensive survey of teenage drug use, found 11.4% of the high school seniors have used the synthetic substances, often packaged as potpourri or herbal incense and sold in convenience stores, which mimic the effects of marijuana. K2 and Spice emerged as a problem in 2008, and their popularity appears to be rising. People who smoke the chemical-coated herbs may experience euphoria, but bad reactions are common, including convulsions, anxiety attacks, dangerously elevated heart rates, vomiting, and suicidal thoughts. Most teens who smoke Spice or K2 report using other illicit drugs.

Marijuana remains the most popular drug among teens. Marijuana use increased for the fourth year in a row after a decade of decline. Nearly 7% of high school seniors report smoking marijuana daily, which is the highest rate seen in 30 years. In addition, half of high school seniors reported having tried an illicit drug at some time, 40% reported using one or more drugs in the past year, and a quarter said they had used one or more drugs in the past month, the survey found. Tobacco and alcohol use are at their lowest levels since the survey began in 1975.

Group-Administered Surveys Surveys can be distributed to individuals who have gathered together in a group. In fact, you have probably participated in a group-administered survey in one of your college classes. It is common for surveys to be administered to students in college and high school classrooms as well as to professionals in the criminal justice system who have gathered for in-service training or conference participation. The researcher will address the group regarding the purpose of the survey and to request participation. The researcher will then hand out the survey to each member of the group. The survey participants will typically complete the survey at the time of distribution and immediately return it to the researcher.

The major strengths of group-administered surveys are listed below.

1. Response rates are typically very high.

2. Since the researcher is at least present, he has the opportunity to explain the study and answer questions respondents may have about the survey.

3. Generally, group-administered surveys are inexpensive to complete since numerous surveys can be completed and returned at one time.

The major weakness of group-administered surveys is that it only applies to the small number of participants than can be easily gathered as a group. It is practically impossible to have a random sample of community residents gather to take a survey. However, some groups of people naturally congregate (e.g.,

students and prisoners), making group-administered surveys a viable means of survey distribution for some populations.

Internet and E-mail Surveys A recent development in survey distribution is to send an e-mail invitation to the sample. The selected subjects are then asked to answer questions by replying to a survey that is included in the e-mail or they are provided a link to a website where the survey can be completed online. Several commercial companies (e.g., Survey Monkey) make the process of creating, distributing, and collecting and coding data from an Internet survey easy and affordable. Although Internet and e-mail surveys are fairly new, the process and challenges mirror those for mail surveys.

The major strengths of Internet and e-mail surveys are listed below.

1. Internet and e-mail surveys are inexpensive to complete. The researcher does not even incur the printing, postage, and data entry costs associated with a mail survey.

2. The data from Internet and e-mail surveys can be collected quickly. An e-mail survey can be distributed instantaneously to hundreds of email addresses and since the survey is answered online, there is no delay in the researcher obtaining the completed survey. Once the respondent hits "submit" or "send" the researcher obtains the completed survey immediately.

The major weaknesses of Internet and e-mail surveys are listed below.

1. Internet and e-mail surveys are limited to individuals with e-mail addresses and Internet access. There are variations in computer ownership and use by race, ethnicity, age, income, and education, which can significantly impact the generalizability of results.

2. Depending on the sampled group and the topic, response rates to Internet and e-mail surveys are frequently low. A significant problem with Internet and e-mail surveys is inducing people to respond to the survey since there is no personal interaction between the researcher and potential respondent.

Personal Interviews

Surveys are often conducted by interviewers who read the survey items to respondents and record their responses in a face-to-face or telephone interview. A persistent issue with interviews involves the reliability (i.e., consistency) of the responses. Since there is a personal interaction between the interviewer and the respondent, the interviewer may influence the responses provided to the questions, which impacts the interrater reliability of the study. Different interviewers obtain somewhat different answers to the same questions. The interviewer's style and personal characteristics (such as gender, race, and age) can impact the answers provided by respondents. Also, since the survey questions are read to the respondent, the interviewer's tone and body language can lead to a different meaning to the question for different respondents. As discussed in the reliability section of this chapter, it is critical to the reliability of survey questions and responses that the questions mean the same thing to all respondents. The way certain questions are phrased by different interviewers can impact the responses given, thus impacting the reliability of the study. It is critical that interviewers are trained prior to data collection and monitored throughout the interview process so inconsistencies between interviewers can be minimized.

Face-to-Face Interviews   Face-to-face interviews are typically completed in the respondent's residence. Recall from the opening case study that the initial interview of the National Crime Victimization Survey is completed face-to-face.

The major strengths of face-to-face interviews are listed below.

1. Surveys which utilize face-to-face interviews typically have high response rates.

2. Lengthy surveys can be completed through face-to-face interviews. Although it is not always the case, some face-to-face interviews take more than one hour to complete.

3. The interviewer can answer any questions the respondent may have and can probe for additional information when an inadequate or incomplete answer is provided.

The major weaknesses of face-to-face interviews are listed below.

1. Due to the cost of interview staff and perhaps travel to the interview locations, face-to-face interviews are typically the most expensive survey distribution method.

2. The amount of time it takes to complete all the face-to-face interviews means that the data collection period is usually longer than other methods of survey distribution.

Telephone Interviews   Telephone interviews are usually completed through the use of a computer-assisted telephone interviewing (CATI) system. With CATI, the interviewer reads the question from a computer screen and then enters the respondent's answer directly into the CATI software so it is readily available for analysis. The CATI system then automatically shows the next question on the computer screen. This process increases the speed with which interviews are completed and reduces interviewers' errors. Telephone interviews are less expensive, less time consuming, and less subject to the reliability threats that can occur when conducting face-to-face interviews.

The major strengths of telephone interviews are listed below.

1. The telephone interviewing process can be completed very quickly. A staff of 15 interviewers can complete over 1,000 telephone interviews in a few days.

2. Through the use of random digit dialing (RDD), probability sampling can be utilized in telephone interviews. RDD is used because a large percentage of household telephone numbers are not listed in the current telephone book, either because they are new or at the request of the customer. RDD offers each

telephone number an equal probability of being selected, which is required in probability sampling, by randomly generating the last four digits of each telephone number selected in the sample.

The major weaknesses of telephone interviews are listed below.

1. Even though RDD is used, there are sampling limitations with telephone surveys because many people do not have landline telephones. According to the 2011 National Health Interview Survey, 36.8% of the respondents did not have a working landline telephone in their home, up from 20% in 2008.[31] Furthermore, 31% of the respondents stated they receive all or almost all of their calls on cell phones.[32] People without landline phones and those who only use cell phones are generally excluded from RDD sampling. This limits the generalizability of findings generated from RDD samples.

2. In addition to the rise of cell phone use, telephone survey response rates suffer from the increased use of caller ID, which has decreased the rate at which people answer their landline telephones. Also, because many telephone calls are for sales and fundraising purposes, some people react negatively to calls from strangers, which further reduces the response rates for telephone surveys.[33]

Which Method of Survey Distribution Should a Researcher Use?

It would be much easier if we just said that there is one preferred method of survey distribution, but the reality is that a survey researcher needs to consider his research questions, survey structure, population under study, and the strengths and weaknesses of each method of distribution in deciding which is best for his research project. For example, when the researcher has a limited budget, one of the self-administered techniques (i.e., mail, group-administered, Internet, and e-mail surveys) is preferable. Numerous Ph.D. dissertations in criminal justice and criminology have utilized self-administered surveys because of their low cost. However, self-administered surveys are not a good option if the researcher is concerned about the reading and writing capabilities of the sample members. Furthermore, self-administered surveys are not a good option when the survey consists of several open-ended questions. Personal interviews are more appropriate for several open-ended questions while self-administered surveys should include almost exclusively closed-ended questions. There is no simple answer to the stated question at the start of this section. The researcher needs to consider the research question and survey and then needs to maximize the strengths and minimize the weaknesses of the chosen survey distribution method.

C H A P T E R   S U M M A R Y

This chapter began with a brief overview of the three main components of survey research (i.e., sampling, question design, and methods of survey distribution) followed by a discussion of nonresponse and its impact on survey results. Comprehensive discussions of validity and reliability followed. The four ways of assessing the validity of survey questions and responses were illustrated, including face validity, content validity, criterion-related validity, and construct validity. Preferred mechanisms to increase the validity of embarrassing and stigmatizing questions as well as to control for social desirability bias were explained. For reliability, the three main mechanisms to assess reliability (i.e., test-retest reliability, interrater reliability, and split-half reliability) were presented as well as mechanisms to increase reliability such as ensuring consistent question meaning for all respondents. Finally, the methods of survey distribution were presented along with the strengths and weaknesses of each.

C R I T I C A L   T H I N K I N G   Q U E S T I O N S

1. What are the three categories of nonrespondents, and how does nonresponse impact survey results?

2. What are the main ways to assess validity, and what strategies exist to increase the validity of survey questions and responses?

3. What are the main ways to assess reliability, and what strategies exist to increase the reliability of survey questions and responses?

4. What are the strengths and weaknesses of each survey distribution method?

K E Y   T E R M S

construct validity: Assesses the extent to which a particular measure relates to other measures consistent with theoretically derived hypotheses concerning the concepts/variables that are being measured

content validity: When the survey questions measure the full breadth and depth of the concept being studied

criterion-related validity: An assessment to determine the strength of the relationship between the responses to the survey and another measurement, the criterion, to which it should be related if the measurement is valid

Cronbach's alpha: A statistic used to assess the internal consistency/reliability of an index

face validity: An assessment of the survey questions to see if on "face value" the questions seem to be measuring the concepts and variables they are supposed to be measuring

index: A set of items that measure some underlying concept

interrater reliability: A ratio established to determine the agreement among multiple raters

reliability: Addresses the consistency of a measurement and refers to whether or not a researcher gets the same results if the same instrument is used to measure something more than once

response rate: The number of people who respond to a survey divided by the number of people sampled

scale: A set of questions that are ordered in some sequence

self-administered surveys: The distribution of surveys for respondents to complete on their own; includes surveys distributed by mail, group-administered surveys, and surveys distributed via the Internet

social desirability bias: When respondents provide answers to survey questions that do not necessarily reflect the respondent's beliefs but instead reflect social norms

split-half reliability: An assessment of reliability in which the correspondence between two halves of a measurement is determined

telescoping: When a respondent brings behaviors and actions that occurred outside the recall period into the recall period

test-retest reliability: An assessment of reliability in which a measurement is reliable over time if the same measurement is repeated using the same subjects and yields the same results

validity: Addresses the accuracy of the measurement and refers to the extent to which researchers measure what they planned to measure

E N D N O T E S

1 Truman, Jennifer L. (September 2011). *Criminal victimization, 2010.* Washington D.C.: Bureau of Justice Statistics.

2 Fowler, Floyd J., Jr. (2009). *Survey research methods,* 4th ed. Thousand Oaks, CA: Sage.

3 Ibid.

4 Ibid.

5 Ibid.

6 Ibid.

7 Truman, September 2011.

8 Fowler, 2009.

9 Earl Babbie. (2013). *The practice of social research,* 13th ed. Belmont, CA: Wadsworth.

10 Wilsnack, R. "Explaining collective violence in prisons: Problems and possibilities." 61–78 in Cohen, A., G. Cole, and R. Bailey. (1976). *Prison violence.* Lexington, MA: Lexington Books. This study was excerpted from Amy B. Thistlethwaite and John D. Wooldredge. (2010).

Forty studies that changed criminal justice: Explorations into the history of criminal justice research. Upper Saddle River, NJ: Prentice Hall.

11 Sykes, G. (1958). *The society of captives: A study of a maximum security prison.* Princeton, NJ: Princeton University Press.

12 Henderson, J., W. Rauch, and R. Phillips. (1987). *Guidelines for developing a security program,* 2nd ed. Washington D.C.: National Institute of Corrections, NIC Accession Number 006045.

13 Useem, B., and A. Piehl. (2006). "Prison buildup and disorder." *Punishment and Society* 8, 87–115.

14 Fowler, 2009.

15 Rosenberg, M. (1965). *Society and the adolescent self-image.* Princeton, NJ: Princeton University Press.

16 ICPSR can be accessed at http://www.icpsr.umich.edu /icpsrweb/ICPSR/

17 Maltais, Michelle. (July 9, 2012). "Want a job? Check the spelling on your Facebook profile." *Los Angeles Times*. http://www.latimes.com/business/technology/la-fi-social-recruiting-jobs-20120709,0,2693929.story. Retrieved on July 10, 2012.

18 Fowler, 2009.

19 Ibid.

20 LaPiere, Richard T. (1934). "Attitudes vs. actions." *Social Forces* 13, 230–237.

21 Jacobs, J., and L. Kraft. (1978). "Integrating the keepers: A comparison of black and white prison guards in Illinois." *Social Problems* 23, 304–318. This study was excerpted from Amy B. Thistlethwaite and John D. Wooldredge. (2010). *Forty studies that changed criminal justice: Explorations into the history of criminal justice research.* Upper Saddle River, NJ: Prentice Hall.

22 Jacobs and Kraft, p. 317.

23 Jurik, N. (1985). "An officer and a lady: Organizational barriers to women working as correctional officers in men's prisons." *Social Problems* 32, 375–388.

24 Bjerregaard, Beth, and Carolyn Smith. (1993). "Gender differences in gang participation, delinquency, and substance use. *Journal of Quantitative Criminology* 9, 329–355.

25 Hudson, W. (1982). *The clinical measurement package: A field manual.* Homewood, IL: Dorsey Press.

26 Bjerregaard and Smith, 1993.

27 Bjerregaard and Smith, 1993, p. 339.

28 Fowler, 2009.

29 Ibid.

30 Leger, Donna Leinwand. (December 14, 2011). "Survey: More teens using synthetic drugs." *USA Today*. http://www.usatoday.com/news/nation/story/2011-12-14/more-teens-using-synthetic-drugs/51900736/1. Retrieved on June 15, 2012.

31 http://www.cdc.gov/nchs/nhis/quest_data_related_1997_forward.htm. Retrieved on July 12, 2012.

32 Ibid.

33 Fowler, 2009.

Experimental and Quasi-Experimental Designs

The Impact of Teen Court

Research Study

An Experimental Evaluation of Teen Courts[1]

Research Question

Is teen court more effective at reducing recidivism and improving attitudes than traditional juvenile justice processing?

Methodology

Researchers randomly assigned 168 juvenile offenders ages 11 to 17 from four different counties in Maryland to either teen court as experimental group members or to traditional juvenile justice processing as control group members. (Note: Discussion on the technical aspects of experimental designs, including random assignment, is found in detail later in this chapter.) Of the 168 offenders, 83 were assigned to teen court and 85 were assigned to regular juvenile justice processing through random assignment. Of the 83 offenders assigned to the teen court experimental group, only 56 (67%) agreed to participate in the study. Of the 85 youth randomly assigned to normal juvenile justice processing, only 51 (60%) agreed to participate in the study.

Upon assignment to teen court or regular juvenile justice processing, all offenders entered their respective sanction. Approximately four months later, offenders in both the experimental group (teen court) and the control group (regular juvenile justice processing) were asked to complete a post-test survey inquiring about a variety of behaviors (frequency of drug use, delinquent behavior, variety of drug use) and attitudinal measures (social skills, rebelliousness, neighborhood attachment, belief in conventional rules, and positive self-concept). The study researchers also collected official re-arrest data for 18 months starting at the time of offender referral to juvenile justice authorities.

Results

Teen court participants self-reported higher levels of delinquency than those processed through regular juvenile justice processing. According to official re-arrests, teen court youth were re-arrested at a higher rate and incurred a higher average number of total arrests than the control group. Teen court offenders also reported significantly lower scores on survey items designed to measure their "belief in conventional rules" compared to offenders processed through regular juvenile justice avenues. Other attitudinal and opinion measures did not differ significantly between the experimental and control group members based on their post-test responses. In sum, those youth randomly assigned to teen court fared worse than control group members who were not randomly assigned to teen court.

Limitations with the Study Procedure

Limitations are inherent in any research study and those research efforts that utilize experimental designs are no exception. It is important to consider the potential impact

that a limitation of the study procedure could have on the results of the study.

In the current study, one potential limitation is that teen courts from four different counties in Maryland were utilized. Because of the diversity in teen court sites, it is possible that there were differences in procedure between the four teen courts and such differences could have impacted the outcomes of this study. For example, perhaps staff members at one teen court were more punishment-oriented than staff members at the other county teen courts. This philosophical difference may have affected treatment delivery and hence experimental group members' belief in conventional attitudes and recidivism. Although the researchers monitored each teen court to help ensure treatment consistency between study sites, it is possible that differences existed in the day-to-day operation of the teen courts that may have affected participant outcomes. This same limitation might also apply to control group members who were sanctioned with regular juvenile justice processing in four different counties.

A researcher must also consider the potential for differences between the experimental and control group members. Although the offenders were randomly assigned to the experimental or control group, and the assumption is that the groups were equivalent to each other prior to program participation, the researchers in this study were only able to compare the experimental and control groups on four variables: age, school grade, gender, and race. It is possible that the experimental and control group members differed by chance on one or more factors not measured or available to the researchers. For example, perhaps a large number of teen court members experienced problems at home that can explain their more dismal post-test results compared to control group members without such problems. A larger sample of juvenile offenders would likely have helped to minimize any differences between the experimental and control group members. The collection of additional information from study participants would have also allowed researchers to be more confident that the experimental and control group members were equivalent on key pieces of information that could have influenced recidivism and participant attitudes.

Finally, while 168 juvenile offenders were randomly assigned to either the experimental or control group, not all offenders agreed to participate in the evaluation. Remember that of the 83 offenders assigned to the teen court experimental group, only 56 (67%)

agreed to participate in the study. Of the 85 youth randomly assigned to normal juvenile justice processing, only 51 (60%) agreed to participate in the study. While this limitation is unavoidable, it still could have influenced the study. Perhaps those 27 offenders who declined to participate in the teen court group differed significantly from the 56 who agreed to participate. If so, it is possible that the differences among those two groups could have impacted the results of the study. For example, perhaps the 27 youths who were randomly assigned to teen court but did not agree to be a part of the study were some of the least risky of potential teen court participants—less serious histories, better attitudes to begin with, and so on. In this case, perhaps the most risky teen court participants agreed to be a part of the study, and as a result of being more risky, this led to more dismal delinquency outcomes compared to the control group at the end of each respective program. Because parental consent was required for the study authors to be able to compare those who declined to participate in the study to those who agreed, it is unknown if the participants and nonparticipants differed significantly on any variables among either the experimental or control group. Moreover, of the resulting 107 offenders who took part in the study, only 75 offenders accurately completed the post-test survey measuring offending and attitudinal outcomes.

Again, despite the experimental nature of this study, such limitations could have impacted the study results and must be considered.

Impact on Criminal Justice

Teen courts are generally designed to deal with nonserious first time offenders before they escalate to more serious and chronic delinquency. Innovative programs such as "Scared Straight" and juvenile boot camps have inspired an increase in teen court programs across the country, although there is little evidence regarding their effectiveness compared to traditional sanctions for youthful offenders. This study provides more specific evidence as to the effectiveness of teen courts relative to normal juvenile justice processing. Researchers learned that teen court participants fared worse than those in the control group. The potential labeling effects of teen court, including stigma among peers, especially where the offense may have been very minor, may be more harmful than doing less or nothing. The real impact of this study lies in the recognition that teen courts and similar sanctions for minor offenders may do more harm than good.

One important impact of this study is that it utilized an experimental design to evaluate the effectiveness of a teen court compared to traditional juvenile justice processing. Despite the study's limitations, by using an experimental design it improved upon previous teen court evaluations by attempting to ensure any results were in fact due to the treatment, not some difference between the experimental and control group. This study also utilized both official and self-report measures of delinquency, in addition to self-report measures on such factors as self-concept and belief in conventional rules, which have been generally absent from teen court evaluations. The study authors also attempted to gauge the comparability of the experimental and control groups on factors such as age, gender, and race to help make sure study outcomes were attributable to the program, not the participants. ●

IN THIS CHAPTER YOU WILL LEARN

The four components of experimental and quasi-experimental research designs and their function in answering a research question

The differences between experimental and quasi-experimental designs

The importance of randomization in an experimental design

The types of questions that can be answered with an experimental or quasi-experimental research design

About the three factors required for a causal relationship

That a relationship between two or more variables may appear causal, but may in fact be spurious, or explained by another factor

That experimental designs are relatively rare in criminal justice and why

About common threats to internal validity or alternative explanations to what may appear to be a causal relationship between variables

Why experimental designs are superior to quasi-experimental designs for eliminating or reducing the potential of alternative explanations

---

INTRODUCTION

The teen court evaluation that began this chapter is an example of an experimental design. The researchers of the study wanted to determine whether teen court was more effective at reducing recidivism and improving attitudes compared to regular juvenile justice case processing. In short, the researchers were interested in the relationship between **variables**—the relationship of teen court to future delinquency and other outcomes. When researchers are interested in whether a program, policy, practice, treatment, or other intervention impacts some outcome, they often utilize a specific type of research method/design called **experimental design.** Although there are many types of experimental designs, the foundation for all of them is the **classic experimental design.** This research design, and some typical variations of this experimental design, are the focus of this chapter.

Although the classic experiment may be appropriate to answer a particular research question, there are barriers that may prevent researchers from using this or another type of experimental design. In these situations, researchers may turn to **quasi-experimental designs.** Quasi-experiments include a group of research designs that are missing a key element found in the classic experiment and other experimental designs (hence the term "quasi" experiment). Despite this missing part, quasi-experiments are similar in structure to experimental designs and are used to answer similar types of research questions. This chapter will also focus on quasi-experiments and how they are similar to and different from experimental designs.

Uncovering the relationship between variables, such as the impact of teen court on future delinquency, is important in criminal justice and criminology, just as it is in other scientific disciplines such as education, biology, and medicine. Indeed, whereas criminal justice researchers may be interested in whether a teen court reduces recidivism or improves attitudes, medical field researchers may be concerned with whether a new drug reduces cholesterol, or an education researcher may be focused on whether a new teaching style leads to greater academic gains. Across these disciplines and topics of interest, the experimental design is appropriate. In fact, experimental designs are used in all scientific disciplines; the only thing that changes is the topic. Specific to criminal justice, below is a brief sampling of the types of questions that can be addressed using an experimental design:

Does participation in a correctional boot camp *reduce* recidivism?

What is the *impact* of an in-cell integration policy on inmate-on-inmate assaults in prisons?

Does police officer presence in schools *reduce* bullying?

Do inmates who participate in faith-based programming while in prison have a *lower* recidivism rate upon their release from prison?

Do police sobriety checkpoints *reduce* drunken driving fatalities?

What is the *impact* of a no-smoking policy in prisons on inmate-on-inmate assaults?

Does participation in a domestic violence intervention program *reduce* repeat domestic violence arrests?

A focus on the classic experimental design will demonstrate the usefulness of this research design for addressing criminal justice questions interested in **cause and effect relationships.** Particular attention is paid to the classic experimental design because it serves as the foundation for all other experimental and quasi-experimental designs, some of which are covered in this chapter. As a result, a clear understanding of the components, organization, and logic of the classic experimental design will facilitate an understanding of other experimental and quasi-experimental designs examined in this chapter. It will also allow the reader to better understand the results produced from those various designs, and importantly, what those results mean. It is a truism that the results of a research study are only as "good" as the design or method used to produce them. Therefore, understanding the various experimental and quasi-experimental designs is the key to becoming an informed consumer of research.

THE CHALLENGE OF ESTABLISHING CAUSE AND EFFECT

Researchers interested in explaining the relationship between variables, such as whether a treatment program impacts recidivism, are interested in causation or causal relationships. In a simple example, a causal relationship exists when X (**independent variable**) causes Y (**dependent variable**), and there are no other factors

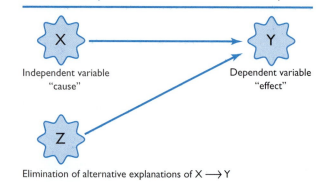

FIGURE 5.1 | The Cause and Effect Relationship

Elimination of alternative explanations of X ⟶ Y

1. Timing—X comes before Y in time
2. Association—X and Y are related/associated/correlated
3. Elimination of alternative explanations

(Z) that can explain that relationship. For example, offenders who participated in a domestic violence intervention program (X–domestic violence intervention program) experienced fewer re-arrests (Y–re-arrests) than those who did not participate in the domestic violence program, and no other factor other than participation in the domestic violence program can explain these results. The classic experimental design is superior to other research designs in uncovering a causal relationship, if one exists. Before a causal relationship can be established, however, there are three conditions that *must* be met (see Figure 5.1).[2]

Timing   The first condition for a causal relationship is **timing.** For a causal relationship to exist, it must be shown that the independent variable or cause (X) preceded the dependent variable or outcome (Y) in time. A decrease in domestic violence re-arrests (Y) cannot occur before participation in a domestic violence reduction program (X), if the domestic violence program is proposed to be the cause of fewer re-arrests. Ensuring that cause comes before effect is not *sufficient* to establish that a causal relationship exists, but it is one *requirement* that must be met for a causal relationship.

Association   In addition to timing, there must also be an observable **association** between X and Y, the second necessary condition for a causal relationship. Association is also commonly referred to as **covariance** or **correlation.** When an association or correlation exits, this means there is some pattern of relationship between X and Y—as X changes by increasing or decreasing, Y also changes by increasing or decreasing. Here, the notion of X and Y increasing or decreasing can mean an actual increase/decrease in the quantity of some factor, such as an increase/decrease in the number of prison terms or days in a program or re-arrests. It can also refer to an increase/decrease in a particular category, for example, from nonparticipation in a program to participation in a program. For instance, subjects who participated in a domestic violence reduction program (X) incurred fewer domestic violence re-arrests (Y) than those who did not participate in the program. In this example, X and Y are associated—as X changes or increases from nonparticipation to participation in the domestic violence program, Y or the number of re-arrests for domestic violence decreases.

Associations between X and Y can occur in two different directions: positive or negative. A **positive association** means that as X increases, Y increases, or, as X decreases, Y decreases. A **negative association** means that as X increases, Y decreases, or, as X decreases, Y increases. In the example above, the association is negative—participation in the domestic violence program was associated with a *reduction* in re-arrests. This is also sometimes called an inverse relationship.

Elimination of Alternative Explanations   Although participation in a domestic violence program may be *associated* with a reduction in re-arrests, this does not mean for certain that participation in the program was the cause of reduced re-arrests. Just as timing by itself does not imply a causal relationship, association by itself does not imply a causal relationship. For example, instead of the program being the cause of a reduction in re-arrests, perhaps several of the program participants died shortly after completion of the domestic violence program and thus were not able to engage in domestic violence (and their deaths were unknown to the researcher tracking re-arrests). Perhaps a number of the program participants moved out of state and domestic violence re-arrests occurred but were not able to be uncovered by the researcher. Perhaps those in the domestic violence program experienced some other event, such as the trauma of a natural disaster, and that experience led to a reduction in domestic violence, an event not connected to the domestic violence program. If any of these situations occurred, it might appear that the domestic violence program led to fewer re-arrests. However, the observed reduction in re-arrests can actually be attributed to a factor unrelated to the domestic violence program.

The previous discussion leads to the third and final necessary consideration in determining a causal relationship—**elimination of alternative explanations.**

This means that the researcher must rule out any other potential explanation of the results, except for the experimental condition such as a program, policy, or practice. Accounting for or ruling out alternative explanations is much more difficult than ensuring timing and association. Ruling out all alternative explanations is difficult because there are so many potential other explanations that can wholly or partly explain the findings of a research study. This is especially true in the social sciences, where researchers are often interested in relationships explaining human behavior. Because of this difficulty, associations by themselves are sometimes mistaken as causal relationships when in fact they are **spurious.** A spurious relationship is one where it appears that X and Y are causally related, but the relationship is actually explained by something other than the independent variable, or X.

One only needs to go so far as the daily newspaper to find headlines and stories of mere associations being mistaken, assumed, or represented as causal relationships. For example, a newspaper headline recently proclaimed "Churchgoers live longer."[3] An uninformed consumer may interpret this headline as evidence of a causal relationship—that going to church by itself will lead to a longer life—but the astute consumer would note possible alternative explanations. For example, people who go to church may live longer because they tend to live healthier lifestyles and tend to avoid risky situations. These are two probable alternative explanations to the relationship independent of simply going to church. In another example, researchers David Kalist and Daniel Yee explored the relationship between first names and delinquent behavior in their manuscript titled "First Names and Crime: Does Unpopularity Spell Trouble?"[4] Kalist and Lee (2009) found that unpopular names are associated with juvenile delinquency. In other words, those individuals with the most unpopular names were more likely to be delinquent than those with more popular names. According to the authors, is it not necessarily someone's name that leads to delinquent behavior, but rather, the most unpopular names also tend to be correlated with individuals who come from disadvantaged home environments and experience a low socioeconomic status of living. Rightly noted by the authors, these alternative explanations help to explain the link between someone's name and delinquent behavior—a link that is not causal.

A frequently cited example provides more insight to the claim that an association by itself is not sufficient to prove causality. In certain cities in the United States, for

CLASSICS IN CJ RESEARCH
Minneapolis Domestic Violence Experiment

RESEARCH STUDY
The Minneapolis Domestic Violence Experiment (MDVE)[5]

RESEARCH QUESTION
Which police action (arrest, separation, or mediation) is most effective at deterring future misdemeanor domestic violence?

METHODOLOGY
The experiment began on March 17, 1981, and continued until August 1, 1982. The experiment was conducted in two of Minneapolis's four police precincts—the two with the highest number of domestic violence reports and arrests. A total of 314 reports of misdemeanor domestic violence were handled by the police during this time frame.

This study utilized an experimental design with the random assignment of police actions. Each police officer involved in the study was given a pad of report forms. Upon a misdemeanor domestic violence call, the officer's action (arrest, separation, or mediation) was predetermined by the order and color of report forms in the officer's notebook. Colored report forms were randomly ordered in the officer's notebook and the color on the form determined the officer response once at the scene. For example, after receiving a call for domestic violence, an officer would turn to his or her report pad to determine the action. If the top form was pink, the action was arrest. If on the next call the top form was a different color, an action other than arrest would occur. All colored report forms were randomly ordered through a lottery assignment method. The result is that all police officer actions to misdemeanor domestic violence calls were randomly assigned. To ensure the lottery procedure was properly carried out, research staff participated in ride-alongs with officers to ensure that officers did not skip the order of randomly ordered forms. Research staff also made sure the reports were received in the order they were randomly assigned in the pad of report forms.

To examine the relationship of different officer responses to future domestic violence, the researchers examined official arrests of the suspects in a 6-month follow-up period. For example, the researchers examined those initially arrested for misdemeanor domestic violence and how many were subsequently arrested for domestic violence within a 6-month time frame. They did the same procedure for the police actions of separation and mediation. The researchers also interviewed the victim(s) of each incident and asked if a repeat domestic violence incident occurred with the same suspect in the 6-month follow-up period. This allowed researchers to examine domestic violence offenses that may have occurred but did not come to the official attention of police. The researchers then compared official arrests for domestic violence to self-reported domestic violence after the experiment.

RESULTS
Suspects arrested for misdemeanor domestic violence, as opposed to situations where separation or mediation was used, were significantly less likely to engage in repeat domestic violence as measured by official arrest records and victim interviews during the 6-month follow-up period. According to official police records, 10% of those initially arrested engaged in repeat domestic violence in the follow-up period, 19% of those who initially received mediation

example, as ice cream sales increase on a particular day or in a particular month so does the incidence of certain forms of crime. If this association were represented as a causal statement, it would be that ice cream or ice cream sales causes crime. There is an association, no doubt, and let us assume that ice cream sales rose before the increase in crime (timing). Surely, however, this relationship between ice cream sales and crime is spurious. The alternative explanation is that ice cream sales and crime are associated in certain parts of the country because of the weather. Ice cream sales tend to increase in warmer temperatures, and it just so happens that certain forms of crime tend to increase in warmer temperatures as well. This coincidence or association does not mean a causal relationship exists. Additionally, this does not mean that warm temperatures cause crime either. There are plenty of other alternative explanations for the increase in certain forms of crime and warmer temperatures.[6] For another example of a study subject to alternative explanations, read the June 2011 news article titled "Less Crime in U.S. Thanks to Videogames."[7] Based on your reading, what are some other potential explanations for the crime drop other than videogames?

The preceding examples demonstrate how timing and association can be present, but the final needed condition for a causal relationship is that all alternative explanations are ruled out. While this task is difficult, the classic experimental design helps to ensure these additional explanatory factors are minimized. When other designs are used, such as quasi-experimental designs, the chance that alternative explanations emerge is greater. This potential should become clearer as we explore the organization and logic of the classic experimental design.

engaged in repeat domestic violence, and 24% of those who randomly received separation engaged in repeat domestic violence. According to victim interviews, 19% of those initially arrested engaged in repeat domestic violence, compared to 37% for separation and 33% for mediation. The general conclusion of the experiment was that arrest was preferable to separation or mediation in deterring repeat domestic violence across both official police records and victim interviews.

LIMITATIONS WITH THE STUDY PROCEDURE

A few issues that affected the random assignment procedure occurred throughout the study. First, some officers did not follow the randomly assigned action (arrest, separation, or mediation) as a result of other circumstances that occurred at the scene. For example, if the randomly assigned action was separation, but the suspect assaulted the police officer during the call, the officer might arrest the suspect. Second, some officers simply ignored the assigned action if they felt a particular call for domestic violence required another action. For example, if the action was mediation as indicated by the randomly assigned report form, but the officer felt the suspect should be arrested, he or she may have simply ignored the randomly assigned response and substituted his or her own. Third, some officers forgot their report pads and did not know the randomly assigned course of action to take upon a call of domestic violence. Fourth and finally, the police chief also allowed officers to deviate from the randomly assigned action in certain circumstances. In all of these situations, the random assignment procedures broke down.

IMPACT ON CRIMINAL JUSTICE

The results of the MDVE had a rapid and widespread impact on law enforcement practice throughout the United States. Just two years after the release of the study, a 1986 telephone survey of 176 urban police departments serving cities with populations of 100,000 or more found that 46 percent of the departments preferred to make arrests in cases of minor domestic violence, largely due to the effectiveness of this practice in the Minneapolis Domestic Violence Experiment.[8]

In an attempt to replicate the findings of the Minneapolis Domestic Violence Experiment, the National Institute of Justice sponsored the Spouse Assault Replication Program. Replication studies were conducted in Omaha, Charlotte, Milwaukee, Miami, and Colorado Springs from 1986–1991. In three of the five replications, offenders randomly assigned to the arrest group had higher levels of continued domestic violence in comparison to other police actions during domestic violence situations.[9] Therefore, rather than providing results that were consistent with the Minneapolis Domestic Violence Experiment, the results from the five replication experiments produced inconsistent findings about whether arrest deters domestic violence.[10]

Despite the findings of the replications, the push to arrest domestic violence offenders has continued in law enforcement. Today many police departments require officers to make arrests in domestic violence situations. In agencies that do not mandate arrest, department policy typically states a strong preference toward arrest. State legislatures have also enacted laws impacting police actions regarding domestic violence. Twenty-one states have mandatory arrest laws while eight have pro-arrest statutes for domestic violence.[11]

THE CLASSIC EXPERIMENTAL DESIGN

Table 5.1 provides an illustration of the classic experimental design.[12] It is important to become familiar with the specific notation and organization of the classic experiment before a full discussion of its components and their purpose.

Major Components of the Classic Experimental Design

The classic experimental design has four major components:

1. Treatment
2. Experimental Group and Control Group
3. Pre-Test and Post-Test
4. Random Assignment

Treatment   The first component of the classic experimental design is the **treatment**, and it is denoted by X in the classic experimental design. The treatment can be a

TABLE 5.1 | The Classic Experimental Design

Experimental Group	R	O_1	X	O_2
Control Group	R	O_1		O_2
		Pre-Test		**Post-Test**

Experimental Group = Group that receives the treatment
Control Group = Group that does not receive the treatment
R = Random assignment
O_1 = Observation before the treatment, or the pre-test
X = Treatment or the independent variable
O_2 = Observation after the treatment, or the post-test

number of things—a program, a new drug, or the implementation of a new policy. In a classic experimental design, the primary goal is to determine what effect, if any, a particular treatment had on some outcome. In this way, the treatment can also be considered the independent variable.

Experimental and Control Groups
The second component of the classic experiment is an experimental group and a control group. The **experimental group** receives the treatment, and the **control group** does not receive the treatment. There will always be at least one group that receives the treatment in experimental and quasi-experimental designs. In some cases, experiments may have multiple experimental groups receiving multiple treatments.

Pre-Test and Post-Test
The third component of the classic experiment is a pre-test and a post-test. A **pre-test** is a measure of the dependent variable or outcome *before* the treatment. The **post-test** is a measure of the dependent variable *after* the treatment is administered. It is important to note that the post-test is defined based on the stated goals of the program. For example, if the stated goal of a particular program is to reduce re-arrests, the post-test will be a measure of re-arrests after the program. The dependent variable also defines the pre-test. For example, if a researcher wanted to examine the impact of a domestic violence reduction program (treatment or X) on the goal of reducing re-arrests (dependent variable or Y), the pre-test would be the number of domestic violence arrests incurred before the program. Program goals may be numerous and all can constitute a post-test, and hence, the pre-test. For example, perhaps the goal of the domestic violence program is also that participants learn of different pro-social ways to handle domestic conflicts other than resorting to violence. If researchers wanted to examine this goal, the post-test might be subjects' level of knowledge about pro-social ways to handle domestic conflicts other than violence. The pre-test would then be subjects' level of knowledge about these pro-social alternatives to violence before they received the treatment program.

Although all designs have a post-test, it is not always the case that designs have a pre-test. This is because researchers may not have access or be able to collect information constituting the pre-test. For example, researchers may not be able to determine subjects' level of knowledge about alternatives to domestic violence before the intervention program if the subjects are already enrolled in the domestic violence intervention program. In other cases, there may be financial barriers to collecting

pre-test information. In the teen court evaluation that started this chapter, for example, researchers were not able to collect pre-test information on study participants due to the financial strain it would have placed on the agencies involved in the study.[13] There are a number of potential reasons why a pre-test might not be available in a research study. The defining feature, however, is that the pre-test is determined by the post-test.

Random Assignment
The fourth component of the classic experiment is random assignment. **Random assignment** refers to a process whereby members of the experimental group and control group are assigned to the two groups through a random and unbiased process. Random assignment should not be mistaken for **random selection** as discussed in Chapter 3. Random selection refers to selecting a smaller but representative sample from a larger population. For example, a researcher may randomly select a sample from a larger city population for the purposes of sending sample members a mail survey to determine their attitudes on crime. The goal of random selection in this example is to make sure the sample, although smaller in size than the population, accurately represents the larger population.

Random assignment, on the other hand, refers to the process of assigning subjects to either the experimental or control group with the goal that the *groups are similar or equivalent to each other in every way* (see Figure 5.2). The exception to this rule is that one group gets the treatment and the other does not (see discussion

FIGURE 5.2 | Random Assignment

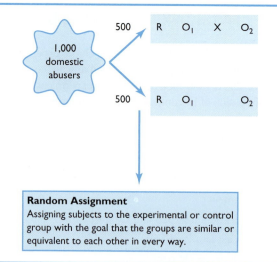

Random Assignment
Assigning subjects to the experimental or control group with the goal that the groups are similar or equivalent to each other in every way.

below on why equivalence is so important). Although the concept of random is similar in each, the goals are different between random selection and random assignment.[14] Experimental designs all feature random assignment, but this is not true of other research designs, in particular quasi-experimental designs.

The classic experimental design is the foundation for all other experimental and quasi-experimental designs because it retains all of the major components discussed above. As mentioned, sometimes designs do not have a pre-test, a control group, or random assignment. Because the pre-test, control group, and random assignment are so critical to the goal of uncovering a causal relationship, if one exists, we explore them further below.

The Logic of the Classic Experimental Design

Consider a research study using the classic experimental design where the goal is to determine if a domestic violence treatment program has any effect on re-arrests for domestic violence. The randomly assigned experimental and control groups are comprised of persons who had previously been arrested for domestic violence. The pre-test is a measure of the number of domestic violence arrests before the program. This is because the goal of the program is to determine whether re-arrests are impacted after the treatment. The post-test is the number of re-arrests following the treatment program.

Once randomly assigned, the experimental group members receive the domestic violence program, and the control group members do not. After the program, the researcher will compare the pre-test arrests for domestic violence of the experimental group to post-test arrests for domestic violence to determine if arrests increased, decreased, or remained constant since the start of the program. The researcher will also compare the post-test re-arrests for domestic violence between the experimental and control groups. With this example, we explore the usefulness of the classic experimental design, and the contribution of the pre-test, random assignment, and the control group to the goal of determining whether a domestic violence program reduces re-arrests.

The Pre-Test   As a component of the classic experiment, the pre-test allows an examination of change in the dependent variable from before the domestic violence program to after the domestic violence program. In short, a pre-test allows the researcher to determine if re-arrests increased, decreased, or remained the same following the domestic violence program. Without a pre-test, researchers would not be able to determine the extent of change, if any, from before to after the program for either the experimental or control group.

Although the pre-test is a measure of the dependent variable before the treatment, it can also be thought of as a measure whereby the researcher can compare the experimental group to the control group before the treatment is administered. For example, the pre-test helps researchers to make sure both groups are similar or equivalent on previous arrests for domestic violence. The importance of equivalence between the experimental and control groups on previous arrests is discussed below with random assignment.

Random Assignment   Random assignment helps to ensure that the experimental and control groups are equivalent before the introduction of the treatment. This is perhaps one of the most critical aspects of the classic experiment and all experimental designs. Although the experimental and control groups will be made up of different people with different characteristics, assigning them to groups via a random assignment process helps to ensure that any differences or bias between the groups is eliminated or minimized. By minimizing bias, we mean that the groups will balance each other out on all factors except the treatment. If they are balanced out on all factors prior to the administration of the treatment, any differences between the groups at the post-test must be due to the treatment—the only factor that differs between the experimental group and the control group. According to Shadish, Cook, and Campbell: "If implemented correctly, random assignment creates two or more groups of units that are probabilistically similar to each other on the average. Hence, any outcome differences that are observed between those groups at the end of a study are likely to be due to treatment, not to differences between the groups that already existed at the start of the study."[15] Considered in another way, if the experimental and control group differed significantly on any relevant factor other than the treatment, the researcher would not know if the results observed at the post-test are attributable to the treatment or to the differences between the groups.

Consider an example where 500 domestic abusers were randomly assigned to the experimental group and 500 were randomly assigned to the control group. Because they were randomly assigned, we would likely find more frequent domestic violence arrestees in both groups, older and younger arrestees in both groups, and so on. If random assignment was implemented correctly, it would be highly unlikely that all of the experimental group members were the most serious or frequent arrestees and all of the control group members were less serious and/or less frequent arrestees. While there are no guarantees, we know the chance of this happening is extremely small with random assignment because it is based on known probability theory. Thus, except for a chance occurrence, random assignment will result in equivalence between the experimental and control group in much the same way that flipping a coin multiple times will result in heads approximately 50% of the time and tails approximately 50% of the time. Over 1,000 tosses of a coin, for example, should result in roughly 500 heads and 500 tails. While there is a chance that flipping a coin 1,000 times will results in heads 1,000 times, or some other major imbalance between heads and tails, this potential is small and would only occur by chance.

The same logic from above also applies with randomly assigning people to groups, and this can even be done by flipping a coin. By assigning people to groups through a random and unbiased process, like flipping a coin, only by chance (or researcher error) will one group have more of one characteristic than another, on average. If there are no major (also called statistically significant) differences between the experimental and control group before the treatment, the most plausible explanation for the results at the post-test is the treatment.

As mentioned, it is possible by some chance occurrence that the experimental and control group members are significantly different on some characteristic prior to administration of the treatment. To confirm that the groups are in fact similar after they have been randomly assigned, the researcher can examine the pre-test if one is present. If the researcher has additional information on subjects before the treatment is administered, such as age, or any other factor that might influence post-test results at the end of the study, he or she can also compare the experimental and control group on those measures to confirm that the groups are equivalent. Thus, a researcher can confirm that the experimental and control groups are equivalent on information known to the researcher.

Being able to compare the groups on known measures is an important way to ensure the random assignment process "worked." However, perhaps most important is that randomization also helps to ensure similarity across unknown variables between the experimental and control group. Because random assignment is based on known probability theory, there is a much higher probability that *all* potential differences between the groups that could impact the post-test should balance out with random assignment—known or unknown. Without random assignment,

A football referee flipping a coin is viewed as a fair and unbiased way to determine which team gets to make the decision to take the ball, kick to the other team, or defer their choice to the second half of the football game.

it is likely that the experimental and control group would differ on important but unknown factors and such differences could emerge as alternative explanations for the results. For example, if a researcher did not utilize random assignment and instead took the first 500 domestic abusers from an ordered list and assigned them to the experimental group and the last 500 domestic abusers and assigned them to the control group, one of the groups could be "lopsided" or imbalanced on some important characteristic that could impact the outcome of the study. With random assignment, there is a much higher likelihood that these important characteristics among the experimental and control groups will balance out because no individual has a different chance of being placed into one group versus the other. The probability of one or more characteristics being concentrated into one group and not the other is extremely small with random assignment.

To further illustrate the importance of random assignment to group equivalence, suppose the first 500 domestic violence abusers who were assigned to the experimental group from the ordered list had significantly fewer domestic violence arrests before the program than the last 500 domestic violence abusers on the list. Perhaps this is because the ordered list was organized from least to most chronic domestic abusers. In this instance,

The 1978 documentary *Scared Straight* introduced to the public the "Lifer's Program" at Rahway State Prison in New Jersey. This program sought to decrease juvenile delinquency by bringing at-risk and delinquent juveniles into the prison where they would be "scared straight" by inmates serving life sentences. Participants in the program were talked to and yelled at by the inmates in an effort to scare them. It was believed that the fear felt by the participants would lead to a discontinuation of their problematic behavior so that they would not end up in prison themselves. Although originally touted as a success based on anecdotal evidence, subsequent evaluations of the program and others like it proved otherwise.

Using a classic experimental design, Finckenauer evaluated the original "Lifer's Program" at Rahway State Prison.[16] Participating juveniles were randomly assigned to the experimental group or the control group. Results of the evaluation were not positive. Post-test measures revealed that juveniles who were assigned to the experimental group and participated in the program were actually more seriously delinquent afterwards than those who did not participate in the program. Also using an experimental design with random assignment, Yarborough evaluated the "Juvenile Offenders Learn Truth" (JOLT) program at the State Prison of Southern Michigan at Jackson.[17] This program was similar to that of the "Lifer's Program" only with fewer obscenities used by the inmates. Post-test measurements were taken at two intervals, 3 and 6 months after program completion. Again, results were not positive. Findings revealed no significant differences between those juveniles who attended the program and those who did not.

Other experiments conducted on *Scared Straight*-like programs further revealed their inability to deter juveniles from future criminality.[18] Despite the intuitive popularity of these programs, these evaluations proved that such programs were not successful. In fact, it is postulated that these programs may have actually done more harm than good.

the control group would be lopsided concerning number of pre-program domestic violence arrests—they would be more chronic than the experimental group. The arrest imbalance then could potentially explain the post-test results following the domestic violence program. For example, the "less risky" offenders in the experimental group might be less likely to be re-arrested regardless of their participation in the domestic violence program, especially compared to the more chronic domestic abusers in the control group. Because of imbalances between the experimental and control group on arrests before the program was implemented, it would not be known for certain whether an observed reduction in re-arrests after the program for the experimental group was due to the program or the natural result of having less risky offenders in the experimental group. In this instance, the results might be taken to suggest that the program significantly reduces re-arrests. This conclusion might be spurious, however, for the association may simply be due to the fact that the offenders in the experimental group were much different (less frequent offenders) than the control group. Here, the program may have had no effect—the experimental group members may have performed the same regardless of the treatment because they were low-level offenders.

The example above suggests that differences between the experimental and control groups based on previous arrest records could have a major impact on the results of a study. Such differences can arise with the lack of random assignment. If subjects were randomly assigned to the experimental and control group, however, there would be a much higher probability that less frequent and more frequent domestic violence arrestees would have been found in both the experimental and control groups and the differences would have balanced out between the groups—leaving any differences between the groups at the post-test attributable to the treatment only.

In summary, random assignment helps to ensure that the experimental and control group members are balanced or equivalent on all factors that could impact the dependent variable or post-test—known or unknown. The only factor they are not balanced or equal on is the treatment. As such, random assignment helps to isolate the impact of the treatment, if any, on the post-test because it increases confidence that the only difference between the groups should be that one group gets the treatment and the other does not. If that is the only difference between the groups, any change in the dependent variable between the experimental and control group must be attributed to the treatment and not an alternative explanation, such as significant arrest history imbalance between the groups (refer to Figure 5.2). This logic also suggests that if the experimental group and control group are imbalanced on any factor that may be relevant to the outcome, that factor then becomes a potential alternative explanation for the results—an explanation that reduces the researcher's ability to isolate the real impact of the treatment.

The Control Group   The presence of an equivalent control group (created through random assignment) also gives the researcher more confidence that the findings at the post-test are due to the treatment and not some other alternative explanation. This logic is perhaps best demonstrated by considering how interpretation of results is affected without a control group. Absent an equivalent control group, it cannot be known whether the results of the study are due to the program or some other factor. This is because the control group provides a baseline of comparison or a "control." For example, without a control group, the researcher may find that domestic violence arrests declined from pre-test to post-test. But the researcher would not be able to definitely attribute that finding to the program without a control group. Perhaps the single experimental group incurred fewer arrests because they matured over their time in the program, regardless of participation in the domestic violence program. Having a randomly assigned control group would allow this consideration to be eliminated, because the *equivalent* control group would also have naturally matured if that was the case.

Because the control group is meant to be similar to the experimental group on all factors with the exception that the experimental group receives the treatment, the logic is that any differences between the experimental and control group after the treatment must then be attributable only to the treatment itself—everything else occurs equally in both the experimental and control groups and thus cannot be the cause of results. The bottom line is that a control group allows the researcher more confidence to attribute any change in the dependent variable from pre- to post-test and between the experimental and control groups to the treatment—and not another alternative explanation. Absent a control group, the researcher would have much less confidence in the results.

Knowledge about the major components of the classic experimental design and how they contribute to an understanding of cause and effect serves as an important foundation for studying different types of experimental and quasi-experimental designs and their organization. A useful way to become familiar with the components of the experimental design and their important role is to consider the impact on the interpretation of results when one or more components are lacking. For example, what if a design lacked a pre-test? How could this impact the interpretation of post-test results and knowledge about the comparability of the experimental and control group? What if a design lacked random assignment? What are some potential problems that could occur and how could those potential problems impact interpretation of results?

What if a design lacked a control group? How does the absence of an equivalent control group affect a researcher's ability to determine the unique effects of the treatment on the outcomes being measured? The ability to discuss the contribution of a pre-test, random assignment, and a control group—and what is the impact when one or more of those components is absent from a research design—is the key to understanding both experimental and quasi-experimental designs that will be discussed in the remainder of this chapter. As designs lose these important parts and transform from a classic experiment to another experimental design or to a quasi-experiment, they become less useful in isolating the impact that a treatment has on the dependent variable and allow more room for alternative explanations of the results.

One more important point must be made before further delving into experimental and quasi-experimental designs. This point is that rarely, if ever, will the average consumer of research be exposed to the symbols or specific language of the classic experiment, or other experimental and quasi-experimental designs examined in this chapter. In fact, it is unlikely that the average consumer will ever be exposed to the terms pre-test, post-test, experimental group, or random assignment in the popular media, among other terms related to experimental and quasi-experimental designs. Yet, consumers are exposed to research results produced from these and other research designs every day. For example, if a national news organization or your regional newspaper reported a story about the effectiveness of a new drug to reduce cholesterol or the effects of different diets on weight loss, it is doubtful that the results would be reported as produced through a classic experimental design that used a control group and random assignment. Rather, these media outlets would use generally nonscientific terminology such as "results of an experiment showed" or "results of a scientific experiment indicated" or "results showed that subjects who received the new drug had greater cholesterol reductions than those who did not receive the new drug." Even students who regularly search and read academic articles for use in course papers and other projects will rarely come across such design notation in the research studies they utilize. Depiction of the classic experimental design, including a discussion of its components and their function, simply illustrates the organization and notation of the classic experimental design. Unfortunately, the average consumer has to read between the lines to determine what type of design was used to produce the reported results. Understanding the key components of the classic experimental design allows educated consumers of research to read between those lines.

In 2009, Richard Stephens, John Atkins, and Andrew Kingston of the School of Psychology at Keele University conducted a study with 67 undergraduate students to determine if swearing affects an individual's response to pain. Researchers asked participants to immerse their hand in a container filled with ice-cold water and repeat a preferred swear word. The researchers then asked the same participants to immerse their hand in ice-cold water while repeating a word used to describe a table (a non-swear word). The results showed that swearing increased pain tolerance compared to the non-swearing condition. Participants who used a swear word were able to hold their hand in ice-cold water longer than when they did not swear. Swearing also decreased participants' perception of pain.

1. This study is an example of a repeated measures design. In this form of experimental design, study participants are exposed to an experimental condition (swearing with hand in ice-cold water) and a control condition (non-swearing with hand in ice-cold water) while repeated outcome measures are taken with each condition, for example, the length of time a participant was able to keep his or her hand submerged in ice-cold water. Conduct an Internet search for "repeated measures design" and explore the various ways such a study could be conducted, including the potential benefits and drawbacks to this design.

2. After researching repeated measures designs, devise a hypothetical repeated measures study of your own.

3. Retrieve and read the full research study "Swearing as a Response to Pain" by Stephens, Atkins, and Kingston while paying attention to the design and methods (full citation information for this study is listed below). Has your opinion of the study results changed after reading the full study? Why or why not?

Full Study Source: Stephens, R., Atkins, J., and Kingston, A. (2009). "Swearing as a response to pain." *NeuroReport* 20, 1056–1060.

VARIATIONS ON THE EXPERIMENTAL DESIGN

The classic experimental design is the foundation upon which all experimental and quasi-experimental designs are based. As such, it can be modified in numerous ways to fit the goals (or constraints) of a particular research study. Below are two variations of the experimental design. Again, knowledge about the major components of the classic experiment, how they contribute to an explanation of results, and what the impact is when one or more components are missing provides an understanding of all other experimental designs.

Post-Test Only Experimental Design

The post-test only experimental design could be used to examine the impact of a treatment program on school disciplinary infractions as measured or **operationalized** by referrals to the principal's office (see Table 5.2). In this design, the researcher randomly assigns a group of discipline problem students to the experimental group and control group by flipping a coin—heads to the experimental group and tails to the control group. The experimental group then enters the 3-month treatment program. After the program, the researcher compares the number of referrals to the principal's office between

A 2009 experimental suggests that swearing makes pain more tolerable.

TABLE 5.2 | Post-Test Only Experimental Design

Experimental Group	R	X	O
Control Group	R		O
			Post-Test

TABLE 5.3 | Experimental Design with Two Treatments and a Control Group

Experimental Group	R	O_1	X_1	O_2
Experimental Group	R	O_1	X_2	O_2
Control Group	R	O_1		O_2
		Pre-Test		**Post-Test**

the experimental and control groups over some period of time, for example, discipline referrals at 6 months after the program. The researcher finds that the experimental group has a much lower number of referrals to the principal's office in the 6 month follow-up period than the control group.

Several issues arise in this example study. The researcher would not know if discipline problems decreased, increased, or stayed the same from before to after the treatment program because the researcher did not have a count of disciplinary referrals prior to the treatment program (e.g., a pre-test). Although the groups were randomly assigned and are presumed equivalent, the absence of a pre-test means the researcher cannot confirm that the experimental and control groups were equivalent before the treatment was administered, particularly on the number of referrals to the principal's office. The groups could have differed by a chance occurrence even with random assignment, and any such differences between the groups could potentially explain the post-test difference in the number of referrals to the principal's office. For example, if the control group included much more serious or frequent discipline problem students than the experimental group by chance, this difference might explain the lower number of referrals for the experimental group, not that the treatment produced this result.

Experimental Design with Two Treatments and a Control Group

This design could be used to determine the impact of boot camp versus juvenile detention on post-release recidivism (see Table 5.3). Recidivism in this study is operationalized as re-arrest for delinquent behavior. First, a population of known juvenile delinquents is randomly assigned to either boot camp, juvenile detention, or a control condition where they receive no sanction. To accomplish random assignment to groups, the researcher places the names of all youth into a hat and assigns the groups in order. For example, the first name pulled goes into experimental group 1, the next into experimental group 2, and the next into the control group, and so on.

Once randomly assigned, the experimental group youth receive either boot camp or juvenile detention for a period of 3 months, whereas members of the control group are released on their own recognizance to their parents. At the end of the experiment, the researcher compares the re-arrest activity of boot camp participants to detention delinquents to control group members during a 6-month follow-up period.

This design has several advantages. First, it includes all major components of the classic experimental design, and simply adds an additional treatment for comparison purposes. Random assignment was utilized and this means that the groups have a higher probability of being equivalent on all factors that could impact the post-test. Thus, random assignment in this example helps to ensure the only differences between the groups are the treatment conditions. Without random assignment, there is a greater chance that one group of youth was somehow different, and this difference could impact the post-test. For example, if the boot camp youth were much less serious and frequent delinquents than the juvenile detention youth or control group youth, the results might erroneously show that the boot camp reduced recidivism when in fact the youth in boot camp may have been the "best risks"—unlikely to get re-arrested with or without boot camp. The pre-test in the example above allows the researcher to determine change in re-arrests from pre-test to post-test. Thus, the researcher can determine if delinquent behavior, as measured by re-arrest, increased, decreased, or remained constant from pre- to post-test. The pre-test also allows the researcher to confirm that the random assignment process resulted in equivalent groups based on the pre-test. Finally, the presence of a control group allows the researcher to have more confidence that any differences in the post-test are due to the treatment. For example, if the control group had more re-arrests than the boot camp or juvenile detention experimental groups 6 months after their release from those programs, the researcher would have more confidence that the programs produced fewer re-arrests because the control group members were the same as the experimental groups; the only difference was that they did not receive a treatment.

The one key feature of experimental designs is that they all retain random assignment. This is why they are considered "experimental" designs. Sometimes, however, experimental designs lack a pre-test. Knowledge of the usefulness of a pre-test demonstrates the potential problems with those designs where it is missing. For example, in the post-test only experimental design, a researcher would not be able to make a determination of change in the dependent variable from pre- to post-test. Perhaps most importantly, the researcher would not be able to confirm that the experimental and control groups were in fact equivalent on a pre-test measure before the introduction of the treatment. Even though both groups were randomly assigned, and probability theory suggests they should be equivalent, without a pre-test measure the researcher could not confirm similarity because differences could occur by chance even with random assignment. If there were any differences at the post-test between the experimental group and control group, the results might be due to some explanation other than the treatment, namely that the groups differed prior to the administration of the treatment. The same limitation could apply in any form of experimental design that does not utilize a pre-test for conformational purposes.

Understanding the contribution of a pre-test to an experimental design shows that it is a critical component. It provides a measure of change and also gives the researcher more confidence that the observed results are due to the treatment, and not some difference between the experimental and control groups. Despite the usefulness of a pre-test, however, perhaps the most critical ingredient of any experimental design is random assignment. It is important to note that all experimental designs retain random assignment.

Experimental Designs Are Rare in Criminal Justice and Criminology

The classic experiment is the foundation for other types of experimental and quasi-experimental designs. The unfortunate reality, however, is that the classic experiment, or other experimental designs, are few and far between in criminal justice.[20] Recall that one of the major components of an experimental design is random assignment. Achieving random assignment is often a barrier to experimental research in criminal justice. Achieving random assignment might, for example, require the

approval of the chief (or city council or both) of a major metropolitan police agency to allow researchers to randomly assign patrol officers to certain areas of a city and/or randomly assign police officer actions. Recall the MDVE. This experiment required the full cooperation of the chief of police and other decision-makers to allow researchers to randomly assign police actions. In another example, achieving random assignment might require a judge to randomly assign a group of youthful offenders to a certain juvenile court sanction (experimental group), and another group of similar youthful offenders to no sanction or an alternative sanction as a control group.[21] In sum, random assignment typically requires the cooperation of a number of individuals and sometimes that cooperation is difficult to obtain.

Even when random assignment can be accomplished, sometimes it is not implemented correctly and the random assignment procedure breaks down. This is another barrier to conducting experimental research. For example, in the MDVE, researchers randomly assigned officer responses, but the officers did not always follow the assigned course of action. Moreover, some believe that the random assignment of criminal justice programs, sentences, or randomly assigning officer responses may be unethical in certain circumstances, and even a violation of the rights of citizens. For example, some believe it is unfair when random assignment results in some delinquents being sentenced to boot camp while others get assigned to a control group without any sanction at all or a less restrictive sanction than boot camp. In the MDVE, some believe it is unfair that some suspects were arrested and received an official record whereas others were not arrested for the same type of behavior. In other cases, subjects in the experimental group may receive some benefit from the treatment that is essentially denied to the control group for a period of time and this can become an issue as well.

There are other important reasons why random assignment is difficult to accomplish. Random assignment may, for example, involve a disruption of the normal procedures of agencies and their officers. In the MDVE, officers had to adjust their normal and established routine, and this was a barrier at times in that study. Shadish, Cook, and Campbell also note that random assignment may not always be feasible or desirable when quick answers are needed.[22] This is because experimental designs sometimes take a long time to produce results. In addition to the time required in planning and organizing the experiment, and treatment delivery, researchers may need several months if not years to collect and analyze the data before they have answers. This is particularly important because time is often of the essence in criminal justice research, especially in research efforts testing the effect of some policy or program where it is not feasible to wait years for answers. Waiting for the results of an experimental design means that many policy-makers may make decisions without the results.

QUASI-EXPERIMENTAL DESIGNS

In general terms, quasi-experiments include a group of designs that lack random assignment. Quasi-experiments may also lack other parts, such as a pre-test or a control group, just like some experimental designs. The absence of random assignment, however, is the ingredient that transforms an otherwise experimental design into a quasi-experiment. Lacking random assignment is a major disadvantage because it increases the chances that the experimental and control groups differ on relevant factors before the treatment—both known and unknown—differences that may then emerge as alternative explanations of the outcomes.

Just like experimental designs, quasi-experimental designs can be organized in many different ways. This section will discuss three types of quasi-experiments: nonequivalent group design, one-group longitudinal design, and two-group longitudinal design.

Nonequivalent Group Design

The nonequivalent group design is perhaps the most common type of quasi-experiment.[23] Notice that it is very similar to the classic experimental design with the exception that it lacks random assignment (see Table 5.4). Additionally, what was labeled the experimental group in an experimental design is sometimes called the **treatment group** in the nonequivalent group design. What was labeled the control group in the experimental design is sometimes called the **comparison group** in the nonequivalent group design. This terminological distinction is an indicator that the groups were not created through random assignment.

TABLE 5.4 | Nonequivalent Group Design

Treatment Group	NR	O_1	X	O_2
Comparison Group	NR	O_1		O_2
		Pre-Test		**Post-Test**

NR = Not Randomly assigned

One of the main problems with the nonequivalent group design is that it lacks random assignment, and without random assignment, there is a greater chance that the treatment and comparison groups may be different in some way that can impact study results. Take, for example, a nonequivalent group design where a researcher is interested in whether an aggression-reduction treatment program can reduce inmate-on-inmate assaults in a prison setting. Assume that the researcher asked for inmates who had previously been involved in assaultive activity to volunteer for the aggression-reduction program. Suppose the researcher placed the first 50 volunteers into the treatment group and the next 50 volunteers into the comparison group. Note that this method of assignment is not random but rather first come, first serve.

Because the study utilized volunteers and there was no random assignment, it is possible that the first 50 volunteers placed into the treatment group differed significantly from the last 50 volunteers who were placed in the comparison group. This can lead to alternative explanations for the results. For example, if the treatment group was much younger than the comparison group, the researcher may find at the end of the program that the treatment group still maintained a higher rate of infractions than the comparison group—even after the aggression-reduction program! The conclusion might be that the aggression program actually increased the level of violence among the treatment group. This conclusion would likely be spurious and may be due to the age differential between the treatment and comparison groups. Indeed, research has revealed that younger inmates are significantly more likely to engage in prison assaults than older inmates. The fact that the treatment group incurred more assaults than the comparison group after the aggression-reduction program may only relate to the age differential between the groups, not that the program had no effect or that it somehow may have increased aggression. The previous example highlights the importance of random assignment and the potential problems that can occur in its absence.

Although researchers who utilize a quasi-experimental design are not able to randomly assign their subjects to groups, they can employ other techniques in an attempt to make the groups as equivalent as possible *on known or measured factors* before the treatment is given. In the example above, it is likely that the researcher would have known the age of inmates, their prior assault record, and various other pieces of information (e.g., previous prison stays). Through a technique called **matching,** the researcher could make sure the treatment and comparison groups were "matched" on these important factors before administering the aggression reduction program to the treatment group. This type of matching can be done individual to individual (e.g., subject #1 in treatment group is matched to a selected subject #1 in comparison group on age, previous arrests, gender), or aggregately, such that the comparison group is similar to the treatment group overall (e.g., average ages between groups are similar, equal proportions of males and females). Knowledge of these and other important variables, for example, would allow the researcher to make sure that the treatment group did not have heavy concentrations of younger or more frequent or serious offenders than the comparison group—factors that are related to assaultive activity independent of the treatment program. In short, matching allows the researcher some control over who goes into the treatment and comparison groups so as to balance these groups on important factors absent random assignment. If unbalanced on one or more factors, these factors could emerge as alternative explanations of the results. Figure 5.3 demonstrates the logic of matching both at the individual and aggregate level in a quasi-experimental design.

Matching is an important part of the nonequivalent group design. By matching, the researcher can approximate equivalence between the groups on important variables that may influence the post-test. However, it is important to note that a researcher can only match subjects on factors that they have information about—a researcher cannot match the treatment and comparison group members on factors that are unmeasured or otherwise unknown but which may still impact outcomes. For example, if the researcher has no knowledge about the number of previous incarcerations, the researcher cannot match the treatment and comparison groups on this factor. Matching also requires that the information used for matching is valid and reliable, which is not always the case. Agency records, for example, are notorious for inconsistencies, errors, omissions, and for being dated, but are often utilized for matching purposes. Asking survey questions to generate information for matching (for example, how many times have you been incarcerated?) can also be problematic because some respondents may lie, forget, or exaggerate their behavior or experiences.

In addition to the above considerations, the more factors a researcher wishes to match the group members on, the more difficult it becomes to find appropriate matches. Matching on prior arrests or age is less complex than matching on several additional pieces of information. Finally, matching is never considered superior to random assignment when the goal is to construct equitable groups. This is because there is a much higher likelihood of equivalence

FIGURE 5.3 | (a) Individual Matching (b) Aggregate Matching

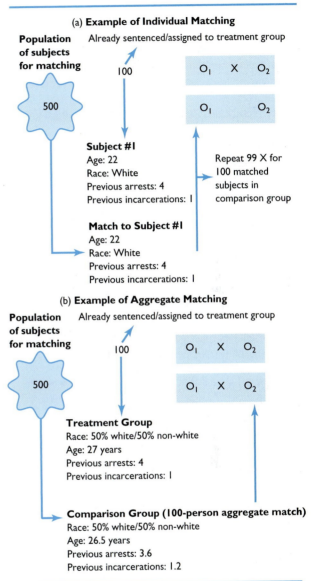

(a) **Example of Individual Matching**

with random assignment on factors that are both measured and unknown to the researcher. Thus, the results produced from a nonequivalent group design, even with matching, are at a greater risk of alternative explanations than an experimental design that features random assignment.

The previous discussion is not to suggest that the nonequivalent group design cannot be useful in answering important research questions. Rather, it is to suggest that the nonequivalent group design, and hence any quasi-experiment, is more susceptible to alternative explanations than the classic experimental design because

RESEARCH IN THE NEWS
The Effects of Red Light Camera (RLC) Enforcement

On March 15, 2009, an article appeared in the *Santa Cruz Sentinel* entitled "Ticket's in the Mail: Red-Light Cameras Questioned." The article stated "while studies show fewer T-bone crashes at lights with cameras and fewer drivers running red lights, the number of rear-end crashes increases."[24] The study mentioned in the newspaper, which showed fewer drivers running red lights with cameras, was conducted by Richard Retting, Susan Ferguson, and Charles Farmer of the Insurance Institute for Highway Safety (IIHS).[25] They completed a quasi-experimental study in Philadelphia to determine the impact of red light cameras (RLC) on red light violations. In the study, the researchers selected nine intersections—six of which were experimental sites that utilized RLCs and three comparison sites that did not utilize RLCs. The six experimental sites were located in Philadelphia, Pennsylvania, and the three comparison sites were located in Atlantic County, New Jersey. The researchers chose the comparison sites based on the proximity to Philadelphia, the ability to collect data using the same methods as at experimental intersections (e.g., the use of cameras for viewing red light traffic), and the fact that police officials in Atlantic County had offered assistance selecting and monitoring the intersections.

The authors collected three phases of information in the RLC study at the experimental and comparison sites:

Phase 1 Data Collection: Baseline (pre-test) data collection at the experimental and comparison sites consisting of the number of vehicles passing through each intersection, the number of red light violations, and the rate of red light violations per 10,000 vehicles.

Phase 2 Data Collection: Number of vehicles traveling through experimental and comparison intersections, number of red light violations after a 1-second yellow light increase at the experimental sites (treatment 1), number of red light violations at comparison sites without a 1-second yellow light increase, and red light violations per 10,000 vehicles at both experimental and comparison sites.

Phase 3 Data Collection: Red light violations after a 1-second yellow light increase and RLC enforcement at the experimental sites (treatment 2), red light violations at comparison sites without a 1-second yellow increase or RLC enforcement, number of vehicles passing through the experimental and comparison intersections, and the rate of red light violations per 10,000 vehicles.

The researchers operationalized "red light violations" as those where the vehicle entered the intersection one-half of a second or more after the onset of the red signal where the vehicle's rear tires had to be positioned behind the crosswalk or stop line prior to entering on red. Vehicles already in the intersection at the onset of the red light, or those making a right turn on red with or without stopping were not considered red light violations.

The researchers collected video data at each of the experimental and comparison sites during Phases 1–3. This allowed the researchers to examine red light violations before, during, and after the implementation of red light enforcement and yellow light time increases. Based on an analysis of data, the researchers revealed that the implementation of a 1-second yellow light increase led to reductions in the rate of red light violations from Phase 1 to Phase 2 in all of the experimental sites. In 2 out of 3 comparison sites, the rate of red light violations also decreased, despite no yellow light increase. From Phase 2 to Phase 3 (the enforcement of red light camera violations in addition to a 1-second yellow light increase at experimental sites), the authors noted decreases in the rate of red light violations in all experimental sites, and decreases among 2 of 3 comparison sites without red light enforcement in effect.

Concluding their study, the researchers noted that the study "found large and highly significant incremental reductions in red light running associated with increased yellow signal timing followed by the introduction of red light cameras." Despite these findings, the researchers noted a number of potential factors to consider in light of the findings: the follow-up time periods utilized when counting red light violations before and after the treatment conditions were instituted; publicity about red light camera enforcement; and the size of fines associated with red light camera enforcement (the fine in Philadelphia was $100, higher than in many other cities), among others.

After reading about the study used in the newspaper article, has your impression of the newspaper headline and quote changed?

For more information and research on the effect of RLCs, visit the Insurance Institute for Highway Safety at http://www.iihs.org/research/topics/rlr.html.

---

of the absence of random assignment. As a result, a researcher must be prepared to rule out potential alternative explanations. Quasi-experimental designs that lack a pre-test or a comparison group are even less desirable than the nonequivalent group design and are subject to additional alternative explanations because of these missing parts. Although the quasi-experiment may be all that is available and still can serve as an important

TABLE 5.5 | One-Group Longitudinal Design

Treatment	NR	O_1	O_1	O_1	O_1	X	O_2	O_2	O_2	O_2
				Pre-Test				Post-Test		

design in evaluating the impact of a particular treatment, it is not preferable to the classic experiment. Researchers (and consumers) must be attuned to the potential issues of this design so as to make informed conclusions about the results produced from such research studies.

One-Group Longitudinal Design

Like all experimental designs, the quasi-experimental design can come in a variety of forms. The second quasi-experimental design (above) is the one-group longitudinal design (also called a simple interrupted time series design).[26] An examination of this design shows that it lacks both random assignment and a comparison group (see Table 5.5). A major difference between this design and others we have covered is that it includes multiple pre-test and post-test observations.

The one-group longitudinal design is useful when researchers are interested in exploring longer-term patterns. Indeed, the term **longitudinal** generally means "over time"—repeated measurements of the pre-test and post-test over time. This is different from **cross-sectional designs,** which examine the pre-test and post-test at only one point in time (e.g., at a single point before the application of the treatment and at a single point after the treatment). For example, in the nonequivalent group design and the classic experimental design previously examined, both are cross-sectional because pre-tests and post-tests are measured at one point in time (e.g., at a point 6 months after the treatment). Yet, these designs could easily be considered longitudinal if researchers took repeated measures of the pre-test and post-test.

The organization of the one-group longitudinal design is to examine a baseline of several pre-test observations, introduce a treatment or intervention, and then examine the post-test at several different time intervals. As organized, this design is useful for gauging the impact that a particular program, policy, or law has, if any, and how long the treatment impact lasts. Consider an example whereby a researcher is interested in gauging the impact of a tobacco ban on inmate-on-inmate assaults in a prison setting. This is an important question, for recent years have witnessed correctional systems banning all tobacco products from prison facilities. Correctional administrators predicted that there would be a major

increase of inmate-on-inmate violence once the bans took effect. The one-group longitudinal design would be *one* appropriate design to examine the impact of banning tobacco on inmate assaults.

To construct this study using the one-group longitudinal design, the researcher would first examine the rate of inmate-on-inmate assaults in the prison system (or at an individual prison, a particular cellblock, or whatever the **unit of analysis**) prior to the removal of tobacco. This is the pre-test, or a baseline of assault activity before the ban goes into effect. In the design presented above, perhaps the researcher would measure the level of assaults in the preceding four months prior to the tobacco ban. When establishing a pre-test baseline, the general rule is that, in a longitudinal design, the more time utilized, both in overall time and number of intervals, the better. For example, the rate of assaults in the preceding month is not as useful as an entire year of data on inmate assaults prior to the tobacco ban. Next, once the tobacco ban is implemented, the researcher would then measure the rate of inmate assaults in the coming months to determine what impact the ban had on inmate-on-inmate assaults. This is shown in Table 5.5 as the multiple post-test measures of assaults. Assaults may increase, decrease, or remain constant from the pre-test baseline over the term of the post-test.

If assaults increased at the same time as the ban went into effect, the researcher might conclude that the increase was due only to the tobacco ban. But, could there be alternative explanations? The answer to this question is yes, there may be other plausible explanations for the increase even with several months of pre-test data. Unfortunately, without a comparison group there is no way for the researcher to be certain if the increase in assaults was due to the tobacco ban, or some other factor that may have spurred the increase in assaults and happened at the same time as the tobacco ban. What if assaults decreased after the tobacco ban went into effect? In this scenario, because there is no comparison group, the researcher would still not know if the results would have happened anyway without the tobacco ban. In these instances, the lack of a comparison group prevents the researcher from confidently attributing the results to the tobacco ban, and interpretation is subject to numerous alternative explanations.

TABLE 5.6 | Two-Group Longitudinal Design

Treatment	NR	O_1	O_1	O_1	O_1	X	O_2	O_2	O_2	O_2
Comparison	NR	O_1	O_1	O_1	O_1		O_2	O_2	O_2	O_2
		Pre-Test					**Post-Test**			

Two-Group Longitudinal Design

A remedy for the previous situation would be to introduce a comparison group (see Table 5.6). Prior to the full tobacco ban, suppose prison administrators conducted a **pilot program** at one prison to provide insight as to what would happen once the tobacco ban went into effect systemwide. To conduct this pilot, the researcher identified one prison. At this prison, the researcher identified two different cellblocks, C-Block and D-Block. C-Block constitutes the treatment group, or the cellblock of inmates who will have their tobacco taken away. D-Block is the comparison group—inmates in this cellblock will retain their tobacco privileges during the course of the study and during a determined follow-up period to measure post-test assaults (e.g., 12-months). This is a two-group longitudinal design (also sometimes called a multiple interrupted time series design), and adding a comparison group makes this design superior to the one-group longitudinal design.

The usefulness of adding a comparison group to the study means that the researcher can have more confidence that the results at the post-test are due to the tobacco ban and not some alternative explanation. This is because any difference in assaults at the post-test between the treatment and comparison group should be attributed to the only difference between them, the tobacco ban. For this interpretation to hold, however, the researcher must be sure that C-Block and D-Block are similar or equivalent on all factors that might influence the post-test. There are many potential factors that should be considered. For example, the researcher will want to make sure that the same types of inmates are housed in both cellblocks. If a chronic group of assaultive inmates constitutes members of C-Block, but not D-Block, this differential could explain the results, not the treatment.

The researcher might also want to make sure equitable numbers of tobacco and non-tobacco users are found in each cellblock. If very few inmates in C-Block are smokers, the real effect of removing tobacco may be hidden. The researcher might also examine other areas where potential differences might arise, for example, that both cellblocks are staffed with equal numbers of officers, that officers in each cellblock tend to resolve inmate

disputes similarly, and other potential issues that could influence post-test measure of assaults. Equivalence could also be ensured by comparing the groups on additional evidence before the ban takes effect: number of prior prison sentences, time served in prison, age, seriousness of conviction crime, and other factors that might relate to assaultive behavior, regardless of the tobacco ban. Moreover, the researcher should ensure that inmates in C-Block do not know that their D-Block counterparts are still allowed tobacco during the pilot study, and vice versa. If either group knows about the pilot program being an experiment, they might act differently than normal, and this could become an explanation of results. Additionally, the researchers might also try to make sure that C-Block inmates are completely tobacco free after the ban goes into effect—that they do not hoard, smuggle, or receive tobacco from officers or other inmates during the tobacco ban in or outside of the cellblock. If these and other important differences are accounted for at the individual and cellblock level, the researcher will have more confidence that any differences in assaults at the post-test between the treatment and comparison groups are related to the tobacco ban, and not some other difference between the two groups or the two cellblocks.

The addition of a comparison group aids in the ability of the researcher to isolate the true impact of a tobacco ban on inmate-on-inmate assaults. All factors that influence the treatment group should also influence the comparison group because the groups are made up of equivalent individuals in equivalent circumstances, with the exception of the tobacco ban. If this is the only difference, the results can be attributed to the ban. Although the addition of the comparison group in the two-group longitudinal design provides more confidence that the findings are attributed to the tobacco ban, the fact that this design lacks randomization means that alternative explanations cannot be completely ruled out—but they can be minimized. This example also suggests that the quasi-experiment in this instance may actually be preferable to an experimental design—noting the realities of prison administration. For example, prison inmates are not typically randomly assigned to different cellblocks by prison officers. Moreover, it is highly unlikely that a prison would have two open cellblocks waiting for a researcher to randomly assign incoming inmates to the prison for a tobacco ban study. Therefore, it is likely there would be differences among the groups in the quasi-experiment.

Fortunately, if differences between the groups are present, the researcher can attempt to determine their potential impact before interpretation of results. The researcher can also use statistical models after the ban takes effect to determine the impact of any differences between the groups on the post-test. While the two-group longitudinal quasi-experiment just discussed could also take the form of an experimental design, if random assignment could somehow be accomplished, the previous discussion provides one situation where an experimental design might be appropriate and desired for a particular research question, but would not be realistic considering the many barriers.

THE THREAT OF ALTERNATIVE EXPLANATIONS

Alternative explanations are those factors that could explain the post-test results, other than the treatment. Throughout this chapter, we have noted the potential for alternative explanations and have given several examples of explanations other than the treatment. It is important to know that potential alternative explanations can arise in any research design discussed in this chapter. However, alternative explanations often arise because some design part is missing, for example, random assignment, a pre-test, or a control or comparison group. This is especially true in criminal justice where researchers often conduct field studies and have less control over their study conditions than do researchers who conduct experiments under highly controlled laboratory conditions. A prime example of this is the tobacco ban study, where it would be difficult for researchers to ensure that C-Block inmates, the treatment group, were completely tobacco free during the course of the study.

Alternative explanations are typically referred to as **threats to internal validity.** In this context, if an experiment is internally valid, it means that alternative explanations have been ruled out and the treatment is the only factor that produced the results. If a study is *not* internally valid, this means that alternative explanations for the results exist or potentially exist. In this section, we focus on some common alternative explanations that may arise in experimental and quasi-experimental designs.[27]

Selection Bias

One of the more common alternative explanations that may occur is **selection bias.** Selection bias generally indicates that the treatment group (or experimental group) is somehow different from the comparison group (or control group) on a factor that could influence the post-test results. Selection bias is more often a threat in quasi-experimental designs than experimental designs due to the lack of random assignment. Suppose in our study of the prison tobacco ban, members of C-Block were substantially younger than members of D-Block, the comparison group. Such an imbalance between the groups would mean the researcher would not know if the differences in assaults are real (meaning the result of the tobacco ban) or a result of the age differential. Recall that research shows that younger inmates are more assaultive than older inmates and so we would expect more assaults among the younger offenders independent of the tobacco ban.

In a quasi-experiment, selection bias is perhaps the most prevalent type of alternative explanation and can seriously compromise results. Indeed, many of the examples above have referred to potential situations where the groups are imbalanced or not equivalent on some important factor. Although selection bias is a common threat in quasi-experimental designs because of lack of random assignment, and can be a threat in experimental designs because the groups could differ by chance alone or the practice of randomization was not maintained throughout the study (see Classics in CJ Research-MDVE above), a researcher may be able to detect such differentials. For example, the researcher could detect such differences by comparing the groups on the pre-test or other types of information before the start of the study. If differences were found, the researcher could take measures to correct them. The researcher could also use a statistical model that could account or control for differences between the groups and isolate the impact of the treatment, if any. This discussion is beyond the scope of this text but would be a potential way to deal with selection bias and estimate the impact of this bias on study results. The researcher could also, if possible, attempt to re-match the groups in a quasi-experiment or randomly assign the groups a second time in an experimental design to ensure equivalence. At the least, the researcher could recognize the group differences and discuss their potential impact on the results. Without a pre-test or other pre-study information on study participants, however, such differences might not be able to be detected and, therefore, it would be more difficult to determine how the differences, as a result of selection bias, influenced the results.

History

Another potential alternative explanation is **history.** History refers to any event experienced differently by the treatment and comparison groups in the time between the pre-test and the post-test that could impact results. Suppose during the course of the tobacco ban study several riots occurred on D-Block, the comparison group. Because of the riots, prison officers "locked down" this cellblock numerous times. Because D-Block inmates were locked down at various times, this could have affected their ability to otherwise engage in inmate assaults. At the end of the study, the assaults in D-Block might have decreased from their pre-test levels because of the lockdowns, whereas in C-Block assaults may have occurred at their normal pace because there was not a lockdown, or perhaps even increased from the pre-test because tobacco was also taken away. Even if the tobacco ban had no effect and assaults remained constant in C-Block from pre- to post-test, the lockdown in D-Block might make it appear that the tobacco ban led to increased assaults in C-Block. Thus, the researcher would not know if the post-test results for the C-Block treatment group were attributable to the tobacco ban or the simple fact that D-Block inmates were locked down and their assault activity was artificially reduced. In this instance, the comparison group becomes much less useful because the lockdown created a historical factor that imbalanced the groups during the treatment phase and nullified the comparison.

Maturation

Another potential alternative explanation is **maturation.** Maturation refers to the natural biological, psychological, or emotional processes we all experience as time passes—aging, becoming more or less intelligent, becoming bored, and so on. For example, if a researcher was interested in the effect of a boot camp on recidivism for juvenile offenders, it is possible that over the course of the boot camp program the delinquents naturally matured as they aged and this produced the reduction in recidivism—not that the boot camp somehow led to this reduction. This threat is particularly applicable in situations that deal with populations that rapidly change over a relatively short period of time or when a treatment lasts a considerable period of time. However, this threat could be eliminated with a comparison group that is similar to the treatment group. This is because the maturation effects would occur in both groups and the effect of the boot camp, if any, could be isolated.

This assumes, however, that the groups are matched and equitable on factors subject to the maturation process, such as age. If not, such differentials could be an alternative explanation of results. For example, if the treatment and comparison groups differ by age, on average, this could mean that one group changes or matures at a different rate than the other group. This differential rate of change or maturation as a result of the age differential could explain the results, not the treatment. This example demonstrates how selection bias and maturation can interact at the same time as alternative explanations. This example also suggests the importance of an equivalent control or comparison group to eliminate or minimize the impact of maturation as an alternative explanation.

Attrition or Subject Mortality

Attrition or **subject mortality** is another typical alternative explanation. Attrition refers to differential loss in the number or type of subjects between the treatment and comparison groups and can occur in both experimental and quasi-experimental designs. Suppose we wanted to conduct a study to determine who is the better research methods professor among the authors of this textbook. Let's assume that we have an experimental design where students were randomly assigned to professor 1, professor 2, or professor 3. By randomly assigning students to each respective professor, there is greater probability that the groups are equivalent and thus there are no differences between the three groups with one exception—the professor they receive and his or her particular teaching and delivery style. This is the treatment. Let's also assume that the professors will be administering the same tests and using the same textbook. After the group members are randomly assigned, a pre-treatment evaluation shows the groups are in fact equivalent on all important known factors that could influence post-test scores, such as grade point average, age, time in school, and exposure to research methods concepts. Additionally, all groups scored comparably on a pre-test of knowledge about research methods, thus there is more confidence that the groups are in fact equivalent.

At the conclusion of the study, we find that professor 2's group has the lowest final test scores of the three. However, because professor 2 is such an outstanding professor, the results appear odd. At first glance, the researcher thinks the results could have been influenced by students dropping out of the class. For example, perhaps several of professor 2's students dropped the course but none did from the classes of professor 1 or 3.

It is revealed, however, that an equal number of students dropped out of all three courses before the post-test and, therefore, this could not be the reason for the low scores in professor 2's course. Upon further investigation, however, the researcher finds that although an equal number of students dropped out of each class, the dropouts in professor 2's class were some of his best students. In contrast, those who dropped out of professor 1's and professor 3's courses were some of their poorest students. In this example, professor 2 appears to be the least effective teacher. However, this result appears to be due to the fact that his best students dropped out, and this highly influenced the final test average for his group. Although there was not a differential loss of subjects in terms of numbers (which can also be an attrition issue), there was differential loss in the types of students. This differential loss, not the teaching style, is an alternative explanation of the results.

Testing or Testing Bias

Another potential alternative explanation is **testing** or **testing bias.** Suppose that after the pre-test of research methods knowledge, professor 1 and professor 3 reviewed the test with their students and gave them the correct answers. Professor 2 did not. The fact that professor 1's and professor 3's groups did better on the post-test final exam may be explained by the finding that students in those groups remembered the answers to the pre-test, were thus biased at the pre-test, and this artificially inflated their post-test scores. Testing bias can explain the results because students in groups 1 and 3 may have simply remembered the answers from the pre-test review. In fact, the students in professor 1's and 3's courses may have scored high on the post-test without ever having been exposed to the treatment because they were biased at the pre-test.

Instrumentation

Another alternative explanation that can arise is **instrumentation.** Instrumentation refers to changes in the measuring instrument from pre- to post-test. Using the previous example, suppose professors 1 and 3 did not give the same final exam as professor 2. For example, professors 1 and 3 changed the final exam and professor 2 kept the final exam the same as the pre-test. Because professors 1 and 3 changed the exam, and perhaps made it easier or somehow different from the pre-test exam, results that showed lower scores for professor 2's students may be related only to instrumentation changes from pre- to post-test. Obviously, to limit the influence of instrumentation, researchers should make sure that instruments remain consistent from pre- to post-test.

Reactivity

A final alternative explanation is **reactivity.** Reactivity occurs when members of the treatment or experimental group change their behavior simply as a result of being part of a study. This is akin to the finding that people tend to change their behavior when they are being watched or are aware they are being studied. If members of the experiment know they are part of an experiment and are being studied and watched, it is possible that their behavior will change independent of the treatment. If this occurs, the researcher will not know if the behavior change is the result of the treatment, or simply a result of being part of a study. For example, suppose a researcher wants to determine if a boot camp program impacts the recidivism of delinquent offenders. Members of the experimental group are sentenced to boot camp and members of the control group are released on their own recognizance to their parents. Because members of the experimental group know they are part of the experiment, and hence being watched closely after they exit boot camp, they may artificially change their behavior and avoid trouble. Their change of behavior may be totally unrelated to boot camp, but rather, to their knowledge of being part of an experiment.

Other Potential Alternative Explanations

The above discussion provided some typical alternative explanations that may arise with the designs discussed in this chapter. There are, however, other potential alternative explanations that may arise. These alternative explanations arise only when a control or comparison group is present.

One such alternative explanation is **diffusion of treatment.** Diffusion of treatment occurs when the control or comparison group learns about the treatment its members are being denied and attempts to mimic the behavior of the treatment group. If the control group is successful in mimicking the experimental group, for example, the results at the end of the study may show similarity in outcomes between groups and cause the researcher to conclude that the program had no effect. In fact, however, the finding of no effect can be explained by the comparison group mimicking the treatment group.[28] In reality, there may be no effect of the treatment, but the researcher would not know this for sure because the control group effectively transformed into another experimental group—there is then no baseline of comparison. Consider a study where a researcher wants to determine the impact of a training program on class behavior and participation. In this study, the experimental group is exposed to several sessions of training on how to act appropriately in class and how to engage in class participation. The control group does not receive such training, but they are aware that they are part of an experiment. Suppose after a few class sessions the control group starts to mimic the behavior of the experimental group, acting the same way and participating in class the same way. At the conclusion of the study, the researcher might determine that the program had no impact because the comparison group, which did not receive the new program, showed similar progress.

In a related explanation, sometimes the comparison or control group learns about the experiment and attempts to compete with the experimental or treatment group. This alternative explanation is called **compensatory rivalry.** For example, suppose a police chief wants to determine if a new training program will increase the endurance of SWAT team officers. The chief randomly assigns SWAT members to either an experimental or control group. The experimental group will receive the new endurance training program and the control group will receive the normal program that has been used for years. During the course of the study, suppose the control group learns that the treatment group is receiving the new endurance program and starts to compete with the experimental group. Perhaps the control group runs five more miles per day and works out an extra hour in the weight room, in addition to their normal endurance program. At the end of the study, and due to the control group's extra and competing effort, the results might show no effect of the new endurance program, and at worst, experimental group members may show a decline in endurance compared to the control group. The rivalry or competing behavior actually explains the results, not that the new endurance program has no effect or a damaging effect. Although the new endurance program may in reality have no effect, this cannot be known because of the actions of the control group, who learned about the treatment and competed with the experimental group.

Closely related to compensatory rivalry is the alternative explanation of comparison or control group **demoralization.**[29] In this instance, instead of competing with the experimental or treatment group, the control or comparison group simply gives up and changes their normal behavior. Using the SWAT example, perhaps the control group simply quits their normal endurance program when they learn about the treatment group receiving the new endurance program. At the post-test, their endurance will likely drop considerably compared to the treatment group. Because of this, the new endurance program might emerge as a shining success. In reality, however, the researcher will not know if any changes in endurance between the experimental and control groups are a result of the new endurance program or the control group giving up. Due to their giving up, there is no longer a comparison group of equitable others, the change in endurance among the treatment group members could be attributed to a number of alternative explanations, for example, maturation. If the comparison group behaves normally, the researcher will be able to exclude maturation as a potential explanation. This is because any maturation effects will occur in both groups.

The previous discussion suggests that when the control or comparison group learns about the experiment and the treatment they are denied, potential alternative explanations can arise. Perhaps the best remedy to protect from the alternative explanations just discussed is to make sure the treatment and comparison groups do not have contact with one another. In laboratory experiments this can be ensured, but sometimes this is a problem in criminal justice studies, which are often conducted in the field.

The previous discussion also suggests that there are numerous alternative explanations that can impact the interpretation of results from a study. A careful researcher would know that alternative explanations must be ruled out before reaching a definitive conclusion about the impact of a particular program. The researcher must be attuned to these potential alternative explanations because they can influence results and how results are interpreted. Moreover, the discussion shows that several alternative explanations can occur at the same time. For example, it is possible that selection bias, maturation, attrition, and compensatory rivalry all emerge as alternative explanations in the same study. Knowing about these potential alternative explanations and how they can impact the results of a study is what distinguishes a consumer of research from an educated consumer of research.

CHAPTER SUMMARY

The primary focus of this chapter was the classic experimental design, the foundation for other types of experimental and quasi-experimental designs. The classic experimental design is perhaps the most useful design when exploring causal relationships. Often, however, researchers cannot employ the classic experimental design to answer a research question. In fact, the classic experimental design is rare in criminal justice and criminology because it is often difficult to ensure random assignment for a variety of reasons. In circumstances where an experimental design is appropriate but not feasible, researchers may turn to one of many quasi-experimental designs. The most important difference between the two is that quasi-experimental designs do not feature random assignment. This can create potential problems for researchers. The main problem is that there is a greater chance the treatment and comparison groups may differ on important characteristics that could influence the results of a study. Although researchers can attempt to prevent imbalances between the groups by matching them on important known characteristics, it is still much more difficult to establish equivalence than it is in the classic experiment. As

such, it becomes more difficult to determine what impact a treatment had, if any, as one moves from an experimental to a quasi-experimental design.

Perhaps the most important lesson to be learned in this chapter is that to be an educated consumer of research results requires an understanding of the type of design that produced the results. There are numerous ways experimental and quasi-experimental designs can be structured. This is why much attention was paid to the classic experimental design. In reality, all experimental and quasi-experimental designs are variations of the classic experiment in some way—adding or deleting certain components. If the components and organization and logic of the classic experimental design are understood, consumers of research will have a better understanding of the results produced from any sort of research design. For example, what problems in interpretation arise when a design lacks a pre-test, a control group, or random assignment? Having an answer to this question is a good start toward being an informed consumer of research results produced through experimental and quasi-experimental designs.

CRITICAL THINKING QUESTIONS

1. Why is randomization/random assignment preferable to matching? Provide several reasons with explanation.

2. What are some potential reasons a researcher would not be able to utilize random assignment?

3. What is a major limitation of matching?

4. What is the difference between a longitudinal study and a cross-sectional study?

5. Describe a hypothetical study where maturation, and not the treatment, could explain the outcomes of the research.

KEY TERMS

association (or covariance or correlation): One of three conditions that must be met for establishing cause and effect, or a causal relationship. Association refers to the condition that X and Y must be related for a causal relationship to exist. Association is also referred to as covariance or correlation. Although two variables may be associated (or covary or be correlated), this does not automatically imply that they are causally related

attrition or subject mortality: A threat to internal validity, it refers to the differential loss of subjects between the experimental (treatment) and control (comparison) groups during the course of a study

cause and effect relationship: A cause and effect relationship occurs when one variable causes another, and no other explanation for that relationship exists

classic experimental design or experimental design: A design in a research study that features random assignment to an experimental or control group. Experimental designs can vary tremendously, but a constant feature is random assignment, experimental and control groups, and a post-test. For example, a classic experimental design features random assignment, a treatment, experimental and control groups, and pre- and post-tests

comparison group: The group in a quasi-experimental design that does not receive the treatment. In an experimental design, the comparison group is referred to as the control group

compensatory rivalry: A threat to internal validity, it occurs when the control or comparison group attempts to compete with the experimental or treatment group

control group: In an experimental design, the control group does not receive the treatment. The control group serves as a baseline of comparison to the experimental group. It serves as an example of what happens when a group equivalent to the experimental group does not receive the treatment

cross-sectional designs: A measurement of the pre-test and post-test at one point in time (e.g., six months before and six months after the program)

demoralization: A threat to internal validity closely associated with compensatory rivalry, it occurs when the control or comparison group gives up and changes their normal behavior. While in compensatory rivalry the group members compete, in demoralization, they simply quit. Both are not normal behavioral reactions

dependent variable: Also known as the outcome in a research study. A post-test is a measure of the dependent variable

diffusion of treatment: A threat to internal validity, it occurs when the control or comparison group members learn that they are not getting the treatment and attempt to mimic the behavior of the experimental or treatment group. This mimicking may make it seem as if the treatment is having no effect, when in fact it may be

elimination of alternative explanations: One of three conditions that must be met for establishing cause and effect. Elimination of alternative explanations means that the researcher has ruled out other explanations for an observed relationship between X and Y

experimental group: In an experimental design, the experimental group receives the treatment

history: A threat to internal validity, it refers to any event experienced differently by the treatment and comparison groups—an event that could explain the results other than the supposed cause

independent variable: Also called the cause

instrumentation: A threat to internal validity, it refers to changes in the measuring instrument from pre- to post-test

longitudinal: Refers to repeated measurements of the pre-test and post-test over time, typically for the same group of individuals. This is the opposite of cross-sectional

matching: A process sometimes utilized in some quasi-experimental designs that feature treatment and comparison groups. Matching is a process whereby the researcher attempts to ensure equivalence between the treatment and comparison groups on known information, in the absence of the ability to randomly assign the groups

maturation: A threat to internal validity, maturation refers to the natural biological, psychological, or emotional processes as time passes

negative association: Refers to a negative association between two variables. A negative association is demonstrated when X increases and Y decreases, or X decreases and Y increases. Also known as an inverse relationship—the variables moving in opposite directions

operationalized or operationalization: Refers to the process of assigning a working definition to a concept. For example, the concept of intelligence can be operationalized or defined as grade point average or score on a standardized exam, among others

pilot program or test: Refers to a smaller test study or pilot to work out problems before a larger study and to anticipate changes needed for a larger study. Similar to a test run

positive association: Refers to a positive association between two variables. A positive association means as X increases, Y increases, or as X decreases, Y decreases

post-test: The post-test is a measure of the dependent variable after the treatment has been administered

pre-test: The pre-test is a measure of the dependent variable or outcome before a treatment is administered

quasi-experiment: A quasi-experiment refers to any number of research design configurations that resemble an experimental design but primarily lack random assignment. In the absence of random assignment, quasi-experimental designs feature matching to attempt equivalence

random assignment: Refers to a process whereby members of the experimental group and control group are assigned to each group through a random and unbiased process

random selection: Refers to selecting a smaller but representative subset from a population. Not to be confused with random assignment

reactivity: A threat to internal validity, it occurs when members of the experimental (treatment) or control (comparison) group change their behavior unnaturally as a result of being part of a study

selection bias: A threat to internal validity, selection bias occurs when the experimental (treatment) group and control (comparison) group are not equivalent. The difference between the groups can be a threat to internal validity, or, an alternative explanation to the findings

spurious: A spurious relationship is one where X and Y appear to be causally related, but in fact the relationship is actually explained by a variable or factor other than X

testing or testing bias: A threat to internal validity, it refers to the potential of study members being biased prior to a treatment, and this bias, rather than the treatment, may explain study results

threat to internal validity: Also known as alternative explanation to a relationship between X and Y. Threats to internal validity are factors that explain Y, or the dependent variable, and are not X, or the independent variable

timing: One of three conditions that must be met for establishing cause and effect. Timing refers to the condition

that X must come before Y in time for X to be a cause of Y. While timing is necessary for a causal relationship, it is not sufficient, and considerations of association and eliminating other alternative explanations must be met

treatment: A component of a research design, it is typically denoted by the letter X. In a research study on the impact of teen court on juvenile recidivism, teen court is the treatment. In a classic experimental design, the treatment is given only to the experimental group, not the control group

treatment group: The group in a quasi-experimental design that receives the treatment. In an experimental design, this group is called the experimental group

unit of analysis: Refers to the focus of a research study as being individuals, groups, or other units of analysis, such as prisons or police agencies, and so on

variable(s): A variable is a concept that has been given a working definition and can take on different values. For example, intelligence can be defined as a person's grade point average and can range from low to high or can be defined numerically by different values such as 3.5 or 4.0

E N D N O T E S

1 Povitsky, W., N. Connell, D. Wilson, & D. Gottfredson. (2008). "An experimental evaluation of teen courts." *Journal of Experimental Criminology,* 4, 137–163.

2 Hirschi, T., and H. Selvin (1966). "False criteria of causality in delinquency." *Social Problems,* 13, 254–268.

3 Robert Roy Britt, "Churchgoers Live Longer." April, 3, 2006. http://www.livescience.com/health/060403_church_good.html. Retrieved on September 30, 2008.

4 Kalist, D., and D. Yee (2009). "First names and crime: Does unpopularity spell trouble?" *Social Science Quarterly,* 90 (1), 39–48.

5 Sherman, L. (1992). *Policing domestic violence.* New York: The Free Press.

6 For historical and interesting reading on the effects of weather on crime and other disorder, see Dexter, E. (1899). "Influence of weather upon crime." *Popular Science Monthly,* 55, 653–660 in Horton, D. (2000). *Pioneering Perspectives in Criminology.* Incline Village, NV: Copperhouse.

7 http://www.escapistmagazine.com/news/view/111191-Less-Crime-in-U-S-Thanks-to-Videogames, retrieved on September 13, 2011. This news article was in response to a study titled "Understanding the effects of violent videogames on violent crime." See Cunningham, Scott,

Engelstätter, Benjamin, and Ward, (April 7, 2011). Available at SSRN: http://ssrn.com/abstract=1804959.

8 Cohn, E. G. (1987). "Changing the domestic violence policies of urban police departments: Impact of the Minneapolis experiment." *Response,* 10 (4), 22–24.

9 Schmidt, Janell D., & Lawrence W. Sherman (1993). "Does arrest deter domestic violence?" *American Behavioral Scientist,* 36 (5), 601–610.

10 Maxwell, Christopher D., Joel H. Garner, & Jeffrey A. Fagan. (2001). *The effects of arrest on intimate partner violence: New evidence for the spouse assault replication program.* Washington D.C.: National Institute of Justice.

11 Miller, N. (2005). *What does research and evaluation say about domestic violence laws? A compendium of justice system laws and related research assessments.* Alexandria, VA: Institute for Law and Justice.

12 The sections on experimental and quasi-experimental designs rely heavily on the seminal work of Campbell and Stanley (Campbell, D.T., & J. C. Stanley. (1963). *Experimental and quasi-experimental designs for research.* Chicago: RandMcNally) and more recently, Shadish, W., T. Cook, & D. Campbell. (2002). *Experimental and quasi-experimental designs for generalized causal inference.* New York: Houghton Mifflin.

13   Povitsky et al. (2008). p. 146, note 9.

14   Shadish, W., T. Cook, & D. Campbell. (2002). Experimental and quasi-experimental designs for generalized causal inference. New York: Houghton Mifflin Company.

15   Ibid, 15.

16   Finckenauer, James O. (1982). *Scared straight! and the panacea phenomenon.* Englewood Cliffs, N.J.: Prentice Hall.

17   Yarborough, J.C. (1979). Evaluation of JOLT (Juvenile Offenders Learn Truth) as a deterrence program. Lansing, MI: Michigan Department of Corrections.

18   Petrosino, Anthony, Carolyn Turpin-Petrosino, & James O. Finckenauer. (2000). "Well-meaning programs can have harmful effects! Lessons from experiments of programs such as Scared Straight." *Crime and Delinquency,* 46, 354–379.

19   "Swearing makes pain more tolerable" retrieved at http://www.livescience.com/health/090712-swearing-pain.html (July 13, 2009). Also see "Bleep! My finger! Why swearing helps ease pain" by Tiffany Sharples, retrieved at http://www.time.com/time/health/article/0,8599,1910691,00.html?xid=rss-health (July 16, 2009).

20   For an excellent discussion of the value of controlled experiments and why they are so rare in the social sciences, see Sherman, L. (1992). *Policing domestic violence.* New York: The Free Press, 55–74.

21   For discussion, see Weisburd, D., T. Einat, & M. Kowalski. (2008). "The miracle of the cells: An experimental study of interventions to increase payment of court-ordered financial obligations." *Criminology and Public Policy,* 7, 9–36.

22   Shadish, Cook, & Campbell. (2002).

23   Ibid.

24   Kelly, Cathy. (March 15, 2009). "Tickets in the mail: Red-light cameras questioned." *Santa Cruz Sentinel.*

25   Retting, Richard, Susan Ferguson, & Charles Farmer. (January 2007). "Reducing red light running through longer yellow signal timing and red light camera enforcement: Results of a field investigation." Arlington, VA: Insurance Institute for Highway Safety.

26   Shadish, Cook, & Campbell. (2002).

27   See Shadish, Cook, & Campbell. (2002), pp. 54–61 for an excellent discussion of threats to internal validity. Also see Chapter 2 for an extended discussion of all forms of validity considered in research design.

28   Trochim, W. (2001). *The research methods knowledge base,* 2nd ed. Cincinnati, OH: Atomic Dog.

29   Ibid.

C h a p t e r **6**

Qualitative Research in Criminal Justice

CASE STUDY

Exploring the Culture of "Urban Scrounging"[1]

Research Purpose

To describe the culture of urban scrounging, or dumpster diving, and the items that can be found in dumpsters and trash piles.

Methodology

This field study, conducted by Dr. Jeff Ferrell, currently a professor of sociology at Texas Christian University, began in 2002. In December of 2001, after resigning from an academic position in Arizona, Ferrell returned home to Fort Worth, Texas. An avid proponent for and participant in field research throughout his career, he decided to use the next eight months, prior to the 2002 academic year beginning, to explore a culture in which he had always been interested, the urban underground of "scrounging, recycling, and secondhand living" (p. 1). Using the neighborhoods of central Fort Worth as a backdrop, Ferrell embarked, often on his bicycle, into the life of a dumpster diver. While he was not completely homeless at the time, he did his best to fully embrace the lifestyle of an urban scrounger and survive on what he found. For this study, Ferrell was not only learning how to survive off of the discarded possessions of others, he was systematically recording and describing the contents of the dumpsters and trash piles he found and kept. While in the field, Ferrell was also exploring scrounging as a means of economic survival and the social aspects of this underground existence. A broader theme of Ferrell's research emerged as he encountered the number and vast array of items he found discarded in trash piles and dumpsters. This theme concerns the "hyperconsumption" and "collective wastefulness" (pp. 5–6) by American citizens and the environmental destruction created by the accumulating and discarding of so many material goods.

Results and Implications

Ferrell's time spent among the trash piles and dumpsters of Fort Worth resulted in a variety of intriguing yet disturbing realizations regarding not only material excess but also social and personal change. While encounters with others were kept to a minimum, as they generally are for scroungers, Ferrell describes some

As Ferrell described, urban scrounging is a way of life for many, particularly the homeless and under- or unemployed.

123

of the people he met along the way and their conversations. Whether food, clothes, building materials, or scrap metal, the commonality was that scroungers could usually find what they were looking for among the trash heaps and alleyways. Throughout his book, Ferrell often focuses on the material items that he discovered while scrounging. He found so much, he was able to fill and decorate a home with perfectly good items that had been discarded by others, including the bicycle he now rides and a turquoise sink and bathtub. He found books and even old photographs and other mementos meant to document personal history. While discarded, these social artifacts tell the stories of society and often have the chance to find altered meaning when possessed by someone new.

Beyond the things found and people met, Ferrell discusses the boundary shift that has taken urban scrounging from deviant to criminal as lines are often blurred between public access and ownership. Not only do these urban scroungers face the stigma associated with their scrounging activities, those who dive in dumpsters and dig through trash piles can face criminal charges for trespassing. While this makes scrounging more challenging, due to basic survival or interest, the wealth of items and artifacts to be found are often worth the risk. Ultimately, Ferrell's experiences as an urban scrounger provide not only a description of this subculture but also a critique on American consumption and wastefulness, a theme that becomes more important as Americans and others continue in economically tenuous times. ●

IN THIS CHAPTER YOU WILL LEARN:

To explain what it means for research to be qualitative

To describe the advantages of field research

To explain the challenges of field studies for researchers

To provide examples of field research in the social sciences

To discuss the case study approach

INTRODUCTION

In Chapter 2, you read about the differences between quantitative and qualitative methodologies. Whereas methods that are quantitative in nature focus on numerical measurements of phenomena, qualitative methods are focused on developing a deeper understanding regarding groups of people, or subcultures, about which little is known. Using detailed description, findings from qualitative research are generally more sensitizing, providing the research community and the interested public information about these generally elusive groups and their behaviors. A debate rages between criminologists as to which type of research should be achieved and referenced more often. The truth is that both have something valuable to offer regarding the study of deviance, crime, and victimization.

FIELD RESEARCH

Qualitative methodologies involve the use of **field research,** where researchers are out among these groups collecting information rather than studying participant behavior through surveys or experiments that have been developed in artificial settings. Field research provides

some of the most fascinating reading because the researcher is observing closely or acting as part of the group and is therefore able to describe in depth not only the subjects' behaviors, but also consider the motivations that drive their behaviors. This chapter focuses on the use of qualitative methods in the social sciences, particularly the use of participant observation to study deviant, and sometimes criminal, behaviors. The many challenges as well as advantages of conducting this type of research will be discussed as will well-known examples of past field research and suggestions for conducting this type of research. First, however, it is important to understand what sets qualitative field research apart from the other methodologies discussed in this text.

The Study of Behavior

It is common for criminal justice researchers to rely on survey or interview methodologies to collect data. One advantage of doing so is being able to collect data from many respondents in a short period of time. Technology has created other advantages with survey methodology. For example, Internet surveys are a convenient, quick, and inexpensive way to reach respondents who may or may not reside nearby. Researchers often survey community residents and university students, but may also focus specifically on offender or victim samples. One significant limitation of using survey methodologies is that they rely on the truthfulness of the respondents. If researchers are interested in attitudes and behaviors that may be illegal or otherwise controversial, it could be that respondents will not be truthful in answering the questions placed before them. Survey research has focused on past or current drug use (see the Monitoring the Future Program), past victimization experiences (see the National Criminal Victimization Survey), and prison sexual assault victimization (see the Prison Rape Elimination Act data collection procedures conducted by the Bureau of Justice Statistics), just to name a few. If a student uses marijuana but does not want anyone to know, they may choose to falsify their survey responses when asked about marijuana use. If a citizen or prison inmate has been sexually assaulted but is too ashamed or afraid to tell anyone, they may be untruthful when asked about such victimization experiences on a survey. The point is, although researchers attempt to better understand the attitudes and behaviors of a certain population through the use of surveys, there is one major drawback to consider: the disjunction between what people say and what they actually do. As mentioned previously, a student may be a drug user but not admit to it. Someone may be a gang member, but say they are not when asked directly about it. Someone may respond that they have never committed a crime or been victimized when in fact they have. In short, people sometimes lie and there are many potential reasons for doing so. Perhaps the offender or drug user has not yet been caught and does not want to be caught. Whatever the reason, this is a hazard of measuring attitudes and behaviors through the use of surveys. One way to overcome the issue of untruthfulness is to conduct research using various forms of actual participation or observation of the behaviors we want to study. By observing someone in their natural environment (or, "the field"), researchers have the ability to observe behaviors firsthand, rather than relying on survey responses. These research strategies are generally known as participant observation methods.

Types of Field Research: A Continuum

Participant observation strategies involve researchers studying groups or individuals in their natural setting. Think of participant observation as a student internship. Students may read about law enforcement in their textbooks and discuss law enforcement issues in class, but only through an internship with a law enforcement agency will a student have a chance to understand how things actually happen from firsthand observation. Field strategies were first developed for social science, and particularly crime, research in the 1920s by researchers working within the University of Chicago's Department of Sociology. The "Chicago School," as this group of researchers is commonly known, focused on ethnographic research to study urban crime problems. Emerging from the field of anthropology, **ethnographic research** relies on field research methodologies to scientifically examine human culture in the natural environment. Significant theoretical developments within the field of criminology, such as social disorganization, which focused on the impact of culture and environment, were advanced at this time. For example, researchers such as Shaw and McKay, Thrasher, and others used field research to study the activities of subcultures, particularly youth gangs, as well as areas of the city that were most impacted by crime. These researchers were not interested in studying these problems from afar. Instead, they were interested in understanding social problems, including the impact of environmental disintegration, from the field.

There are various ways to conduct field research, and these can be placed on a continuum from most to least invasive and also from more qualitative to more quantitative. In attempting to understand phenomena from the standpoint of the actors, a researcher may participate fully in the behaviors of the group or may instead choose to observe from afar as activities unfold. The most invasive, and also most qualitative, form of participant observation is complete participation. The least invasive, and also most quantitative, is complete observation. In between these two are participant as observer and observer as participant. Each of these strategies will now be discussed in more detail.

Complete participation, sometimes referred to as disguised observation, is a method that involves the researcher becoming a full-fledged member of a particular group. For example, if a researcher is interested in understanding the culture of correctional officers, she may apply to be hired on as a correctional officer. Once hired on, the researcher will wear the uniform and obtain firsthand experience working in a prison environment. To study urban gangs, a researcher may attempt to be accepted as a member or associate of the gang. In complete participation, the true identity of the researcher is not known to the members of the group. Therefore, they are ultimately just like any other member of the group under study. Not only will the researcher have the ability to observe the group from the inside, he can also manipulate the direction of group activity through participation or through the use of **confederates.** This method is considered the most qualitative because, as a complete participant, the researcher will be fully sensitized to what it is like to be a member of the group under study, and will fully participate in the group's activities. The researcher can then share the information he has gathered on the group's inner workings, motivations, and activities from the perspective of a group member.

Researchers utilizing the **participant as observer** method will also participate in the activities of the group under study. The difference between the complete participant strategy and participant as observer strategy is that in the participant as observer method, the researcher reveals herself as a researcher to the group. Her presence as a researcher is known. Accordingly, the researcher does not overtly attempt to influence the direction of group activity. While she does participate, the researcher is more interested in observing the group's activity and corresponding behaviors as they occur naturally. So, if a researcher wanted to examine life as a homeless person, she might go to where a group of homeless persons congregate. The researcher would introduce herself as such but, if safe, stay one or many days and nights out with the homeless she meets in order to conduct observations and participate in group activities.

The third participant observation strategy is **observer as participant.** As with the participant as observer method, researchers using the observer as participant method reveal themselves to the group as a researcher. Here again, their presence as a researcher is known. What makes this strategy different from the first two is that the researcher does not participate in the group's activities. While he may interact with the participants, he does not participate. Instead, the researcher is there only to observe. An example of this method would be a researcher who conducts "ride-alongs" in order to study law enforcement behavior during traffic stops. The researcher will interact with the officers, but he will not participate or even exit the car during the traffic stops being observed.

The least invasive participant observation strategy is **complete observation.** As you will learn in Chapter 7, this is a totally unobtrusive method; the research subjects are not aware that they are being observed for purposes of research. Think of a law enforcement officer being on a stakeout. These officers generally sit in unmarked vehicles down the street as they observe the

Using complete observation methods, researchers can study human behavior from afar, eliminating reactivity among study subjects.

movements and activities of a certain person or group of people. Researchers who are complete observers work much the same way. While being the least invasive, complete observation is also the least qualitative. Studying an individual or group from afar means that there is no interaction with that individual. Without this interaction, researchers are unable to gain a more sensitized understanding of the motivations of the group. This strategy is considered to be more quantitative because researchers must rely on counts of activities or movements. For example, if you are a researcher interested in studying how many drivers run a stop sign on campus, you may sit near the intersection and observe driver behavior. In collecting the data, you will count how many drivers make a complete stop, how many come to a rolling stop, and how many run the stop sign altogether. Now, although you may have these counts, you will not know why drivers stopped or not. It could be that one driver had a sick passenger who he was rushing to the hospital and that is why he did not come to a complete stop. As with most quantitative research, as a complete observer, questions of "why?" often go unanswered.

FIGURE 6.1 | Differences among Participant Observation Methods

	Researcher Identity Known	Researcher Participation
Complete Participation	No	Yes
Participant as Observer	Yes	Yes
Observer as Participant	Yes	No
Complete Observation	No	No

Advantages and Disadvantages of Field Research by Method

As with any particular research method, there are advantages and disadvantages to conducting field research. Some of these are specific to the type of field research a researcher decides to conduct. One general advantage to participant observation methods is that researchers are able to study "hard to reach" populations. A disadvantage is that these groups may be difficult to study for a number of reasons. It could be that the group is criminal in nature, such as a youth gang, a biker gang, or the Mafia. While perhaps not criminal, the individual or group may be involved in deviant behaviors that they are unwilling to discuss even with people they know. An additional disadvantage is that there could be administrative roadblocks to conducting such research. If a researcher wants to understand the correctional officer culture but the prison will not allow the researcher to conduct the study, she may have to get hired on and conduct the research as a full participant. Examples of research involving each of these situations will be discussed later in this chapter.

Another challenge for field researchers is the ability to maintain objectivity. In Chapter 2, the importance of objectivity for scientific research was discussed. If data gathered is subjective or biased in some way, research findings will be impacted by this subjectivity and will therefore not be reflective of reality. While objectivity would be easier to maintain from afar, the closer a researcher becomes to a group and its members, the easier it may be to lose objectivity. This is true particularly for complete participants. For researchers who participate as members of the group under study, it may become difficult not to begin to identify with the group. When this occurs, and the researcher loses sight of the research goals in favor of group membership, it is called "**going native.**" This is a hazard of field research in which the researcher spends a significant amount of time, perhaps years, within a group. The researcher may begin to see things from the group's perspective and therefore not be able to objectively

complete the intended study. To balance this possible hazard of complete participation is the advantage of not having **reactivity.** Because the research subjects do not know they are being observed, they will not act any differently than they would under normal circumstances. Researchers therefore avoid the **Hawthorne Effect** when conducting field research as a complete participant.

There is the possibility that a researcher who incorporates the participant as observer strategy may also go native. Although his presence as a researcher is known, he is interacting with the group and participating in group activities. Therefore, it is possible he may begin to lose objectivity due to an attachment to or identification with the group under study. Whereas complete participants can avoid the Hawthorne Effect, participants as observers do not have this luxury. Even though these researchers may be participating in group activities, because their presence as a researcher is known, it can be expected that the group may in some way alter their behavior because they are being observed. An additional disadvantage to this strategy is that it may take time for a researcher to be accepted by group members who are aware of the researcher's presence. If certain group members are uncomfortable with the researcher's presence, they may make it difficult for the researcher to interact with other members or join in group activities.

Researchers on the observing end of the participant observation continuum face some similar and some unique challenges. Those who conduct observer as participant field studies will also face reactivity, or the Hawthorne Effect, because their presence as a researcher is known to the group under study. As in the ride-along example discussed previously, if a patrol officer knows she is being observed, she may alter her behavior in such a way that the researcher is not observing a realistic traffic stop. Additionally, these researchers may face difficulties gaining access or being accepted into the group under study, especially since they are there only to observe and not to participate with the group. In this case, the researcher may be ostracized even further by the group because she is not acting as one of them.

Researchers acting as complete observers to gather data on an individual or group are not limited by reactivity. Because the research subjects are unaware they are being observed, the Hawthorne Effect will not impact study findings. The advantage is that this method is totally unobtrusive, or noninvasive. The main disadvantage here is that the researcher is too far away to truly understand the group and their behaviors. As mentioned previously, at this point, the research becomes quite quantitative because the researcher can only observe and count movements and interactions from afar. Lacking in context, these counts may not be as useful in understanding a group as findings would be from the use of another participant observation method.

Costs   One of the more important factors to consider when determining whether field research is the best option is the demand such research may place on a researcher. If you remember from the opening case study, Ferrell spent months in the field to collect information on urban scrounging. Researchers may spend weeks, months, and even years participating with and/or observing study subjects. Due to this, they may experience financial, personal, and sometimes professional costs. Time away from family and friends can take a personal toll on researchers. If the researcher is funding his own research or otherwise not able to earn a salary while undergoing the field study, he may suffer financially. Finally, also due to time away and perhaps due to activities that may be considered unethical, fieldwork can have a negative impact on a researcher's career. While these demands are very real, past researchers have found ways to successfully navigate the world of field research resulting in fascinating findings and ultimately coming out unscathed from the experience.

Gaining Access   Gaining access to populations of interest is also a difficult task to accomplish as these populations are often small, clandestine groups who generally keep out of the public eye. Field research is unlike survey research in that there is not a readily available list of gang members or dumpster divers from which you can draw a random sample. Instead, researchers often rely on the snowball sampling technique. If you remember from Chapter 3, snowball sampling entails a researcher meeting one or a handful of group members and receiving introductions to other group members from the initial members. One member leads you to the next, who then leads you to the next.

When gathering information as an observer as participant, a researcher should be straightforward and announce her intentions to group members immediately. It may be best to give a detailed explanation of her presence and purpose to group leaders or other decision-makers. If this does not happen, when the group does find out a researcher is in their presence, they may feel the researcher was trying to hide something. If the identity of the researcher is known, it is important that the researcher be a researcher, and that she not pretend to be one of the group, as this may also cause problems. It may be disconcerting

to group members if an outsider thinks she is closer to the group than members are willing to allow her to be.

While complete participant researchers may be introduced to one or more members, this does not mean that they will be readily accepted as part of the group. This is true even if they are acting as full participants. There are some things researchers can do to increase their chances of being accepted. First, researchers should learn the argot, or language, of the group under study. Study subjects may have a particular way of speaking to one another through the use of slang or other vernacular. If a researcher is familiar with this argot and is able to use it convincingly, he will seem less of an outsider. It is also important to time your approach. A researcher should be aware, as much as possible, about what is happening in the group before gaining access. If a researcher is studying drug dealers and there was just a big drug bust or if a researcher is studying gangs and there was recently a fight between two gangs, it may not be the best time to gain access as members of these groups may be immediately suspicious of people they do not know.

Researchers often must find a **gatekeeper** in order to join a group. Gatekeepers are those individuals who may or may not know about the researcher's true identity, who will vouch for the researcher among the other group members and who will inform the researcher about group norms, territory, and the like. Gatekeepers may lobby to have a researcher become a part of the group or to be allowed access to the place where the group gathers. While this is helpful for the researcher, it can be dangerous for the gatekeeper, especially if something goes wrong. If the researcher is attempting to be a full participant but her identity as a researcher is exposed, the gatekeeper may be held responsible for allowing the researcher in. This may be the case even if the gatekeeper was not aware of the researcher's true identity. If a researcher does not want to enter the group himself, he may find an **indigenous observer,** or a member of the group who is willing to collect information for him. The researcher may pay or otherwise remunerate this person for her efforts as she will be able to see and hear what the researcher could not. A similar problem may arise, however, if this person is caught. There may be negative consequences to pay if it is found out that she is revealing information about the group. Additionally, the researcher must be careful when analyzing the information provided as it may not be objective, or may not even be factual at all.

Maintaining Objectivity   Once a researcher gains access, there is another issue she must face. This is the difficulty of remaining an outsider while becoming an

RESEARCH STUDY

Based on his ethnography of African American youth living in poor, inner-city neighborhoods, Elijah Anderson[2] developed a comprehensive theory regarding youth violence and the "code of the street." Anderson explains that, stemming from a lack of resources, distrust in law enforcement, and an overall lack of hope, aggressive behavior is condoned by the informal street code as a way to resolve conflict and earn respect. Anderson's detailed description and analysis of this street culture provided much needed awareness regarding the context of African American youth violence. Like other research discussed in this chapter, these populations could not be sent an Internet survey or be surveyed in a classroom. The only way for Anderson to gain this knowledge was to go out to the streets and observe and interact with the youth himself. To do this, he conducted four years of field research in both the inner city and the more suburban areas of Philadelphia. During this time, he conducted lengthy interviews with youth and acted as a direct observer of their activities. Anderson's research is touted for bringing attention to and understanding of inner-city life. Not only does he describe the "code of the street," but, in doing so, he provides answers to the problem of urban youth violence.

---

insider. In short, the researcher must guard against going native. Objectivity is necessary for research to be scientific. If a researcher becomes too familiar with the group, she may lose objectivity and may even be able to identify with and/or empathize with the group under study. If this occurs, the research findings will be biased and not an objective reflection of the group, what drives the group, and the activities in which the group members participate. For these reasons, it is not suggested that a researcher conduct field research among a group of which he is a member. If a researcher has been a member of a social organization for many years and is friends, or at least acquaintances, with many of the members, it would be very difficult for her to objectively study the group. The researcher may consider the group and the group's activities as normal and therefore miss out on interesting relationships and behaviors. This is also why external researchers are often brought in to evaluate agency programs. If employees of that program are tasked with evaluating it, they may—consciously or not—design the study in such a way that findings are sure to be positive. This may be because they feel that a negative evaluation will mean an end to the program and ultimately an end to their jobs. Having such a stake in the findings of research is sure to impact the objectivity of the person tasked with conducting the study. While bringing in external researchers may ensure objectivity, these researchers face their own challenges. Trulson, Marquart, and Mullings[3] offer some tips for breaking in to criminal justice agencies, specifically prisons, as an external researcher. The first two tips pertain to obtaining access through the use of a gatekeeper. The third tip focuses on the development and cultivation of relationships within the agency in order to maintain access. The remaining tips describe how a researcher can make a graceful exit once the research project is completed while still maintaining those relationships, as well as building new ones, for potential future research endeavors.

- ❏ Tip #1: Get a Contact
- ❏ Tip #2: Establish Yourself and Your Research
- ❏ Tip #3: Little Things Count
- ❏ Tip #4: Make Sense of Agency Data by Keeping Contact
- ❏ Tip #5: Deliver Competent Readable Reports on Time
- ❏ Tip #6: Request to Debrief the Agency
- ❏ Tip#7: Thank Everyone
- ❏ Tip #8: Deal with Adversity by Planning Ahead
- ❏ Tip #9: Inform the Agency of Data Use
- ❏ Tip #10: Maintain Trust by Staying in for the Long Haul (pp. 477–478)

Documenting the Experience Researchers must also decide how best to document their experiences for later analysis. There is a Chinese Proverb that states, "the palest ink is better than the best memory." Applied here, researchers are encouraged to document as much as they can, as giving a detailed account of things that have occurred from memory is difficult. When taking notes, it is important for researchers to be as specific as possible when describing individuals and their behaviors. It is also important for researchers not to ignore behaviors that may seem trivial at the time, as these may actually signify something much more meaningful.

Particularly as a complete participant, researchers are not going to have the ability to readily pull out their note pad and begin taking notes on things they have seen and heard. Even careful note taking can be dangerous

Participant observation research not only informs criminal justice operations, but police and other investigative agencies use these methods as well. Think about an undercover investigation. While the purpose of going undercover for a law enforcement officer is to collect evidence against a suspect, the officer's methods mirror those of an academic researcher who joins a group as a full participant. In the 1970s, FBI agent Joe Pistone[4] went undercover to obtain information about the Bonnano family, one of the major Sicilian organized crime families in New York at the time. Assuming the identity of Donnie Brasco, the jewel thief, Pistone infiltrated the Bonnano family for six years. Using many of the techniques discussed here—learning the argot and social mores of the group, finding a gatekeeper, documenting evidence through the use of recording devices—by the early 1980s, Pistone provided the FBI with enough evidence to put over 100 Mafioso in prison for the remainder of their lives. Many of you may recognize his alias, as Pistone's experiences as an undercover agent were brought to the big screen with the release of *Donnie Brasco,* starring Johnny Depp. Depp's portrayal of Pistone showed not only his undercover persona but also the difficulties he had maintaining relationships with his loved ones. Now, more than 30 years later, people are still interested in Pistone's experiences as Brasco. As recently as 2005, the National Geographic Channel premiered *Inside the Mafia*, a series focused on Pistone's experiences as Brasco. While this is a more well-known example of an undercover operation, undercover work goes on all the time. Whether making drug busts, infiltrating gangs or other trafficking organizations, or conducting a sting operation on one of their own, investigators employ many of the same techniques as field researchers rely upon.

for a researcher who is trying to hide his identity. If a researcher is found to be documenting what is happening within the group, this may breed distrust and group members may become suspicious of the researcher. This suspicion may cause the group members to act unnaturally around the researcher. Even if research subjects are aware of the researcher's identity, having someone taking notes while they are having a casual conversation can be disconcerting. This may make subjects nervous and unwilling to participate in group activities while the researcher is present. Luckily, with the advance of technology, documentation does not have to include a pen and a piece of paper. Instead, researchers may opt for audio and/or visual recording devices. In one-party consent states, it is legal for one person to record a conversation they are having with another. Not all states are one-party consent states, however, so researchers must be careful not to break any laws with their plan for documentation.

Ethical Dilemmas for Field Researchers

As you can tell, field research poses unique complications for researchers to consider prior to and while conducting their studies. Ethical issues posed by field research, particularly field research in which the researcher's identity is not known to research subjects, include the use of deception, privacy invasion, and the lack of consent. How can a researcher obtain informed consent from research subjects if she doesn't want anyone to know research is taking place? Is it ethical to include someone in a research study without his or her permission? When the first guidelines for human subjects research were handed down, they caused a huge roadblock for field researchers. Later, however, it was determined that social science poses less risk to human subjects, particularly those being observed in their natural setting. Because it was recognized that the risk for harm was significantly less, field researchers were allowed to conduct their studies without conditions involving informed consent. The debate remains, however, as to whether it is truly ethical to conduct research on individuals without them knowing. A related issue is confidentiality and anonymity. If researchers are living among study subjects, anonymity is impossible. One way field researchers protect their subjects in this regard is through the use of **pseudonyms.** A pseudonym is a false name given to someone whose identity needs to be kept secret. In writing up their study findings, researchers will use pseudonyms instead of the actual names of study subjects.

Beyond the ethical nature of the research itself, field studies may introduce other ethical dilemmas for the researcher. For example, what if the researcher, as a participating member of a group, is asked to participate in an illegal activity? This may be a nonviolent activity like vandalism or graffiti, or it may be an activity that is more sinister in nature. Researchers, as full participants, have to decide whether they would be willing to commit the crime in question. After all, if caught and arrests are made, "I was just doing research," will not be a justification the researcher will be able to use for his participation.

In 2009, CBS aired a new reality television series, *Undercover Boss*,[5] in which corporate executives go "undercover" to experience life as an employee of their company. Fully disguised, the executives are quickly thrown into the day-to-day operations of their workplaces. From the co-owner of the Chicago Cubs, to the CEO of Norwegian Cruise Line, to the mayor of Cincinnati, these executives conduct field research on camera to gain a better understanding of how their company, or city administration, runs from the bottom up. Often, they find hardworking, talented employees who are deserving of recognition, which is given as the episode comes to a close and the executive reveals himself and his undercover activities to his employees. Other times, they find employees that are not so good for business. Ultimately, the experience provides these executives with awareness they did not have prior to going undercover, and they hope to be able to utilize this knowledge to position their workplaces for continued success. Not only has this show benefited the companies and other workplaces profiled, with millions of viewers each week, it has certainly brought the adventures of field research into prime time.

Even if not a full participant, a researcher may observe some activity that is unlawful. The researcher will then have to decide whether to report this activity or to keep quiet about it. If a researcher is called to testify, there could be consequences for not cooperating. Depending on what kind of group is being studied, these dilemmas may occur more or less frequently. It is important that researchers understand prior to entering the field that they may have to make difficult decisions that like the research itself, could have great costs to them personally and professionally.

Examples of Field Research in Criminal Justice

If you recall from Chapter 2, Humphreys' Tea Room Trade is an example of field research. Humphreys participated to an extent, acting as a "watchqueen" so that he could observe the sexual activities taking place in public restrooms and other public places. Another study exploring clandestine sexual activity was conducted by Styles.[6] Styles was interested in the use of gay baths, places where men seeking to have sexual relationships with other men could have relatively private encounters. While Styles was a gay man attempting to study other gay men, at the outset his intention was to be a nonparticipant observer. Having a friend vouch for him, he easily gained access into the bath and began figuring out how to best observe the scene. After observing and conducting a few interviews, Styles was approached by another man for sexual activity. Although he was resolved to only observe, this time he gave in. From this point on, he began attending another bath and collecting information as a complete participant. Styles' writing is informative, not only for the description regarding this group's activity, but also for the discussion he provides about his travels through the world of field research, beginning as an observer and ending as a complete participant. His writing on insider versus outsider research resulted in four main reflections for readers to consider:

- There are no privileged positions of knowledge when it comes to scrutinizing human group life;

- All research is conditioned by value biases and factual preconceptions about the group being studied;

- Fieldwork is a process of building up images from one's biases, preconceptions, and new information, testing these images against one's observations and the reports of informants, and accepting, modifying, or discarding these images on the basis of what one observes and what one has been told; and

- Insider and outsider researchers will differ in the ways they go about building and testing their images of the group they study. (pp.148–150)

Researchers, including Marquart, Schmid and Jones, and Conover, have conducted participant observation field studies in the prison environment.

Reviewing the literature, one finds that field researchers often choose sexual deviance as a topic for their field studies. Tewksbury and colleagues have researched gender differences in sex shop patrons[7] and places where men have been found to have anonymous sexual encounters[8] such as sex shop theaters.[9] Another interesting field study was conducted by Ronai and Ellis.[10] For this study, Ronai acted as a complete participant, drawing from her past as a table dancer and also gaining access as an exotic dancer in a Florida strip bar for the purpose of her master's thesis research. Building on Ronai's experiences and her interviews with fellow dancers, the researchers examined the interactional strategies used by dancers, both on the stage and on the floor, to ensure a night where the dancers were well paid for their services. In conducting these studies, these researchers were able to expose places where many are either unwilling or afraid to go, or perhaps afraid to admit they go.

In their study of women who belong to outlaw motorcycle gangs, Hopper and Moore[11] used participant observation methods as well as interviews to better understand the biker culture and where women fit into this culture. Moore provided access, as he was once a member and president of Satan's Dead, an outlaw biker club in Mississippi. Like Styles, Hopper and Moore discuss the challenges of conducting research among the outlaw biker population. Having to observe quietly while bikers committed acts opposite to their personal values and not being able to ask many questions or give uninvited comments were just some of the hurdles the researchers had to overcome in order to conduct their study. The male bikers were, at the least, distrustful of the researchers, and the women bikers even more so. While these challenges existed, Hopper and Moore were able to ascertain quite a bit about the female experience as relates to their role in or among the outlaw biker culture.

Ferrell has been one of the most active field researchers of our time. He is considered a founder and remains a steadfast proponent of cultural criminology,[12] a subfield of criminology that examines the intersections of cultural activities and crime. Not only did he conduct the ethnography on urban scrounging discussed at the beginning of this chapter, he has spent more than a decade in the field studying subcultural groups who defy social norms. Crossing the United States, and the globe, Ferrell has explored the social and political motivations of urban graffiti artists,[13] anarchist bicycle group activists, and outlaw radio operators,[14] just to name a few. The research conducted by Ferrell, and others discussed here, has been described as **edgework,** or radical ethnography.

This means that, as researchers, Ferrell and others have gone to the "edge," or the extreme, to collect information on subjects of interest. Ferrell and Hamm[15] have put together a collection of readings based on edgework, as have Miller and Tewksbury.[16] While dangerous and wrought with ethical challenges, their research has shed light on societal groups who, whether by choice or not, often reside in the shadows.

Although ethnographers have spent years studying criminal and other deviant activities, field research has not been limited to those groups. Other researchers have sought to explore what it's like to work in criminal justice from the inside. In the 1960s, Skolnick[17] conducted field research among police officers to better understand how elements of their occupation impacted their views and behaviors. He wrote extensively about the "working personality" of police officers as shaped by their occupational environment, including the danger and alienation they face from those they are sworn to protect, and the solidarity that builds from shared experiences. Beyond law enforcement, there have also been a variety of studies focused on the prison environment. When Ted Conover,[18] a journalist interested in writing from the correctional officer perspective, was denied permission from the New York Department of Correctional Services to do a report on correctional life, he instead applied and was hired on as an actual correctional officer. In *Newjack: Guarding Sing Sing*, Conover offers a compelling account of his **journalistic field research,** which resulted in a one-year stint as a corrections officer. From his time in training until his last days working in the galleries, Conover's experiences provide the reader a look into the challenges faced by correctional officers, stemming not only from the inmates but the correctional staff as well.

Prior to Conover's writing, Marquart was also interested in correctional work and strategies utilized by prison guards to ensure control over the inmate population. Specifically, in the 1980s, Marquart[19] examined correctional officials' use of physical coercion and Marquart and Crouch[20] explored their use of inmate leaders as social control mechanisms. In order to conduct this field study, Marquart, with the warden's permission, entered a prison unit in Texas and proceeded to work as a guard from June 1981 until January 1983. He was able to work in various posts within the institution so that he could observe how prison guards interacted with inmates. Marquart not only observed the prison's daily routine, he examined institutional records, conducted interviews, and also developed close relationships with 20 prison guards and inmate leaders, or building tenders, whom he relied on for their insider knowledge of prison life and inmate control. Based on his fieldwork, Marquart shared his findings regarding the intimidation and physical coercion used by prison guards to discipline inmates. This fieldwork also provided a fascinating look into the building tender system that was utilized as a means of social control in the Texas prison system prior to that system being discontinued.

In the early 1990s, Schmid and Jones[21] used a unique strategy to study inmate adaptation from inside the prison walls. Jones, an offender serving a sentence in a prison located in the upper midwestern region of the United States, was given permission to enroll in a graduate sociology course focused on methods of research. This course was being offered by Schmid and led to collaborative work between the two men to study prison culture. They specifically focused on the experiences of first-time, short-term inmates. With Jones acting as the complete participant and Schmid acting as the complete observer, the pair began their research covertly. While they were aware of Jones's meeting with Schmid for purposes of the research methods course in which he was enrolled, correctional authorities and other inmates perceived Jones to be just another inmate. In the 10 months that followed, Jones kept detailed notes regarding his daily experiences and his personal thoughts about and observations of prison life. Also included in his notes was information about his participation in prison activities and his communications with other similar, first-time, short-term inmates. Once his field notes were prepared, Jones would mail them to Schmid for review. Over the course of these letters, phone calls, and intermittent meetings, new observation strategies and themes began to develop based on the observations made by Jones. Upon his release from prison and their analyzing of the initial data, Jones and Schmid reentered the prison to conduct informed interviews with 20 first-time, short-term inmates. Using these data, Schmid and Jones began to write up their findings, which focused on inmate adaptations over time, identity transformations within the prison environment,[22] and conceptions of prison sexual assault,[23] among other topics. Schmid and Jones discussed how their roles as a complete observer and a complete participant allowed them the advantage of balancing scientific objectivity and intimacy with the group under study. The unfettered access Jones had to other inmates within the prison environment as a complete participant added to the unusual nature of this study yielding valuable insight into the prison experience for this particular subset of inmates.

CASE STUDIES

Beyond field research, **case studies** provide an additional means of qualitative data. While more often conducted by researchers in other disciplines, such as psychology, or by journalists, criminologists also have a rich history of case study research. In conducting case studies, researchers use in-depth interviews and **oral/life history,** or autobiographical, approaches to thoroughly examine one or a few illustrative cases. This method often allows individuals, particularly offenders, to tell their own story, and information from these stories, or case studies, may then be extrapolated to the larger group. The advantage is a firsthand, descriptive account of a way of life that is little understood. Disadvantages relate to the ability to generalize from what may be an atypical case and also the bias that may enter as a researcher develops a working relationship with their subject. Most examples of case studies involving criminological subjects were conducted more than 20 years ago, which may be due to criminologists' general inclination toward more quantitative research during this time period.

The earliest case studies focused on crime topics were conducted in the 1930s. Not only was the Chicago School interested in ethnographic research, these researchers were also among the first to conduct case studies on individuals involved in criminal activities. Shaw's *The Jack Roller* (1930)[24] and Sutherland's *The Professional Thief* (1937)[25] are not only the oldest but also the most well-known case studies related to delinquent and criminal figures. Focused on environmental influences on behavior, Shaw profiled an inner city delinquent male, "Stanley" the "jack roller," who explained why he was involved in delinquent behavior, specifically the crime of mugging intoxicated men. Fifty years later, Snodgrass[26] updated Shaw's work, following up with an elderly "Stanley" at age 70. Sutherland's case study, resulting in the publication of *The Professional Thief,* was based on "Chic Conwell's" account of his personal life and professional experience surviving off of what could be stolen or conned from others. The 1970s and 1980s witnessed numerous publications based on case studies. Researchers examined organized crime figures and families,[27] heroin addicts,[28] thieves,[29] and those who fence stolen property.[30] As with participant observation research, case studies have not been relegated to offenders

RESEARCH IN THE NEWS
Making Critical Choices as a Field Researcher

In conducting field studies, researchers often must make decisions that impact the viability of their research. Sometimes, researchers don't make the best choices. In the 1990s, Dr. Ansley Hamid was an esteemed anthropologist, well-known for his field research focused on the drug subculture.[31] Based on his previous success as a researcher documenting the more significant trends in drug use and addiction, he, through his position as a university professor, was awarded a multimillion-dollar federal research grant to examine heroin use on the streets of New York. It was not long after the grant was awarded, however, that Hamid was accused of misusing the funds provided by the National Institute on Drug Abuse, even going so far as to use the funds to purchase heroin for his own use and the use of his research subjects. While the criminal charges were eventually dismissed, Hamid paid the ultimate professional price for his behavior, particularly his use of the drug, which was documented in his handwritten field notes.[32] As of 2003, the professor was no longer connected to John Jay College of Criminal Justice at the City University of New York. In fact, Hamid is no longer working in higher education at all due to the accusations and accompanying negative publicity. Instead, he owns a candle shop in a small Brooklyn neighborhood. He does not plan to stop researching and writing though. His book, *Ganja Complex: Rastafari and Marijuana,* was published in 2002. This case is a prime example of what can happen when researchers cross the boundary of objectivity. Hamid's brief experience in the shoes of a heroin user led to his ultimate downfall as an objective and respected researcher.

only. In fact, more recently the case study approach has been applied to law enforcement and correctional agencies.[33] These studies have examined activities of the New York City Police Department,[34] the New Orleans Police Department's response in the aftermath of Hurricane Katrina,[35] and Rhode Island's prison system.[36]

As with field research, the case study approach can provide a deeper understanding of individuals or groups of individuals, such as crime families, who live outside of the mainstream. Case studies inform us about the motivations for why individuals or groups behave the way they do and how those experiences or activities were either beneficial or detrimental for them. The same goes for agency research. One department or agency can learn from the experiences of another department or agency. With more recent research utilizing the case study approach, it could be that this methodology will be seen more often in the criminal justice literature.

C H A P T E R   S U M M A R Y

Qualitative research strategies allow researchers to enter into groups and places that are often considered off limits to the general public. The methods and studies discussed here provide excellent examples of the use of field research to discover motivations for the development and patterns of behavior within these groups. These qualitative endeavors offer a unique look into the lives of those who may live or work on the fringes of modern society. As it would be nearly impossible to conduct research on these groups using methods such as experiments, surveys, and formal interviews, participant observation techniques extend the ability of researchers to study activities beyond the norm by participating with and observing subjects in their natural environment and later describing in detail their experiences in the field.

C R I T I C A L   T H I N K I N G   Q U E S T I O N S

1. What are the advantages to using a more qualitative research method?

2. Compare and contrast the four different participant observation strategies.

3. What must a researcher consider before conducting field research?

4. What did Styles learn about conducting research as an insider versus an outsider?

5. How has the case study approach been applied to criminal justice research?

K E Y   T E R M S

case study: In-depth analysis of one or a few illustrative cases

complete observation: A participant observation method that involves the researcher observing an individual or group from afar

complete participation: A participant observation method that involves the researcher becoming a full-fledged member of a particular group; sometimes referred to as disguised observation

confederates: Individuals, who are part of the research team, used to speed up the events of interest when observations are being made

edgework: This refers to researchers going to the "edge," or the extreme, to collect information on subjects of interest

ethnographic research: Relies on field research methodologies to scientifically examine human culture in the natural environment

field research: Research that involves researchers studying individuals or groups of individuals in their natural environment

gatekeeper: A person within the group under study whom the researcher can use to learn about and access the group

going native: A challenge to field research in which the researcher loses her identity as a researcher and begins to identify more with her role as a member of the group under study

Hawthorne Effect: Based on a study of worker productivity, this term refers to changes in behavior caused by being observed

indigenous observer: A person within the group under study who is willing to collect information about the group for compensation

journalistic field research: Field research conducted by journalists and used to write books or articles about a certain topic of interest

observer as participant: A participant observation strategy in which the researcher is known to the group and is only there to observe

oral/life history: Methods used to conduct case studies; similar to an autobiographical account

participant as observer: A participant observation strategy in which the researcher will participate with the group but his identity as a researcher is known

participant observation strategies: First used for social science in the 1920s, these are research methodologies that involve participation and/or observation with the group under study; there are four such strategies

pseudonym: A false name given to someone whose identity needs to be kept secret

reactivity: The problem of having research subjects change their natural behavior in reaction to being observed or otherwise included in a research study

E N D N O T E S

1   Ferrell, J. (2006). *Empire of scrounge: Inside the urban underground of dumpster diving, trash picking, and street scavenging.* New York: New York University Press.

2   Anderson, E. (1999). *Code of the street: Decency, violence, and the moral life of the inner city.* New York: W.W. Norton & Co.

3   Trulson, C., J. Marquart, & J. Mullings. (2004). "Breaking in: Gaining entry to prisons and other hard-to-access criminal justice organizations." *Journal of Criminal Justice Education*, 15(2), 451–478.

4   Lovgren, S. (2005, June 10). "FBI Agent 'Donnie Brasco' recalls life in the Mafia." Retrieved March 7, 2012 from http://news.nationalgeographic.com/news/pf/34063528 .html.

5   See series website, http://www.cbs.com/shows /undercover_boss/.

6   Styles, J. (1979). "Outsider/insider: Researching gay baths." *Urban Life*, 8(2), 135–152.

7   McCleary, R., & R. Tewksbury. (2010). "Female patrons of porn." *Deviant Behavior*, 31, 208–223.

8   Tewksbury, R. (2008). "Finding erotic oases: Locating the sites of men's same-sex anonymous sexual encounters." *Journal of Homosexuality*, 55(1), 1–19.

9   Douglas, B., & R. Tewksbury. (2008). "Theaters and sex: An examination of anonymous sexual encounters in an erotic oasis." *Deviant Behavior*, 29(1), 1–17.

10   Ronai, C. R., & C. Ellis. (1989). "Turn-ons for money: Interactional strategies of the table dancer." *Journal of Contemporary Ethnography*, 18, 271–298.

11   Hopper, C. B., & J. Moore. (1990). "Women in outlaw motorcycle gangs." *Journal of Contemporary Ethnography*, 18(4), 363–387.

12   Ferrell, J., & C. Sanders (Eds.). (1995). *Cultural criminology*. Boston: Northeastern University Press.

13   Ferrell, J. (1996). *Crimes of style: Urban graffiti and the politics of criminality*. Boston: Northeastern University Press.

14   Ferrell, J. (2002). *Tearing down the streets: Adventures in urban anarchy*. New York: Palgrave Mcmillan.

15   Ferrell, J., & M. Hamm (Eds.). (1998). *Ethnography at the edge: Crime, deviance, and field research*. Boston: Northeastern University Press

16   Miller, J., & R. Tewksbury (Eds.). (2001). *Extreme methods: Innovative approaches to social science research*. Boston: Allyn & Bacon.

17   Skolnick, J. (1966). *Justice without trial: Law enforcement in a democratic society*: New York: Wiley & Sons.

18   Conover, T. (2000). *Newjack: Guarding Sing Sing*. New York: Random House, Inc.

19   Marquart, J. (1986). "Prison guards and the use of physical coercion as a mechanism of prisoner control." *Criminology*, 24(2), 347–366.

20   Marquart, J. & B. Crouch. (1984). "Coopting the kept: Using inmates for social control in a southern prison." *Justice Quarterly*, 1(4), 491–509.

21   Schmid, T. J., & R. S. Jones. (1993). "Ambivalent actions: Prison adaptation strategies of first-time, short-term inmates." *Journal of Contemporary Ethnography*, 21(4), 439–463.

22   Schmid, T. J., & R. S. Jones. (1991). "Suspended identity: Identity transformation in a maximum security prison." *Symbolic Interaction*, 14, 415–432.

23   Jones, R. S., & T. J. Schmid. (1989). "Inmates' conceptions of prison sexual assault." *Prison Journal*, 69, 53–61.

24   Shaw, C. (1930). *The jack-roller*. Chicago: University of Chicago Press.

25   Sutherland, E. (1937). *The professional thief*. Chicago: University of Chicago Press.

26   Snodgrass, J. (1982). *The jack-roller at seventy: A fifty year follow-up*. Lexington, MA: D.C. Heath.

27   Abadinsky, H. (1983). *The criminal elite: Professional and organized crime*. Wesport, CT: Greenwood Press.; Anderson, A. (1979). *The business of organized crime*. Stanford: Hoover Institution Press.; Ianni, F., & E. Reuss-Ianni. (1972). *A family business: kinship and social control in organized crime*. New York: Russell Sage.

28   Agar, M. (1973). *Ripping and running: A formal ethnography of urban heroin users*. New York: Seminar Press.; Rettig, R., M. Torres, & G. Garrett. (1977). *Manny: A criminal addict's story*. Boston: Houghton Mifflin.

29   Chambliss, W. (1972). *Boxman: A professional thief's journal, with Harry King*. New York: Harper and Row.; King, H., & W. Chambliss. (1984). *Harry King: A professional thief's journal*. New York: Wiley.

30   Klockars, C. (1974). *The professional fence*. New York: Free Press; Steffensmeier, D. (1986). *The fence: In the shadow of two worlds*. Totowa, NJ: Rowman and Littlefield.

31   Forero, J. (1999, November, 1). "Charges unravel drug-use scholar's career." *The New York Times* Archives. Retrieved March 7, 2012 from http://www.nytimes.com/1999/11/01/nyregion/charges-unravel-drug-use-scholar-s-career.html?pagewanted=print&src=pm.

32   Smallwood, S. (2002, October 25). "Crossing the line: A heroin researcher partakes and pays the price." *The Chronicle of Higher Education*. Retrieved March 7, 2012 from http://chronicle.com/article/Crossing-the-Line/2839.

33   Travis, L. III (1983). "The case study in criminal justice research: Applications to policy analysis." *Criminal Justice Review*, 8, 46–51.

34   Eterno, J. (2003). *Policing within the law: A case study of the New York City Police Department*. Westport, CT: Praeger.

35   Wigginton, M. (2007). "The New Orleans police emergency response to Hurricane Katrina: A case study." A Dissertation completed for the University of Southern Mississippi.

36   Carroll, L. (1998). *Lawful order: A case study of correctional crisis and reform*. New York: Garland.

C h a p t e r **7**

Unobtrusive Methods

CASE STUDY

Crime Reporting on Cable News

Research Exposure

An Examination of Crime Reporting on Cable News[1]

Research Question

To what extent are scholars in the fields of criminal justice and criminology participating in crime reporting on major cable news television programs?

Methodology

For this study researchers utilized content analysis, an unobtrusive method of information collecting, to explore crime reporting across different television media outlets. They first selected the most highly rated news programs from three different 24-hour cable news networks. Included in the study were *Anderson Cooper 360°* (CNN), *The O'Reilly Factor* (FOX), and *Countdown with Keith Olbermann* (MSNBC). Researchers recorded these programs on Tuesdays and Thursdays from June to September, 2006. Episodes of each program were coded first for the inclusion of crime segments and later for discussion of crime causation and crime control, taking into consideration the guests appearing on the programs. Data from 64 episodes were included for final analysis. From these episodes, 180 crime segments were analyzed by the researchers. As there were two researchers, or raters, analyzing the media content, an interrater reliability analysis was conducted to determine coding consistency between the raters.

Results and Implications

Of the three programs analyzed, *Anderson Cooper 360°* devoted the most time to crime reporting (40%) and, across all three programs, crime reporting segments lasted approximately five minutes. As for type of crime discussed most often, the majority of time spent discussing crime (90%) was devoted to street crime, terrorism, and sexual offenses. More than one-third of segments

focused on high-profile cases such as the yet unsolved murder of JonBenet Ramsey in Colorado.

During the crime segments analyzed, there were 347 guest appearances. Scholars and researchers represented 4% of guests while politicians and practitioners (e.g., law enforcement officials, attorneys) were called upon the most (37.5%). During the crime-related segments, the researchers revealed that little discussion was devoted to crime causation and/or crime control. Indeed, only 17% of guests incorporated crime causation into the interview and only 14% of guests mentioned crime control. These findings were similar for both academic and nonacademic guest appearances. When crime causation was discussed, it was found to involve the nonprofessional diagnosing of individual pathology, most frequently mental illness. For those incorporating crime control and policy into their discussions, the majority of guests were in favor of more severe penalties for offenders. Of all of the guest appearances, there were only nine in which guests supported less severe penalties such as rehabilitation or decriminalization. Finally, regarding what type of content the guest appearances provided, more guests were found to be sharing facts or their experience to develop the crime-related story, although 22.5% provided only speculation regarding the case in question. Researchers found that when speculation did not occur naturally, program hosts often encouraged such discussion through the questions they posed during the interview.

Ultimately the findings of this study lend support to past research in the area of crime reporting. Academic guest appearances remain as few and far between as they were two decades ago, and the conversations continue to lack insight regarding crime causation or appropriate preventative measures for and/or responses to criminal events. Of course, as the researchers note, perhaps cable news programs are not the place for such discourse. While one cannot deny that news audiences are aware of the "what," it remains questionable as to whether they will understand the "why," or the context of criminal events, from the information received from cable news media outlets. ●

To explain the reasons for conducting unobtrusive research

To discuss reactivity and the Hawthorne Effect

To locate archives of existing data

To discuss the advantages and disadvantages of using secondary data

To compare and contrast the various methods for conducting unobtrusive research

INTRODUCTION

Previous chapters in this text have examined the many types of data collection techniques most often used by social scientists to study crime. So far you have learned about the variations of the experimental design, data collection utilizing surveys and interviews, as well as participant observation data-gathering techniques. Which technique is chosen by a researcher may depend on any number of factors, including the time available to conduct the study, the monetary or personal costs the study may entail, and the specific research question being examined. The decision on what technique to use may also be influenced by the population of interest. For example, if a researcher wanted to examine gang affiliation among prison inmates, he would seemingly need access to a prison facility, but that is not necessarily the case. This chapter continues the discussion on data-gathering techniques by focusing on additional methodologies that are often described as "unobtrusive."

REACTIVITY AND THE NEED FOR UNOBTRUSIVE RESEARCH

There are many ways in which researchers can implement unobtrusive methodologies, or indirect methods, to answer their research questions. The most popular unobtrusive method in criminal justice research is the use of secondary data. Other techniques include content analysis (as discussed in the example at the beginning of this chapter), the use of archival records, the analyzing of physical traces, simulations, and, as was discussed in Chapter 6, the use of observation. This chapter explores each of these techniques in more depth, giving examples of how they have been used to advance the study of crime-related and other social science topics.

The Impact of Reactivity on Research Findings

Being **unobtrusive**, or nonreactive, implies that what or who is being studied is unaware of its/her role as research participant. Therefore, the information obtained will not be tainted by reactivity. As was discussed in Chapter 6, methodologies that are obtrusive, and therefore known to the study participants, can cause limitations to information gathering. For example, can you recall the Hawthorne Effect? The Hawthorne Effect represents a threat to the internal validity of a study by providing an alternative explanation for study findings. It describes how a research participant may change her behavior (i.e., act unnaturally) due to their role as a research participant. If such an unnatural change in behavior occurs, researchers are no longer measuring a true or natural reaction to what is being studied. Researchers therefore cannot contend that it was the study components alone that influenced the behavior of the study participants. Additionally, reactivity limits the generalizability of study findings as such findings can only be said to be true regarding subjects under the same conditions (i.e., those who are being observed at the time the behavior took place).

The Hawthorne Effect was coined from a research study on the relationship between worker productivity and work environment, which was conducted at the Western Electric–Hawthorne Works factory in the early 20th century. At the time, researchers were interested in understanding whether slight changes to the workers' environment, particularly the lighting in the environment, would alter the workers' productivity. Study findings revealed that there were increases in productivity during the time of the experiments (even when lighting conditions deteriorated); however, these were later attributed not to the change in environment, but rather the perceived interest in and attention being received by the workers (to read more about the Hawthorne Effect, visit the Harvard Business School's Baker Library Historical Collections website). The Hawthorne Effect, and the research on which it is based, continues to be discussed relative to research methods as well as management in the workplace. Interestingly, in 2009, a group of researchers at the University of Chicago reanalyzed the original Hawthorne Works factory data, finding that the original results may have been overstated and that factors other than reactivity may have influenced productivity among the workers being observed.[2] While these new findings have come to light, **reactivity** continues to be recognized as a limitation to research involving human subjects.

As another example of how reactivity may affect researcher findings, let's say a research team wants to examine a program for discipline-problem students. To resolve discipline problems at school, a special program was implemented in which discipline-problem children were taken from their normal classroom and put in an environment where there were fewer students, more one-on-one attention from the teacher, and a specialized learning program. While researchers may be interested specifically in changes in the children's behavior based on the program curriculum, it could be that such behavioral changes were due instead to the extra attention the children were receiving from the teacher and/or from the researchers conducting the program evaluation. Therefore, reactivity may limit the researchers' ability to say with certainty that changes in student performance and behavior were due solely to the program curriculum. Additionally, let's say researchers want to examine how patients in a doctor's office react to longer-than-usual wait times. Under normal circumstances, patients may get agitated and respond negatively to office staff. However, if the same patients knew they were being observed as part of a study, they may respond with more patience. There are numerous situations in which an individual's behaviors may be influenced by the presence of observers or by the simple knowledge that he is part of a research study. Think about how you would respond in a particular situation, such as the example involving the doctor's office, if you knew you were being observed and your actions were being documented.

Advantages of Measuring from Afar

Although there are disadvantages to using unobtrusive measures, there are also advantages to using them in the research process. Perhaps the greatest advantage is the ability to diminish or eliminate reactivity, or the Hawthorne Effect. Utilizing unobtrusive methods, researchers are able to observe, measure, and study subjects without them being aware they are being studied.

In certain unobtrusive methods, such as archival records and secondary data, human subjects are not directly involved in the research, and this eliminates most concerns related to reactivity. The records and data to be analyzed are already in existence, and it is the researcher's job to analyze the information only. This can save valuable resources including time and money and can also allow researchers to study populations that they may not be able to otherwise. For example, if a researcher wanted to explore what the writers of the U.S. Constitution were

thinking at the time of the American Revolution, they could not ask Thomas Jefferson or Benjamin Franklin personally. They could, however, look back to letters, diaries, and other written documents to better understand what was being thought and felt at the time. As another example, if researchers wanted to conduct a study of sexual assault victims but did not have access to such a population, they may look to analyze data, originally collected for a different purpose by a secondary source. National Crime Victimization Survey data, for example, could be used for this purpose. The following sections will examine in more detail the many types of unobtrusive methods utilized by researchers.

Unobtrusive Methods

Secondary Data Analysis   By far the most popular type of unobtrusive research method, secondary data analysis involves the reanalyzing of existing data. Secondary data analysis entails researchers obtaining and reanalyzing data that were originally collected for a different purpose. This is considered unobtrusive because researchers are utilizing data that already exists and therefore do not have to enter the lives of subjects to collect information needed for their study.

Secondary data analysis is a popular methodology among criminal justice researchers due to its many advantages.

The Lost Letter Technique

The same Stanley Milgram responsible for the classic *Obedience to Authority* study discussed in Chapter 2 is also responsible for implementing what is now referred to as the lost letter technique.[3] In the 1960s, Milgram conducted studies in which letters preaddressed and stamped were dropped in pedestrian areas. These letters were preaddressed to organizations that were controversial in nature, such as the Ku Klux Klan and other white supremacist groups. The address, however, was the study site address and not the actual organization address. As a way of indirectly measuring attitudes toward these organizations, specifically acceptability, Milgram determined the rate at which these letters were returned. The letter being returned indicated that someone had taken the time to pick up the letter and send it on. The study revealed low rates of return, which Milgram believed pointed to a general lack of acceptability of these types of organizations.

In the 1990s, Stern and Faber[4] introduced Milgram's lost letter technique to the electronic age. Using e-mails, the researchers conducted two separate experiments. In the first experiment, faculty at a small college were sent one of four prewritten "lost" e-mail messages differing in tone and urgency. Of the faculty who received the "lost" messages, 19% returned the message to the sender. No message was sent on to the person to whom the e-mail was originally addressed. There was also no difference found on rates of return based on the type of message received. In the second experiment, the researchers sought to measure attitudes regarding Ross Perot, a presidential candidate at the time. Using a selection of 200 e-mails obtained from the online "white pages," the researchers sent a variation of e-mails that included a request for assistance with fundraising for Perot's campaign. Of the messages sent, 29% were returned. Based on a content analysis of returned messages, it was found that respondents showed either a negative or neutral attitude toward the Perot campaign. While ethical considerations and limits to generalizability abound when conducting a study using such a technique, it seems that with the aide of technology, this data-gathering tool is not yet lost to the history books.

There exist numerous sources of data that can be useful for developing criminal justice studies. All criminal justice and other government agencies collect official data, of varying extent, for records purposes. The Census Bureau collects information regarding the characteristics of U.S. residents. The Federal Bureau of Investigation (FBI) collects and compiles crime data each year from local and state law enforcement agencies for its Uniform Crime Reports and National Incident Based Reporting System. State prison systems and county and city jail administrators collect data on their inmates. Beyond official data, the U.S. Department of Justice, through its Bureau of Justice Statistics, facilitates numerous surveys including the National Crime Victimization Survey and surveys of inmates in jails, state correctional facilities, and federal correctional facilities. Local program staff who perform evaluations of their work may choose to make data collected for evaluation purposes available to others as may individual researchers who have collected extensive data for research projects. If receiving federal funding to conduct research, it may be a stipulation of the funding agreement that the data be made available for public use after a certain period of time has passed. The National Institute of Justice was the first to have such a requirement, specifying that data collected through NIJ-funded research projects must be given to NIJ once the research had concluded. These data and numerous other datasets are available to researchers for secondary use.

Application processes to obtain original data vary greatly depending on the agency that holds the data, the type of data being requested, and other factors. Sometimes obtaining data requires a phone call only, or establishing a contact within an agency. Other times, especially with datasets that are restricted due to identifying information contained within, there are lengthy applications and in-person meetings with agency administrators required for consideration. Today, data archives exist that make obtaining data as easy as a click of a button. Data archives such as the Interuniversity Consortium for Political and Social Research (ICPSR) at the University of Michigan, which houses the National Archive of Criminal Justice Data, provide access to a broad range of data that can be downloaded quickly by researchers. All that needs to be done is a keyword search to see if archives such as ICPSR have data that may be useful to a researcher beginning a new research project.

Advantages and Disadvantages of Secondary Data

The main reason secondary data analysis is employed so often by criminal justice researchers is that it can save

Research utilizing Geographic Information System (GIS) technology involves the use of mapping hardware, software, and data to examine structural, social, and other area characteristics and how these relate to criminal activity, program delivery, and other criminal justice topics. GIS technology can be used to map where things are, to map quantities, to map densities, to find what is inside or nearby an area, and/or to map change.[5] In the 1950s and 1960s, multiple disciplines contributed to the development of GIS; however, today most academic GIS programs are housed in geography departments on university campuses.

Digital mapping was first adopted by the federal government in the 1960s through its use by the U.S. Census Bureau.[6] In the 1970s and 1980s, private vendors began to offer smaller systems, making GIS analysis affordable for state and city use and eventually for use by community and other smaller organizations. With its increased use for criminal justice applications, the National Institute of Justice (NIJ) developed a Crime Mapping Research Center, which supports research using computerized crime mapping. One NIJ funded research project examined computerized crime mapping use among law enforcement agencies. Surveying over 2,000 law enforcement agencies, Mamalian and LaVigne (1999)[7] found that the majority of agencies sampled used some form of analysis, whether to fulfill reporting requirements to the Uniform Crime Reports (73%) or to calculate agency statistical reports (52%). Very few agencies, however, used computerized crime mapping (13%). When used, the vast majority (91%) reported using computerized crime mapping to conduct geocoding and mapping offense data. As would be expected due to resource allocation, larger departments (36%), those with more than 100 officers, were more likely than smaller departments (3%) to use computerized crime mapping.

GIS has also made its way into the criminal justice academic literature base. Manhein, Listi, and Leitner (2006)[8] used GIS and spatial analysis to examine dumped and scattered human remains in the state of Louisiana. Medina, Siebeneck, and Hepner (2011)[9] used GIS to explore patterns of terrorist incidents occurring in Iraq between 2004 and 2009. Davidson, Scholar, and Howe (2011)[10] utilized GIS-based methods to determine where needle exchange programs were most needed in San Francisco and Los Angeles. As a final example, Caplan, Kennedy, and Miller (2011)[11] relied upon GIS modeling to determine whether risk terrain modeling was more effective than hot spot mapping in the forecasting of shootings, finding that risk terrain modeling was significantly more accurate. As these examples show, GIS, as an unobtrusive method, can be very helpful in answering a wide variation of questions related to the investigation of crime and other behaviors. With more resources allocated to this type of analysis, the future is wide open for GIS to take root in criminal justice research.

valuable time and resources. It may allow the analyzing of data from a place that is normally restricted to researchers such as correctional environments. For research projects that are unfunded, secondary data analysis provides a means for answering research questions that is much less costly than collecting original data. That is not to say that all data is free to researchers. There are datasets that may be difficult to obtain due to fees that must be paid for their use or due to the cost in time and effort that must be put forth to obtain the dataset. Another limitation with the use of official and other existing data is that researchers have no control over the original data collection. There may be issues with the methodology of the original data collection or problems with agency recordkeeping leading to questions of accuracy. Certain variables may not have been included in the original data collection, limiting the questions that can be answered by analyzing the existing data. There may also have been certain biases impacting the original data collection. For example, if an agency or program wanted the original study to show favorable results, it could be that data was "fudged" in such a way that findings were as wanted, instead of as actually existed. While the advantages to the use of secondary data are many, these limitations should be taken into serious consideration prior to beginning a study reliant on secondary data.

Historical Research

The saying that "history repeats itself" may apply to the interest some researchers have in studying the past. Historical research is a form of secondary data analysis that involves obtaining information from historical documents and archival records to answer a research question. An abundance of information exists in libraries and other places where **archives** are kept such as city, county, or state agencies where researchers can examine past events, trends over time, and the like. With the advent of the Internet, retrieving such records has become much less cumbersome.

Archival Records   Archival records are not only used for examining criminal justice-related questions. Outside of our discipline, historical records have been explored by those interested in weather patterns and also by those interested in environmental change. Simonton[12] chronicled the use of historical data in psychological research and concluded that the use of such applications should and will continue. He contends that "methodological advances [including the use of advanced statistical techniques]…render the historical record a far more useful source of scientific data" than may have been previously realized. One recent study[13] utilizing archival records examined the combat histories of veterans seeking treatment for Post-Traumatic Stress Disorder. For this study, researchers explored archival records detailing Vietnam combat from the U.S. National Military Personnel Records Center, finding that Vietnam-era veterans seeking treatment for PTSD may misrepresent their combat involvement, at least according to their documented military record. As relates to criminal justice, archives holding arrest records, prison records, and death row records may be analyzed. Theoretically, Durkheim's influential work on suicide from which his theory of anomie was developed was based on archived records. Additionally, there are numerous examples of the use of historical data to examine criminal offenders from Albini's (1971)[14] study tracing the origins of the Mafia to Sicily to Clarke's (1982)[15] study of assassins and their motivations.

While archival data has been and continues to be utilized for scientific inquiry, it is important to understand the limitations of such data. First, historical data are only available through archives that must be "mined" for their information. In some cases, this may be easy to do, especially if the archive is online and able to be easily searched. In other cases, accessing such data may involve traveling far distances to visit libraries or records offices to gather the information needed. Questions of reliability and validity also confound the use of archival data. Gidley,[16] citing Scott (1990), notes that such data should be judged based on four criteria, its authenticity or genuine nature, its credibility or whether the record is free from distortion, its representativeness as compared to other records of its kind, and its meaning or clarity of the evidence in question. Researchers should also take into consideration the original methods used to collect the data as well as the intentions of the original data collectors when using archival data. As mentioned previously, if the data were biased in some way when originally collected, they will continue to be so in their current use.

Diaries, Letters, and Autobiographies   Aside from archival records, historical research may also involve the analysis of personal documents, including diaries and letters, or other accounts of life events as told by the person under study. Diaries of those who have gone before us have been examined to better understand the time or event in question and to gain insight into what that person was like or what they were thinking at the time. Often exhibitions of historical diaries and letters travel from library to library. The Library of Congress allows online access to a number of such diaries, including those from George Washington and Theodore Roosevelt; however, research involving this type of data does not have to be historical. Current research endeavors may also involve diaries through what is known as the **diary method.** In this method, subjects are asked to keep a record of their behaviors as they relate to the study being conducted. For example, a study on substance abuse may ask a user to chronicle his or her daily use during the time the research is being conducted. A study on unemployment may ask a study subject to keep a diary of the challenges faced as he or she searches for a job.

Historical research involves obtaining archived and other vintage documents, such as this letter, for analysis.

Autobiographies have also been used to chronicle histories, many of which focus on a life of crime. Although its validity is now questioned, Tufts' autobiographical account of his life as a career criminal was the first to be published in 1930.[17] Since that time, many accounts have been published, especially by former organized crime members.[18] While there is much interest in the telling of these stories, readers should be aware that not everything told has been backed up by evidence and therefore, as with Tufts' autobiography, the validity of the accounts is somewhat unknown.

Content Analysis

The opening case study of this chapter described a research study in which media content was analyzed to answer a research question, namely to what extent criminal justice and criminology scholars were contributing to popular cable news programs. This method is referred to as **content analysis,** and such analysis may be conducted using any form of mass communication, including television, newspapers, magazines, and the like. In the past, such methods have relied on written material, but today, television and films and any other source of mass media (e.g., Facebook and Twitter posts) may also be utilized for purposes of content analysis. The procedural elements of content analysis as described by Berelson[19] (1952) include subject selection, the development of inclusion criteria, classification, and analysis of results. The establishment and reporting of the inclusion criteria and classification schemes are important elements of content analysis because they allow a path to be followed for other raters within the project or future researchers attempting to replicate the study findings.

Recent examples of research involving content analysis include the examination of criminal justice pioneer importance as measured by existing biography length,[20] crime drama portrayals of "prime time justice,"[21] last words of Death Row inmates and news coverage of executions in Texas,[22] portrayals of gay and lesbian police officer depictions in the "core cop film genre,"[23] and constructions of crime and justice as portrayed in American comic books.[24] While such research can be found in mainstream criminal justice and criminology journals, journals devoted to media topics, such as the *Journal of Criminal Justice and Popular Culture*, and *Crime, Media, Culture: An International Journal*, have been established to focus primarily on such issues and research methodologies.

A recent contribution to the content analysis process is the development of computer software programs that can be used to aide researchers with counts and classification particularly when it is written content being measured. Whereas content analysis was, in the past, primarily done by hand, now content can be copied into such programs and the software will conduct the counts. This allows larger amounts of content to be analyzed in a much shorter amount of time.

Issues most discussed regarding content analysis are those of reliability and validity. That is, ratings, counts, or classifications may be considered subjective and therefore differ from person to person. There are ways to increase the reliability and validity of such research findings. For example, it is important to have clearly established inclusion criteria and classification schemes for others to follow. This lends to a more objective system of classification. Additionally, many research projects involve multiple raters. Once each rater has completed their ratings, a ratio is established to determine agreement among the raters. This ratio is measuring **interrater reliability.** Such an analysis is generally included in study findings for research involving content analysis by more than one rater.

Meta-Analysis   **Meta-analysis** is a type of content analysis in which researchers review, organize, integrate, and summarize the existing research literature on a certain topic. Researchers conducting meta-analyses will gather existing quantitative information on studies that have been conducted in the past in order to compare their methodology and findings. In the 1970s, Glass[25] was the first to coin this term and to describe the quantitative process, which utilizes statistical methodologies to code, analyze, and interpret the similarities and differences found among the literature relating to a certain research question. Most commonly, this method has been used to assess the effectiveness of certain interventions, such as correctional boot camp programs, drug treatment programs, and the like.[26] Although most of such research has developed out of the field of psychology, there has been an increase in the use of meta-analysis as a method for researching criminal justice topics. Two recent academic journal articles[27] have addressed this increase, the methods best suited, and the usefulness of meta-analysis for the field, finding that, while such analyses are time consuming and labor intensive, they are, as Pratt (2010) states, "a welcome addition to the criminologists' toolbox" (pg. 165).

Physical Trace Analysis   "Crime Scene Investigation," need we say more? Of course we do, although you are probably most familiar with this type of unobtrusive method from courses involving crime scene investigation or the many television shows that devote time to such information-gathering techniques. For example, if a law enforcement officer were examining a crime scene in which a sexual assault was alleged to have taken place, what would she look for? The officer would most likely be examining the scene for semen, blood, contraceptive materials, and/or other substances that may have been left behind from such an incident. **Physical trace analysis** is similar and refers to the examination of physical substances that have been created and left by individuals as they come in contact with their environment. As with other unobtrusive methods, physical trace analysis represents an indirect method of measuring certain phenomena.

Examples of the use of physical trace analysis for social science research include the study of museum exhibit popularity by examining wear on the floor attributed to heavy foot traffic[28] and the determination of crowd size as estimated by trash accumulation after a social event has taken place.[29] As another example using garbage, researchers may attempt to measure how popular certain establishments are by examining

Like crime scene investigators, criminal justice researchers can focus on physical traces to conduct a study.

how much trash is accumulated on a given night or how many homeless persons stay under a certain highway bridge by examining garbage or other waste left behind. It would be assumed that a bar with more trash was more heavily frequented the night before than a bar with less trash, and a highway bridge under which there was more trash, is a more popular stopping-over point for transient populations than one with little trash or waste accumulated. Such an examination could also be conducted using public restrooms. If a university administrator was interested in adding restrooms to campus and he needed to know where these additional restrooms would be most utilized, how could this be measured? Once again, looking at trash accumulation or "wear and tear" on doors, floors, and toilets would be indirect ways to answer such a question. If you were interested in exploring where most students sit in a given classroom, what kinds of things would you look for as you examined the classroom after the class had ended? Perhaps you would look at the disarray of the seats or tables. You might also look at where trash has accumulated in the classroom or if there is writing on tables where it had not been before. These would also be indirect ways to measure which sections of classroom seating are most used, and such observations could be made once or multiple times after the class has ended. Furthermore, with the rise of technology, particularly the use of the Internet, also come avenues for unobtrusive research. For example, visits to a webpage could indicate popularity of that website. Celebrity popularity is often measured by the number of times that person's name is entered into an online search engine.

Researchers have also been able to apply analysis of physical traces to the study of crime and deviance. For example, studies of vandalism in certain neighborhoods and graffiti in public areas have been conducted to indicate the presence of lawbreakers and/or subcultures or gang activity.[30] Additionally, the sale of burglar alarms or other home protection devices has been used as a proxy measure for fear of crime.[31] That is, if there is an increase in the installation of burglar alarms, it is assumed that fear of crime in that area is on the rise. With the use of the Internet, popularity of pornography sites, particularly those that are unlawful due to posting pornographic content involving children, can be measured. Additionally, for purposes of investigation, electronic physical traces (i.e., IP addresses) can be tracked as a means to find out who is viewing or from which computer these websites are being viewed.

One important thing to remember about physical trace analysis is that the resulting evidence is not direct; these are indirect measures of phenomena. Just because a law enforcement officer finds semen and blood at a crime scene, it does not automatically prove that a crime has occurred. Also, just because the sale of burglar alarms increases, it does not necessarily indicate that fear of crime is also on the rise. Alarm companies could have dropped their fees, leading to an increase in sales. Therefore, while interesting, such measures are generally seen as being inferentially weak. When using such methods, it is always important to triangulate, or attempt to validate your findings through the use of other measures when possible. The more evidence you have, the more secure you can be that your findings are indeed measuring what you propose they are measuring. A final issue with the collection of physical trace data is an individual's right to privacy; however, if information is public, the collection of that information would not involve a violation of that right.

Observation

In Chapter 6, you learned about the many variations of participant-observation research. On the spectrum of intrusiveness, complete observation is the least intrusive. In conducting research as a complete observer, a researcher only observes the individuals and behaviors under study. The researcher makes no advances or attempts to be involved with the individual(s) or to change the natural chain of events. He or she is only there to witness what occurs. As an example of complete observation, you may be wondering how often store patrons park in a handicap parking spot without the proper tags on their vehicle. To answer this question, you may sit near the parking spot in question and observe how many vehicles park there illegally. You are not interacting with the store patrons, nor are you interfering with their decision to park in the handicap parking spot. You are merely observing their behavior. Acting as a complete observer is quite similar to being on a stake-out. A limitation is that you could be sitting for some time waiting for events to occur as you have no control over when or how things may happen. For example, if you were observing the handicap parking spot, you may sit there for hours or even days without anyone actually parking there.

In **disguised observation,** the researcher may actually take part in the behavior or group under study. As a disguised observer, the researcher's identity and purpose for being there is hidden from the group, making the gathering of information unobtrusive. Because the subjects do not know they are being studied, the researcher is able to observe individuals in their natural environment. As was discussed in Chapter 6, there are numerous examples of disguised observation in criminal justice research. If you remember the case study from Chapter 2, Humphreys acted as a disguised observer when researching the phenomenon of anonymous sex in public places.

While these examples exist, disguised observation is not without its critics. While being able to observe individuals in their natural environment without the researcher's presence being known is what makes this data collection method so valuable, some disagree with its use due to privacy concerns. As the subject is not asked for his or her permission before being observed for research purposes, an invasion of their privacy has occurred. Another issue, as mentioned previously, is the waiting that an observer, even a disguised observer, must do during their observations. To circumvent this, actors, referred to as confederates, have been implemented to speed up the events of interest. As is done for the ABC Primetime television show, "What Would You Do," actors play out a scenario in the hopes of eliciting a response from those around them. John Quinones, the host of the show, watches the scene from afar as do hidden cameras. After the event takes place, he moves forward to interview those who either did or did not react to the event that took place in front of them. Scenes of domestic violence, drunk driving, and racism have all been set up by the television show with varied responses by individuals present. Researchers have also examined such topics through the use of confederates. For example, Formby and Smykla (1984) studied pedestrians' reactions to a student actor's attempt to drive under the influence. To set the scene, the actor, smelling of alcohol, stumbled to his car and pretended to have difficulty opening the car door. Amazingly, out of the pedestrians who passed, over 60% assisted the "drunk" driver open his car door. While the use of confederates is helpful to researchers, there are instances where public reaction to the event being observed can be dangerous to the research team, particularly the confederates. For example, in the case of a staged domestic violence altercation, a passerby may respond physically to the person acting as the abuser. Researchers never truly know how people will respond, which makes this type of research exciting, albeit risky.

RESEARCH IN THE NEWS
Mock Jury Decides Scott Peterson Case

On Christmas Eve in 2002 the disappearance of Laci Peterson, a young pregnant woman in Modesto, California, sparked a media frenzy.[32] Laci, who was nearing eight months into her pregnancy, was married to Scott Peterson, a man whom she had met in college and married in 1997. The night before she disappeared, Laci was seen by her mother and sister. The following morning there was no sign of her. Her car was left parked in the driveway and her purse, keys, and cell phone were found on the kitchen table inside the home she shared with Scott. The day Laci disappeared, her husband was fishing and did not return until that evening, which was when he called Laci's family to see if she was with them. That evening the search began and did not conclude until early April 2003 when a male fetus and badly decomposed body of a recently pregnant woman were discovered days apart on the San Francisco Bay shore, north of Berkeley. Investigation into their marriage revealed Scott's multiple extramarital affairs and other unseemly behavior. He was arrested on April 18, 2003, in southern California. With an altered appearance and carrying thousands of dollars in cash, he looked as if he were planning to leave the country. His trial began in June 2004.

In October 2004, prior to the end of Peterson's trial, CBS aired an episode of *48 Hours Mystery* entitled, "On the Verge of a Verdict," for which a jury consultant team was asked to put together a mock jury similar to the jury hearing the Scott Peterson case.[33] Using the mock jury, a study was conducted to see how individuals resembling the actual jurors in the case might decide the outcome. The mock jurors were shown the same evidence presented by the prosecution and defense at trial, which included the infamous conversations recorded between Scott Peterson and Amber Frey, the woman involved with Scott at the time of Laci's disappearance. After hearing and discussing the evidence, as an actual jury would, the mock jury deadlocked, with all but two of the mock jurors deciding Scott Peterson was guilty of murdering his wife and unborn son. Following this outcome, the mock jury shared that they thought the actual jury would also end in a deadlock. This was not the case, however. On November 12, 2004, the actual jury convicted Scott Peterson following only eight hours of deliberation. He was later sentenced to death and is currently awaiting execution in California's San Quentin State Prison.

Simulation

The use of simulation in criminal justice research has, for the most part, involved studies of jury behavior. Because it is difficult, if not impossible, to study juror behavior in real time, mock juries have been instituted using mostly community and college student samples. This type of research began with the Chicago Jury Project of the 1950s.[34] Since that time, mock juries and mock trials have become commonplace and, beyond research, are often used as educational tools for criminal justice students. **Simulations** can be defined as artificial research settings that have been carefully created so that their features mimic reality as much as possible. The two most prominent research projects involving simulation were discussed in Chapter 2, Zimbardo's Stanford Prison Experiment and Milgram's study on *Obedience to Authority*. Zimbardo recreated the prison environment for his study of inmate and correctional officer behavior, and Milgram set up an artificial "learning" experiment where the "teacher," or person under study, was directed to give shocks at increasingly high levels when wrong answers were given. While these two studies are remembered most for the psychological toll exerted on their participants, the subjects' nonartificial response was due in large part to the realistic nature of the simulation.

With the advent of new technologies, it is possible that simulations will be utilized more often for research. Advanced simulation setups are already utilized for criminal justice training, and their use could be extended for research purposes. For example, the Incident Command Simulation Training (InCoSiT) Program[35] is facilitated at the Bill Blackwood Law Enforcement Management Institute at Sam Houston State University. This program mimics a command center during a crisis event, and those being trained use the simulation to practice what they would do during such an event. While this program is currently used for training, there are research applications that could also make use of such a simulated scenario. For example, if a researcher wanted to examine gender differences in crisis command response, InCoSiT would provide a platform for that study to be conducted.

There exist numerous sources of archival records in the United States and abroad. These are available for researchers and other interested parties to search, and interesting and surprising finds often result. To increase awareness of archives and archival records research, the Society of American Archivists[36] holds a national "I Found It in the Archives!" competition where archive users are able to submit their experiences for review. Archie Rison, the 2011 winner of the competition, relied on archives at the Stephen F. Austin University East Texas Research Center to conduct extensive genealogy research on his family. Recent news stories have also related interesting archival finds. One story revealed how heroin was found in a United Kingdom National Archives file.[37] The heroin, which was part of a 1928 court case, was found by a citizen who had requested the file to review. When the substance was found, it was sent off for analysis, which confirmed the presence of heroin. After being handed over to the Metropolitan Police, the package containing the heroin was replaced with a picture in the archive folder. Jeff James, the UK National Archives Director of Operations noted that, while extremely rare, finds like that are sometimes unexpectedly discovered in their collection of 11 million records. With archives such as these existing across the globe, it is only a matter of time before another fascinating discovery is made.

CHAPTER SUMMARY

As this chapter has shown, there are many ways to avoid reactivity in gathering data for a research project. Whether you obtain data from an online archive, use GIS mapping, or observe others from a distance, by being unobtrusive you can generally ensure that reactivity is not a limitation to your research findings. While these methods have numerous advantages including the savings in time and cost and access to restricted populations, they are not without their shortcomings. The biggest limitation of using unobtrusive methods is that measurements are often indirect and therefore should be substantiated by other measures of the same phenomenon. Additional shortcomings include the lack of control over original data collection in the use of secondary data and the chance that obtaining data may not in fact be quick or without cost. In a nutshell, unobtrusive methods offer another way of data gathering. In some situations, they may be the only available option for a researcher besides doing nothing. Whether such methods are the best choice must be determined by individual researchers based on the needs of their research projects.

CRITICAL THINKING QUESTIONS

1. What is reactivity, and how do unobtrusive methods serve to decrease this?

2. Why is secondary data analysis a popular option for criminal justice researchers?

3. What is physical trace analysis, and how has it been used for criminal justice research?

4. What are the advantages and disadvantages to being a disguised observer?

5. Explain how technology has advanced unobtrusive data-gathering techniques. Give at least three examples.

KEY TERMS

archives: A place, either physical or electronic, where records and other data are stored

content analysis: A method requiring the analyzing of content contained in mass communication outlets such as newspapers, television, magazines, and the like

diary method: A data-gathering technique that asks research subjects to keep a diary, or written record, of their time participating in the research study

disguised observation: A researcher joins the group under study to observe their behavior but does not reveal his or her identity as a researcher or purpose for being there

interrater reliability: A ratio established to determine agreement in a content analysis with multiple raters

meta-analysis: A type of content analysis in which researchers quantitatively review, organize, integrate, and summarize the existing research literature on a certain topic

physical trace analysis: The examination of physical substances that have been created and left by individuals as they come in contact with their environment

secondary data analysis: Occurs when researchers obtain and reanalyze data that were originally collected for a different purpose

simulations: Artificial research settings that have been carefully created so that their features mimic reality as much as possible

unobtrusive: A method that is nonreactive; indicates that what or who is being studied is unaware of its/their role as research participant

E N D N O T E S

1   Frost, N. A., & N. D. Phillips. (2011). Talking heads: Crime reporting on cable news. *Justice Quarterly*, 28 (1), 87–112.

2   The Economist. (June 4, 2009). Questioning the Hawthorne Effect—Light work: Being watched may not affect behaviour, after all. Retrieved online, http://www.economist.com/node/13788427.

3   Milgram, S. (1977). *The individual in a social world*. New York: McGraw-Hill.

4   Stern, S. E., & J. E. Faber. (1997). "The lost e-mail method: Milgram's lost-letter technique in the age of the Internet." *Behavior Research Methods, Instruments & Computers*, 29 (2), 260–263.

5   See ESRI website, http://www.gis.com/

6   Coppock, J. T., & D. W. Rhind. (1991). "The history of GIS." In Maguire, D. J., M. F. Goodchild, & D. W. Rhind (eds.) *Geographical Information Systems: Principles and Applications* (Volume 1, pgs. 21–43). Harlow, Essex, England: Longman Scientific & Technical.

7   Mamalian, C. A., & N. G. LaVigne. (1999). *The use of computerized crime mapping by law enforcement: Survey results*. U.S. Department of Justice—National Institute of Justice. Retrieved from http://www.nij.gov/pubs-sum/fs000237.htm.

8   Manhein, M. H., G. A. Listi, & M. Leitner. (2006). "The application of geographic information systems and spatial analysis to assess dumped and subsequently scattered human remains." *Journal of Forensic Sciences*, 51(3), 469–474.

9   Medina, R. M., L. K. Siebeneck, & G. F. Hepner. (2011). "A geographic information systems (GIS) analysis of spatiotemporal patterns of terrorist incidents in Iraq 2004–2009." *Studies in Conflict & Terrorism*, 34(11), 862–882.

10 Davidson, P. J., S. Scholar, & M. Howe. (2011). "A GIS-based methodology for improving needle exchange service delivery." *International Journal of Drug Policy*, 22(2), 140–144.

11 Caplan, J. M., L. W. Kennedy, & J. Miller. (2011). "Risk terrain modeling: Brokering criminological theory and GIS methods for crime forecasting." *Justice Quarterly*, 28(2), 360–381.

12 Simonton, D. K. (2003). "Qualitative and quantitative analyses of historical data." *Annual Review of Psychology*, 54, 617–640.

13 Frueh, B. C., J. D. Elhai, A. L. Grubaugh, J. Monnier, T. B. Kashdan, J. A. Sauvageot, M. B. Hamner, B. G. Burkett, & G. W. Arana. (2005). "Documented combat exposure of U.S. veterans seeking treatment for combat-related post-traumatic stress disorder." *The British Journal of Psychiatry*, 186, 467–472.

14 Albini, J. (1971). *The American mafia: Genesis of a legend*. New York: Appleton.

15 Clarke, J. W. (1982). *American assassins: The darker side of politics*. Princeton, N.J.: Princeton University Press.

16 Gidley, B. (2004). "Doing historical and archival research." In C. Seale (ed.), *Researching Society and Culture* (249–264). Thousand Oaks, CA: Sage.

17 Tufts, H. (1930). *The autobiography of a criminal*. Upper Saddle River, NJ: Pearson.

18 See for example, Maas, P. (1968). *The Valachi Papers*. New York: Bantam Books; Teresa, V., with T. C. Renner. (1973). *My life in the Mafia*. Greenwich, CN: Fawcett; Pileggi, N. (1985). *Wiseguy: Life in a Mafia family*. New York: Simon and Schuster.

19 Berelson, B. (1952). *Content analysis in communication research*. New York: Free Press.

20 Ross, L. E. (2008). "Criminal justice pioneers: A content analysis of biographical data." *Journal of Criminal Justice*, 36(2), 182–189.

21 Eschholz, S., M. Mallard, & S. Flynn. (2004). "Images of prime time justice: A content analysis of 'NYPD Blue' and 'Law & Order.'" *Journal of Criminal Justice and Popular Culture*, 10(3), 161–180.

22 Malone, D. F. (2006). *Dead men talking: Content analysis of prisoners' last words, innocence claims and news coverage from Texas' death row*. A Master's thesis completed for the Department of Journalism at the University of North Texas.

23 Wilson, F. T., D. R. Longmire, & W. Swymeler. (2009). "The absence of gay and lesbian police officer depictions in the first three decades of the core cop film genre: Moving towards a cultivation theory perspective." *Journal of Criminal Justice and Popular Culture*, 16(1), 27–39.

24 Phillips, N. D., & S. Strobl. (2006). "Cultural criminology and kryptonite: Apocalyptic and retributive constructions of crime and justice in comic books." *Crime, Media, Culture: An International Journal*, 2(3), 304–331.

25 Glass, G. V. (1976). "Primary, secondary, and meta-analysis of research." *Educational Researcher*, 5(10), 3–8.

26 Smith, P., P. Gendreau, & K. Swartz. (2009). "Validating the principles of effective intervention: A systematic review of the contributions of meta-analysis in the field of corrections." *Victims & Offenders*, 4(2), 148–169.

27 Pratt, T. C. (2010). "Meta-analysis in criminal justice and criminology: What it is, when it's useful, and what to watch out for." *Journal of Criminal Justice Education*, 21(2), 152–168; Wells, E. (2009). "Uses of meta-analysis in criminal justice research: A quantitative review." *Justice Quarterly*, 26(2), 268–294.

28 Webb, E. J. (1966). *Unobtrusive measures: Nonreactive research in the social sciences*. Chicago: Rand McNally.

29 Webb, E. J., D. T. Campbell, R. D. Schwartz, L. Sechrest, & J. B. Grove. (1981). *Nonreactive measures in the social sciences* (2nd ed.). Boston: Houghton Mifflin.

30 Klofas, J., & C. Cutshall. (1985). "Unobtrusive research methods in criminal justice: Using graffiti in the reconstruction of institutional cultures." *Journal of Research in Crime and Delinquency*, 22(4), 355–373; Sechrest, L., & A. K. Olson. (1971). "Graffiti in four types of institutions of higher education." *Journal of Sex Research*, 7, 62–71.

31 Clinard, M. B., & R. Quinney. (1973). *Criminal behavior systems: A typology* (2nd ed.). New York: Holt.

32 The Modesto Bee. *The Peterson Case*. See website, http://www.modbee.com/peterson.

33 Klug, R. (October 30, 2004). On the verge of a verdict. In S. Zirinsky, *48 Hours Mystery* [Season 18, Episode 7]. Los Angeles, CA; CBS.

34 Bornstein, B. H. (1999). "The ecological validity of jury simulations: Is the jury still out?" *Law and Human Behavior*, 23(1), 75–91.

35 See InCoSiT website, http://www.incosit.org/

36 See the Society of American Archivists website, http://www2.archivists.org/initiatives/i-found-it-in-the-archives/i-found-it-in-the-archives-2011-national-competition

37 BBC News. (December 19, 2011). "Heroin found in national archives file." Retrieved from http://www2.archivists.org/.

Chapter 8

Putting It All Together: Understanding and Assessing Criminal Justice Research

Developing a Valid Racial Profiling Benchmark

Research Study

Testing for Racial Profiling in Traffic Stops from Behind a Veil of Darkness[1]

Research Question

Can a valid benchmark for racial profiling be established?

Methodology

As part of an effort to address public concerns about racial profiling, many police departments collect data on the traffic stops that their officers make. For each traffic stop made, the officer documents the race of the driver. The department can then determine what percentage of traffic stops involves white drivers and what percentage involves black drivers. The key problem in testing for racial profiling in traffic stops is identifying a valid benchmark against which to compare the race distribution of the stopped drivers. Departments know the racial breakdown of traffic stops, but what do they compare the numbers to in an effort to assess racial disparities in traffic stops?

A benchmark should approximate the racial composition of the population that could be legitimately stopped by the police, given their patrol deployment patterns and race neutrality in stopping vehicles.[2] Currently, there are two common benchmarks used in racial profiling analysis. First, many studies use residential

population data as the benchmark. It is widely recognized that residential population data, obtained through the U.S. Census, provide poor estimates of the population at risk of a traffic stop. In other words, residential population data is not a valid benchmark with which to compare traffic stop data. The residential population includes people who do not drive, and the driving population in many places includes people who are not residents. Second, some police departments have commissioned traffic surveys that then serve as the benchmark to which the agency compares its traffic stop data. Traffic surveys involve hiring trained observers that tally the race distribution of drivers at certain locations within the city. Traffic surveys also have limitations and are costly to carry out. It is estimated that a traffic survey costs $30,000 at a minimum, which few departments can afford.[3]

In this study, the researchers propose a new benchmark to test for racial profiling. The approach makes use of what the researchers call the "veil of darkness" hypothesis. This hypothesis asserts that police are less likely to know the race of a motorist before making a stop after dark than they are during daylight. If we assume that racial differences in traffic patterns, driving behavior, and exposure to law enforcement do not vary between daylight and darkness, then we can test for racial profiling by comparing the race distribution of stops made during daylight to the race distribution of stops made after dark. Basically, the racial distribution of traffic stops at night serves as the benchmark that we then compare to the racial distribution of traffic stops during the day. Evidence of racial profiling exists, for example, if black motorists are more likely to be stopped during the day than at night.

The location for this study was Oakland, California. The Oakland Police Department (OPD) had received several complaints by motorists and advocates that OPD officers engaged in racial profiling, discriminating in particular against black drivers. The data provided to substantiate the allegations involved the use of residential population data as the benchmark; 56% of the drivers stopped by the OPD were black, whereas blacks comprised only 35% of the city's residential population. The OPD entered into a legal settlement agreement with the U.S. Department of Justice requiring that they collect traffic stop data on an ongoing basis and regularly monitor the data to detect racial profiling.

The data analyzed included all reported vehicle stops carried out by OPD officers between June 15 and December 30, 2003, amounting to a total of 7,607 stops. The data included the race of the stopped driver and the time of the stop. The authors defined daylight as extending from sunrise to sunset. The remaining times were considered dark. Of the 7,607 stops in the database, the authors omitted 329 that were made pursuant to a criminal investigation, where the use of race as an identifying factor is explicitly allowed by law. Another 549 stops were lacking race or time information, so they were excluded as well.

Results

Overall, 45% of the drivers stopped were white and 55% were black. When divided by time of day, 51% of the drivers stopped during daylight were white while 49% were black. During dark hours, 35% of the stopped drivers were white while 65% were black. Recall that the racial distribution of traffic stops at night serves as the benchmark that we then compare to the racial distribution of traffic stops during the day. Evidence of racial profiling exists if black motorists are more likely to be stopped during the day than at night. This study found the direct opposite. Black drivers were more likely to be stopped at night (65% of the stops involved black drivers) than during the day (49% of the stops involved black drivers). If anything, the numbers and comparison discussed previously suggest reverse profiling, because it shows that white drivers are disproportionately stopped during daylight when visibility is high.

However, the researchers assumed that racial differences in travel patterns, driving behavior, and exposure to law enforcement do not vary between daylight and darkness, but these assumptions may not be true.

The assumption that travel patterns are similar in the day and the night may be inaccurate, because the time of employment is known to vary by race.[4] To deal with this issue, the researchers made use of the natural variation in hours of daylight over the year. In the winter, it is dark by early evening, whereas in the summer it stays light much later. Recall that the data used in this study were from June 15 through December 30, 2003. Limiting the analysis to stops occurring during the intertwilight period (i.e., between roughly 5 and 9 PM), the researchers could test for differences in the racial distribution of traffic stops between night and day, while controlling for racial variation in travel patterns by time of day.

The second analysis done by researchers was of traffic stops that occurred between 5 and 9 PM, which we will refer to as the intertwilight sample. Depending on the date of the stop, some of the stops were made during daylight and some during dark. Using the intertwilight sample, the authors found that 52% of the drivers stopped during daylight hours were black while 57% of the drivers stopped when it was dark were black. Recall that evidence of racial profiling exists if black motorists are more likely to be stopped during the day than at night. Once again, this analysis provides little evidence of racial profiling in the OPD.

Limitations with the Study Procedure

Although the previous results suggest there is no racial profiling in traffic stops in the OPD, those results hinge on the assumptions that racial differences in travel patterns, driving behavior, and exposure to law enforcement do not vary between daylight and darkness. As noted previously, the assumptions may not be true. The researchers were able to control for differences in travel patterns between daylight and darkness by limiting their analysis to only those traffic stops that occurred between 5 PM and 9 PM (i.e., intertwilight sample). However, the researchers were unable to control for any racial differences in driving behavior and exposure to law enforcement between daylight and darkness. If the assumptions are not true, then the results can be questioned.

Despite the terms of the court settlement that require data collection on every traffic stop conducted by the OPD, there is evidence of a substantial non-reporting problem in the data. An audit of the traffic stop reports led the OPD's Independent Monitoring Team to estimate that as many as 70% of all motor

FIGURE 8.1 | Jurisdictions Currently Collecting Traffic Stop Data—2012

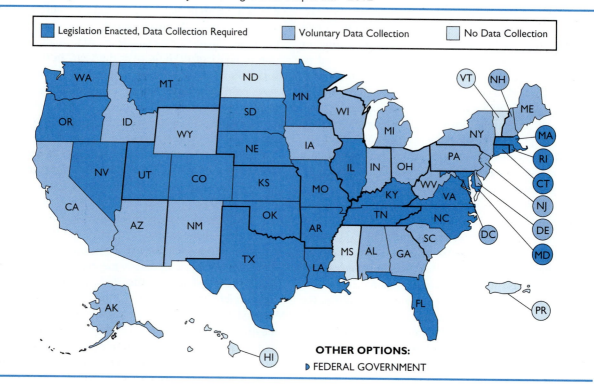

vehicle stops were not reported in the early phases of this study. Court-ordered oversight and increased officer sanctions for noncompliance raised the number of completed stop forms, especially in October, November, and December. Therefore, the data are not a reflection of all traffic stops but just those that were documented by the officer who made the stop. The extent to which there were racial disparities in reporting (i.e., officers were more likely to not provide documentation on stops of black drivers), then the results can be questioned.

In order to validate the proposed benchmark, replication is required. No one study can by itself establish a sufficient base of knowledge to validate this benchmark. As of the middle of 2012, only four studies utilizing this methodology have been done, so we have a long way to go in validating the veil of darkness as a benchmark in racial profiling research. [5]

Impact on Criminal Justice

Police agencies throughout the country collect information on the race of drivers stopped by police (see Figure 8.1). As of 2012, 25 states had enacted legislation requiring racial profiling data collection by law enforcement agencies in the state. [6] Another 21 states and the District of Columbia have some police agencies that voluntarily collect data on traffic stops for racial profiling analysis. Only the states of Hawaii, Mississippi, North Dakota, and Vermont do not have any known police agencies that collect traffic stop information for racial profiling assessment purposes. [7]

There is plenty of data collection on racial profiling happening throughout the country. This data is then analyzed by the police agency or researchers to determine if racial profiling is occurring within the agency. As is clear from the preceding research article, the problem is there is no valid benchmark for racial profiling assessments. Without a valid benchmark, the traffic stop data cannot be used to make a determination if a police agency is engaging in racial profiling.

The veil of darkness method described in this article might be the right approach. There is still plenty of work that needs to be done to demonstrate that the veil of darkness method is a valid benchmark for racial profiling analysis, but this approach is currently the most useful, cost-effective benchmark yet devised. [8] ●

The steps in the research process

The structure of research articles and reports

What questions to ask and answer about each section of a research article

About external indicators of research quality

How to assess the internal indicators of research quality

How to critique a research article

INTRODUCTION

We hope your adventure through research methods has been an enjoyable one. It is now time to put the material you have learned into practice. In this chapter, we will revisit the steps in the research process covered in Chapter 1. Since the past several chapters have focused on specific research tools, it is important to once again see the big picture of research methods, so we will review the steps in the research process once again. After this, we will discuss the structure of research articles and reports so you will be prepared to read research articles. Understanding the structure of these documents will greatly assist you as you move forward as an educated consumer of research. Along with an overview of the structure of research articles and reports, a set of questions that you should ask as you read each section of a research article will be presented. The questions will serve as a helpful guide as you move forward in evaluating research documents and putting what you have learned in this book and in your class into practice.

The next two sections of this chapter will discuss how to determine the quality of a research article. In other words, how do you know if a research article is "good" and how do you go about assessing the specific details provided in research articles? This section is the culmination of your efforts throughout this semester. Now that you have the knowledge necessary to be an educated consumer of research, this section will provide you the specific tools necessary to know what questions to ask and what documentation to look for as you review and assess research articles. The sections are divided into two categories: external indictors of quality research and internal indicators of quality research. Finally, the last section of this chapter will provide an example of a research article critique. Using experimental design as the template, we will ask and answer a set of questions regarding the Minneapolis Domestic Violence Experiment (also covered in Chapter 5). The questions and answers will allow you to make an educated decision regarding the quality of the research. This will serve as a practical example of what you can do in the future as you put your knowledge of research methods into practice in both your academic and professional careers and your personal life.

THE RESEARCH PROCESS

Although this section was previously covered in Chapter 1, it is important to, once again, review the steps in the research process. Over the past several chapters, we have reviewed several specific research tools, designs, and methods. As you studied the specifics of research methods in each separate chapter, you may have lost focus of the "big picture" and how these different pieces fit together to form a comprehensive understanding of research methods. At the beginning of this chapter, it is important once again to look at the "big picture" to see how all these different tools, designs, and methods come together in the research process. When you read this information the first time in Chapter 1, you were in your first week of class and still may have been quite anxious about understanding this material. Now that you have almost completed the course, the steps should be easy to understand. What was once possibly a foggy understanding of the steps in the research process in Chapter 1 should now be crystal clear.

One of the nice things about studying research methods is it is about learning a process. Research methods can be seen as a sequential process with the first step being followed by the second step, and so on. There are certainly times when the order of the steps may be modified, but researchers typically follow the same process for each research study they complete regardless of the research topic. Very simply, a research problem or question is identified, and a methodology is selected, developed, and implemented to answer the research question. This sequential process is one of the advantages of understanding research methods, because once you understand the process, you can apply that process to any research question that interests you. In addition, research methods are the same across disciplines. So, sampling is the same in business as it is in health education as it is in criminal justice. Certainly the use of a particular method will be more common in one discipline in comparison to another, but the protocol for implementing the method to complete the research study is the same. For example, field research (discussed in Chapter 6) is used much more frequently in anthropology than in criminal justice. However, the research protocol to implement field research is the same whether you are studying an indigenous Indian tribe in South America in anthropology or a group of heroin users in St. Louis in criminal justice.

Some authors have presented the research process as a wheel or circle, with no specific beginning or end. Typically, the research process begins with the selection of a research problem and the development of research questions or hypotheses (discussed in Chapter 2). It is common for the results of previous research to generate new research questions and hypotheses for the researcher. This suggests that research is cyclical, a vibrant and continuous process. When a research study answers one question, the result is often the generation of additional questions, which plunges the researcher right back into the research process to complete additional research to answer these new questions.

In this section, a brief overview of the research process will be presented. Although you will probably not be expected to conduct a research study on your own, it is important for an educated consumer of research to understand the steps in the research process. The steps are presented in chronological order and appear neatly presented. In practice, the researcher can go back and forth between the steps in the research process.

Step 1: Select a Topic and Conduct a Literature Review

The first step in the research process is typically the identification of a problem or topic that the researcher is interested in studying. Research topics can arise from a wide variety of sources, including the findings of a current study, a question that a criminal justice agency needs to have answered, or the result of intellectual curiosity. Once the researcher has identified a particular problem or topic, the researcher assesses the current state of the literature related to the problem or topic. The researcher will often spend a considerable amount of time in determining what the existing literature has to say about the topic. Has the topic already been studied to the point that the questions in which the researcher is interested have been sufficiently answered? If so, can the researcher approach the subject from a previously unexamined perspective? Many times, research topics have

been previously explored but not brought to completion. If this is the case, it is certainly reasonable to examine the topic again. It is even appropriate to replicate a previous study to determine whether the findings reported in the prior research continue to be true in different settings with different participants. This step in the research process was discussed in Chapter 2.

Step 2: Develop a Research Question

After a topic has been identified and a comprehensive literature review has been completed on the topic, the next step is the development of a research question or questions. The research question marks the beginning of your research study and is critical to the remaining steps in the research process. The research question determines the research plan and methodology that will be employed in the study, the data that will be collected, and the data analysis that will be performed. Basically, the remaining steps in the process are completed in order to answer the research question or questions established in this step. The development of research questions was discussed in Chapter 2.

Step 3: Develop a Hypothesis

After the research questions have been established, the next step is the formulation of hypotheses, which are statements about the expected relationship between two variables. For example, a hypothesis may state that there is no relationship between heavy metal music preference and violent delinquency. The two variables stated in the hypothesis are music preference and violent delinquency. Hypothesis development was discussed in Chapter 2.

Step 4: Operationalize Concepts

Operationalization involves the process of giving the concepts in your study a working definition and determining how each concept in your study will be measured. For example, in Step 3, the variables were music preference and violent delinquency. The process of operationalization involves determining how music preference and violent delinquency will be measured. Operationalization was discussed in Chapter 2.

Step 5: Develop the Research Plan and Methodology

The next step is to develop the methodology that will be employed to answer the research questions and test the hypotheses. The research methodology is the blueprint for the study, which outlines how the research is to be

RESEARCH IN THE NEWS
Road Rage Common Among Commuters[9]

A recent survey found that almost 60% of the respondents who drive to work said they experience road rage at times while traveling to and from the office. These findings are similar to the results found in 2006, which was the last time the study was conducted. Nearly one in ten (9%) workers who drive to work have gotten into a fight with another commuter. While incidents of road rage are more prevalent among those with long commutes, workers with short trips to their jobs are not immune. Of workers with commutes of less than 5 minutes, 37% said they experience road rage from time to time. The same goes for 54% of workers with commutes of less than 10 minutes.

Women are more apt to feel road rage; 61% compared to 56% of men. In terms of age groups, workers ages 25 to 34 were the most likely to experience road rage at 68%, while workers 55 and older were the least likely to experience road rage at 47%. The survey was completed online by 3,892 U.S. workers who were employed full-time. Workers who were self-employed or worked for the government were excluded from the survey. The survey was completed by workers 18 years of age and older and was conducted between May 14 and June 4, 2012.

conducted. The research questions will determine the appropriate methodology for the study. The research design selected should be driven by the research questions asked. In other words, the research questions dictate the methods used to answer them. The methodology is basically a research plan on how the research questions will be answered and will detail:

1. What group, subjects, or population will be studied and selected? Sampling was discussed in Chapter 3.

2. What research design will be used to collect data to answer the research questions? Various research designs were covered in Chapters 4–7.

You need to have familiarity with all research designs so that you can become an educated consumer of research. A survey cannot answer all research questions, so knowing a lot about surveys but not other research designs will not serve you well as you assess research studies. There are several common designs used in criminal justice and criminology research, and brief descriptions of some of them are presented next. At this point in the semester, you should be completely familiar with each of these designs since they have been detailed in prior chapters.

Survey Research   Survey research is one of the most common research designs employed in criminal justice research. It obtains data directly from research participants by asking them questions and is often conducted through self-administered questionnaires and personal interviews. For example, a professor might have her students complete a survey during class to understand the relationship between drug use and self-esteem. Survey research was discussed in Chapter 4.

Experimental Design   Experimental designs are used when researchers are interested in determining whether a program, policy, practice, or intervention is effective. For example, a researcher may use an experimental design to determine if boot camps are effective at reducing juvenile delinquency. Experimental designs were discussed in Chapter 5.

Field Research   Field research involves researchers studying individuals or groups of individuals in their natural environment. The researcher is observing closely or acting as part of the group under study and is able to describe in depth not only the subject's behaviors, but also consider the motivations that drive their behaviors. For example, if a researcher wanted to learn more about gangs and their activities, he may "hang out" with a gang in order to observe their behavior. Field research was discussed in Chapter 6.

Case Studies   A case study is an in-depth analysis of one or a few illustrative cases. This design allows the story behind an individual, a particular offender, to be told, and then information from cases studied can be extrapolated to a larger group. Often these studies require the review and analysis of documents such as police reports and court records and interviews with the offender and others. For example, a researcher may explore the life history of a serial killer to try and understand why the offender killed. Case studies were discussed in Chapter 6.

Secondary Data Analysis   Secondary data analysis occurs when researchers obtain and reanalyze data that was originally collected for a different purpose. This can include reanalyzing data collected from a prior research study, using criminal justice agency records to answer a research question, or conducting historical research. For example, a researcher using secondary data analysis may analyze inmate files from a nearby prison to understand the relationship between custody level assignment and disciplinary violations inside prison. Secondary data analysis was discussed in Chapter 7.

Content Analysis   Content analysis requires the assessment of content contained in mass communication outlets such as newspapers, television, magazines, and the like. In this research design, documents, publications, or presentations are reviewed and analyzed. For example, a researcher utilizing content analysis might review true crime books involving murder to see how the characteristics of the offender and victim in the true crime books match reality as depicted in the FBI's Supplemental Homicide Reports. Content analysis was discussed in Chapter 7.

Despite the options these designs offer, other research designs are available and were discussed in previous chapters. Ultimately, the design used will depend on the nature of the study and the research questions asked.

Step 6: Execute the Research Plan and Collect Data

The next step in the research process is the collection of the data based on the research design developed. For example, if a survey is developed to study the relationship between gang membership and violent delinquency, the distribution and collection of surveys from a group of high school students would occur in this step. Data collection was discussed in several chapters throughout this text.

Step 7: Analyze Data

After the data have been collected, the next phase in the research process involves analyzing the data through various and appropriate statistical techniques. The most common means for data analysis today is through the use of a computer and statistically oriented software. Data analysis and statistics are discussed in Chapter 9.

Step 8: Report Findings, Results, and Limitations

Reporting and interpreting the results of the study are the final steps in the research process. The findings and results of the study can be communicated through reports, journals, or books. At this step, the results are reported and the research questions are answered. In addition, an assessment is made regarding the support or lack of support for the hypotheses tested. It is also at this stage that the researcher can pose additional research questions that may now need to be answered as a result of the research study. In addition, the limitations of the study will be described by the researcher as well as the impact the limitations may have on the results of the study. All research has limitations, so it is incumbent on the researcher to identify those limitations for the reader.

STRUCTURE OF RESEARCH ARTICLES AND REPORTS

As noted in the prior section, research methods can be seen as a sequential process as depicted in the steps in the research process. The question then becomes, what do researchers do with all the data and information they collect in their research projects? The answer is they write journal articles, research reports, and books. One of the advantages of reading research articles is their structures are usually very similar. It is helpful as an educated consumer of research to understand the common structure of research articles and reports. You will be able to easily identify these sections as you review research articles and reports in the future.

Before we discuss the structure of research articles and reports, it is necessary to mention the three main publication outlets for research articles. First, a common outlet for a researcher's study and results is a journal article. Journal articles appear in thousands of journals covering the gamut of academic disciplines from accounting to zoology. Researchers write manuscripts based on their research projects and then submit them to journals for publication. Later in this section, we will discuss how to assess the quality of a journal. For now, it is important to recognize that journals are a critical outlet for research articles. Second, another place to find research is in reports that are published by government agencies, private companies, and businesses. For our specific purposes, this includes government documents produced by state and federal agencies such as the U.S. Department of Justice and local, state, and federal criminal justice agencies. Thousands of documents each year are published as reports with many available online. Reports are similar in structure to journal articles; however, reports are usually more detailed than journal articles, which have limited space for details such as the research methods used in the study and the results. Furthermore, reports typically do not include a literature review. Due to these similarities, reports can be evaluated in much the same way as journal articles. Third, books are sometimes used as a primary source to document a research study. Due to the magnitude of the study, a book-length manuscript is developed to document the research methodology and findings. University presses (e.g., Cornell University Press and University of Texas Press) commonly print research projects and their results as books.

Most published research follows a basic format, which will be reviewed in this section. Although the structure described next will vary slightly depending on the research methods utilized and will vary by discipline and the requirements of the publication outlet, most research reports that are published follow a similar format. Consumers of research grow accustomed to seeing the same basic information in each published research article. By knowing the structure of a research article and the general information that is included in each of the sections, research consumers can be less anxious about reading published research. This format also provides a structure for researchers to follow when writing up their research. This format includes a title, abstract, introduction, literature review, methodology, findings, discussion, conclusion, and references. Each will be described next along with questions that an educated consumer of research should ask regarding each part of a research article.

Title

Titles help research consumers quickly identify if the journal, article, or book may be of interest to them. The title should provide the research consumer with a general idea of the article topic and perhaps the main variables assessed in the study. Some evaluative questions to ask regarding the title of a research article include:

1. Is the title concise and specific?
2. Are the main variables and research subjects included in the title?
3. Is the title free of jargon and acronyms that may not be generally recognized by research consumers? [10]

Abstract

The abstract is typically limited to 150–200 words, depending on the publication outlet. The abstract gives a short synopsis of the article, including the topic covered, the methodology, and the major findings of the research. The abstract provides a quick way for the research consumer to get an overview of the research study to see if

more in-depth exploration is warranted. Some evaluative questions to ask regarding the abstract of a research article include:

1. Is the purpose of the study clearly stated in the abstract?
2. Does the abstract include the main points of the methodology used?
3. Does the abstract include the main findings? [11]

Introduction

In the introduction, the researcher should establish for the reader the importance of the research topic, the historical background of the problem, and the need for research in the area. For example, several strategies have been developed to reduce recidivism among convicted sex offenders (e.g., sex offender registration, community notification, residency restrictions, and civil commitment). This is obviously an important topic, and researchers want to find out which strategy works best at reducing recidivism. After the researcher has introduced the topic and its significance, the introduction should be narrowed down to the specific research project discussed in the article. Some evaluative questions to ask about the introduction include:

1. Does the researcher identify a specific problem area in the introduction?
2. Does the researcher establish the importance of the problem area?
3. Does the introduction start broadly and then narrow down to the specific research topic?

Literature Review

The literature review section provides a framework for the research by assessing the prior studies that have already been conducted on the topic. Basically, the literature review includes the pertinent prior studies that have addressed the topic of your research and have answered your research questions. The literature review provides a compilation of what is currently known about the topic under study. The literature review should also be critical and note the limitations in the prior research and identify the gaps in the literature where adequate research has not been conducted. The literature review should contain the most recent research studies on the topic as well. However, the literature review should not dismiss history, but instead should discuss the seminal studies on the topic. For example, if you are conducting a study on the factors that impact the decisions of police officers

WHAT RESEARCH SHOWS: IMPACTING CRIMINAL JUSTICE OPERATIONS

Civil Commitment of Sex Offenders: Are the Right Offenders Identified and Public Safety Increased?[12]

In response to a growing perceived need to protect the public from sexual offenses, numerous public policies have been developed to manage and track convicted sex offenders. Although the most widely known of these initiatives are sex offender registration and community notification laws, many states have recently also enacted sex offender civil management laws (also commonly referred to as civil confinement/commitment laws or sexually violent predator [SVP] laws). These civil management laws are designed to protect the public while offering treatment to the offender, by allowing the civil confinement of those sex offenders deemed to be at high risk for sexual recidivism after they have completed their criminal justice sentences for certain sexual crimes. Twenty-two jurisdictions (20 states, District of Columbia, and the federal government) have enacted such laws.

New York is one of these states. In 2007, the State of New York enacted its Sex Offender Management and Treatment Act (SOMTA) to civilly manage those sex offenders deemed to be at high risk for sexual recidivism. Specifically, SOMTA allows the state to civilly manage sex offenders about to be released from state supervision who have mental abnormalities that predispose them to engage in repeated sex offenses, by either:

a. placing the offenders in the community on strict and intensive supervision and treatment (SIST); or

b. civilly confining those offenders deemed to be dangerous (i.e., unable to control their sexual offending behavior).

The study sought to inform the SOMTA review process by answering the following research questions:

1. Which variables are most influential in the SOMTA review process? and

2. Is the sex offender civil management process in New York correctly identifying high-risk offenders (and, therefore, likely increasing public safety)?

To answer the first research question, the researchers obtained data on all offenders reviewed for possible civil management from April 13, 2007, to November 12, 2008 (N = 1,991). Since SOMTA had only been enacted a year and a half before the study, a sufficient length of time had not yet passed for the sexual recidivism rates of the 1,991 offenders screened under SOMTA to be adequately judged. To overcome this challenge, the researchers created a historical cohort of New York sex offenders before the enactment of SOMTA. Offenders in the historical cohort were matched (on variables found to be important to the SOMTA review process) to those offenders actually reviewed under SOMTA. In other words, the offenders used to answer the second research question (i.e., the recidivism analysis) were never reviewed under SOMTA but were matched on risk factors to SOMTA-reviewed

Research has shown that unlike sex offender registration, community notification, and residency restrictions, sex offender civil management appears to be reducing sexual victimizations.

offenders. A total of 1,546 offenders were included in the matched historical cohort.

To answer the first research question, the researchers identified the demographic, criminal history, and victim variables that contributed most significantly to being deemed high risk and receiving a psychiatric exam. The greatest increase in the odds of an offender receiving a psychiatric exam was associated with the offender's Static-99 score. The Static-99 is the most widely used instrument to conduct male sex offender risk assessments and has been found to be reliable and valid. Three other variables that made the SOMTA review process likely were having a male victim, age of the offender (with older offenders more likely to be reviewed), and number of prior sexual convictions. To answer the second research question, the researchers used the matched historical cohort. The data analysis revealed an overall 5-year sexual rearrest rate of 7.2%.

Taken as a whole, the results of the study supported the efficacy of the risk assessment process used in New York to identify those offenders most likely to recidivate sexually. The factors identified by the research most likely to be associated with an offender being high risk are the same ones identified in prior literature (i.e., Static-99 score, male victim, older offender, and number of prior sexual convictions). The researchers concluded that the results of the current study indicate that sex offender civil management is successful and is likely increasing public safety. This is important to the operation of the criminal justice system because the growing body of research indicates little, no, and sometimes even negative impacts on public safety resulting from sex offender registration and community notification,[13] as well as sex offender residency restrictions.[14] Thus, unlike sex offender registries, community notification, and residency restrictions, sex offender civil management appears from this study to be reducing sexual victimizations.

to arrest juvenile offenders, you would definitely want to include the article, discussed later in this chapter, by Piliavin and Briar: the seminal work on police discretion and juveniles.

The review of the literature may also include a description of the theoretical framework that was used for the study. The theoretical framework can put the development of the researchers' hypotheses into context. To demonstrate the link between the theoretical framework and hypothesis construction, some publications will place the hypotheses at the end of the literature review instead of at the beginning of the methodology section. Some evaluative questions to ask about the literature review include:

1. Does the literature review include current as well as seminal citations?

2. Is the literature review critical of the prior literature by noting its limitations?

3. Have gaps in the current literature been identified in the literature review?[15]

Methods

The methods section is where the material discussed in the prior chapters of this text is put into action to let readers know the details of how the research was conducted. It should provide details on the methods used by the researchers to gather data and answer the research questions and/or test the hypotheses. The methodology section includes a description of the research design, data sources, sampling strategy, variables and how they were measured, and data collection instruments used. Methods sections are often longer in quantitative studies than in qualitative studies. Explicit details of the methods used should be provided, because this section of the article provides much of the material needed by the consumer of research to evaluate the quality of the article. Unfortunately, this detail is not always provided, which leaves the consumer to make assumptions about the methods and their limitations.

Depending on the publication outlet, the limitations of the research study may also be included in the methods section of the research article. If the limitations are not discussed in the methods section, then they will be reviewed in the discussion or conclusion section. Complete transparency and full candor are expected as the researcher shows the reader that he acknowledges the limitations of the research and has thought through how the limitations can impact the results. For example, if the experimental design had several participants drop out of

the program between the pre-test and the post-test, then the researcher needs to discuss how subject mortality can influence the results of the study. Similarly, if the survey researcher discovers some wording issues with one of the questions on the survey, then he should address this reliability issue and how it may impact the results of the study. No research is perfect, so it is incumbent upon the researcher to state the limitations and flaws in the research and to provide the information needed by the educated consumer of researcher to decide the magnitude of the limitations and their cumulative impact on the research findings.

In the methods section, the researcher should also discuss the statistical analysis of the data to be performed and reported in the results section of the article. Although the statistical tests performed can become quite technical and complex, it is important for the researcher to present information about the statistical tests so the consumer can become familiar with the techniques used in analyzing the data. Statistics will be discussed in Chapter 9.

It is impossible to develop a single checklist of the topics that need to be addressed in a methods section because the details that need to be provided depend on the methods used. For example, the response rate only needs to be included in the methods section when a survey has been conducted. Likewise, the sampling protocol is frequently a component of the methods section, but sampling is irrelevant when a case study is completed. Specific evaluative questions about the methodology section will not be presented here, but instead will be provided when the internal indicators of research quality are presented later in this chapter.

Results/Findings

The results section is a straightforward discussion of the research findings, but it is frequently the most difficult part of a research article to understand due to the statistical tests that may be used, especially for a newly educated consumer of research. At the beginning of the results section, a discussion of the sample is provided, along with appropriate statistical description, so the reader can understand the characteristics of the research subjects. The results section presents the findings of the research and answers each research question and/or tests each hypothesis.

For quantitative studies, the statistical analysis presented in the results section is typically presented in tables, charts, and graphs as well as described in the text. The tables often provide greater detail than what is described in words and also allow the reader to follow the description of the results provided in the article. In the results section, the researchers will also state whether there were any unexpected findings or findings that have not been discovered in the prior literature. The researcher will wait until the discussion section to discuss the reasons for the anomaly in detail, but she will typically point out the interesting finding when it is initially presented in the results section.

The presentation of data flows logically and a straightforward discussion of the main findings and their significance are presented in the results section. In qualitative research, the data are organized in a manner that illustrates a line of reasoning or tells a story. Some evaluative questions to ask about the results include:

1. What findings are statistically significant? (discussed in Chapter 9)
2. Does the author answer each research question and/or address each hypothesis?
3. If there are tables, are the highlights discussed in the narrative of the results?
4. Are the results of qualitative studies adequately supported with examples of quotations or descriptions of observations?[16]

Discussion

Some research articles combine the discussion section with the results section, while others combine the discussion section with the conclusion section, while still others keep all three sections separate. We will present them as separate sections. In the discussion section of the article, the researcher is expected to interpret the findings of the research study and discuss their implications. The major findings are discussed and examined for agreement or disagreement with prior research findings as presented in the literature review portion of the article.

The researchers basically answer the following question: "Did the findings support the results of prior literature?" If yes, the author will note that his findings are consistent with prior research. If the answer is no, then the researcher will identify potential reasons for the unexpected finding. The unexpected finding may be due to a research limitation or the researcher may provide an analytical or theoretical framework to explain the odd finding. In a sense, the research article is presented in a circular manner. The literature review is presented followed by the methods and results section,

and then in the discussion section, the findings are tied back to the prior literature presented in the literature review.

Depending on the type of research completed, the researchers will present in the discussion section the implications of the findings for prior literature, theory development, and policy and practice in the criminal justice system. Depending on the publication outlet, some research articles may include a few paragraphs on the policy implications of the research findings. Some evaluative questions to ask about the discussion include:

1. Do the researchers acknowledge specific methodological limitations and their potential impact on the findings (limitations may be covered in methods section)?
2. Are the results discussed in terms of the literature cited in the literature review?
3. Are the results discussed in terms of any relevant theories?[17]
4. Does the author offer speculations about what the results may mean and their implications?

Conclusion

In the conclusion, the researchers will first briefly summarize the research problem addressed in the study, the major results, and any significant unexpected findings. Then, the researchers provide the reader a broad perspective on the research findings and put the findings into context by demonstrating where the study results fit into the larger literature. The researchers will explain the benefits derived from the research and identify areas in need of further research.

Also, the researcher will discuss the generalizability of the findings. Can the findings be generalized to other populations, other settings, and other contexts? If so, the researcher will justify why the findings can be generalized within the selected parameters. If not, the researcher will discuss this limitation and its causes along with providing an explanation of what research needs to be done in the future to improve the generalizability of the results. Some evaluative questions to ask about the conclusion include:

1. Are specific implications discussed?
2. Are suggestions for future research specified?
3. Does the research extend the boundaries of the knowledge on a topic?[18]

4. Do the researcher's conclusions concur with the results that were reported or does the author over-generalize the findings?

References

The reference section of a research article gives the reader complete information about the previous research that was used in the study. Researchers need to provide citations for each source that was used in the research article. Many of the sources will have been used in the literature review section. The reader can use the reference list to obtain additional primary sources on the research topic. If you compare the references of several research articles on the same topic, you will be able to determine what seminal and critical articles exist on the research topic.

Some evaluative questions to ask about the references include:

1. Has the most recent research on the topic been included in the references?

2. Have the seminal articles on the topic been included in the references?

EXTERNAL INDICATORS OF RESEARCH QUALITY

This section will focus on the external indicators of research quality. The external indicators can be identified without reading the research article. It is important to recognize that reading the article and identifying the internal indicators of research quality, which will be discussed in the next section, is a more valid measure of, and therefore a better way to assess, research quality. However, the external indicators can serve as a shortcut method to determine if the research article is worth further attention and assessment.

As previously discussed, the three main publication outlets for research articles are journal articles, reports, and books. Most of the focus of this section will be on journal articles since academic journals are the primary way that researchers disseminate the results of their research. Some of the indicators discussed next, such as university affiliation and researcher reputation, apply equally to journal articles, books, and reports, but a few comments about the indicators of quality books and reports are necessary before we delve into those topics.

For this section, we are referring to books used as a primary source to document a research study. In other

words, due to the magnitude of the study, a book-length manuscript is developed to document the research methodology and findings. Secondary sources include textbooks, encyclopedias, and news reports. Secondary sources usually involve summaries of primary source work and, while they may offer some information related to the research methods used in the study, they often do not provide the detail you need to assess the quality of the research article without tracking down the original article (i.e., primary source).

For books as a primary source, one of the main factors to consider when determining the quality of research reported is to look at the book's publisher. Books published by university presses (e.g., Cornell University Press and University of Texas Press) are typically high-quality manuscripts involving high-quality research. University presses, similar to some of the academic journals discussed next, have stringent manuscript review processes, so only the best manuscripts are printed by these publishers.

Similarly, for reports, you need to look at what organization published the research. If the report is published by a federal agency such as the U.S. Department of Justice, then it should be considered high quality. The U.S. Department of Justice and other federal agencies have full-time researchers that write research reports on data obtained by the agency, so the research is conducted and written by trained researchers. The same can be said for reports published by state agencies. There are also private companies (e.g., Rand Corporation) that routinely conduct research in criminal justice agencies and then publish the reports, which are frequently available on their websites. Much of this work completed by respected companies is high quality as well because trained, full-time researchers are conducting the research and reporting the results. The theme is that if the research is completed by a full-time researcher, then it is probably a quality piece of research. Of course, there will be exceptions to the general rule, but it is a good piece of information to remember as you move forward in assessing research articles.

You should be more skeptical of research reports completed by city or county criminal justice agencies. Most of these agencies do not have full-time researchers, so there is concern about the capabilities of the person who completed the research. That does not mean that a report completed by a county or city criminal justice agency cannot be high quality but rather that you should not assume it to be high quality based on the agency that produced it. These reports need further assessment to determine their quality. We will discuss three external indicators of quality research: researcher reputation, institutional reputation, and journal quality.

Researcher Reputation

Some researchers consistently produce top-quality research, so the research articles they write—whether as a book, report, or journal article—can be assumed to be high quality. There are researchers that are the best in their particular area of expertise and everything they produce is high quality. Often, the largest body of research in a particular area is done by the same person or the same group of people at a few different institutions. We will not name specific researchers who meet these requirements, but maybe your professor will. If you or your professor does not know the researcher, you can search for information about her on the Internet. You should be able to easily find the researcher's curriculum vita (like a resume) online and look at her prior publications to see if she has written in this area before and where the prior research articles have been published.

Institutional Reputation

Another external indicator is the institutional affiliation of the researcher and its reputation. Just like journals discussed in the following section, some universities are better than others when it comes to research. Researchers who work at top-ranked research universities are going to have strict requirements to produce high-quality research and high-quality publications in order to maintain their employment. Although even the top-ranked research universities have some deadwood (we definitely are not going to name names), institutional reputation is a quick way to determine if the research article is high quality.

Journal Quality

As previously stated, academic journals are the primary way that researchers disseminate the results of their research. The journals vary in quality though. One measure of the quality of a journal is their manuscript review process. There are two types of journals: refereed and nonrefereed journals. Refereed journals use a peer-review process to review manuscripts. Peer review is a form of quality control most commonly related to academic journals. If a journal follows a peer review process, when a manuscript is submitted to the journal, it

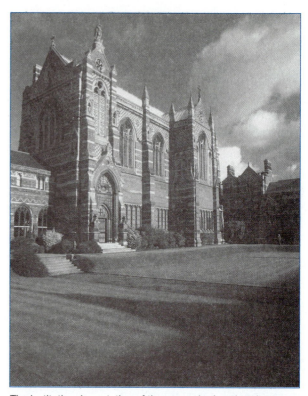

The institutional reputation of the researcher's university can be used as an external indicator of research quality.

is sent out to be reviewed by two or more experts in the field to determine whether the manuscript is suitable for publication. The review is almost always a blind review, which means the reviewer does not know the name of the researcher who wrote the manuscript. This limits bias in the review process.

When a manuscript is submitted to a refereed journal, the journal editor will review the manuscript to see if it is of sufficient quality to send out for external review. Those that are not of sufficient quality are rejected by the journal editor and returned to the author. For those that are good enough to be externally reviewed, the editor will send the manuscript to two or more reviewers. Sometimes, these reviewers are members of the journal's editorial board. Each reviewer evaluates the article, provides written comments to the editor, and recommends to either accept, reject, or send the manuscript back to the authors for revisions and reassessment after the revisions are made (commonly called "revise and resubmit"). After the reviews are completed, the editor makes the final decision on whether the manuscript will be accepted for publication, rejected, or sent back to the authors with a request to "revise and resubmit."

Nonrefereed journals do not utilize the peer review process. The articles in nonrefereed journals will be reviewed by the journal editor and published in the order in which they are received or according to a fee that the author pays. Journals that are not peer reviewed do not garner as much respect from fellow researchers as there is less quality control of the material published. If you are not familiar with a particular journal, you can usually determine if it is a peer-reviewed journal by reading the material at the front of the journal. There is a section at the beginning of the journal (sometimes it is in the back) that will be titled something like "information for potential contributors," which will provide information on the manuscript review process for the journal.

As an external indicator of research quality, research articles appearing in refereed journals will be higher quality than articles appearing in nonrefereed journals. Of course, there are exceptions to this statement, but it is a good principle to remember as you move forward as an educated consumer of research.

You have identified that the journal utilizes a peer-review process and so it is a refereed journal. Now what? Well, all refereed journals are not the same quality; some are better than others. So, how do you determine if the refereed journal is a high-quality journal? One indicator is the journal's acceptance rate. The acceptance rate is the number of manuscripts accepted for publication divided by the number of manuscripts submitted to the journal for publication consideration. The lower the acceptance rate, presumably the better the quality of the journal. The acceptance rate can be difficult to obtain without directly contacting the journal editor, so it is not always available to the consumer of research.

Another indicator of the quality of the journal is the reputation of the journal editor. As stated previously regarding the reputation of the researcher, if the journal editor is one of the top researchers in the area covered by the journal, then that is an indication that the journal is high quality as well. Similarly, the reader can review the names of the editorial board members listed at the beginning of the journal. The better the reputations of the editorial board members, the better the reputation of the journal. In addition, the university affiliation of each editorial board member will be presented in the journal. If the journal has several editorial board members that come from major research universities, then this is an

indication that the journal is of high quality. These three indicators (acceptance rate, editor reputation, and editorial board composition) are used by research consumers to assess the quality of the journal, but a new indicator has been developed in recent years to measure journal quality: the impact factor.

Impact Factor   The impact factor is a measure of the frequency with which the average article in a journal has been cited in a particular year. It is an evaluation tool that is annually provided by the company Thomson Reuters in the *Journal Citation Reports*. A journal's impact factor is the average number of times articles from the journal, published in the past two years, have been cited. The latest year available at the time of this writing is 2011. The impact factor for 2011 was calculated as the number of citations in 2011 to articles published in the journal in 2009 and 2010 divided by the number of articles published in the journal in 2009 and 2010. The higher the impact factor, the higher the journal quality. The idea behind the impact factor is that if other researchers are citing the material from the journal's articles, then this is an indication that the journal's articles are high quality and thus the journal is a quality venue for published research.

The top-ranked journals of the 2011 *Journal Citation Reports* in the criminology and penology category which is where criminal justice and criminology journals are ranked, are:

1. *Trauma Violence and Abuse* (impact factor—3.265);
2. *Criminology* (impact factor—2.467);
3. *Journal of Research in Crime and Delinquency* (impact factor—2.231);
4. *Crime and Justice: A Review of Research* (impact factor—2.188), and;
5. *British Journal of Criminology* (impact factor—2.130)

A list of the top 50 journals in criminal justice and criminology are presented in Figure 8-2. You can assume that the articles in the higher ranked journals are high quality before you even begin to read the journal article.

When judging the quality of a research article using external indicators, the bottom line is to look at it from as many different perspectives as possible, including the author's credentials, the author's professional affiliation, and where the work is published.

FIGURE 8.2 | Criminal Justice and Criminology Journal Rankings by Impact Factor—2011

Rank	Journal Title	Impact Factor
1	Trauma Violence and Abuse	3.265
2	Criminology	2.467
3	Journal of Research in Crime and Delinquency	2.231
4	Crime and Justice: A Review of Research	2.188
5	British Journal of Criminology	2.130
6	Journal of Quantitative Criminology	2.120
7	Aggression and Violent Behavior	1.949
8	Crime & Delinquency	1.750
9	Criminal Justice and Behavior	1.708
10	Journal of Interpersonal Violence	1.639
11	Justice Quarterly	1.631
12	Sexual Abuse: A Journal of Research and Treatment	1.538
13	Punishment & Society: International Journal of Penology	1.419
14	Youth Violence and Juvenile Justice	1.366
15	Legal and Criminological Psychology	1.286
16	Violence and Victims	1.283
17	Criminal Behaviour and Mental Health	1.277
18	Journal of Criminal Justice	1.235
19	Journal of Experimental Criminology	1.171
20	European Journal of Criminology	1.000
21	Theoretical Criminology	0.950
22	International Journal of Speech Language and the Law	0.920
23	Journal of Forensic Psychiatry & Psychology	0.884
24	International Journal of Offender Therapy and Comparative Criminology	0.840
25	Canadian Journal of Criminology and Criminal Justice	0.791
26	Journal of Criminal Law & Criminology	0.703
27	Psychology Crime & Law	0.694
28	Policing & Society	0.686
29	Police Quarterly	0.684
30	Homicide Studies	0.619
31	Feminist Criminology	0.613
32	Australian and New Zealand Journal of Criminology	0.609
33	Security Journal	0.605
34	Criminology & Criminal Justice	0.565
35	Policing: An International Journal of Police Strategies & Management	0.547
36	Journal of Investigative Psychology and Offender Profiling	0.533
37	Social & Legal Studies	0.531
38	European Journal on Criminal Policy and Research	0.526
39	Crime Media Culture	0.433
40	Prison Journal	0.400
41	Journal of Forensic Psychology Practice	0.366
42	Psychiatry, Psychology and Law	0.349
43	Crime Law and Social Change	0.346
44	Monatsschrift fur Kriminologie und Strafrechtsreform (Germany)	0.346
45	Revija za Kriminalistiko in Kriminologijo (Slovenia)	0.340
46	Criminal Law Review	0.273
47	Recht & Psychiatrie (Germany)	0.241
48	Deviance et Societe (Switzerland)	0.197
49	International Journal of Law Crime and Justice	0.107
50	Kriminalistik (Germany)	0.073

In a 2007 study on the effects of popular videos such as the "Baby Einstein" and "Brainy Baby" series, researchers found that these products may be doing more harm than good and may actually delay language development in toddlers. Parents aiming to put their babies on the fast track, even if they are still working on walking, spend hundreds of millions of dollars each year on the videos.

The study was conducted by researchers from the University of Washington. The data was obtained through telephone interviews with 1,008 parents of children age 2 months to 24 months. Each telephone interview took about 45 minutes to complete. Questions were asked about child and parent demographics, child-parent interactions, and child's viewing of several content types of television and DVDs/videos. Parents were also asked to complete the short form of the MacArthur-Bates Communicative Development Inventory (CDI), which measures infant language development and has been shown to be both reliable and valid. The associations between CDI scores and media exposure were evaluated using multivariate regression (see Chapter 9), controlling for parent and child demographics and parent-child interactions.[20] Among infants (age 8 to 16 months), each hour per day of viewing baby DVDs/videos was associated with a 17-point decrease in the CDI score. Infants who watched videos learned six to eight fewer new vocabulary words than babies who never watched the videos. Among toddlers (age 17 to 24 months), there were no significant associations between any type of media exposure and CDI scores.[21] In fact, the American Academy of Pediatrics has recommended no television for children under 24 months.

The University of Washington press release[22] regarding the study led to a letter from Bob Iger, the CEO of Disney and proprietor of Baby Einstein, to Mark Emmert, the president of the University of Washington, calling the press statement "misleading, irresponsible, and derogatory"[23] and claiming the "methodology [used in the study] is doubtful, its data seem anomalous and the inferences it posits unreliable."[24] In response, President Emmert stated "The Journal of Pediatrics is a prestigious, peer-reviewed journal. Papers submitted to this journal undergo a rigorous review by experts in the field before they are accepted for publication. This process ensures that the work represented in the paper meets high standards of scientific inquiry required by the editors of the journal and its editorial panel of distinguished scientists. . . . The University of Washington will not retract its news release." [25]

INTERNAL INDICATORS OF RESEARCH QUALITY

Although the external indicators of research quality serve as a quick screening mechanism for research articles, it is not a substitute for a detailed, internal review of the article. Even though many journals utilize a peer-review process and some have low manuscript acceptance rates, articles within those journals will vary in quality, so an internal assessment of research quality is essential. A reader who critically assesses a research article will evaluate the methodology used by the researcher, assess the analysis performed, and verify that the conclusions drawn by the authors are supported by the research findings. When we reviewed the structure of research articles earlier in the chapter, we provided evaluative questions you should ask about the title, abstract, introduction, literature review, results, discussion, conclusion, and references. We did not provide any evaluative questions for the methods section at the time, but now we're ready to address those in this section, in which the internal indicators of research quality will be presented. These indicators will assist in answering the question "How good is this research article?" We will focus on the methods section of the article.

Throughout this book you have been provided with the tools necessary to critically evaluate research. We have covered a comprehensive list of research methods topics and have consistently discussed issues and challenges faced by researchers when conducting research. For example, in Chapter 3 we discussed probability and non-probability sampling and the issues of representativeness, generalizability, sampling error, and sample size. In Chapter 4, we discussed surveys and issues such as nonresponse, social desirability, ensuring truthful responses, and ensuring consistent question meaning for all respondents. We also provided a comprehensive discussion of reliability and validity, focusing on mechanisms to assess and increase each. In Chapter 5, we discussed experimental and quasi-experimental designs, focusing on the critical importance of the pretest, control group, and random assignment. In addition, we discussed several threats to internal validity that may impact the results found utilizing these designs. In Chapter 6, we discussed field research and the issues of going native, reactivity and the Hawthorne Effect, maintaining objectivity, and ethical dilemmas faced by field researchers. We also discussed case studies and the issues of generalizability and researcher bias. In Chapter 7, we discussed unobtrusive measures, such as secondary data analysis and the issues of having no control over the original data collection and problems with the validity of agency records. We also discussed the use of archival data and the reliability and validity issues that arise from this method, along with content analysis and the challenge of interrater reliability.

At this point, you may be thinking that no piece of research is going to withstand the rigors set forth in this chapter and book. We have stated it before, but it should be clear after the last paragraph that there is no perfect research. Researchers make a series of decisions when conducting a research study and not everyone will agree with those decisions. Each decision creates the potential for error, and each step in the research process creates the potential for error as well. There is plenty of high-quality research, though. The issue is not whether the research has limitations but how the flaws impact the research results. Are the errors of the magnitude that they can significantly impact the results of the study, which then leads you to question the results?

Your ability to read and critically evaluate research articles will improve with practice by reading many journal articles, books, and reports, but it does take practice. Remember, research involves a process and research articles are structured in a similar manner each time. Once you are comfortable with the process for conducting research and the structure of research articles, your review of articles will become easier and more routine. Once you have developed your ability to critically assess research articles, those skills will remain with you forever. You will not have to relearn the research process and evaluative issues every five years in order to maintain your skills. The reality is research methods do not change that much. Yes, it is true that new techniques are developed (e.g., Internet and e-mail surveys), but the foundation of research methods developed decades ago will be the same foundation in 100 years.

We will present several evaluative questions next. As you put your research methods knowledge into practice and review research articles, revisit the earlier chapters. But, do not think of research quality as a dichotomy of good and bad. In reality, research quality should be reflected as a continuum, and every research article can be placed somewhere on the continuum.

Questions to Ask about Research Articles

Following are some evaluative questions you should ask about a research article. Some of the questions will differentially apply, depending on the methods used in the research study. The questions will be categorized by chapter so you can easily refer back to the chapter for additional information.

Evaluative Questions from Chapter 2 Material—Ethics and Terminology

- What is/are the basic research question(s)?
- What were the major concepts in the research study?
- How were the concepts operationalized and measured?
- Would other measurements have been better? Why or why not?
- What were the independent and dependent variables in the study?
- Were any hypotheses stated?
- Were these hypotheses justified adequately in terms of prior research?
- Did the study seem consistent with current ethical standards? Explain how ethical standards were upheld.
- Did the author adequately represent the findings in the discussion and/or conclusions sections?
- Did the researcher overgeneralize the findings? If yes, how?

Evaluative Questions from Chapter 3 Material—Sampling
In the methods section of a research article, the researcher should describe the sampling procedures used in the study and describe the subjects who participated in the research. When you are reading about the sampling procedures, be sure to evaluate who the research subjects were, taking into account available demographic characteristics such as age, race, ethnicity, and gender. Be sure to assess whether the composition of the sample will limit the generalizability of the results. Some evaluative questions about sampling follow.

- Was a sample or the entire population used in the study?
- What type of sampling method was employed?
- Was a probability sampling method used?

- If a non-probability sampling method was used, does the researcher justify its use and discuss its limitations?

- Did the authors think the sample was generally representative of the population from which it was drawn? Why or why not?

- Do you think the sample was generally representative of the population from which it was drawn? Why or why not?

- Was the sample size large enough? Why or why not?

- Overall, is the sample appropriate for generalizing to the population?

Evaluative Questions from Chapter 4 Material—Surveys, Validity, and Reliability

- Was survey research used? Was this design suited to the research question posed? Why or why not?

- Was the response rate reported? If yes, what was it?

- Does it appear likely that those who did not respond or participate were markedly different from those who did participate? Why or why not?

- What is the likelihood that characteristics of the nonrespondents introduced bias into the results? Did the authors adequately discuss this issue?

- What evidence did the authors provide to show the representativeness/generalizability of the sample to the population? What comparisons between the respondents, sample, and population were presented?

- Did the survey used, the measures of the variables, seem valid and reliable? Why or why not?

- How did the author attempt to establish the validity of the survey?

- When delving into sensitive matters (e.g., past victimization or criminal/delinquent history), is there reason to believe that accurate data were obtained?

- Do you believe that social desirability is an issue in the study? Why or why not?

- How did the author attempt to establish the reliability of the survey?

- If an index was used in the survey, does it have adequate internal consistency?

- How did the researcher ensure consistent meaning of the questions?

- How was the survey distributed? What factors influenced the author's decision to distribute the survey in this manner?

Evaluative Questions from Chapter 5 Material— Experimental and Quasi-Experimental Designs

- What type of research design was used in this study?

- What were the parameters/criteria for inclusion in the study?

- What cases were excluded from the study?

- What was/were the treatment(s)?

- What was/were the dependent variable(s)?

- What pre-test(s) was/were conducted? Be sure to discuss how each dependent variable was measured and the time frame.

- What post-test(s) was/were conducted? Be sure to discuss how each dependent variable was measured and the time frame.

- What was/were the experimental/treatment group(s)?

- What was/were the control/comparison group(s)? Was the control/comparison group adequate?

- Were the groups established through randomization or matching? Be sure to discuss the procedures used to establish and monitor equivalence.

- What threats to internal validity could impact the results of this study? For each threat to internal validity identified, define the threat, describe how it applies to this study, and explain how it could impact the results of this study.

- Were any causal assertions made or implied in the hypotheses or in subsequent discussion? If yes, were all three criteria for establishing causal relationships addressed? How did the author establish the existence of the three criteria for causality? What, if any, variables were controlled in the analysis to reduce the risk of spurious relationships?

Evaluative Questions from Chapter 6 Material—Field Research and Case Studies

- Was field research or a case study used in this study? Was the design suited to the research question posed? Why or why not?

CLASSICS IN CJ RESEARCH
Factors that Influence Police Decisions Regarding Juveniles

RESEARCH STUDY[26]
In the mid-1960s, very few research studies had been conducted on police discretion. The use of police discretion was recognized by researchers and law enforcement personnel at the time, but few studies had addressed the factors that police consider when making decisions to arrest. Piliavin and Briar were the first to assess the factors that impact police decisions regarding juveniles.

RESEARCH QUESTION
What factors influence police decisions regarding juveniles?

METHODOLOGY
The setting for the research was a metropolitan police department in the United States serving an industrial city with approximately 450,000 residents. Data for this study came from observations of police officers on the street over a 9-month period and interviews with these same officers (27 of the 30 officers were interviewed). Utilizing field research, systematic data were collected on police encounters with 76 juveniles. Observations took place on a variety of days and shifts, but more observations occurred in the evenings and on weekends when police officers were more likely to interact with juveniles.

The subjects under study were 30 police officers assigned to the Juvenile Bureau. These police officers were responsible for delinquency prevention as well as law enforcement for the police department. In the field, juvenile officers operated essentially as patrol officers. They were assigned to beats, answered calls for service, and although concerned primarily with juvenile offenders, frequently had occasion to arrest adults. The study is limited to police interaction with juveniles though. The researchers had an opportunity to observe all officers in the Bureau during the study, but their observations were concentrated on those who had been working in the Bureau for a minimum of one year. The officers were observed in the course of their regular patrol shifts. Observations were completed for the following encounters with juveniles:

1. Encounters taking place at or near the scene of offenses reported to the police department; and

2. Encounters occurring as the result of officers' directly observing youths either committing offenses or in suspicious circumstances.

For these encounters, officers could choose among five dispositional alternatives:

1. Outright release;

2. Release and submission of a field interrogation report briefly describing the circumstances surrounding the police-juvenile encounter;

3. Official reprimand and release to parents or guardian;

4. Citation to juvenile court; and

5. Arrest and confinement in juvenile detention.

Dispositions 3, 4, and 5 involved the juvenile being taken to the police station and resulted in an official record for the juvenile because his name was officially recorded in Bureau files as a juvenile violator.

For purposes of this analysis, each youth's demeanor in the encounter was classified as either cooperative or uncooperative. The data used for the classification of demeanor were the written records of observations made by the researchers. The classifications were made by an independent assessor not associated with this study. In classifying a youth's demeanor as cooperative or uncooperative, particular attention was paid to: 1) the youth's responses to police officers' questions and requests; 2) the respect and deference, or lack of these qualities, shown by the youth toward police officers, and 3) police officers assessments of the youth's demeanor.

RESULTS
The researchers reported several results. First, the researchers found that broad discretion was exercised by police officers in dealing with juvenile offenders. All offenses, even serious ones, received each of the five dispositional alternatives

---

- How much interaction was present between the researcher and the research subjects?

- What steps were taken to keep the researcher from influencing the behavior of the research subjects?

- Were any ethical dilemmas faced by the researcher? If yes, how did the researcher handle the dilemmas?

- Did the researcher maintain objectivity? If not, how did this influence the results of the study?

- Did the researcher acknowledge any biases or reactivity in the study? If so, how did they impact the results?

- Did the researcher discuss the generalizability of the findings?

previously discussed. Therefore, the commission of a serious offense did not automatically result in arrest.

Second, the exercise of discretion was affected by a few readily observable criteria, including the seriousness of the current offense, the juveniles' prior offense record, race, and demeanor. The first two criteria (i.e., seriousness of offense and prior record) are legal factors and are expected to be taken into consideration by the police when making decisions.

However, the demeanor of the youth was identified as a major factor in determining what police disposition he would be given. Overall, 67% of the juveniles who were categorized as uncooperative in their interaction with police were arrested while less than 5% of the juveniles who were deemed cooperative were arrested. During interviews, officers estimated that 50–60% of dispositions for first-time juvenile offenders were based on the demeanor of the juvenile. Besides legal factors like seriousness of the offense and prior record, demeanor of the juvenile was the most important factor influencing the decisions of officers.

Third, the differential in arrest and apprehension rates between blacks and whites was not simply a consequence of a greater offense rate among blacks. To some extent, the differential was due to the fact that blacks more often than whites were viewed as uncooperative. Blacks were more likely to receive one of the more severe outcomes. This finding was attributed to police officer prejudice against blacks. Researchers interviewed 27 of the officers assigned to the Juvenile Bureau, and 18 of them candidly expressed their disapproval of blacks.

LIMITATIONS WITH THE STUDY PROCEDURE

Piliavin and Briar offered one of the first empirical studies of police discretion by observing police encounters with juveniles. They based their conclusions, however, on a small sample of police observations (i.e., 76 total observations were made in a 9-month period). Also, the 76 observations were not randomly selected. These limitations, small sample size and non-random sample, bring the generalizability of the findings into question. What the researchers observed in this particular city with these officers may not apply in other jurisdictions with different officers.

There are possible reliability issues with how demeanor was coded for the research. Whether or not the juvenile was cooperative and respectful to the police could be a highly subjective decision. The researchers did use an independent assessor to categorize the data on demeanor, but the assessor's interpretation of the data may have been different from another person's interpretation. Utilizing an interrater reliability protocol where two independent assessors categorize the data on demeanor and then the two assessments are compared would have improved the reliability of the categorization.

In Piliavin and Briar's study, the researchers' role of observer as participant (discussed in Chapter 6) was known to the police officers being studied. The police knew exactly who the researchers were and that their encounters with juveniles were being examined. A potential source of bias with this type of observational research is known as the Hawthorne Effect (see Chapter 6). When research subjects are aware that their behavior is being observed, the observation itself may influence their behavior. The extent to which the police officers in Piliavin and Briar's study altered their behavior because they were being observed was unknown. However, the candor shown by the officers in their interviews with the investigators and the use of officially frowned-upon practices while under observation provide some assurance that the observations were valid and reflected the typical activities of the police officers studied.

IMPACT ON CRIMINAL JUSTICE

Piliavin and Briar were among the first to conduct an empirical study that explored the influence of demeanor on police decision-making. Their systematic observations of police-juvenile encounters revealed that the police were more likely to arrest uncooperative juveniles. Over the past half century, numerous studies of police discretion have demonstrated the relationship between suspect demeanor and arrest. Piliavin and Briar also observed that police unfairly targeted black juveniles because they fit a stereotype held by the police that most delinquents were black. Today, the influence of race and police discretion centers on the topic of racial profiling as discussed in the chapter opening case study.

- Did the instruments used, the measures of the variables, seem valid and reliable? Why or why not?

- How did the author attempt to establish the reliability of the measurement?

- How did the author attempt to establish the validity of the measurement?

- What more could have been done in the study to establish reliability and validity?

Evaluative Questions from Chapter 7 Material—Unobtrusive Methods

- Was an unobtrusive method such as secondary data analysis used? Was this design suited to the research question posed? Why or why not?

- Did the instruments used, the measures of the variables, seem valid and reliable? Why or why not?

- How did the author attempt to establish the reliability of the measurement?

- How did the author attempt to establish the validity of the measurement?

- What more could have been done in the study to establish reliability and validity?

ARTICLE CRITIQUE: MINNEAPOLIS DOMESTIC VIOLENCE EXPERIMENT

Sherman, Lawrence W., and Richard A. Berk. (1984). "The specific deterrent effects of arrest for domestic assault." *American Sociological Review.* 49, 261–272. Portions of the article are included in Appendix A.

As the final section in this chapter, we will present an example of an article critique utilizing the internal indicators of research quality discussed in the previous section. Recall that it is impossible to develop a single checklist of the topics that need to be addressed in a methods section of a research article, because the details that need to be provided depend on the methods used. Similarly, it is impossible to develop a single set of questions that can be asked and answered to comprehensively assess every research article, because the questions depend on the methods used in the article. Therefore, we will present an example of an article critique tailored to the experimental and quasi-experimental designs discussed in Chapter 5. We selected the Minneapolis Domestic Violence Experiment (MDVE) as the example, because it is probably the best known piece of research in criminal justice and criminology. You not only hear about the results of the MDVE (arrest is most effective in reducing domestic violence recidivism) in research methods, but also hear about it in policing classes and policy courses. The MDVE is to research methods what *Miranda v. Arizona* is to criminal procedure: the most recognized example on the topic.

Next, we ask and answer several questions regarding the MDVE. Portions of the article are in Appendix A. You can review the article to see where we obtained the information to answer each question. This is the type of activity you will be able to perform, although probably not as structured as the questions and answers that follow, as you begin to apply your knowledge as an educated consumer of research.

1. *In one sentence, state the purpose of this study.*
The purpose of the MDVE was to determine which of three police responses (arrest, separation, or

The Minneapolis Domestic Violence Experiment concluded that arrest leads to fewer incidences of repeat domestic violence in comparison to separation and mediation.

mediation) produced the lowest recidivism rates for domestic violence offenders.

2. *What type of research design was used in this study?*
A randomized experimental design was used in the MDVE.

3. *What were the parameters/criteria for inclusion in the study?*
In order to be included in the study, the calls for police service had to involve a misdemeanor (simple) domestic assault, and both the suspect and the victim had to be present when the police arrived.

4. *What cases were excluded from the study?*
The following cases were excluded from the study: (1) cases involving felony domestic assaults; (2) cases where both parties were not present when the police arrived; (3) cases where the suspect attempted to assault police officers; (4) cases where a victim persistently demanded an arrest, and (5) cases involving injuries to both parties.

5. *What was/were the treatment(s)?*
The treatment was the police response to domestic violence, which included arrest, separation, or mediation.

6. *What was/were the dependent variable(s)?*
The dependent variable was repeat domestic violence (i.e., recidivism).

7. *What pre-test(s) was/were conducted? Be sure to discuss how each dependent variable was measured and the time frame.*
Since the dependent variable was recidivism, no pre-test was conducted in the MDVE.

8.   *What post-test(s) was/were conducted? Be sure to discuss how each dependent variable was measured and the time frame.*

The post-test involved a 6-month follow-up period to measure the frequency and seriousness of domestic violence after each police intervention of arrest, separation, or mediation. The dependent variable (i.e., repeat domestic violence) was measured in two ways. First, the researchers obtained police offense and arrest reports for domestic violence that mentioned the suspect's name during the 6-month follow-up period. Second, victim interviews were completed 2 weeks after the police intervention and every 2 weeks thereafter for 24 weeks. The first victim interview was face-to-face while each subsequent interview was conducted over the telephone. The victim interviews allowed researchers to examine domestic violence offenses that may have occurred but did not come to the official attention of police.

9.   *What was/were the experimental group(s)?*

Since three interventions were used in the MDVE, there are three different groups of people, totaling 314 cases. There were two experimental groups. First, the 136 people arrested during the study comprised one experimental group. Second, the 89 people separated during the study comprised the second experimental group.

10. *What was/were the control group(s)?*

Since the common police practice at the time for cases of misdemeanor domestic violence was to advise and mediate the situation, leaving both parties at the location, the control group was the 89 people advised/mediated during the domestic violence calls for service.

11. *How was random assignment established? Be sure to discuss the procedures used to establish and monitor equivalence.*

The three different police actions were randomly distributed based on color-coded report forms carried by the officers. Upon a misdemeanor domestic violence call with both parties present, the officer's action (arrest, separation, or mediation) was predetermined by the order of report forms in the officer's notebook. The colored report forms were randomly ordered in the officer's notebook and the color on the form determined the officer response at the scene. All colored report forms were randomly ordered through a lottery assignment

method. The result was that all police officer actions in misdemeanor domestic violence calls were randomly assigned. To ensure the random assignment was carried out as planned, research staff participated in ride-alongs with officers to ensure that officers did not skip the order of randomly ordered forms. In addition, the research staff logged the domestic violence reports in the order received to make sure the sequence corresponded to the original assignment of police interventions. Table 1 in the research article located in Appendix A shows the degree to which the treatments were delivered as designed.

12. *Identify two threats to internal validity that may impact the results of this study. For each threat to internal validity identified, define the threat, describe how it applies to this study, and explain how it may impact the results of this study.*

The first threat to internal validity is selection bias. As depicted in Table 1 in the article in Appendix A, the officers did not always follow the random assignment protocol. For example, some officers decided to violate the random assignment protocol, which violated the randomized experimental design, because they found the upcoming treatment inappropriate for the situation. The officers did not always follow the randomly assigned action (arrest, separation, or mediation) as a result of other circumstances that occurred at the scene. In fact, some officers simply ignored the assigned action if they felt a particular call for domestic violence required another action. Selection bias generally indicates that the experimental group is somehow different from the control group on a factor that could influence the post-test results. Since the officers violated the random assignment protocol and self-selected some subjects for arrest, the arrested group may be different from the other two groups on factors that may impact repeat domestic violence.

The second threat to internal validity is attrition or subject mortality. Attrition refers to differential loss in the number or type of subjects between the experimental and control groups. In the MDVE, attrition occurred with the victim interviews. Only 205 of the victims (65% response rate) could be located and initial interviews obtained two weeks after the police intervention. Only 161 victims (51% response rate) provided all 12 follow-up interviews over the 6-month follow-up period. The question then is, "Are there differences between the respondents and the nonrespondents that could then impact the results of the MDVE?" We do not know how the two groups differed so are unable to adequately answer the question. We do know from Chapter 4 that as the response rate decreases, it becomes more likely that the nonrespondents will differ from the survey respondents. When

there are significant differences between respondents and nonrespondents, each group represents biased subgroups of the total population. Bias means that in some systematic way the individuals responding to a survey are different from the overall population. Therefore, the results based on the survey respondents are not reflective of the overall population.

CHAPTER SUMMARY

In this chapter, we reviewed the steps in the research process to provide the "big picture" of research endeavors. We also reviewed the structure of research articles. It is helpful as an educated consumer of research to understand the common structure of research articles and reports. You will be able to easily identify these sections as you review research articles and reports in the future. We specifically discussed three external indicators of research quality, including researcher reputation, institutional reputation, and journal quality. The external indicators can serve as a short-cut method to determine if the research article is worth further attention and assessment. Although the external indicators of research quality serve as a quick screening mechanism for research articles, it is not a substitute for a

detailed, internal review of the article. A reader who critically assesses a research article will evaluate the methodology used by the researcher, assess the analysis performed, and verify that the conclusions drawn by the authors are supported by the research findings. We reviewed the internal indicators of research quality in this chapter. The discussion was a culmination of the tools provided throughout this book to critically evaluate research. Finally, this chapter provided an example of a research article critique to demonstrate how the internal indicators of research quality can be used to assess a research article. Now that you have finished this chapter, you have the tools necessary to thoroughly review and evaluate research, with one exception: statistics. Statistics will be covered in the next chapter.

CRITICAL THINKING QUESTIONS

1. What are the steps in the research process, and what activities occur at each step?
2. What are the primary sections of a research article, and what material is covered in each section?
3. What are the three main external indicators of research quality? How is journal quality determined?
4. How would you apply the internal indicators of research quality to a research article? Be sure to provide the types of questions you would ask in your assessment.

ENDNOTES

1 Grogger, Jeffrey, and Greg Ridgeway. (2006). "Testing for racial profiling in traffic stops from behind a veil of darkness." *Journal of the American Statistical Association* 101, 878–887.
2 Worden, Robert E., Sarah J. McLean, and Andrew P. Wheeler. (2012). "Testing for racial profiling with the veil-of-darkness method." *Police Quarterly* 15, 92–111.
3 Ibid.
4 Hamermesh, D. S. (1996). *Workdays, workhours, and work schedules: Evidence for the United States and*
Germany. Kalamazoo, MI: W. E. Upjohn Institute for Employment Research.
5 Worden, et al., 2012.
6 http://www.racialprofilinganalysis.neu.edu/background/jurisdictions.php. Retrieved on July 28, 2012.
7 Ibid.
8 Worden, et al., 2012.
9 http://www.forbes.com/sites/jacquelynsmith/2012/07/20/how-road-rage-endangers-your-commute-and-how-to-prevent-it-in-yourself/; http://www.careerbuilder.com/

share/aboutus/pressreleasesdetail.aspx?sd=7/18/2012&id=pr708&ed=12/31/2012

10 Pyrczak, Fred. (2008). *Evaluating research in academic journals: A practical guide to realistic evaluation.* Glendale, CA: Pyrczak Publishing.

11 Ibid.

12 McReynolds, Larkin S., and Jeffrey C. Sandler. (2012). "Evaluating New York State's Sex Offender Management and Treatment Act: A matched historical cohort analysis." *Criminal Justice Policy Review* 23, 164–185.

13 Sandler, J. C., N. J. Freeman, and K. M. Socia. (2008). "Does a watched pot boil? A time-series analysis of New York State's sex offender registration and notification." *Psychology, Public Policy, and Law* 14, 284–302; Zgoba, K., P. Witt, M. Dalessandro, and B. Veysey. (2008). *Meghan's Law: Assessing the practical and monetary efficacy.* Washington, D.C.: U.S. Department of Justice.

14 Duwe, G., W. Donnay, and R. Tewksbury. (2008). "Does residential proximity matter? A geographic analysis of sex offense recidivism." *Criminal Justice and Behavior* 35, 484–504.

15 Pyrczak, 2008.

16 Ibid.

17 Ibid.

18 Ibid.

19 Dance, Amber. (August 7, 2007). "Videos as a baby brain drain: A study finds infants who view some popular educational products learn fewer words." *Los Angeles Times.* http://articles.latimes.com/2007/aug/07/science/sci-babyeinstein7. Retrieved on July 28, 2012; Park, Alice. (August 6, 2007). "Baby Einsteins: Not so smart after all." *Time Science.* http://www.time.com/time/health/article/0,8599,1650352,00.html. Retrieved on July 28, 2012.

20 Zimmerman, Frederick J., Dimitri A. Christakis, & Andrew N. Meltzoff. (2007). "Associations between media viewing and language development in children under age 2 years." *Journal of Pediatrics* 151, 364–368.

21 Ibid.

22 http://www.washington.edu/alumni/uwnewslinks/200709/videos.html. Retrieved on July 28, 2012.

23 http://www.seattlepi.com/local/article/The-full-text-of-Walt-Disney-Co-s-letter-1246455.php. Retrieved on July 28, 2012.

24 Ibid.

25 uwnews.washington.edu/ni/article.asp?articleID=36148. Retrieved on July 28, 2012.

26 Piliavin, Irving, and Scott Briar. (1964). "Police encounters with juveniles." *American Journal of Sociology* 70, 206–214. This study was also included in Amy B. Thistlethwaite and John D. Wooldredge. (2010). *Forty studies that changed criminal justice: Explorations into the history of criminal justice research.* Upper Saddle River, NJ: Prentice Hall.

Chapter 9

Basic Statistics for Consumers

CASE STUDY

Gang Involvement and Violent Victimization

Research Study

Understanding the Relationship between Violent Victimization and Gang Membership[1]

Research Question

Is gang involvement, along with involvement in gang crime and other risky lifestyles, related to being the victim of a violent crime?

Methodology

This study, conducted by Katz, Webb, Fox, and Shaffer, examined data collected through the Arrestee Drug Abuse Monitoring (ADAM) program. ADAM was established in 1987 by the National Institute of Justice (NIJ) and consisted of surveys of recently jailed juveniles and adults. The ADAM survey covered a number of topics from drug use to participation in other risky behavior and was administered across a variety of cities. A supplement to the ADAM survey also inquired about gang membership, victimization, and gang-related activity, among other related areas.

The final survey sample for the current study included 909 juvenile arrestees from Maricopa and Pima counties in Arizona. Of all potential juveniles eligible for interview, only 5% declined to participate in the survey.

In determining gang membership, the researchers separated juvenile arrestees into four different types: 1) Never in a gang, 2) Gang associate, 3) Former gang member, and 4) Current gang member. In terms of being the victim of a crime, the researchers collected information on lifetime victimization and violent victimization in the past 30 days. Several types of violent victimization
were measured by the survey, including but not limited to being threatened, shot, or shot at with a gun, non-gun weapon victimizations, and assaults.

Results

Following interviews with juvenile arrestees, the researchers examined relationships among variables, for example, cross-tabulating gang status with violent victimization. Overall, bivariate analyses revealed that current gang members were more likely to be the victim of a violent crime than all other members of the study sample, including non-gang members, gang associates, and former gang members. For example, current gang members were more likely to be threatened with a gun, shot at, and shot than gang associates, non-gang members, or former gang members.

Beyond bivariate associations, the authors also conducted a multivariate analysis. Multivariate logistic regression models (see discussion on logistic regression later in this chapter) were utilized to determine if the type of gang membership was associated with being the victim of a violent crime (in the past 30 days). The researchers examined this relationship even after accounting for the effects of other variables collected by researchers, such as whether the juvenile was involved in gang-related crime in the past 30 days, the number of prior arrests of the juvenile, and whether or not the juvenile was still in school, among others. Accounting for the influence of these factors on violent victimization in the past 30 days, the authors revealed that being involved in gang-related crime in the past 30 days was the strongest predictor of violent victimization. Being involved in a gang-related crime increased the juvenile's likelihood of being the victim of a violent crime by 51%—regardless of gang membership status. Thus, it is not so much a matter of gang membership that contributes to violent victimization, according to the authors, but rather, whether the juvenile engages in gang-related activity or not.

Limitations with the Study Procedure

In the current study, a potential limitation is that juvenile offenders were surveyed or asked questions about delinquent acts, victimizations, and gang status, among others. Particular to gang status, for example, juveniles were asked to self-report gang status through questions such as "Have you ever been in a gang?" or "Are you currently a member of a gang?" When questioning juveniles, in jail or another custodial setting, there is always the potential that the offenders may have exaggerated their ties to a gang to be boastful, or conversely, played down their true level of gang membership for fear of legal repercussions. The same could also be said for any number of questions asked of the juvenile arrestees, for example, their gang-related activity or levels of victimization. Unfortunately, official data (e.g., arrest records) were not available to the authors so as to confirm juvenile self-reports. These and other potential limitations should be considered from the perspective of an informed consumer of research and how such limitations could have impacted the findings of the study.

Impact on Criminal Justice

The results of this study furthered the recognition that those who participate in criminal and delinquent activities are more prone to be victimized. The authors label this effect as the victim-offender overlap. In this study, the authors revealed that being a member of a gang, per se, does not automatically translate into violent victimization. What counts is the type of behavior demonstrated by the individual, and specifically, participation in gang-related crime. Among other potential impacts, such research has much relevance to prevention and intervention programs targeting gang members. Indeed, the results of the research suggest that providing information to gang members on the link between gang-related crime (not simply just gang membership) and being the victim of a violent crime might prove effective concerning the reduction of gang-related crime. As the authors rightly note, "… policy-makers might be wise to focus on the problems associated with gang membership rather than on gang membership itself."[2] ●

IN THIS CHAPTER YOU WILL LEARN

That statistical tests are best considered as a set of tools to help organize, understand, and interpret data collected through a research study

Basic information related to variable coding and measurement

About univariate statistics—such as the mean, mode, and median—or statistics for examining the characteristics of one variable

About bivariate statistics—such as a correlation—or statistics for examining the association or relationship between two variables

About the origin of the .05 level of significance

How to interpret an alpha level of .05, .01, and .001

That the nature of the data being nominal, ordinal, interval, or ratio will dictate the appropriate type of statistical test required to examine the data

About two common statistical techniques for examining the relationship among more than two variables (also called multivariate statistical techniques)

INTRODUCTION

This text originated with research consumers in mind. As opposed to a guide on training researchers, it was driven by the reality that most students of research methods are unlikely to ever design and conduct a research study of their own. As a result, previous chapters provided an overview of various research methods and designs focused on the basics of research consumerism—which type of methods and designs are appropriate for different types of research questions and the advantages, disadvantages, and caveats associated with different research

CLASSICS IN CJ RESEARCH
The Criminal Investigation Process

RESEARCH STUDY
The Criminal Investigation Process

METHODOLOGY
The goal of this classic study in criminal justice was to come to an understanding of the role and functions of police investigators (as opposed to patrol officers, for example). According to the study authors, Greenwood and Petersilia, there has always been the belief that investigators were crucial to solving crimes. Unfortunately, there was simply little information at the time (1970s) on the role, function, and success of investigators in solving criminal incidents.

To explore the role and function of investigators, Greenwood and Petersilia sent mail surveys to 300 large police departments. Of these 300 departments, 153, or just over 50%, responded to the survey. The mail survey inquired about a number of areas of investigative work, for example, the training and evaluation of investigators, the clearance and arrest rates associated with investigative work, and the organizational structure of investigations, among others. The researchers also conducted interviews with investigators at several police departments and also observed firsthand the work of some investigators. In short, the researchers utilized survey methods and field work to understand the role and function of police investigators.

RESULTS
The results of the Greenwood and Petersilia study called into question the notion that investigators were absolutely essential in solving crime. Survey data indicated that only a small portion of investigators' time was actually spent in activities that resulted in an arrest. For example, almost half of investigators' time was spent on such activities as questioning victims, locating witnesses, and gathering evidence. Moreover, it was revealed that investigators were responsible for clearing only a small percent of index crimes they investigated (under 3%).

Perhaps one of the more interesting findings of the study was that routine police procedures, often conducted by patrol officers or other first responders to the crime scene, were most important in solving crimes. Such routine police procedures required no special training or investigative experience beyond what a typical patrol officer would receive. Indeed, when the researchers compared survey findings across the different

departments, their overall conclusion was that the contribution of investigators to clearance and arrest rates was minimal.

LIMITATIONS WITH THE STUDY PROCEDURE
Predictably, this study was criticized on a number of fronts. Critics attacked the fact that only 153 of 300 agencies responded to the survey (or just over 50% response rate) and surmised that the authors received a biased picture on the investigative police function. In short, critics rightly questioned whether the 50% of agencies that responded may have differed significantly from the 50% of agencies that did not respond to the mail survey. Moreover, the surveys consisted only of large police departments with at least 150 full-time employees and in areas that served at least 100,000 individuals in the population. Thus, the study looked mostly at large urban settings. Critics argued that the findings likely were not applicable to smaller jurisdictions.

Despite these and other criticisms, this was the first major examination of the role and function and relevance of investigators in large police agencies across the United States.

IMPACT ON CRIMINAL JUSTICE
This study was important to criminal justice in a number of ways. Specific to criminal justice practice, the findings of this study led to changes in how police agencies trained patrol officers. For example, patrol officers in several jurisdictions received extended training and were given greater responsibility in conducting investigations when they responded to a crime incident. This was in direct recognition of the finding that one of the most important aspects to crime solvability was the information gathered by first responders to the crime scene, typically the patrol officer. Specific to criminal justice research, two researchers replicated this study nearly a decade later utilizing a suburban police department in Los Angeles, CA. Overall, their findings were consistent with those found by Greenwood and Petersilia, but their study was more supportive of the important role of investigators. At the most basic level, however, this study was the first of its kind and questioned long-held beliefs on the role of investigators in police agencies. Through the use of data, including face-to-face interviews and field observations, this study spurred additional research into the role and function of investigators to help improve police performance in the solving of crimes.

Source: Greenwood, P., & Petersilia, J. (1975). *The criminal investigation process.* Santa Monica, CA: Rand.

---

designs. Consistent with our focus on consumerism, what remains in this text is an introduction to basic statistics.

As opposed to a chapter on how to conduct statistics, this chapter focuses on the function of statistical

tests in the research process. For researchers, statistics are best considered as a set of tools to help organize, understand, and interpret data collected during the course of a research study. These tools then help researchers provide answers to the questions that led to a research study in the first place. For consumers, however, a basic knowledge of statistics—the different types of statistical tests available, when they are appropriate to use, what they accomplish, and how they are interpreted—will help provide better insight into the reported results of a research study. We do not believe that research consumers necessarily need to know how to conduct a full complement of statistical tests to be able to understand the results produced by such tests. As a result, little attention in this chapter is paid to the specific procedures for conducting statistical tests. Rather, this chapter places more emphasis on the use, presentation, and basic interpretation of common statistical tests.

This chapter begins by presenting a hypothetical dataset based on a hypothetical research question. This hypothetical dataset and its associated research question will serve as a foundation for the statistical tests covered in this chapter. This chapter then revisits levels of measurement. Revisiting measurement levels is important because the level at which a variable is measured drives the type of statistical test(s) appropriate to examine the variable. Next, this chapter covers a number of common statistical tests used to explore single variables. Included in this section are typical examples of how statistics on a single variable are presented and interpreted, and generally, their function in the research process. This chapter then covers another set of common statistical tests utilized for exploring relationships or associations between two variables, again with an emphasis on presentation and interpretation. This chapter ends with a discussion of two common statistical tests used to explore relationships among more than two variables, and some important caveats of statistical analyses relevant to consumers of research.

HYPOTHETICAL RESEARCH SCENARIO: PRISON SMOKING BAN

The Situation

As a result of state laws banning smoking in a number of public places such as restaurants and parks, the director of a large state prison system was notified that smoking would likely be banned inside the state prison system in the near future. In anticipation of this change, the prison system director hired a researcher from a local university to conduct a **pilot test** to determine the potential impact of a full smoking ban in the state's prison system. The prison director feared that a prison system

smoking ban would possibly inflame tensions among inmates and lead to an increase of violent incidents. As a result, the director believed that a pilot test gauging the potential impact of this change in the prison system would allow prison authorities to anticipate and plan for any potential negative consequences once a full smoking ban went into effect.

The Design

After several meetings with the prison director and other prison officials, the researcher decided to conduct the pilot test at one prison. The researcher designed the study so that one cellblock at one prison was banned from smoking. Designing the study this way, the researcher wanted to compare the number of violent incidents that occurred among prison inmates in the selected cellblock 4 months prior to the pilot smoking ban to the number of violent incidents that occurred during a 4-month period after the ban went into effect.

To more accurately specify the impact that a smoking ban might have on violent incidents, the researcher decided to select a comparison cellblock. Selecting a comparison cellblock of inmates not subject to the smoking ban provides a baseline for comparison. As discussed in Chapter 5, the addition of a comparison cellblock allowed the researcher more insight as to whether any change in the level of violent incidents during the smoking ban was due to the ban or some other rival causal factor.

Because inmates already occupied all cells in each cellblock in the prison system, the researcher was not able to utilize an experimental design for the pilot study. This was because inmates were not able to be randomly assigned to cellblocks prior to the study, nor could other conditions be randomized prior to the smoking ban, such as the number and type of officers in the cellblock. Therefore, the researcher designed the pilot smoking ban as a two-group longitudinal design (also known as a multiple interrupted time series design), a quasi-experiment. In this design, the researcher compared two equivalent cellblocks in one prison—one cellblock whose inmates had their smoking privileges removed (smoking ban cellblock) and a comparison cellblock that was not subject to the ban. At a basic level, the logic of this design is that if incidents increase in the cellblock subject to the smoking ban compared to the equivalent cellblock not subject to the ban, the increase must be attributable only to the ban.

A prisoner smoking in his cell. Many prison systems across the United States have banned all tobacco products in prison. Some fear that banning tobacco products in prison could lead to violence.

Selection of Cellblocks

In selecting two different cellblocks, the researcher first chose Cellblock A, which is one of four cellblocks within a larger separate prison building located at the south end of the prison grounds. Cellblock A is a smoking cellblock and contains 40 inmates. It is designated as a maximum security cellblock, although inmates are generally free during the day to roam the cellblock to work and participate in a number of other activities. Cellblock A was the cellblock subject to the smoking ban.

After searching for an equivalent cellblock, the researcher identified Cellblock B, which is located in a larger

prison building at the north end of the prison grounds. Like Cellblock A, it was also a smoking cellblock, designated as maximum security, and in a building with three additional cellblocks. Cellblock B also held 40 inmates and the researcher believed that it was the most comparable cellblock at the prison in terms of the types and number of inmates that are housed in that cellblock, in addition to other attributes such as number of correctional staff monitoring inmates. Additionally, because Cellblocks A and B are at opposite ends of the prison grounds, there was virtually no contact between inmates of the two cellblocks, a factor that the researcher felt was important to the pilot study. In short, the researcher wanted to ensure that inmates in Cellblock B did not find out about the pilot test smoking ban in Cellblock A, or vice versa. In short, the researcher wanted the inmates to behave normally, without knowledge that they might be part of a study.

Collection of Additional Secondary Data

After selecting the treatment and comparison cellblocks, the researcher was allowed access to agency files to collect certain types of secondary or agency collected data on inmates, for example, the number of previous incarcerations, age at first incarceration, and the number of years incarcerated on current sentence for which the inmate was committed to prison (see Table 9.2 for all variables collected by the researcher). The researcher believed that these and other variables would help explain participation in violent incidents by inmates, independent of the effects of a potential smoking ban in prison. The design of the study is portrayed in Table 9.1.

Although the design is considered a quasi-experiment because the inmates residing in each cellblock were not randomly assigned, the researcher attempted to ensure equivalence among inmates and cellblock characteristics by selecting cellblocks with similar types of inmates and by considering other factors that might relate to involvement in or discovery of violent incidents. Also note that because the researcher was collecting

TABLE 9.1 | Hypothetical Smoking Ban Research Design

Cellblock A	NR	O_1	O_1	O_1	O_1	X Smoking Ban	O_2	O_2	O_2	O_2
Cellblock B	NR	O_1	O_1	O_1	O_1		O_2	O_2	O_2	O_2
		Pre-Test **Violent Incidents Before** **Smoking Ban**					**Post-Test** **Violent Incidents During** **Smoking Ban**			

TABLE 9.2 | Smoking Ban Variables

Variable Name	Label	Coding	Level of Measurement
Race	Race of inmate	0 = Nonwhite 1 = White	Nominal
Previnc	Previous incarcerations	Number	Ratio
Agefirst	Age at first incarceration	Age in years	Ratio
Yearinc	Years incarcerated on current sentence	Years	Ratio
Classrisk	Classification risk category within custody level	1 = Low 2 = Medium 3 = High	Ordinal
Cigsday	Cigarettes smoked per day before the ban	Number	Ratio
Cellblock	Cellblock assignment	0 = Cellblock B 1 = Cellblock A	Nominal
Inc4moprior	Violent incidents 4 months prior to smoking ban	Number	Ratio
Inc4modur	Violent incidents 4 months during smoking ban	Number	Ratio

information on the number of violent incidents in each month before and during the smoking ban, this design can be considered longitudinal. However, because the researcher is also interested in the final number of incidents during the entire 4-month pre-test and 4-month post-test period, and not necessarily the number of incidents in any particular month of the pre-test and post-test, this design could have also been conducted as a nonequivalent group design, which is cross-sectional.

Recall from Chapter 5 that anytime two or more groups of individuals (or cellblocks of inmates) are being compared in an experimental or quasi-experimental design, one consideration is that the groups be equivalent so as to be able to isolate the unique effects of the treatment after it is implemented. In an experimental design, the randomization process helps to ensure that group differences are minimized or eliminated. In a quasi-experiment, such as the two-group longitudinal design discussed previously or the nonequivalent group design, the absence of randomization means that there could indeed be differences between the groups of inmates at the pre-test, and hence, such differences could impact the post-test. For example, if inmates in Cellblock A perpetrated a significantly higher number of incidents than inmates in Cellblock B prior to the smoking ban, whatever led to the higher number of incidents in Cellblock A might lead to higher incidents after the smoking ban is put into place. Fortunately, the availability of data on inmates allowed the researcher to explore, through the use of statistics, how similar or different each group of inmates was with respect to factors that might be linked to participation in violent incidents following implementation of the smoking ban. Such information allows a more precise interpretation of what effect,

if any, a smoking ban had on participation in violent inmate-on-inmate incidents.

Table 9.2 presents all of the variables collected by the researcher to help examine the impact that a smoking ban may have on the prison setting. The table provides the name of the variable collected, the label or what the variable is measuring, how the variable is coded, and finally, at what level the variable is measured.

LEVELS OF MEASUREMENT REVISITED

Table 9.2 includes nine variables collected by the researcher to help determine the impact of a smoking ban on violent incidents among inmates. Two of the variables are nominal level variables (Race and Cellblock). This means that the variable provides a name or label to some value. For example, labels such as nonwhite and white are characteristics of variables measured at the nominal level as are indicators of Cellblock A and Cellblock B. Although nominal variables and their labels may be designated by numerical codes, the codes are not numerically meaningful. For example, inmates who occupy Cellblock A are coded as 1 and inmates in Cellblock B are coded as 0. However, the coding scheme of 1 and 0 do not represent numbers useful for mathematical manipulation nor do they indicate rankings; rather, they are simply labels used to indicate a particular category. This is a property of variables measured at the nominal level.

Further examination of Table 9.2 reveals there is one ordinal level variable included in the data collected by the researcher. This variable, Classrisk, is a measure of each inmate's risk level within their designated prison custody level. For example, all inmates in the smoking

A Just Measure of Crime: The Uniform Crime Reports (UCR)

When considering crime rates, fluctuations in crime over time, or the level of crime in a particular location, there is no better source than the Uniform Crime Reports (UCR). Beginning in 1930, the uniform crime reporting program has relied on city, university and college, and county, state, tribal and federal law enforcement agencies to voluntary report information on known offenses committed and persons arrested each year. To be sure, the UCR only collects information on known offenses and persons arrested—it is not a count of processes and outcomes following arrest such as findings of the court or decisions of the prosecutor.

The UCR reporting program is perhaps the most accurate count of crime that occurs in the United States each year. This does not mean it is perfect, for it does have many limitations. For example, the UCR cannot account for crimes that go unreported. Moreover, the UCR utilizes what is considered a hierarchy rule. This means that if multiple crimes are committed in one criminal incident, only the highest level or most serious crime is counted—therefore underestimating some crime. Despite these and other limitations, the UCR currently functions as a count of crime for roughly 95% of the total population of the United States.

Despite the important nature of the UCR, it is critical to remember that with any compilation of data, there is always the potential for error and other mistakes. Errors and mistakes can occur during any stage of the collection process, from the initial crime report completion by the individual officer, to the collection of the information by the local law enforcement agency, to the transmission of data to the FBI. Other potential errors can include differential interpretation of information requested by the FBI, missing or incomplete information, or simply failing to report an accurate number of crimes. There have even been reports of law enforcement agencies intentionally omitting some crimes from their UCR reporting sheets or otherwise skewing their local crime data.[3] In light of these potentials, there are significant training procedures in place for law enforcement agencies and quality standards and reviews to make sure the data is as accurate as possible. Visit www.fbi.gov and explore information about the UCR, including the history of the program, quality control guidelines, limitations of the data, and what is and is not included in the UCR. Also examine other national data crime collection programs such as the National Crime Victimization Survey (NCVS), the National Incident Based Reporting System (NIBRS), and Supplemental Homicide Reports (SHR), to name a few.

Adapted from: http://www.fbi.gov/about-us/cjis/ucr/frequently-asked-questions/ucr_faqs, retrieved August 26, 2011.

---

ban study were maximum security inmates. However, within that maximum security custody level, Classrisk measures whether each inmate was considered low, medium, or high-risk. As opposed to the nominal level variables, the fact that Classrisk is measured at the ordinal level means that the labels of low, medium, and high and the codes of 1, 2, and 3 are ranked or ordered, from low to high risk. However, one of the properties of a variable measured at the ordinal level is that although the categories are ranked (e.g., low to high), it is not known by how much each of the ranks differs. For example, high-risk maximum security inmates are riskier than both low- and medium-risk maximum security inmates; it is just not known how much risk separates these ranked categories.

There are no interval level variables available in this study. Unlike variables measured at the nominal or ordinal level, interval level variables are measured on a scale where the numerical distance between two different intervals or points on the scale is equal. However, an interval scale of measurement does not feature a true or meaningful zero point. For example, temperature is an often cited example of an interval level measurement. With temperature, the distance between 30° and 60° is 30 intervals. However, when the temperature is 0, there is still warmth. This is what is meant by the absence of a true or meaningful zero point.[4]

As opposed to an interval level of measurement, Table 9.2 indicates that there are six variables measured at the ratio level of measurement. One important characteristic of a variable measured at the ratio level is that two different values are equally spaced apart, just like in an interval level of measurement. For example, an inmate with four previous incarcerations has exactly two more previous incarcerations than an inmate with two previous incarcerations. Another important characteristic is that there is a meaningful or true zero point—where zero actually equals zero and is not arbitrary as with variables measured at the interval level of measurement. For example, variables such as age, height, weight, and number of previous incarcerations are considered variables measured at the ratio level of measurement because zero is meaningful—zero actually means zero.

Because of the preceding properties, variables measured at the interval or ratio level can be subject to a number of statistical tests that would not be appropriate for nominal or ordinal level variables. Additionally, variables measured at these levels can be "scaled down" or "recoded" to create nominal or ordinal level variables. For example, an interval level variable measuring temperature can be scaled down into categories—30°–50°F, 60°–70°F, or "warm" and "cool," and so on. Although interval and ratio variables can be scaled down to resemble nominal or ordinal level variables, nominal and ordinal level variables cannot be "scaled up" or recoded into interval or ratio level variables. As a result, interval and ratio level variables are much more versatile than nominal or ordinal variables when it comes to statistical tests. Finally, it is important to note that variables are not often called nominal, ordinal, interval, or ratio in research reports and other publications. Often, researchers simply refer to the variables as **categorical** or **qualitative** (nominal and ordinal) or **quantitative** or **metric** (interval or ratio).

Regardless of how they are labeled, revisiting the different levels of measurement is important for the primary reason that certain statistical tests apply only to variables measured at a particular level of measurement. For example, it would not make much sense to compute the average of an inmate's race as measured in the current hypothetical study because this is a nominal level variable. This aspect about levels of measurement should become clearer as we explore statistics for examining one variable in the following section.

STATISTICS FOR EXAMINING ONE VARIABLE

One of the fundamental functions of certain statistical tests is to explore and describe the characteristics of a single variable. For producers of research, the purpose of analyzing a single variable is to determine certain attributes or characteristics of the variable. These characteristics become important in determining which types of statistical tests are appropriate to use with the variable. For research consumers, information on a single variable (or a number of single variables) may lead to a better understanding of the characteristics of data, and ultimately, a better understanding of the outcomes of a research study based on that data.

Measures of Central Tendency

The beginning point to understanding the role of statistics in the research process is **measures of central tendency.**

Measures of central tendency include a number of statistics "designed to find a single number that best represents several numbers."[5] Three of the most common statistics for measuring central tendency are the mean, median, and mode. The **mean** represents the average of all scores for a particular variable, for example, the average age at first incarceration or the average number of cigarettes smoked per day for the entire sample of prison inmates. In sum, the mean is a single number that helps to provide an overall view or "average" of a number of different ages at first incarceration.

Averages or means are calculated and meaningful for variables measured at the ratio, interval, and in certain instances at the ordinal level, but are not appropriate for variables measured at the nominal level. One of the most important properties of the mean is that this statistic is influenced by extreme values. Extremely high values, for example, pull the average higher and extremely low values pull the average downward. While extreme values do not change the mathematical accuracy of the mean, such values can affect how accurate a picture the mean represents for any given variable. For example, if among the hypothetical sample of inmates in the smoking ban study of focus in this chapter, a single inmate had 45 previous incarcerations while the remaining 79 inmates each had one previous incarceration, the average would be inflated and would not be an accurate portrayal of the number of previous incarcerations among the majority of the inmate sample. Based on the figures just presented, the mean number of previous incarcerations would equal 1.55. However, nearly 99% of all inmates have only one previous incarceration. While the mean of 1.55 is mathematically accurate to the sample, it probably does not do a good job of clearly portraying the average or "typical" inmate in terms of the number of previous incarcerations.

As opposed to the mean, the **median** represents the middle value in a series of ordered values. Unlike the mean, the median is not influenced by extreme low or high values. For example, the median in the following list of numbers [1, 3, **4**, 5, 6] is 4, and the median in the next list of numbers [1, 3, **4**, 5, 800] is also 4. Despite the presence of an extreme value of 800 relative to the other values in the ordered list, the median remains the same because the middle number in a ranked series is still the middle number, regardless of the values below or above it. As a consumer of research, sometimes the median provides a more accurate overall representation of the characteristics of a particular variable than the mean, because unlike the mean, it is not influenced by extreme values.

TABLE 9.3 | Summary Statistics for Ratio Level Variables (N = 80)

Variable	Mean	Median	Mode
Previous incarcerations	1.28	1.00	1.00
Age at first incarceration	25.98	23.00	18.00
Years incarcerated on current sentence	3.99	3.00	1.00
Cigarettes smoked per day	11.10	8.50	2.00
Incidents 4 months prior to smoking ban	2.06	2.00	2.00
Incidents 4 months during smoking ban	4.57	3.00	1.00

In addition to the mean and median, the final measure of central tendency is the **mode.** In simple terms, the mode is the most frequent value of any particular variable. Suppose nearly all inmates in the smoking ban study had one previous incarceration, the mode for the number of previous incarcerations would be one. It is also the case that a variable may have more than one mode. In fact, there can be multiple modes depending on the frequency of values of a particular variable. For example, presume that among the 80 prisoners in the smoking ban study, 20 prisoners had one previous incarceration, 20 prisoners had three previous incarcerations, 20 prisoners had four previous incarcerations, 15 prisoners had five previous incarcerations, and 5 prisoners had six previous incarcerations. In this example, there would be three modes (1, 3, and 4 previous incarcerations).

Table 9.3 presents all three measures of central tendency (mean, median, and mode) for the ratio level variables collected by the researcher in the hypothetical smoking ban study. Table 9.4 presents the same information but separates the information by the cellblock in which inmates were assigned.

The information presented in Tables 9.3 and 9.4 represents typical ways the mean, median, and mode might be presented in a research report. Also notice "N" and "n" in the tables. N is an indicator of the size of the population or sample. Although N and n are sometimes used interchangeably, N is usually utilized to denote the size of a population, whereas n is utilized to denote the size of a sample from the population. N can also be used as a sample size indicator with n being used to indicate a subset of a sample. In this example, "N" is indicative of the sample of inmates in the smoking ban study (N=80 inmates total), and n is used to represent a subset of inmates from the larger sample (n = 40 in Cellblock A and n = 40 in Cellblock B). However N or n is used, the bottom line is that this letter is used to demonstrate the number or size of the sample or population under study.

As mentioned, measures of central tendency are a group of measures that attempt to describe the characteristics of a particular variable with a single number. While measures of central tendency can help provide an overall picture of a particular variable, to more fully understand the characteristics of a variable it is best to have access to the original data that produced the measure of central tendency. If that data is not available to the consumer, certain basic assumptions of the data can be accomplished by examining all measures of central tendency together. For example, if the mean and median are extremely different, one could make the assumption that data values for a particular variable vary considerably. If the average age of prisoners in the smoking ban sample was age 35, for example, but the median age was 23, it would be safe to assume that the sample contains a number of older inmates that have influenced the mean upwards. However, one should be careful not to make large assumptions simply from a comparison of the mean, median, and mode. Although careful examination of these measures is important for an informed consumer of research,

TABLE 9.4 | Summary Statistics for Ratio Level Variables (Cellblock A vs. Cellblock B)

Variable	Cellblock A (n = 40 Inmates)			Cellblock B (n = 40 Inmates)		
	Mean	Median	Mode	Mean	Median	Mode
Previous incarcerations	1.13	1.00	1.00	1.43	1.00	1.00
Age at first incarceration	25.35	21.00	18.00	26.60	23.00	23.00
Years incarcerated on current sentence	4.10	3.50	2.00	3.87	3.00	1.00
Cigarettes smoked per day	14.75	14.00	23.00	7.45	4.00	2.00
Incidents 4 months prior to smoking ban	2.15	2.00	2.00	1.98	2.00	2.00
Incidents 4 months during smoking ban	7.40	6.50	5.00	1.75	1.00	1.00

what can actually be assumed about data characteristics from examining these measures is somewhat limited. In short, these forms of summary statistics provide only a broad look at variable characteristics and a basic level of understanding about the nature of the data. More detailed information about the characteristics of particular variables can be found by examining a set of statistics commonly referred to as measures of variation.

Measures of Variation

Like measures of central tendency, measures of variation provide a single number that gives information about a single variable. Three of the most commonly used measures of variation include the range, variance, and standard deviation. In the most common instances, these measures of variation are only appropriate and meaningful with interval and ratio level data.

The first measure of variation is the **range.** The range is calculated by taking the highest value for any individual variable and subtracting the lowest value for that individual variable. For example, the highest age of first incarceration (Agefirst) for any prisoner in the smoking ban sample is age 70, and the lowest age of first incarceration is 18. The range associated with Agefirst is thus 52 (70 − 18 = 52). The range associated with number of previous incarcerations (Previncar) is 3 because the inmate(s) with highest number of previous incarcerations in the sample has 3 and the inmate(s) with the lowest number of previous incarcerations has 0 (3 − 0 = 3). Because the range is calculated using only the highest and lowest values of a particular variable, like the mean, it can be influenced by extremely high or low values. For example, the heaviest smoker in the prisoner sample smoked 41 cigarettes per day, and the least frequent smoker smoked 2 cigarettes per day, resulting in a range of 39 (41 − 2 = 39). Note, however, the range as a measure of variation is used to show how much "variability" exists within a given variable—it is not necessarily meant to depict the typical sample member. As a result, it gives the consumer an idea of how much variation there is between the highest and lowest value for any particular variable.

A second common measure of variation is called the **variance.** Calculating the variance, especially by hand,

is tedious and can sometimes be confusing. Of particular interest for our purposes, however, is what the variance measures. The variance provides an indication of how much each individual value of a particular variable differs from the average or mean of a particular variable. Because the variance is calculated in part by determining how much each individual value of a particular variable differs from the mean of a particular variable, a larger variance is an indication that there is more variability of scores around the mean. Alternatively, a variance that is closer to the mean indicates that individual scores of a particular variable are closer to the mean. For example, the average age at first incarceration for the 80 inmates in the hypothetical study is 25.98 years, but the variance is 115.80. Although the variance statistic of 115.80 does not provide a simple description of the variability of individual values for each inmate regarding their age at first incarceration, the large difference between the mean and variance suggest that there is variability among the sample of inmates regarding their age at first incarceration—some inmates are both younger and older than the mean. Indeed, if the variance is 0, this is an indication that all the values for a particular variable are the same as the mean, thus, no variance.

An even more detailed picture of the characteristics of the age at first incarceration for the sample is found through an examination of the **standard deviation.** The standard deviation is calculated by taking the square root of the variance. Mathematical procedures aside, because the standard deviation is a product of the variance, it too provides an idea of the variation of all particular values of a variable compared to the mean of that particular variable. And, just like the variance, the larger the standard deviation, the more individual values of a particular variable stray from the mean.

Table 9.5 provides an examination of all measures of central tendency (mean, mode, and median) and variation (range, variance, and standard deviation) for the variable age at first incarceration in the hypothetical smoking ban study. Inspection of these statistics together and how they are typically presented helps in understanding the characteristics of data collected for a research study. Examining these statistics combined with basic knowledge of how they are calculated and what they represent is

TABLE 9.5 | Measures of Central Tendency and Variation

Variable	Mean	Median	Mode	Range	Variance	St. Dev.
Age at first incarceration	25.98	23.00	18.00	52	115.80	10.76

also a good first step at being an informed consumer of research. Based on what you know so far, what insight can you gather about Agefirst from the measures of central tendency and variation presented?

Thus far, the previous discussion on statistics for single variables has centered on those statistics that are used to examine the characteristics of interval and ratio level data. What about data that is measured at the nominal or ordinal level? Because measures of central tendency and variation are not meaningful for nominal or ordinal level variables, researchers typically use other methods to understand the characteristics of data measured at these levels. For example, frequency tables, percentages, and an assortment of charts, such as bar charts or pie charts, are often used to examine the characteristics of variables measured at the nominal or ordinal level. Again, the goal of the basic statistics just covered is to provide an understanding of the characteristics of data. For nominal and ordinal level variables, percentages, frequency tables, and charts help accomplish that goal.

STATISTICS FOR EXAMINING TWO VARIABLES

Measures of central tendency and variation provide information on a single variable only. It is often the case, however, that researchers are interested in whether there is a relationship or association between two variables. For example, the researcher conducting the pilot smoking ban study may be interested in whether there is an association between a prisoner's cellblock assignment (Cellblock) and his classification risk upon prison intake (Classrisk), among other associations.

Associations between two variables can be observed by crosstabulating variables. Crosstabulating, or producing a "crosstab," is accomplished by comparing the categories of one variable to the categories of another variable. Because crosstabulation requires data

to be in category form, it is used with nominal and/or ordinal data. As mentioned, however, both interval and ratio level data can be "scaled down" into categories for crosstabulation purposes. For example, suppose the researcher wanted to examine if there was any association between the number of cigarettes inmates in Cellblock A smoked per day before the smoking ban (Cigsday) to the number of violent incidents in Cellblock A in the 4 months after the smoking ban went into effect (Inc 4modur). These ratio level variables can be recoded or scaled down into categories. Once into categories, a crosstabulation can be produced for visual inspection of categories. For example, the researcher could recode the ratio level variable Cigsday into categories (inmates who smoked 0–6 cigarettes per day, 7–12 cigarettes per day, and so on) and do the same with the individual frequencies for the ratio level variable Inc4modur (inmates who engaged in 0–5 incidents, 6–10 incidents, and so on). Table 9.6 demonstrates a crosstabulation of these two recoded variables.

An examination of Table 9.6 shows the number of cigarettes smoked per day by inmates in Cellblock A before the smoking ban went into effect compared to the number of violent incidents perpetrated by Cellblock A inmates during the 4-month smoking ban. Basic visual inspection of Table 9.6 shows there is a slight association between the number of cigarettes smoked per day before the ban and involvement in violent incidents during the 4 months the smoking ban was in place. Indeed, as the number of cigarettes smoked per day increases, there appears to be an increase in the number of inmates who engaged in categories that include the highest number of incidents. For example, of the 22 inmates in Cellblock A that smoked 13 or more cigarettes per day before the ban, 12 had 6–10 violent incidents and 5 had 11 or more violent incidents during the test period.

Although there appears to be a slight positive association between the variables (as the number of cigarettes smoked before the ban increases so does the number of

TABLE 9.6 | Association of Cigarettes Smoked and Incidents during Smoking Ban among Cellblock A Inmates

		Inc4modur recoded			
		0-5	6-10	11+	Totals
	0-6	11 (100%)	0 (0%)	0 (0%)	11 (100%)
	7-12	4 (57%)	2 (29%)	1 (14%)	7 (100%)
Cigsday recoded	13-20	4 (40%)	3 (30%)	3 (30%)	10 (100%)
	21+	1 (8%)	9 (75%)	2 (17%)	12 (100%)
	Totals	20 (50%)	14 (35%)	6 (15%)	40 (100%)

WHAT THE RESEARCH SHOWS: IMPACTING CRIMINAL JUSTICE OPERATIONS
Why is .05 the Traditional Level Indicating Statistical Significance?

A significance level of .05 is the standard threshold for indicating that a relationship among variables, or a difference between two or more variables, is statistically significant. In simple terms, a significance level equal to .05 means that there is a relationship between variables, with only a 5 out of 100 or 5% chance of the relationship being due to a chance occurrence.

But who established this traditional cutoff for determining whether a relationship or difference between variables was "good enough" to be considered real and not a chance occurrence? Surprisingly, not much research exists on this subject. This lack of research is even more surprising considering that the .05 level of significance is so universally used across scientific disciplines. In an important article, researchers Cowles and Davis (1982) searched to uncover the origins of the .05 level of significance. Regarding "who" developed this threshold, they revealed that perhaps the earliest formal recognition of the .05 level of significance came from Sir Ronald Fisher. Fisher, a well-known statistician of the early 1900s, wrote a book called *Statistical Methods for Research Workers* in 1925. In this book he formally introduced the .05 level. But Cowles and Davis found evidence of others using similar thresholds even before this time.

Despite the universal and important nature of the .05 threshold, and regardless of the debate as to who should be credited with creating .05 as the standard threshold of statistical significance, Cowles and Davis revealed that the adoption of the .05 level was more than just some arbitrary threshold. At a basic level, the authors reveal that an event that occurs less than or equal to 5% of the time is generally considered by scientists and nonscientists alike as the result of something other than random chance occurrence. This is also because this threshold has intuitive appeal—something occurring only 5 out of 100 times is quite a rare event, indicating that something special, or other than chance, is occurring. But perhaps the most basic reason it was adopted so universally was because the absence of a common threshold indicating significance would leave the task to individual researchers to establish what is and is not statistically significant for a particular study. The widespread adoption of the .05 level led to a minimum standard in determining the likelihood of an event not being due to chance.

Source: Cowles, M., & C. Davis. (1982). On the origins of the .05 level of statistical significance. *American Psychologist* 37, 553–558.

See also, http://www.jerrydallal.com/LHSP/p05.htm, retrieved on August 26, 2011.

---

incidents during the smoking ban in Cellblock A), this basic association should not be taken as an indication that more frequent smokers will automatically engage in a higher level of violent incidents if smoking privileges are removed. There are perhaps a number of other variables that could explain this association beyond the number of cigarettes per day. Perhaps those inmates who smoked the most cigarettes per day were also the most risky or violent inmates, and perhaps had a large number of violent incidents even before the smoking ban went into effect and simply continued to act accordingly. In short, a mere association offers no proof of a causal relationship.

Also make note of an important attribute of Table 9.6—percentages. Percentages can be calculated in two ways, across (or row percentages) or down (or column percentages). Table 9.6 provides row percentages. A general rule of thumb is that percentages should be performed in the direction of the independent or supposed causal variable. In this example, the recoded variable for the number of cigarettes smoked per day is hypothesized to be a factor associated with violent incidents during the 4-month smoking ban, and therefore, the percentages are row percentages. Indeed, it would make little sense to assume that the number of incidents incurred during the smoking ban caused the number of cigarettes smoked *before* the ban—therefore Cigsday is considered the independent variable.

Often, consumers of research find confusion with row and column percentages, and for good reason. For example, it might easily be misinterpreted from Table 9.6 that 100% of inmates who incurred 0–5 incidents during the ban smoked between 0–6 cigarettes per day before the smoking ban (see the cell in the upper left-hand corner of the table). In fact, the correct interpretation is that 100% of inmates who smoked 0–6 cigarettes a day before the ban (11) were involved in 0–5 incidents during the smoking ban. Indeed, calculation of a column percentage, instead of the row percentages provided, would show that only 55% of inmates who incurred 0–5 incidents during the smoking ban smoked 0–6 cigarettes per day (11/20) before the ban went into effect. In essence, one must be careful when interpreting percentages in a crosstabulation and understand the difference between row and column percentages.

In addition to examining whether there "appears" to be an association between two variables through face value inspection of a crosstabulation table, researchers are often interested in a number of other considerations concerning associations. These considerations include how strong the association is between variables (is the association weak, moderate, or strong), what the direction of the association or relationship is (association positive or negative), and whether the relationship between variables is statistically significant.[6] Depending on the measurement of the variables, statistical tests exist to address all of these issues.

Testing for a Statistically Significant Relationship

Although each of the previous questions is important, we focus on the issue of statistical significance because this is what is often reported in research reports and other outlets and is perhaps of most relevance to our purposes. Note, however, that statistical programs that allow a determination of statistical significance also provide the opportunity to evaluate both the direction and strength of an association between two variables, and this information is also typically found in reported research results. Such tests can be accomplished with variables measured at all levels—nominal, ordinal, interval, and ratio.

Two of the most commonly reported statistics for determining if a relationship between two variables is **statistically significant** include chi-square and t-tests. In a nutshell, **chi-square** statistical tests determine whether the relationship between two nominal or ordinal variables is significant. As a practical matter, a relationship between two variables is considered statistically significant when the observed relationship is greater than what would be expected to occur by chance alone. For example, a chi-square test could be utilized in the hypothetical study to determine whether the difference in the number (or frequency) of white and nonwhite inmates assigned to Cellblock A and B is significantly different than what would be expected by chance. A chi-square test could also be used to examine whether there is a significant relationship between the recoded variables in Table 9.6—Cigsday and Inc4modur.

As opposed to chi-square tests, **t-tests** are primarily used with interval and ratio level data. Although there are different types of t-tests, one of the most common is that which examines whether mean differences between two independent or distinct groups are statistically significant. For example, a t-test could be used by the researcher to answer whether the average number of violent incidents

TABLE 9.7 | Cellblock Mean Comparisons on Cigarettes Smoked Per Day

		N	Mean	Sig.
Cigsday	Cellblock A	40	14.75	.000
	Cellblock B	40	7.45	

among inmates in Cellblock A and Cellblock B were significantly different before the smoking ban went into effect. The researcher could do similar mean comparison t-tests between Cellblock A and B inmates on the mean number of previous incarcerations, years incarcerated on current sentence, number of violent incidents during the smoking ban period, and cigarettes smoked per day before the ban.

Table 9.7 provides results of a t-test that compared the mean number of cigarettes smoked per day by inmates in Cellblock A to the mean number of cigarettes smoked by inmates in Cellblock B prior to the smoking ban. First, note that inmates in Cellblock A, on average, smoked roughly 7 more cigarettes per day than inmates in Cellblock B. Recognizing this difference, a t-test examines whether this mean difference is significant, or alternatively, whether this is a difference that could be expected by chance alone. Examining the significance column in Table 9.7 (Sig.), a value of .000 is presented. This is the significance level produced from the t-test in Table 9.7 and is the number of most interest. In basic terms, this reported significance level (.000) indicates that the difference in the average number of cigarettes smoked per day among inmates in Cellblock A compared to the average number smoked by inmates in Cellblock B is significantly different than a chance occurrence. It indicates that the probability of two means, from this sample, being this different by a chance occurrence is less than one chance out of 1,000—too small a chance to conclude that the difference in the number of cigarettes smoked per day is simply a fluke occurrence or some error in the sampling process. In sum, Cellblock A inmates smoke a significantly greater number of cigarettes than Cellblock B inmates.

Traditionally, the level at which a difference is considered statistically significant is any significance value that is less than .05, typically reported in a research report as $p < .05$ (less than 5 out of 100), or $p < .01$ (less than 1 out of 100), or $p < .001$ or just $p < .000$ (less than 1 out of 1,000). Relative to a t-test of difference between two group means as presented

RESEARCH IN THE NEWS
STATS.ORG: The Numbers behind the News

If you question statistics presented in news articles, stats.org is a website for you. Among other activities, researchers at stats.org examine the numbers and associated findings behind major issues and news stories. This organization advocates scientific methods and statistical analyses to examine a variety of social issues today. Highly trained researchers and

statisticians associated with stats.org also provide independent review and critique of popular media studies, discussing benefits and limitations. In the quest to become an informed consumer of research, stats.org is a must visit.

To visit this organization's website, visit, http://stats.org/index.htm.

in Table 9.7, the reported level of .000 means that in less than 1 chance out of 1,000 should we expect this large a difference in the number of cigarettes smoked to be due to chance. In short, the difference in the average number of cigarettes smoked among inmates in each respective cellblock is a real or true difference and such a large difference is unlikely to be the result of a chance occurrence—in fact, in less than 1 out of 1,000 times would we expect to see this large a difference just by chance.

Let us assume that the researcher is also interested in whether there is a difference in the average number of violent incidents recorded among inmates in Cellblock A compared to inmates in Cellblock B during the 4-month smoking ban period. A t-test could also be utilized to examine this question. Recall, however, that inmates in Cellblock B were not subjected to a smoking ban—only inmates in Cellblock A had their smoking privileges removed. Conducting this analysis reveals that inmates in Cellblock A accumulated an average of 7.40 incidents during the 4-month smoking ban and inmates in Cellblock B accumulated an average of 1.75 incidents. According to the t-test results comparing these averages, there is a statistically significant difference between the mean number of violent incidents between inmates in Cellblock A and Cellblock B. In this analysis, the significance value (Sig.) is .000. This means that the probability of this difference being a chance occurrence is less than 1 out of 1,000.

There are two important considerations worth mentioning at this juncture. First, just because a chi-square test or a t-test (or any other statistical test) may indicate a statistically significant relationship or a statistically significant difference between group means does not indicate a causal relationship. Again, there could be a number of other intervening variables that might explain why, for example, inmates in Cellblock A incurred a significantly greater number of incidents during the smoking ban, none of which

might be related to the fact that their smoking privileges were removed.

Second, sometimes the notion of statistical significance does not translate into practical significance. For example, inmates in Cellblock A may have served a significantly greater number of years incarcerated on their current sentence, but in practical terms, the mean differences between the two groups may be only a few years and not otherwise be meaningful on a practical level. In other words, while a relationship or difference may be statistically significant, it may not indicate anything of practical value. Thus, statistical significance does not indicate a causal relationship between two variables nor does it necessarily equate to practical significance. It is simply an indication of whether differences are greater than what would be expected by chance, relative to the size of the sample and other considerations. Although the notion of practical significance must be viewed in the context of a particular study and relative to a particular research question, the important point here is not to blindly put too much emphasis on statistical significance because it might often be the case that there is no practical or real world significance to such a finding in the larger context of a particular study.

STATISTICS FOR EXAMINING MORE THAN TWO VARIABLES

Thus far, this chapter has introduced the reader to a number of basic statistical tools to explore the characteristics of data and to explore relationships between two variables and whether such relationships are statistically significant. As a whole, this chapter presented only a brief overview of some of the most common statistics typically found in a research report and how they are commonly presented. While there are numerous other types of specific statistical procedures and data considerations that could well fit within this chapter, in our opinion, such a focus detracts from the ultimate goal of providing research consumers with an introductory level of information they need to begin understanding the more complex world of statistical analyses. In short, this chapter was meant as a starting point to help the research consumer, not the potential research producer, to get a basic but important grasp on fundamental statistical concepts and tests to become a more informed consumer of research.

With that said, it is common today to find more advanced statistical analyses presented to research consumers at all levels—general public consumers, field practitioners, and others. As a result, we believe it is important to cover, if only briefly, two of the more common statistical techniques for examining relationships among more than two variables. In statistical terminology, these statistical tests are broadly known as **multivariate (multiple variables) statistical tests.** Although numerous different types of multivariate statistical tests exist, the two most common are Ordinary Least Squares (or OLS) regression and Logistic Regression. We provide a discussion and presentation of these statistical tests in the following section. However, it is important to note that with any statistical procedure, even those examining one variable, the nature of the data is important. For example, a mean can only be meaningful when used with interval or ratio level data. All multivariate statistical tests also come with a set of assumptions and the most basic of all assumptions is the type of data that they are able to analyze.

OLS Regression

Ordinary Least Squares (OLS) regression (hereafter OLS regression) is a multivariate statistical technique where a researcher is interested in the relationship between multiple independent variables and one dependent variable. Although OLS regression includes a number of assumptions about the characteristics of data, what is most important for our purposes is that the dependent variable must be measured at the interval or ratio level. Independent variables can be measured at any level—nominal, ordinal, interval, or ratio.

Suppose the researcher in the smoking ban study is interested in the relationship between cigarettes smoked per day before the smoking ban (Cigsday) and the number of incidents during the 4-month smoking ban (Inc4modur). Let's also suppose that the researcher believes other variables might be related to violent incidents during the smoking ban beyond the number of cigarettes an inmate smokes per day. For example, the researcher might also be interested in whether knowledge about inmates' age at first incarceration (Agefirst), years incarcerated on current

sentence (Yearinc), and the number of violent incidents prior to the smoking ban (Inc4moprior) may also have an effect on the incidence of violence during the 4-month smoking ban (Inc4modur)—even accounting for the number of cigarettes inmates smoked before the ban.

By including the variables mentioned previously, the researcher is interested in whether there is a relationship between the number of cigarettes smoked per day before the smoking ban and violent incidents that occurred during the smoking ban, after accounting for the effects of the other independent variables. More specifically, the researcher wants to know whether a smoking ban will lead to violence or whether this relationship is actually explained by factors other than the smoking ban, such as the types of inmates, how long they have been incarcerated, their age at first incarceration, and their involvement in violence before the smoking ban took effect. Because the dependent variable is measured at the ratio level, and the researcher is interested in the impact of multiple independent variables on the dependent variable, OLS regression would be an appropriate statistical technique to examine this research question.

It is possible that the level of violence during the smoking ban period may have nothing to do with how many cigarettes an inmate smokes and the smoking ban, but rather, the characteristics of inmates and their previous demonstrated violent behavior, among other pieces of information. Alternatively, the level of violence may in part be related to the number of cigarettes smoked per day and the smoking ban, but other factors may also contribute to involvement in violent incidents. OLS regression can help to answer what effect each variable has on the dependent variable, if any, and whether some variables are more important than others in explaining inmate violence.

Table 9.8 summarizes the results of an OLS regression model to help answer the previous considerations. Table 9.8 is a simplified presentation of how the results

TABLE 9.8 | OLS Regression of Violent Incidents during Smoking Ban

Variable	Standardized Coefficient	Sig.
Agefirst	.016	.840
Yearinc	−.072	.376
Cigsday	.385	.000
Cellblock (A)	.510	.000
Inc4moprior	.013	.878
R^2 = .560		

from an OLS regression might be presented in a research report or perhaps an academic article or book. As shown, there were five variables "regressed" on the dependent variable measuring the number of incidents during the 4-month smoking ban (Inc4modur). Because only Cellblock A was subjected to the smoking ban, the variable Cellblock was also included to determine whether being in a smoking cellblock (Cellblock B) as opposed to a nonsmoking cellblock (Cellblock A) also influenced incidents during the ban, in addition to the other variables. One way to answer whether banning smoking leads to an increase of violent incidents is to determine whether cellblock assignment has an effect on incidents. In other words, including the variable Cellblock serves as a proxy measure for losing smoking privileges (Cellblock A) or retaining smoking privileges (Cellblock B).

Notice that there are two major columns in Table 9.8, Standardized Coefficient and Sig. The column Standardized Coefficient is a statistic that has been standardized for each variable. It allows us to determine the importance of each variable in the model in explaining Inc4modur, after accounting for the influence of other variables. For example, it tells us the importance of the number of cigarettes smoked per day on the number of incidents incurred during the smoking ban, after accounting for the effects of the number of years incarcerated and other variables in the model. Because these coefficients are standardized, it allows us to determine which variable is most important in explaining the dependent variable. For example, being assigned to Cellblock A is the most influential variable in explaining violent incidents during the 4-month smoking ban because it has the largest Standardized Coefficient; next most important is the number of cigarettes per day smoked before the smoking ban, and so on.

Also notice the negative (–) sign next to the Standardized Coefficient for Yearinc. This sign indicates whether the independent variable has a positive impact on the dependent variable (meaning it leads to an increase in violent incidents) or a negative influence (meaning it leads to a decrease in violent incidents). For example, Agefirst, Cigsday, Cellblock, and Inc4moprior are all positively related to violent incidents during the smoking ban. This means a 1-unit increase in value of these variables (e.g., such as a 1-year increase in the age at first incarceration) leads to a certain increase in violent incidents. Specific to Cigsday, inmates who smoked more cigarettes per day were predicted to have an increased level of violence during the smoking ban, after taking into consideration the other variables in the model. More specifically, for each additional cigarette smoked per day, the dependent variable increases by a factor of .385 incidents after accounting for the influence of other variables in the model.

The third column of Table 9.8 presents the significance level associated with each variable. It tells us which variables are statistically significant in explaining the number of incidents during the 4-month smoking ban. Indeed, variables may be related to violent incidents, but may not have a statistically significant impact on violent incidents (recall the previous discussion on levels of significance, .05, .01, and .001). After accounting for the effects of all variables in the model, only two of the five variables are statistically significant in relation to the dependent variable, Cellblock and Cigsday. We know this because only two of the variables have a significance level that is less than .05, or the traditional barrier denoting a significant effect.

At the most basic level, the results in Table 9.8 suggest that the number of cigarettes smoked per day and cellblock assignment were statistically significant explanations of violence during the smoking ban. Here, inmates subject to the smoking ban (as a result of being in Cellblock A) and inmates who smoked more were significantly more likely to engage in violent incidents during the smoking ban than inmates in Cellblock B or inmates who smoked fewer cigarettes per day. These findings are statistically significant even after accounting for inmates' violence before the smoking ban, their age at first incarceration, and the number of years inmates had been incarcerated. In sum, this model indicates that a smoking ban will increase violence among more frequent smokers subject to the ban, independent of the effects of other variables in the model.

A final piece of information is included in Table 9.8 and is also typically found in the presentation of OLS regression results. This is the R^2. R^2 is a measure that indicates how much variation in violent incidents during the smoking ban is explained by the variables included in the model. In this example, the effects of all the variables in the model predicted .560 or 56.0% of the variance in inmates' involvement in violent incidents measured for 4 months during the smoking ban. In other words, for the sample in the current hypothetical study, more than 50% of what leads to violent incidents during the smoking ban is included in the model and most of that variance is explained by Cigsday and assignment to Cellblock A, or the smoking ban. The variables that might explain the remaining 50% of the variance in participation in violent incidents are not included in the statistical model.

For example, perhaps the inclusion of variables that measured mental health problems or incarceration as a juvenile offender would explain additional variation in participation in violent incidents. Unfortunately, such variables were not available to the researcher so the contribution of these and other variables, in explaining violent incidents, is unknown.

Logistic Regression

Logistic regression is another multivariate technique that allows a researcher to determine the impact of multiple independent variables on a single dependent variable. Independent variables can be nominal, ordinal, interval, or ratio level variables. However, the dependent variable in a logistic regression analysis must be a binary categorical variable. An example of a binary dependent variable might include re-offense and no re-offense, arrested or not arrested, or involvement in a violent incident and no involvement in a violent incident.

As noted earlier, it is always possible that a researcher can "scale down" or "recode" an interval or ratio level variable into categories. In the current hypothetical study, for example, the researcher could recode the frequency of violent incidents during the 4-month smoking ban into two exclusive categories—inmates who incurred 1–4 incidents, and inmates who incurred 5 or more incidents. Two points are worth mentioning here. First, the choice of categories is entirely up to the researcher and might be informed by a number of things such as previous research and general knowledge about the characteristics of the data. Second, a general rule is that a researcher would never want to scale down a variable from interval or ratio level to a categorical variable simply to conduct a certain type of multivariate analysis. If a researcher has an interval or ratio level variable, they simply could use OLS or another statistical technique appropriate for dependent variables measured at that level. For our purposes, however, let's assume the researcher does not have access to an interval or ratio level dependent variable measure of violence during the smoking ban and only has access to a dichotomous dependent variable.

Suppose the researcher is interested in the same question that formed the basis for the OLS regression previously. Suppose also that the researcher has a dependent variable that measures whether inmates were involved in 1–4 incidents during the smoking ban (no inmates in the current data had 0 incidents during the smoking ban), or 5 or more incidents during the smoking ban. This would be an appropriate analysis for logistic regression.

TABLE 9.9 | Logistic Regression of Category of Violent Incidents during Smoking Ban

Variable	Coefficient	Sig.	Exp(B)
Agefirst	−.001	.979	.999
Yearinc	−.050	.753	.951
Cigsday	.328	.001	1.388
Cellblock (A)	6.02	.004	412.86
Inc4moprior	1.13	.034	3.109
R^2 = .60			

Table 9.9 shows the results of the logistic regression model regressing Agefirst, Yearinc, Cigsday, Cellblock (A), and Inc4moprior on the dichotomous dependent variable.

The table offers a typical presentation of results produced by a logistic regression analysis. It has four columns, but for our purposes, column 3 (Sig.) and column 4 (Exp(B)) are most important. Recall from previous discussions that Sig. indicates whether a particular variable is significant in predicting or explaining the dependent variable. All Sig. values that are less than .05 indicate variables significant in explaining the dependent variable. Knowing this, the results in Table 9.9 show that three variables emerged as significant in explaining the dependent variable (e.g., the category of having 5 or more incidents during the 4-month smoking ban period is the predicted category in the logistic regression model). We know this because three variables have significance values that are less than .05. These variables are Cigsday, Cellblock A, and Inc4moprior. In a nutshell, the results of this analysis suggest that inmates who smoke more per day, those assigned to Cellblock A (those subject to the smoking ban), and those with a greater number of incidents prior to the smoking ban are more likely to be found in the category of inmates with 5 or more incidents during the smoking ban compared to those who accumulated 1–4 incidents during the ban.

Further information can be found in column 4, or Exp(B). Exp(B), also called the odds ratio, is best viewed as a measure of association between variables. Odds ratios that are greater than 1 indicate a positive relationship of the independent to the dependent variable, those less than 1 indicate a negative relationship, and those that are exactly 1 indicate a neutral relationship between the variables. For example, the odds ratio for the variable Cigsday is 1.388. This means that the more cigarettes an inmate smoked before the ban, the more likely they will be found in the category of inmates with 5 or more incidents.

Without getting too complex, the odds ratio simply compares the odds of being in one group (the group with 5 or more violent incidents) to the odds of being in the other group (the group of inmates with 1–4 violent incidents during the smoking ban). In the current example, the number of cigarettes smoked per day significantly increases the odds of being in the group with 5 or more incidents, but this effect is relatively weak as the odds ratio is only slightly more than 1.0. Interestingly, being in Cellblock A, and hence being subject to the smoking ban significantly increased the likelihood of being in the higher incident category after accounting for the effects of all other variables in the model. Moreover, those who demonstrated a higher level of previous violent incidents were much more likely to be found in the category of 5 or more incidents, even after accounting for the effects of other variables in the model.

Summing up Table 9.9, the results indicate that inmates who smoke more, are subject to a smoking ban, and those with more incidents prior to the smoking ban are significantly more likely to be involved in a higher number of incidents. Note, these results are somewhat different from the results found previously on the OLS model. For example, in the OLS model accounting for the number of violent incidents as the dependent variable, an inmate's previous history of violent incidents (Inc4moprior) was not a significant factor explaining violence during the smoking ban. One reason for this discrepancy is that the OLS model was predicting the total number of incidents whereas the logistic regression model is predicting a category of incidents. As a result, the outcome of the data analysis may be different because different outcomes are being measured. If in fact the researcher re-coded the dependent variable into two different categories, for example, those with 1–2 incidents and those with more than 3 incidents, the results may change further. Such differences can also occur because OLS regression and logistic regression operate on different assumptions about the characteristics of data beyond their level of measurement. Although this discussion is well beyond this chapter, this is one reason why it is important for researchers to understand the nature of their data.

As mentioned, there are a number of other multivariate statistical techniques available to researchers, and like all statistics, whether they are appropriate to use depends on a number of considerations. That said, the previous discussion of OLS and logistic regression demonstrated two of the most common statistical tests to examine relationships among multiple variables, and how the results of these tests are typically presented and interpreted. Although there are a number of particulars about each of these statistical tests that were not covered because they are far beyond the scope of this text, the basic presentation of these tests will help consumers have at least a basic understanding of two common tests and how they are used in answering a research question.

CHAPTER SUMMARY

The bad news is that no single chapter can fully prepare consumers for the complex world of statistics and their use in the research process. The good news is that this was not the goal of this chapter. Rather, the goal of this chapter was to help readers come away with a basic understanding of the most common statistical tests, why they are used, what they accomplish, and their basic presentation and interpretation. Despite the foundational nature of this chapter, research consumers should feel more confident about reading and interpreting statistics in many common research outlets, and hopefully, will have greater insight into the role statistics play in the final aspects of the research process.

Although statistics are undoubtedly important in seeing a research study through its final stages, it is important for readers to remember that a study is only as "good" as the methods and design that led to the collection of data so as to allow statistical analyses. The saying—"garbage in, garbage out"—is a truism when it comes to research methods. Poorly designed and implemented research studies, whether the fault of the researcher or not, will lead to the production of data and statistical analyses that will also suffer from problems experienced at the front end. Therefore, statistics should not be viewed as a set of tools that allow shortcomings in method and design to be remedied through fancy number crunching. Rather, statistics are just one ingredient of a good study that also must include appropriate methods and design. As a result, consumers who are educated about the research process, including an understanding of the role of basic statistics, are on the path to becoming informed consumers of research.

CRITICAL THINKING QUESTIONS

1. What is the difference between a variable measured at the ratio level and a variable measured at the interval level? Give one example each of a ratio level and an interval level variable not discussed in this chapter.

2. What are measures of central tendency, and what are measures of variance?

3. What does it mean when a study claims that a variable is significant at the .05 level? Explain.

4. Make a persuasive argument that a study's methods and design are perhaps more important than statistical tests.

5. What does it mean if a study variable, like age at first arrest, has a large standard deviation relative to the mean of that variable?

KEY TERMS

categorical/qualitative: Two terms that are often used to describe variables measured at the nominal and ordinal level

chi-square test: A statistical test that examines the association between two variables measured at the ordinal or nominal level

logistic regression: A multivariate statistical test that regresses the independent variables on a categorical dependent variable (e.g., convicted or not convicted, violent or not)

mean: The average of a set of scores; example would be the average score for an entire research methods class

measures of central tendency: Refers to a set of statistics that produce a single number to represent a larger set of numbers; includes the mean, mode, and median

median: Is the middle score of all scores

mode: Is the most frequent score among a set of scores

multivariate statistical tests: Refers to a set of statistical tests that examine the relationships between multiple independent variables and one dependent variable

N/n: Letter utilized to denote population and/or sample size

Ordinary Least Squares (OLS) regression: A multivariate statistical technique that regresses several independent variables on a metric dependent variable (e.g., number of violent incidents)

pilot test: A pilot test is a "test run" or preliminary study. It can be used to work out any problems before a full study, or to provide a preliminary set of answers to research questions before a full study

quantitative/metric: Term used to sometimes refer to variables measured at the interval or ratio level

range: A measure of variation that is the distance between the lowest and highest score in a set of scores

statistically significant: A relationship between variables, or a difference between variables, is statistically significant when it is larger or smaller than would be expected by chance. The minimum level at which a relationship is considered statistically significant is .05, meaning that in only 5 in 100 chances would the relationship or difference be this small or large

standard deviation: A measure of variation that provides an idea of the variation of all particular values of a variable compared to the mean of that particular variable

t-test: A statistical test that examines the level of association between two interval or ratio level variables. For example, a t-test can examine whether the difference in final test scores between two classes is significantly different

variance: Provides an indication of how much each individual value of a particular variable differs from the average of a particular variable

ENDNOTES

1   Katz, C., V. Webb., K. Fox, & J. Shaffer. (2010). Understanding the relationship between violent victimization and gang membership. *Journal of Criminal Justice, 39,* 48–59.

2   Ibid.

3   Mosher, C., T. Miethe, & T. Hart. (2011). *The mismeasure of crime.* Thousand Oaks, CA: SAGE.

4   Vogt, W. P. (1993). *Dictionary of statistics and methodology: A nontechnical guide for the social sciences.* Newbury Park, CA: SAGE, p. 115.

5   Vogt, P. (1993). p. 32.

6   Babbie, E., F. Halley, & J. Zaino. (2003). *Adventures in social research.* Thousand Oaks, CA: SAGE.

The Appendix includes excerpts from the original article which presented the research known as the Minneapolis Domestic Violence Experiment. The excerpts primarily focus on the methodology portions of the article. The citation to the article is provided to access the full-text article.

The Specific Deterrent Effects of Arrest for Domestic Assault*

LAWRENCE W. SHERMAN
University of Maryland,
College Park and Police Foundation

RICHARD A. BERK
University of California,
Santa Barbara

with
42 Patrol Officers of the Minneapolis Police Department,
Nancy Wester, Donileen Loseke, David Rauma, Debra Morrow, Amy Curtis,
Kay Gamble, Roy Roberts, Phyllis Newton, and Gayle Gubman

The specific deterrence doctrine and labeling theory predict opposite effects of punishment on individual rates of deviance. The limited cross-sectional evidence available on the question is inconsistent, and experimental evidence has been lacking. The Police Foundation and the Minneapolis Police Department tested these hypotheses in a field experiment on domestic violence. Three police responses to simple assault were randomly assigned to legally eligible suspects: an arrest; "advice" (including, in some cases, informal mediation); and an order to the suspect to leave for eight hours. The behavior of the suspect was tracked for six months after the police intervention, with both official data and victim reports. The official recidivism measures show that the arrested suspects manifested significantly less subsequent violence than those who were ordered to leave. The victim report data show that the arrested subjects manifested significantly less subsequent violence than those who were advised. The findings falsify a deviance amplification model of labeling theory beyond initial labeling, and fail to falsify the specific deterrence prediction for a group of offenders with a high percentage of prior histories of both domestic violence and other kinds of crime.

RESEARCH DESIGN

The Police Foundation and the Minneapolis Police Department agreed to conduct a randomized experiment.

The design called for random assignment of arrest, separation, and some form of advice which could include mediation at the officer's discretion. In addition, there was to be a six-month follow-up period to measure the

*Direct all correspondence to: Lawrence W. Sherman, Police Foundation, 1909 K Street N.W., Washington, D.C. 20006.

This paper was supported by Grant #80-IJ-CX-0042 to the Police Foundation from the National Institute of Justice, Crime Control Theory Program. Points of view or opinions stated in this document do not necessarily represent the official position of the U.S. Department of Justice, the Minneapolis Police Department, or the Police Foundation.

We wish to express our thanks to the Minneapolis Police Department and its Chief, Anthony V. Bouza, for their cooperation, and to Sarah Fenstermaker Berk, Peter H. Rossi, Albert J. Reiss, Jr., James Q. Wilson, Richard Lempert, and Charles Tittle for comments on an earlier draft of this paper.

American Sociological Review 1984, Vol. 49 (April:261–272)
© Sherman, Lawrence W. and Richard A. Berk. 1984. "The Specific Deterrent Effects of Arrest for Domestic Assault" American Sociological Review 49:261–272.

frequency and seriousness of domestic violence after each police intervention. The advantages of randomized experiments are well known and need not be reviewed here (see, e.g., Cook and Campbell, 1979).

The design only applied to simple (misdemeanor) domestic assaults, where both the suspect and the victim were present when the police arrived. Thus, the experiment included only those cases in which police were empowered (but not required) to make arrests under a recently liberalized Minnesota state law; the police officer must have probable cause to believe that a cohabitant or spouse had assaulted the victim within the last four hours (but police need not have witnessed the assault). Cases of life-threatening or severe injury, usually labeled as a felony (aggravated assault), were excluded from the design for ethical reasons.

The design called for each officer to carry a pad of report forms, color coded for the three different police actions. Each time the officers encountered a situation that fit the experiment's criteria, they were to take whatever action was indicated by the report form on the top of the pad. We numbered the forms and arranged them in random order for each officer. The integrity of the random assignment was to be monitored by research staff observers riding on patrol for a sample of evenings.

After police action was taken, the officer was to fill out a brief report and give it to the research staff for follow-up. As a further check on the randomization process, the staff logged in the reports in the order in which they were received and made sure that the sequence corresponded to the original assignment of treatments.

Anticipating something of the victims' background, a predominantly minority, female research staff was employed to contact the victims for a detailed face-to-face interview, to be followed by telephone follow-up interviews every two weeks for 24 weeks. The interviews were designed primarily to measure the frequency and seriousness of victimizations caused by the suspect after the police intervention.[1] The research staff also collected criminal justice reports that mentioned the suspect's name during the six-month follow-up period.

CONDUCT OF THE EXPERIMENT

As is common in field experiments, implementation of the research design entailed some slippage from the original plan. In order to gather data as quickly as possible, the experiment was originally located in the two Minneapolis precincts with the highest density of domestic violence crime reports and arrests. The 34 officers assigned to those areas were invited to a three-day planning meeting and asked to participate in the study for one year. All but one agreed. The conference also produced a draft order for the chief's signature specifying the rules of the experiment. These rules created several new situations to be excluded from the experiment, such as if a suspect attempted to assault police officers, a victim persistently demanded an arrest, or if both parties were injured. These additional exceptions, unfortunately, allowed for the possibility of differential attrition from the separation and mediation treatments. The implications for internal validity are discussed later.

The experiment began on March 17, 1981, with the expectation that it would take about one year to produce about 300 cases (it ran until August 1, 1982, and produced 330 case reports). The officers agreed to meet monthly with the project director (Sherman) and the project manager (Wester). By the third or fourth month, two facts became clear: (1) only about 15 to 20 officers were either coming to meetings or turning in cases; and (2) the rate at which the cases were turned in would make it difficult to complete the project in one year. By November, we decided to recruit more officers in order to obtain cases more rapidly. Eighteen additional officers joined the project, but like the original group, most of these officers only turned in one or two cases. Indeed, three of the original officers produced almost 28 percent of the cases, in part because they worked a particularly violent beat, and in part because they had a greater commitment to the study. Since the treatments were randomized by officer, this created no internal validity problem. However, it does raise construct validity problems to which we will later return.

There is little doubt that many of the officers occasionally failed to follow fully the experimental design. Some of the failures were due to forgetfulness, such as leaving the report pads at home or at the police station. Other failures derived from misunderstanding about whether the experiment applied in certain situations; application of the experimental rules under complex circumstances was sometimes confusing. Finally, from time to time there were situations that were simply not covered by the experiment's rules.

Whether any officers intentionally subverted the design is unclear. The plan to monitor randomization with ride-along observers broke down because of the unexpectedly low incidence of cases meeting the experimental criteria. The observers had to ride for many weeks before they observed an officer apply one of the treatments. We tried to solve this problem with "chase-alongs," in which the observers rode in their own car with a portable police radio and drove to the scene of any domestic call dispatched to any officer in the precinct. Even this method failed.

Thus, we are left with at least two disturbing possibilities. First, police officers anticipating (e.g., from the dispatch call) a particular kind of incident, and finding the upcoming experimental treatment inappropriate, may have occasionally decided to void the experiment. That is, they may have chosen to exclude certain cases in violation of the experimental design. This amounts to differential attrition, which is clearly a threat to internal validity. Note that if police officers blindly decided to exclude certain cases (e.g., because they did not feel like filling out the extra forms on a given day), all would be well for internal validity.

Second, since the recording officer's pad was supposed to govern the actions of each pair of officers, some officers may also have switched the assignment of driver and recording officer after deciding a case fit the study in order to obtain a treatment they wanted to apply. If the treatments were switched between driver and recorder, then the internal validity was again threatened. However, this was almost certainly uncommon because it was generally easier not to fill out a report at all than to switch.

Table 1 shows the degree to which the treatments were delivered as designed.[2] Ninety-nine percent of the suspects targeted for arrest actually were arrested, while only 78 percent of those to receive advice did, and only 73 percent of those to be sent out of the residence for eight hours were actually sent. One explanation for this pattern, consistent with the experimental guidelines, is that mediating and sending were more difficult ways for police to control the situation, with a greater likelihood that officers might resort to arrest as a fallback position. When the assigned treatment is arrest, there is no need for a fallback

position. For example, some offenders may have refused to comply with an order to leave the premises.

Such differential attrition would potentially bias estimates of the relative effectiveness of arrest by removing uncooperative and difficult offenders from the mediation and separation treatments. Any deterrent effect could be underestimated and, in the extreme, artifactual support for deviance amplification could be found. That is, the arrest group would have too many "bad guys" relative to the other treatments.

With the interviews of the victims, only 205 (of 330, counting the few repeat victims twice) could be located and initial interviews obtained; a 62 percent completion rate. Many of the victims simply could not be found, either for the initial interview or for follow-ups: they either left town, moved somewhere else or refused to answer the phone or doorbell. The research staff made up to 20 attempts to contact these victims, and often employed investigative techniques (asking friends and neighbors) to find them. Sometimes these methods worked, only to have the victim give an outright refusal or break one or more appointments to meet the interviewer at a "safe" location for the interview.

The response rate to the bi-weekly follow-up interviews was even lower than for the initial interview, as in much research on women crime victims. After the first interview, for which the victims were paid $20, there was a gradual falloff in completed interviews with each successive wave; only 161 victims provided all 12 follow-up interviews over the six months, a completion rate of 49 percent. Whether paying for the follow-up interviews would have improved the response rate is unclear; it would have added over $40,000 to the cost of the research. When the telephone interviews yielded few reports of violence, we moved to conduct every fourth interview in person, which appeared to produce more reports of violence.

In sum, despite the practical difficulties of controlling an experiment and interviewing crime victims in an emotionally charged and violent social context, the experiment succeeded in producing a promising sample of 314 cases with complete official outcome measures and an apparently unbiased sample of responses from the victims in those cases.

RESULTS

Two kinds of outcome measures will be considered. One is a *police-recorded* "failure" of the offender to survive the six-month follow-up period without having police generate a written report on the suspect for domestic

TABLE 1 | Designed and Delivered Police Treatments in Spousal Assault Cases

Designed Treatment	Delivered Treatment			
	Arrest	**Advise**	**Separate**	**Total**
Arrest	98.9%	0.0%	1.1%	29.3%
	(91)	(0)	(1)	(92)
Advise	17.6%	77.8%	4.6%	34.4%
	(19)	(84)	(5)	(108)
Separate	22.8%	4.4%	72.8%	36.3%
	(26)	(5)	(83)	(114)
Total	43.4%	28.3%	28.3%	100%
	(136)	(89)	(89)	(314)

violence, either through an offense or an arrest report written by any officer in the department, or through a subsequent report to the project research staff of a randomized (or other) intervention by officers participating in the experiment. A second kind of measure comes from the *interviews with victims*, in which victims were asked if there had been a repeat incident with the same suspect, broadly defined to include an actual assault, threatened assault, or property damage.

Overall, the police data indicate that the separation treatment produces the highest recidivism, arrest produces the lowest.

When self-report data are used, these results suggest a different ordering of the effects, with arrest still producing the lowest recidivism rate (at 19%), but with advice producing the highest (37%).

An obvious rival hypothesis to the deterrent effect of arrest is that arrest incapacitates. If the arrested suspects spend a large portion of the next six months in jail, they would be expected to have lower recidivism rates. But the initial interview data show this is not the case: of those arrested, 43 percent were released within one day, 86 percent were released within one week, and only 14 percent were released after one week or had not yet been released at the time of the initial victim interview. Clearly, there was very little incapacitation, especially in the context of a six-month follow-up. Indeed, virtually all those arrested were released before the first follow-up interview.

ENDNOTES

1 The protocols were based heavily on instruments designed for an NIMH-funded study of spousal violence conducted by Richard A. Berk, Sarah Fenstermaker Berk, and Ann D. Witte (Center for Studies of Crime and Delinquency, Grant #MH-34616-01). A similar protocol was developed for the suspects, but only twenty-five of them agreed to be interviewed.

2 Sixteen cases were dropped because no treatment was applied or because the case did not belong in the study (i.e., a fight between a father and son).

REFERENCES

Cook, Thomas D. and Donald T. Campbell
    1979   *Quasi-Experimentation: Design and Analysis Issues for Field Settings*. Chicago: Rand McNally.

applied research Practical research that may involve evaluating existing or proposed policies or programs.

archives A place, either physical or electronic, where records and other data are stored.

association (or covariance or correlation) One of three conditions that must be met for establishing cause and effect, or a causal relationship. Association refers to the condition that X and Y must be related for a causal relationship to exist. Association is also referred to as covariance or correlation. Although two variables may be associated (or covary or be correlated), this does not automatically imply that they are causally related.

attrition or subject mortality A threat to internal validity, it refers to the differential loss of subjects between the experimental (treatment) and control (comparison) groups during the course of a study.

authority knowledge Knowledge developed when we accept something as being correct and true just because someone in a position of authority says it is true.

case study An in-depth analysis of one or a few illustrative cases.

categorical/qualitative Two terms that are often used to describe variables measured at the nominal and ordinal level.

cause and effect relationship A cause and effect relationship occurs when one variable causes another, and no other explanation for that relationship exists.

Certificates of Confidentiality Certificates awarded by the U.S. Department of Health and Human Services to protect researchers from court orders to identify information or characteristics of a research participant.

chi-square test A statistical test that examines the association between two variables measured at the ordinal or nominal level.

classic experimental design or experimental design A design in a research study that features random assignment to an experimental or control group. Experimental designs can vary tremendously, but a constant feature is random assignment, experimental and control groups, and a post-test. For example, a classic experimental design features random assignment, a treatment, experimental and control groups, and pre- and post-tests.

cluster/multistage sampling A type of probability sampling in which large geographical areas are clustered, or divided, into smaller parts. From there, random samples of individuals or groups or locations are taken in successive or multiple steps. For example, breaking a state down into regions would be a form of clustering. From there, taking a simple or stratified or systematic random sample of schools from each cluster would be one stage of sampling. A next stage of sampling might be randomly selecting students from each randomly selected school.

common sense knowledge Knowledge developed when the information "just makes sense".

comparison group The group in a quasi-experimental design that does not receive the treatment. In an experimental design, the comparison group is referred to as the control group.

compensatory rivalry A threat to internal validity, it occurs when the control or comparison group attempts to compete with the experimental or treatment group.

complete observation A participant observation method that involves the researcher observing an individual or group from afar.

complete participation A participant observation method that involves the researcher becoming a full-fledged member of a particular group; sometimes referred to as disguised observation.

concept A clear idea regarding a particular subject based on that subject's characteristics.

confederates Individuals, who are part of the research team, used to speed up the events of interest when observations are being made.

construct validity Assesses the extent to which a particular measure relates to other measures consistent with theoretically derived hypotheses concerning the concepts/variables that are being measured.

content analysis A method requiring the analyzing of content contained in mass communication outlets such as newspapers, television, magazines, and the like.

content validity When the survey questions measure the full breadth and depth of the concept being studied.

control group In an experimental design, the control group does not receive the treatment. The control group serves as a baseline of comparison to the experimental group. It serves as an example of what happens when a group equivalent to the experimental group does not receive the treatment.

convenience sampling A form of non-probability sampling in which the sample is composed of persons of first contact; also known as accidental or haphazard sampling, or person-on-the-street sampling.

criterion-related validity An assessment to determine the strength of the relationship between the responses to the survey and another measurement, the criterion, to which it should be related if the measurement is valid.

Cronbach's alpha A statistic used to assess the internal consistency/reliability of an index.

cross-sectional designs A measurement of the pre-test and post-test at one point in time (e.g., six months before and six months after the program).

CSI Effect Due to the unrealistic portrayal of the role of forensic science in solving criminal cases in television shows, jurors are more likely to vote to acquit a defendant when the expected sophisticated forensic evidence is not presented.

deduction The process of using a theory and its tenets to develop one or more specific hypotheses.

demoralization A threat to internal validity closely associated with compensatory rivalry, it occurs when the control or comparison group gives up and changes their normal behavior. While in compensatory rivalry, the group members compete, in demoralization, they simply quit. Both are abnormal behavioral reactions.

dependent variable The outcome variable; the variable dependent on what occurs with the independent variable.

diary method A data-gathering technique that asks research subjects to keep a diary, or written record, of their time participating in the research study.

differential police response Methods that allow police departments to prioritize calls and rapidly dispatch an officer only when an immediate response is needed (i.e., crimes in progress).

diffusion of treatment A threat to internal validity, it occurs when the control or comparison group members learn that they are not getting the treatment and attempt to mimic the behavior of the experimental or treatment group. This mimicking may make it seem as if the treatment is having no effect, when in fact it may be.

disguised observation When a researcher joins the group under study to observe their behavior but does not reveal his identity as a researcher or his purpose for being there.

edgework Refers to researchers going to the "edge," or the extreme, to collect information on subjects of interest.

elimination of alternative explanations One of three conditions that must be met for establishing cause and effect. Elimination of alternative explanations means that the researcher has ruled out other explanations for an observed relationship between X and Y.

ethical relativism The belief that how we think about ethics varies from one time to another, one place to another, and from one person to another.

ethics Recognized rules of conduct that govern a particular group.

ethnographic research Relies on field research methodologies to scientifically examine human culture in the natural environment.

experimental designs Used when researchers are interested in determining whether a program, policy, practice, or intervention is effective.

experimental group In an experimental design, the experimental group receives the treatment.

face validity An assessment of the survey questions to see if on "face value" the questions seem to be measuring the concepts and variables they are supposed to be measuring.

field research Research that involves researchers studying individuals or groups of individuals in their natural environment.

gatekeeper A person within the group under study whom the researcher can use to learn about and access the group.

generalizability In reference to sampling, refers to the ability of the sample findings to generalize or be applied to the larger population. For example, let's say the findings of a sample survey on attitudes toward the death penalty reveal the majority of the sample is in support of the death penalty. If the sample is a good representation of the population, the results from this survey can be generalized or applied to the population.

going native A challenge to field research in which the researcher loses her identity as a researcher and begins to identify more with her role as a member of the group under study.

Halloween sadism The practice of giving contaminated treats to children during trick or treating.

Hawthorne Effect Based on a study of worker productivity; refers to changes in behavior caused by being observed.

history A threat to internal validity, it refers to any event experienced differently by the treatment and comparison groups—an event that could explain the results other than the supposed cause.

hypotheses Statements about the expected relationship between two concepts.

illogical reasoning Occurs when someone jumps to premature conclusions or presents an argument that is based on invalid assumptions.

independent variable The variable that determines and precedes the other variable in time; also called the cause.

index A set of items that measures some underlying concept.

indigenous observer A person within the group under study who is willing to collect information about the group for compensation.

induction The process of applying what is known about one or a few cases to an entire group.

informed consent Voluntary consent required from competent research participants after participants have been given accurate and relevant information about the study regarding procedures and possible risks and benefits to participation.

institutional review board (IRB) A group of individuals selected to review research proposals to check compliance with federal and state law; determines whether research should be conducted based on a risk-benefit ratio.

instrumentation A threat to internal validity, it refers to changes in the measuring instrument from pre- to post-test.

interrater reliability A ratio established to determine agreement among multiple raters.

journalistic field research Field research conducted by journalists and used to write books or articles about a certain topic of interest.

logistic regression A multivariate statistical test that regresses the independent variables on a categorical dependent variable (e.g., convicted or not convicted, violent or not).

longitudinal Refers to repeated measurements of the pre-test and post-test over time, typically for the same group of individuals; the opposite of cross-sectional.

matching A process sometimes utilized in some quasi-experimental designs that feature a treatment and comparison group. Matching is a process whereby the researcher attempts to ensure equivalence between the treatment and comparison group on known information, in the absence of the ability to randomly assign the groups.

maturation A threat to internal validity, maturation refers to the natural biological, psychological, or emotional processes as time passes.

mean The average of a set of scores (e.g., the average score for an entire research methods class).

measures of central tendency Refers to a set of statistics that produces a single number to represent a larger set of numbers; includes the mean, mode, and median.

median The middle score of all scores.

meta-analysis A type of content analysis in which researchers quantitatively review, organize, integrate, and summarize the existing research literature on a certain topic.

methodology The techniques utilized to gather information or data for research purposes.

mode The most frequent score among a set of scores.

multivariate statistical tests Refers to a set of statistical tests that examine the relationships between multiple independent variables and one dependent variable.

myths Beliefs that are based on emotion rather than rigorous analysis.

N/n Letter utilized to denote population and/or sample size.

negative association Refers to a negative association between two variables. A negative association is demonstrated when X increases and Y decreases, or X decreases and Y increases. Also known as an inverse relationship—the variables moving in opposite directions.

non-probability sampling methods As opposed to probability sampling methods, non-probability sampling methods include those sampling techniques in which every member of the population *does not* have an equal chance at being selected for the sample.

observer as participant A participant observation strategy in which the researcher is known to the group and the researcher is there only to observe.

operationalization The process of giving a concept a working definition; determining how each concept in your study will be measured (e.g., the concept of intelligence can be operationalized or defined as grade point average or score on a standardized exam).

oral/life history Methods used to conduct case studies; similar to an autobiographical account.

Ordinary Least Squares (OLS) regression A multivariate statistical technique that regresses several independent variables on a metric dependent variable (e.g., number of violent incidents).

overgeneralization Occurs when people conclude that what they have observed in one or a few cases is true for all cases.

paradigm School of thought; way to organize information within a discipline.

participant as observer A participant observation strategy in which the researcher will participate with the group but his identity as a researcher is known.

participant observation strategies First used for social science in the 1920s, these research methodologies involve participation and/or observation with the group under study; there are four such strategies.

peer review A form of quality control most commonly related to academic journals; process by which submitted manuscripts are sent out to be reviewed by experts in the field to determine whether the manuscript is suitable for publication.

personal experience knowledge Knowledge developed through actual experiences.

physical trace analysis The examination of physical substances that have been created and left by individuals as they come in contact with their environment.

pilot program or test Refers to a smaller test study or pilot to work out problems before a larger study and to anticipate changes needed for a larger study; similar to a test run; also can provide a preliminary set of answers to a research question before a full study.

population A complete group; could be all students at a university, all members of a city, or all members of a church; a defining feature of a population is that it be complete.

positive association Refers to a positive association between two variables. A positive association means as X increases, Y increases, or as X decreases, Y decreases.

post-test A measure of the dependent variable after the treatment has been administered.

pre-test A measure of the dependent variable or outcome before a treatment is administered.

probabilistic An event or outcome is more or less likely when certain conditions are present or not present.

probability sampling methods As opposed to non-probability sampling methods, probability sampling methods include those sampling techniques where every member of the population has an equal chance at being selected for the sample. Such procedures increase the probability that the sample is representative of the population, and hence, that the results produced from the sample are generalizable to the population.

proportionate stratified sampling A sampling method in which each predetermined category of the sample is represented in the sample exactly proportionate to their percentage or fraction of the total population.

pseudonym A false name given to someone whose identity needs to be kept secret.

pure research Research conducted to achieve new knowledge in the development of a discipline.

purposive sampling As a non-probability sample, purposive sampling involves the researcher selecting a specific or purposeful sample based on the needs of the research. If a researcher was interested in the techniques of residential burglars, their sample would be focused only on such burglars.

qualitative research Research that is sensitizing or helps to develop a better understanding about a particular group or activity for which there exists little information; more descriptive and less numerical than quantitative research.

quantitative/metric Term sometimes used to refer to variables measured at the interval or ratio level.

quantitative research Research that involves a numerical measurement of some phenomenon.

quasi experiment Refers to any number of research design configurations that resemble an experimental design but primarily lack random assignment. In the absence of random assignment, quasi-experimental designs feature matching to attempt equivalence.

quota sampling Similar to convenience sampling, quota sampling does involve taking into account a known characteristic of the population. For example, if 50% of the population is female, and the researcher wants a 100-person sample to survey, the researcher must survey exactly 50 females in a quota sample. Once the quota of 50 females is met, no other females will be surveyed.

random assignment Refers to a process whereby members of the experimental group and control group are assigned to each group through a random and unbiased process.

random digit dialing A sampling process involving phone numbers where a computer randomly dials the last 4 digits of a telephone number in a given area code using a known prefix. Random digit dialing, in this way, can help remedy the problem of unlisted phone numbers or numbers for which there is no so-called phone book (e.g., cell phones).

random selection Refers to selecting a smaller but representative subset from a population; not to be confused with random assignment.

randomly drawn sample A sample for which each member of the population has an equal chance at being selected. Samples not drawn through a random process are those in which each member of the population does not have an equal chance at being selected for the sample.

range A measure of variation that is the distance between the lowest and highest score in a set of scores.

reactivity The problem of having research subjects change their natural behavior in reaction to being observed or otherwise included in a research study.

reliability Addresses the consistency of a measurement and refers to whether or not a researcher gets the same results if the same instrument is used to measure something more than once.

representativeness In probability sampling processes, when the smaller sample is an accurate representation of the larger population.

research The scientific investigation of an issue, problem, or subject utilizing research methods.

research methods The tools that allow criminology and criminal justice researchers to systematically study crime and the criminal justice system; include the basic rules, appropriate techniques, and relevant procedures for conducting research.

resistance to change The reluctance to change our beliefs in light of new, accurate, and valid information to the contrary.

response rate The number of people who respond to a survey divided by the number of people sampled.

sample A smaller part of a whole population.

sampling In probability sampling, the process of selecting a smaller group from a larger group, with the goal that the smaller sample accurately represents the total population, despite being smaller in number.

sampling error The percentage of error or difference in using a sample instead of an entire population.

sampling frame A complete list of the population that the researcher will use to take a sample. If the sampling frame does not include each member of the population, and hence is not complete, a researcher must question how those who are listed on the sampling frame differ from those who are not accounted for on the sampling frame.

scale A set of questions that are ordered in some sequence.

secondary data analysis Occurs when researchers obtain and reanalyze data that were originally collected for a different purpose.

selection bias Selection bias occurs when the experimental (treatment) group and the control (comparison) group are not equivalent. The difference between the groups can be a threat to internal validity or an alternative explanation to the findings.

selective observation Choosing, either consciously or unconsciously, to pay attention to and remember events that support our personal preferences and beliefs.

self-administered surveys The distribution of surveys for respondents to complete on their own; includes surveys distributed by mail, group-administered surveys, and surveys distributed via the Internet.

shield laws Laws extending government immunity from prosecution for not divulging confidential and anonymous research information in court.

simple random samples As a form of probability sampling, samples randomly drawn from a larger population. Although each member of the population has an equal chance at being selected for the sample, this form of sample cannot guarantee representativeness.

simulations Artificial research settings that have been carefully created so that their features mimic reality as much as possible.

snowball sampling Also called referral sampling, a non-probability sampling technique utilized when a researcher is attempting to study hard-to-access populations. In snowball sampling, a researcher makes a contact, and that contact refers another, and so on. Over time, the sample snowballs, or gets larger. Because there is no ready-to-use sampling frame for some populations (e.g., gang members), researchers must use contacts and referrals to get a sample.

social desirability bias When a respondent provides answers to survey questions that do not necessarily reflect the respondent's beliefs but instead reflect social norms.

split-half reliability An assessment of reliability in which the correspondence between two halves of a measurement is determined.

spurious A spurious relationship is one where X and Y appear to be causally related, but in fact the relationship is actually explained by a variable or factor other than X.

standard deviation A measure of variation that provides an idea of the variation of all particular values of a variable compared to the mean of that particular variable.

statistically significant A relationship between variables, or a difference between variables, is statistically significant when it is larger or smaller than would be expected by chance. The minimum level at which a relationship is considered statistically significant is .05, meaning that in only 5 in 100 chances would the relationship or difference be this small or large.

stratified random sampling A form of probability sampling where several simple random samples are taken from a

population that has been divided up into strata, such as age, race, gender, or any number of strata based on information about the population.

survey research Obtaining data directly from research participants by asking them questions; often conducted through self-administered questionnaires and personal interviews.

systematic random sampling Involves selecting every *n*th person (e.g., 5th, 10th, etc.) from a list; the starting point on the list must be chosen at random.

target population The population of interest for a particular research study (e.g., all prison inmates, all domestic violence arrestees).

telescoping When a respondent brings behaviors and actions that occurred outside the recall period into the recall period.

testing or testing bias A threat to internal validity, it refers to the potential of study members being biased prior to a treatment, and this bias, rather than the treatment, may explain study results.

test-retest reliability An assessment of reliability in which a measurement is reliable over time if the same measurement is repeated using the same subjects and yields the same results.

theory A statement explaining how two or more factors are related to one another.

threat to internal validity Also known as alternative explanation to a relationship between X and Y. Threats to internal validity are factors that explain Y, or the dependent variable, and are not X, or the independent variable.

timing One of three conditions that must be met for establishing cause and effect; timing refers to the condition that X must come before Y in time for X to be a cause of Y. While timing is necessary for a causal relationship, it is not sufficient, and considerations of association and eliminating other alternative explanations must be met.

tradition knowledge Knowledge developed when we accept something as true because that is the way things have always been (so it must be right).

treatment A component of a research design, it is typically denoted by the letter X. In a research study on the impact of teen court on juvenile recidivism, teen court is the treatment. In a classic experimental design, the treatment is given only to the experimental group, not the control group.

treatment group The group in a quasi-experimental design that receives the treatment. In an experimental design, this group is called the experimental group.

t-test A statistical test that examines the level of association between two interval or ratio level variables (e.g. a t-test can examine whether the difference in final test scores between two classes is significantly different).

unit of analysis Refers to the focus of a research study as being individuals, groups, or other units of analysis, such as prisons or police agencies.

unobtrusive A method that is nonreactive; indicates that what or who is being studied is unaware of its/their role as research participant.

validity Addresses the accuracy of the measurement and refers to the extent to which researchers' measure what they planned to measure.

variable(s) An operationalized concept allowing for specific measurement; a concept that has been given a working definition and can take on different values (e.g., intelligence can be defined as a person's grade point average and can range from low to high or can be defined numerically by different values such as 3.5 or 4.0).

variance Provides an indication of how much each individual value of a particular variable differs from the average of a particular variable.

vulnerable populations Regarding informed consent, those populations for which there are unique risks and a question of whether their consent is fully voluntary or not coerced; examples include prison inmates and terminally ill patients.

Brand X Pictures, page 8; © Hill Street Studios/Blend Images LLC, page 13; Royalty-Free/CORBIS, page 23; CORBIS/Royalty Free, page 31; U.S. Census Bureau, Public Information Office (PIO), page 37; Ralph Nardell/Getty Images, page 44; National Science Foundation, page 53; U.S. Census Bureau, Public Information Office (PIO), page 57; David R. Frazier Photolibrary, Inc., page 64; Lisa F. Young/Alamy, page 70; © Mikael Karlsson, page 74; Design Pics/Steve Nagy, page 80; Aaron Roeth Photography, page 95; © Robert Michael/Corbis, page 104; © Anderson Ross/Blend Images LLC, page 107; Design Pics/Con Tanasluk, page 123; © Colin Anderson/Blend Images LLC, page 126; Ingram Publishing/age Fotostock, page 131; Dimitri Vervits/ImageState, page 139; Circa/Getty Images, page 142; Image Farm/Jupiter Images, page 144; © Comstock/PunchStock, page 158; Royalty-Free/CORBIS, page 162; Purestock/Getty Images, page 170; Imagestate Media (John Foxx), page 175; S. Wanke/PhotoLink/Getty Images, page 178.

INDEX

NOTE: A small *n* following a page reference indicates the appearance of an entry in a note.